THIS IS A CARLTON BOOK

This edition published by Prion Books Limited 2007
20 Mortimer Street
London W1T 3JW

Reprinted 2008

Text © Stephen Arnott and Mike Haskins
Design © Carlton Books Limited

ISBN 978-1-85375-619-1

Editorial: Roland Hall
Design: Darren Jordan
Production: Peter Hinton

Typeset by e-type, Liverpool

Printed in Great Britain

JOKE BOOK

PRION

1ST JOKE

"Thank you for the thunderous round of applause there...
Of course, you weren't to know I've got a headache..."
Jack Dee

2ND JOKE

"In the beginning, the world was without form and void.
And God said, 'Let there be light.' And God separated the
light from the dark. And did two loads of laundry."
Kevin Krisciunas

3RD JOKE

☞ First things first, but not necessarily in that order.

ABUSE

☞ The Pope has issued a proclamation on Michael Jackson. If he hears any
more allegations about little boys, the Pope says he'll have no choice but to
make him a priest.

ACCIDENTS

☞ My uncle died the other day. He was only 30. He got stung by a wasp – the
natural enemy of the tightrope walker.

☞ George had an unpleasant accident the other day. He managed to get a vacuum cleaner hose attachment lodged up his backside. I phoned up the hospital to see how he was; they told me he was picking up nicely.

☞ A coach carrying a hundred professional stuntmen to a convention had an accident on the motorway. It crashed through the central reservation, ploughed into a juggernaut, fell thirty feet down an embankment and turned over six times before hitting a wall, bursting into flames and exploding. No one was injured.

☞ Paddy and Murphy are walking down the road when Murphy falls down a manhole. Paddy shouts, "Is it dark down there?" Murphy replies, "I don't know; I can't see!"

"After her accident, my nan had a plastic hip put in. But I thought they should have replaced it with a Slinky, 'cos if she did fall down the stairs again..."
Steve Williams

☞ Harry goes to the funeral of Tom's father. "I'm so sorry for your loss," says Harry to Tom. "But I've been hearing lots of different stories about how your father died. Was it a climbing accident?" "Oh, no," says Tom. "He did go climbing a lot, and his rope got severed on one trip, but he survived the fall." "Someone mentioned a plane crash," says Harry. "That's right," says Tom. "He was in a plane crash. There was a puncture in the fuel tank of his Cessna and he came down in the sea. He managed to swim to safety though." "Incredible," says Harry. "I also heard something about a car accident." "Yes," says Tom. "He was crossing the road when a car knocked him flying. It was a hit-and-run. He spent three months in hospital, but made a full recovery." "Good grief," says Harry. "He sounds indestructible." "That's what we were beginning to think," says Tom. "In the end, we had to shoot the bastard."

☞ What's the difference between falling out of a first-floor window and falling out of a twentieth-floor window? From a first-floor window you go: Thump – "Argggh!" From a twentieth-floor window you go: "Argggh!" – Thump.

"I broke up with a girl once because she'd lied about her weight. I say that; she actually died in a bungee accident."
Jimmy Carr

☞ A lorry carrying a load of tortoises crashes into a lorry full of terrapins. It's a turtle disaster.

☞ Bill bangs his nose on his bathroom cabinet one morning and immediately it comes up in a big red lump. Then for the rest of the day every person he meets asks, "Hey, Bill, what did you do to your nose?" By the end of the day he's so fed-up telling the story that when Tom asks what he did to his nose, he yells, "I bit it!" Tom says, "Don't be stupid. How could you bite your own nose?" And Bill tells him, "I stood on a chair!"

☞ A man is opening a bottle of sparkling wine when the cork pops out and hits him in the eye. The man yelps with pain. His wife looks into the room and says, "Champagne?" "No," whimpers the man, "It really hurts."

☞ Fred goes to see his friend Harry. When he gets to Harry's house he's surprised to see that the home next door is a burnt-out wreck. There's obviously been a serious fire. Fred knocks on Harry's door and Harry's wife Mary answers. It looks as if she's been crying. "Is Harry in?" asks Fred. "No," says Mary. "He's dead." "Oh, no!" says Fred. "There was a fire next door," continues Mary. "The whole family was trapped upstairs. Harry managed to break down the front door and climb the stairs to rescue the three children. Then, after he'd brought them to safety, he went back for their mother. He managed to carry her out, slung over his shoulder. Then he went back in for the grandmother, but the heat was too fierce. He tried to battle through the flames but he couldn't do it. By the time he escaped, his clothes and hair were on fire. We managed to put out the flames, but he was too far gone for help. He died in my arms on the front lawn." "Good heavens!" says Fred. "What a calamity!" "He was a hero," sobs Mary. "Yes," says Fred. "Yes, he was." There's a few moments' pause: then Fred says. "About Harry..." "What?" says Mary. "Before he died," continues Fred, "did he happen to mention anything about a lawnmower he'd borrowed..?"

☞ Two male firefighters are having sex in a smoke-filled room. Their chief bursts in through the door and shouts, "Holy crap! What the hell are you guys up to?" One of the firefighters looks up and says, "Kowalski's suffering from smoke inhalation, sir!" The chief says, "Well, why aren't you giving him mouth-to-mouth resuscitation?" "I did, sir," replies the firefighter. "How the hell do you think all this got started?"

☞ A truck driver is driving along the freeway. A sign comes up which reads, 'Low Bridge Ahead'. Before he knows it, the bridge is right ahead of him and he gets stuck under it. Cars are backed up for miles. Finally, a police car comes up. A cop gets out and walks up to the truck driver. He puts his hands on his hips and says, "Got stuck, huh?" "No," says the truck driver, "I was delivering this bridge and I ran out of gas."

ACCOUNTANTS

**"Did you ever hear of a kid playing accountant
– even if they wanted to be one?"**
Jackie Mason

☞ A businessman walks into the office of a recruitment consultant. "I'm looking for an accountant," he says. "You are?" says the puzzled consultant. "But didn't we find you a new accountant last week?" "Yes," replies the businessman. "He's the one we're looking for."

☞ What does an accountant's wife say when she can't sleep? "Darling, tell me what you were doing in the office today."

ADDICTION

☞ A man is addicted to cigars and goes to his doctor for a cure. The doctor recommends a drastic form of aversion therapy. "When you go to bed tonight, take one of your cigars, unwrap it and stick it up your rectum," says the doctor. "Next day remove the cigar, rewrap it and place it back with the others so you can't tell which one it is. The aversion is obvious: you won't dare smoke any of the cigars, not knowing which is the treated cigar." "Thanks doc; I'll give it a try," says the man, and off he goes. Three weeks later the man comes back. "Are you still addicted?" says the doctor. "I'm surprised. It's usually a very effective cure." "Oh, it worked okay," replies the man. "I don't smoke cigars any more, but now I can't go to sleep unless I have one shoved up my backside…"

☞ My uncle is addicted to brake fluid. Still, he says he can stop at any time.

ADVERTISING

☞ Advertisement in the 'personal' column of the local paper: "Barry Smith. Get in touch soon! Bring three rings: engagement, wedding and teething. Have news! Julie."

☞ Two advertising executives are having lunch. One says to the other, "Where's James Smith been lately? I haven't seen him for a while." The other replies, "Haven't you heard? James went to the big ad agency in the sky. He dropped dead last Friday." "You're kidding," says the first executive. "What did he have?" "Nothing much," replies the second executive. "A small toothpaste account and a couple of clothes stores, but nothing worth going after…"

AGE – GETTING OLDER

> **"When I turned two I was really anxious, because I'd doubled my age in a year. I thought: if this keeps up, by the time I'm six, I'll be ninety."**
> *Steven Wright*

☞ Age always corresponds inversely to the size of your multi-vitamin tablets.

☞ Age creeps up on everybody eventually; during the 1970s, my wife spent a lot of time and money trying to look like Liz Taylor. Now she spends the same amount of time and money trying *not* to look like Liz Taylor.

☞ Inside every older person there's a younger person wondering what the hell happened.

☞ The Ages of Man in Fruit. At 20, a man is like a coconut: so much to offer, so little to give. At 30, he's like a durian: dangerous, but delicious. At 40, he's like a watermelon: big, round and juicy. At 50, he's like a satsuma; they come only once every year. At 60, he's more like a raisin: dried-out, wrinkled and cheap.

☞ The Ages of Woman in Balls. At 18, she's a football: twenty-two men are running after her from all directions. At 28, she's a hockey ball: eight men are panting to get to her. At 38, she's a golf ball: there's only one man's after her now. At 48, she's a table-tennis ball: two guys are doing their damnedest to get rid of her.

☞ When you're four years old, success is not peeing in your pants. When you're 12, success is having friends. At 17, success is having a driving licence. When you get to 20, success is having sex. At 35, success is having cash. At 50, success is having money. When you turn 60, success is having sex. Aged 70, success is having a driving licence. When you turn 75, success is having friends. At 80, success is not peeing in your pants.

AGE – MIDDLE

> **"Thirty-five is when you finally get your head together and your body starts falling apart."**
> *Caryn Leschen*

☞ A man asks his wife what she'd like for her fortieth birthday. She says she'd like to be six again. Next day, the man buys his wife a party hat and a big sticky cake and hires a clown to show her some magic tricks and sing songs. The wife looks at her husband as if he's crazy. "But I thought you'd be happy," says the husband. "You said you wanted to be six again." "You idiot," she fumes. "I meant my dress size!"

☞ A traffic cop pulls over a lady driver for speeding. "Ma'am," he says. "When I saw you tearing down the street. I guessed 65 as a minimum." "That's ridiculous, officer," says the woman. "I'm 54. It's these damned glasses – they put on ten years."

☞ Middle age is when work is a lot less fun, and fun is a lot more work.

☞ Middle age is when you've stopped growing at both ends, and started to grow in the middle.

☞ My wife turned forty last week. I'm going to try and change her for two twenties.

☞ You know you're middle-aged when the only thing you start to exercise is caution.

AGE – OLD

"First you forget names, then you forget faces. Next you forget to pull your zipper up and, finally, you forget to pull it down."
George Burns

☞ A bus driver looks in his mirror and notices that one of his passengers, an elderly man, is crawling up and down the aisle looking for something on the floor. The man is being a nuisance to the other passengers, so the driver stops the bus and gets out of his seat to see what's going on. "I'm looking for my gum," explains the old man. "Gum?" says the driver. "You're bothering all my other passengers for the sake of some old gum?" "I've got to find my gum," says the old man. "You don't want gum that's been on the floor," says the bus driver. "I've got to find my gum," says the old man. "No, you haven't," says the driver. "Get back in your seat." "But I've got to find my gum," protests the old man. "It's got my teeth in it."

☞ A little old lady goes up to a policeman and says, "Officer; I was sexually molested." "You were?" says the policeman. "Where did it happen?" "In the wood behind the library," replies the old lady. "When did it happen?" asks the policeman. "In 1959," replies the old lady. "What?" exclaims the policeman. "That was more than 40 years ago. Why are you telling me about it now?" "No reason," sighs the old lady. "I just like to reminisce once in a while."

☞ Alf is so old, when he goes into a cafe and orders a three-minute egg, they ask for the money up front.

☞ An attractive lady tourist is staying on a dude ranch in Arizona. On her first day at the ranch, she goes to the stables and passes an old Navajo man. The tourist says hello and the old Navajo raises his hand and says, "Chance." The woman is puzzled by this, but thinks nothing of it. However, exactly the same thing happens the next day; she says hello and the old man raises his hand and says, "Chance." The same thing happens on the third day, and the woman decides to get to the bottom of it. She goes over to the old Navajo and says, "I thought the old Native American greeting was 'How'. Why do you say 'Chance' whenever I go past?" The old man looks her up and down and says, "Lady, I know 'how'; these days the best I hope for is a chance."

☞ An old man goes to his doctor with a complaint about his sex life. He tells the doctor that the last time he had sex with his wife he felt very hot and sweaty; in fact, he thought he might pass out with the heat. But the time before that, he'd felt very cold; his feet had been like blocks of ice and he'd been blue and shivering. The doctor agrees that this sounds like a serious complaint. He calls in the old man's wife to see if she's suffered the same symptoms. The old woman comes in and listens as the doctor describes her husband's symptoms. She thinks for a moment, then says, "Oh: that silly old fool! We only have sex twice a year; the last time it was the middle of summer and before that it was January!"

☞ At the care home for the elderly, it's standard practice for inmates to wear rubber bands around their wrists; they wear the bands so that food allergies can be written on them. Unfortunately, Harry is unaware of this when he has his mother admitted. The next time he visits he blows his top when he finds her labelled 'Bananas'.

☞ Did you hear about the old man who said he was going to celebrate his hundredth birthday by making love? The Queen sent him a telegram. And the Duke of Edinburgh sent him a diagram.

☞ Fred and Bert, both in their eighties, are sitting on a bench. Fred turns to Bert and says, "My memory is getting worse and worse. Can you remind me who died yesterday? Was it Bill or you?"

☞ Harry proposes to Mary, but Mary will only marry him on one condition; he must give her a solid gold Boy Scout pocket-knife. Harry is perplexed by this request, but he loves Mary and looks all over for a solid gold pocket-knife. He can't find one anywhere, and in the end he has one made specially. Once the knife has been created, Harry gives it to Mary. He then asks what she's going to do with it. "Nothing," replies Mary. "I'm going to keep in a drawer 'til I get old." "What will you do with it then?" asks Harry. "Well," says Mary, "by the time I'm seventy my hair will be gray and my skin wrinkled, my teeth will have fallen out and my boobs will be down round my knees. It'll be hard to find anyone who'll want to know me sexually... but I figure that a Boy Scout would do a hell of a lot for a solid gold pocket-knife."

☞ Hilda is talking to Janice, "I may be sixty-five," says Hilda, "but men still look at my boobs. Of course, they have to squat down a bit..."

☞ I don't let old age get me down – it's too hard to get back up again.

☞ If an elderly lady falls in her house when there's no one else there, does she make a sound?

☞ Jim celebrates his sixtieth birthday and toddles off to collect his free bus pass. He finds the bus depot and goes to the information desk to sign up. "I'll need some documentation," says the desk clerk. "I need to see your passport or driving licence to verify your age." Jim looks through his pockets – then realises he's left all his paperwork at home. He groans and turns to leave. The clerk takes pity on him. "Hang on," he says. "Tell you what; let me see your chest." "My chest?" exclaims Jim. "Yeah," says the clerk. "Just undo a few buttons on your shirt." Jim is bemused by this request, but does as he's asked. As he pops the buttons, he reveals a mass of white hair on his chest. "That's all I wanted to see," says the clerk. "All that white chest hair proves you're old enough for a pass." With that, the clerk fills out the necessary paperwork and gives Jim his pass. Jim is delighted, and goes home to tell his wife what's happened. She listens to the story with interest, but when Jim has finished, she sits there shaking her head. "What's the matter?" says Jim. "You *are* a fool," she replies. "If you'd dropped you trousers as well you might have got a disability pension."

☞ Little Jenny is out walking with her mother when they meet Great Aunt Judy, a very elderly relative. Aunt Judy says hello, but Jenny remains silent. "Well; aren't you going to say anything?" asks mother. Jenny stares at the old lady and says, "So why doesn't your skin fit your face?"

☞ Maurice and Melvyn are sitting in deckchairs on the front lawn of their retirement home. "How are you feeling today?" asks Maurice. "Not bad," says Melvyn. "How about you?" "I feel like a new-born baby," replies Maurice. "That's nice," says Melvyn. "No, it ain't," says Maurice. "I got no hair or teeth and I think I just crapped myself."

☞ Mum, Dad, their 16-year-old son Billy and Grandpa are driving out to visit relatives. It's a long trip, so they stop off at a motel for the night. Unfortunately, most of the rooms are already booked and Billy and Grandpa have to sleep in the same bed. All goes well until four in the morning when Grandpa wakes up screaming. "Good God!" he shouts. "Billy! Get me a woman! Get me a woman now!" "Calm down, Grandpa," says Billy. "But, Billy, you've got to get me a woman," wails Grandpa. "I gotta have a woman!" "Calm down, Grandpa!" says Billy. "There are three reasons why you're not getting a woman tonight. Firstly, it's four in the morning. Secondly, you're ninety years old. And thirdly – that's *my* dick you're holding, not yours."

☞ My grandma has 'Furniture Disease'; that's when your chest falls into your drawers.

　☞ My grandmother doesn't believe in growing old gracefully; last week she took part in a wet shawl contest.

☞ Old people love to give good advice; it's compensation for their inability to set a bad example.

　☞ Old people think they've developed more patience, but really they've just stopped giving a crap.

☞ She's so old, she has Jesus' mobile number!

　☞ The average age of people living in Bournemouth has gone sky-high; it's got to the point where all shop windows have to be made out of bifocal glass.

☞ The following letter was sent to the principal of a school which had sponsored a luncheon for the elderly: "Dear principal and students; God bless you for the beautiful radio I won in the raffle at your recent senior citizens' luncheon. I am 85 years old and live in a nursing home. All of my family have passed away and I very much enjoyed coming out for a lovely meal, and winning that radio was such a nice surprise. God bless you for your kindness in inviting an old, forgotten lady to your lunch. My roommate is 94 and she has always had her own radio, but she would never let me listen to it, even when she was napping. The other day her radio fell off the nightstand and it broke. It was smashed right up. It was an awful mess and she was in floods of tears. Then she called over and asked if she could listen to my new radio, and I said 'F*** you'."

☞ There are some nice things about old age: like I can sit here and think about how great it is that wrinkles don't hurt.

☞ Travelling isn't much fun when all the historical sites you visit are younger than you are.

☞ What has lots of little balls and screws old ladies? A bingo machine.

☞ What's blue and screws old ladies? Hypothermia.

☞ You don't know what real embarrassment is until your hip sets off a metal detector.

> **"My Grandmother is over eighty and still doesn't need glasses. She drinks right out of the bottle."**
> *Henny Youngman*

AGEING – THE PERKS OF GETTING OLDER

☞ If you've never smoked, what the hell? Why not start? What's the worst that can happen?

☞ In a hostage situation they're more likely to keep the young, pretty ones.

☞ Kidnappers grow less interested in you.

☞ No one expects you to run a marathon.

☞ No one expects you to run into a burning building.

☞ People no longer view you as a hypochondriac.

☞ The number of cells in your brain finally gets down to a more manageable size.

☞ There's nothing left to learn the hard way.

☞ Things you buy new will never wear out.

☞ You can eat your dinner at four in the afternoon and not feel stupid.

☞ You can stop trying to hold your stomach in, even if a supermodel walks into the room.

☞ You no longer have to think of a speed limit as a challenge.

☞ Your enormous investments in health care insurance finally start to pay off.

☞ Your secrets are finally safe with your friends, because they can't remember them either.

AGEING – YOU KNOW YOU'RE GETTING OLD WHEN...

"You know you're old if your walker has an airbag."
Phyllis Diller

☞ A dripping tap causes an uncontrollable urge to hobble to the bathroom.

☞ A sexy young thing catches your fancy, and your pacemaker opens the garage door.

☞ A strenuous bout of weight-lifting only involves getting out of a chair.

☞ After painting the town red, you have to take a week's rest before applying a second coat.

☞ All you want for your birthday is to not be reminded of your age.

☞ Your midnight oil is all used up by nine-thirty.

☞ Complete strangers feel comfortable calling you 'old-timer'.

☞ Conversations with people your own age usually turn into a bout of 'ailment duelling'.

☞ Even dialling long-distance tires you out.

☞ Every time you suck your belly in, your ankles balloon out.

☞ Everything that works hurts; and what doesn't hurt doesn't work.

☞ Fortune-tellers offer to read your face instead of your palm.

☞ Getting a little action means you don't need to eat any extra fibre today.

☞ Getting lucky means you take less than ten minutes to find your car in the supermarket car park.

☞ Going bra-less pulls all the wrinkles out of your face.

☞ Gravity becomes your worst enemy.

☞ Happy hour is a thirty-minute nap.

☞ Having an 'all-nighter' means you didn't have to get out of bed to go to the toilet.

☞ It gets harder and harder for them to make those sexual harassment charges stick.

☞ It takes longer to rest than it did to get tired in the first place.

☞ It takes you a couple of tries to get over a speed bump.

☞ It takes you twice as long to look half as good.

☞ Most of the names in your address book start with 'Dr'.

☞ Most of your co-workers were born the same year you got your last promotion.

☞ People call at nine in the evening and say, "Did I wake you?"

☞ Someone compliments you on your layered look – and you're wearing a bikini.

☞ The best part of your day is over when your alarm clock goes off.

☞ The car you bought brand-new becomes a vintage model.

☞ The clothes you put away until they come back in style come back in style...for the second time.

☞ The girls at the office start confiding in you.

☞ The little old lady you help across the street is your wife.

☞ The only time you kick up your heels is when you fall down (and can't get up).

☞ The pharmacist has become your new best friend.

☞ The 'snap, crackle, and pop' you hear at breakfast isn't the cereal; it's your joints as you try to get off your chair.

☞ The twinkle in your eye is the reflection of the sun on your bifocals.

☞ Those issues of *Reader's Digest* just can't come fast enough.

☞ 'Tying one on' means fastening your Medic Alert bracelet.

☞ Your wild oats turn to prunes and bran.

☞ You answer to Bill, or George, or Mary...in fact, anyone's name but your own.

☞ You're cautioned to slow down by the doctor instead of by the police.

☞ You begin every other sentence with the word 'Nowadays'.

☞ You begin to outlive enthusiasm.

☞ You can clean your teeth in the dishwasher.

☞ You can date someone three times younger than you and not break any laws.

☞ You can go bowling without drinking.

☞ You can sing and brush your teeth at the same time.

☞ You can't understand all the high-tech newfangled gadgets they have nowadays... like flush toilets.

☞ You chat to your friends about 'good grass', and you're talking about your lawn.

☞ You confuse having a clear conscience with having a bad memory.

☞ You dim the lights for economy, not romance.

☞ You discover that all your favourite movies have been re-released in colour.

☞ You need glasses to find your glasses.

☞ You don't care where your wife goes, just so long as you don't have to go there with her.

☞ You don't get satellite TV for the porn; you get it for the weather channel.

☞ You don't remember being absent-minded.

☞ You feel like you're suffering the 'morning after the night before', then realise you haven't actually been anywhere.

☞ You feel you can get away with a combination of black socks and sandals.

☞ You find yourself on the stairs, and you can't remember if you were downstairs going up, or upstairs going down.

☞ You find yourself telling people what a loaf of bread used to cost.

☞ You get all sweaty and out of breath walking down a flight of stairs.

☞ You get two invitations to go out on the same night and you pick the one that will get you home the earliest.

☞ You get winded playing chess.

☞ You give up all your bad, unhealthy habits, and you still feel crappy.

☞ You go to a museum and find most of your favourite childhood toys are on display.

☞ You go to a restaurant and complain that the butter is too tough for your teeth.

☞ You have to change your underwear after every sneeze.

☞ You have to get up from a couch in stages.

☞ You have too much room in the house and not enough room in the medicine cabinet.

☞ You lean over to pick something up off the floor, then ask yourself if there's anything else you could do while you're down there.

☞ You light the candles on your birthday cake, and a group of campers form a circle round it and start singing "Kumbaya".

☞ You like sitting in a rocking chair, but you can't get the damned thing started.

☞ You look both ways before crossing a room.

☞ You realize that a stamp now costs more than a cinema ticket did when you were fourteen.

☞ You remember when the Dead Sea was only sick.

☞ You spend an hour turning the house over, looking for your glasses – then find them on your head.

☞ You start to answer questions with the phrase, "Because I said so!"

☞ You start to appreciate the attractions of accordion music.

☞ You start to clean out your ear with a cotton bud, then realise you forgot to take out your hearing aid.

☞ You start videotaping daytime gameshows.

☞ You take a metal detector to the beach.

☞ You tap your feet and hum along to the music in lifts.

☞ You think you know all the answers, but nobody will ask you the questions.

☞ You wake up looking like the picture on your driving licence.

☞ You walk around barefoot and get compliments about your new alligator shoes.

☞ You wonder how you could be over the hill when you don't even remember getting on top of it.

☞ You wonder why you waited so long to take up macramé.

☞ Your birthday cake can no longer support the weight of the candles.

☞ Your children start saying, "Hey! That looks like a nice place, doesn't it?" when driving past nursing homes.

☞ Your doctor doesn't bother giving you X-rays any more; he just holds you up against a sunny window.

☞ Your idea of a night out is spending an evening on the patio rocking chair.

☞ Your joints become more accurate forecasters than the National Weather Service.

☞ Your knees buckle, but your belt won't.

☞ Your mind starts to make contracts your body can't meet.

☞ Your new reclining chair has more optional extras than your car.

☞ Your semi-annual erection becomes an annual semi-erection!

☞ Your teeth sink into a juicy steak... and stay there.

☞ You're driving in your car but can't remember where you're going – but it doesn't matter; you're not in a hurry.

☞ You're eighteen around the neck, forty-four around the waist and one hundred and five around the golf course.

☞ You're sitting on a park bench and have to ask a passing Boy Scout for help crossing your legs.

☞ You're trying to straighten out the wrinkles in your socks, then discover you aren't wearing any.

ALTERNATIVE THERAPIES

☞ Bernard had to fire his masseuse today. She kept rubbing him up the wrong way.

☞ Meditation is not what you think.

☞ This morning, right in the middle of my yoga class, my instructor confessed that he found me very physically attractive. Obviously he left me in a very awkward position.

☞ Tom recently took up meditation. He says it's better than sitting round doing nothing.

AMISH

☞ How can you tell if your neighbour is an Amish redneck? There's a dead horse on cinderblocks in his front yard.

☞ How many Amish people does it take to change a lightbulb? What's a lightbulb?

☞ Signs your Amish teenager is in trouble: Sometimes he stays in bed till after five in the morning. You find a hidden horde of magazines full of pictures of bonnetless women. When you criticize him, he storms off yelling, "Thou sucketh!" His name is Jebediah, but he goes by 'Jeb Daddy'. You come across his secret stash of colourful socks. You ask him to rake out the stable and he says, "Talk to the hand, 'cos the beard ain't listening." He wears his big black hat backwards.

☞ What's an Amish man's idea of lingerie? A flannel nightdress with only eight buttons.

AMISH – AMISH TEEN MOVIES

☞ 10 Things I Hate About Atheists

☞ American Cheese

☞ Dude, Where's My Cow?

☞ Ferris Bueller's Day Cleaning the Wheat Silo

☞ I Know What You Did Last Harvest

☞ Legally Bearded

☞ Pretty in Sackcloth

☞ The Princess Dairies

ANATOMY

☞ Why does the crack between your buttocks go up and down instead of across? So you don't mumble when you go down a slide.

ANIMAL TESTING

☞ I think animal testing is a terrible idea; they get all nervous and give the wrong answers.

ANNOYANCE

☞ When someone annoys you, just tell them it takes forty-two muscles to frown, but only four muscles to stretch out your arm and whack them across the forehead.

ANTHROPOLOGY

☞ Two anthropologists fly to the South Sea islands to study the natives. They go to adjacent islands and set to work. A few months later, one of them takes a canoe over to the other island to see how his colleague is doing. When he gets there, he finds the other anthropologist standing among a group of natives. "Greetings!" says the visiting anthropologist. "How's it going?" "Wonderful!" says the other anthropologist. "I've discovered an important fact about the local language! Watch!" He points at a palm tree and says, "What is that?" The natives, in unison, say, "Umbalo-gong!" He then points at a rock and says, "And that?" The natives again intone, "Umbalo-gong!" "You see?" says the beaming anthropologist. "They use the same word for 'rock' and for 'palm tree'!" "That *is* amazing," says the visiting anthropologist. "On the other island, the same word means 'index finger'."

ANTIQUES

☞ An infuriated customer storms into an antiques shop holding a small figurine. She goes up to the antique dealer and says, "You sold me this figurine telling me it was genuine ivory; it turns out to be plastic!" "I didn't say it was ivory," replies the dealer. "I just said it was from an elephant." "How can it be from an elephant AND plastic?" fumes the customer. The dealer replies, "When they shot it, they found it was wearing dentures."

ARCHAEOLOGY

☞ Some Russian scientists dig to a depth of 100 metres and find traces of copper wiring dating back 1,000 years. They come to the conclusion that, a thousand years ago, their ancestors had an ancient telephone network. Not to be outdone, Chinese scientists dig down to 200 metres and find traces of 2,000-year-old optical fibres. From this they conclude that their ancestors had an advanced high-tech digital telephone system 1,000 years before the Russians developed their primitive copper-based technology. After these startling finds, a group of Irish scientists dig down 500 metres. The Irish scientists find absolutely nothing. From this they conclude that, 5,000 years ago, the Irish were already using mobile phones.

ARCHERY

☞ A king and his men-at-arms are riding through a forest when they come across a tree. Painted on the tree is a circle, and in the dead centre is an arrow. It looks like an impressive piece of marksmanship and the King is even more impressed when he comes across another target with an arrow dead-centre: then another, then another. Finally, the King comes across an archer examining yet another arrow in the centre of a target. "Is this your arrow?" asks the King. "Yes, sire," replies the archer. "An impressive piece of work, to be sure," says the King. "From what distance did you shoot the arrow?" The archer replies, "300 yards, sire." The King and his men gasp in astonishment. This is superb archery. "And have all the arrows we have seen in the forest been yours?" "Yes, sire," replies the archer. "And have all these arrows been shot from 300 yards?" asks the King. "Indeed, sire," replies the archer. "Then I shall put you in my army," declares the King. "I will be fighting a battle next week and I shall need every good man I can find. You will be in the most dangerous position, in the thick of the fighting, but with your skill you can easily shoot down anyone who attacks you." The archer looks worried, "That might not be such a good idea, my Lord," he says. "I'm not really that good a shot, to be honest." "Have you dared lie to me, then?" cries the King. "Were all these arrows not yours?" "They were mine, sire," gulps the archer. "And did you not shoot them from 300 yards?" demands the King. "I did, sire," says the archer. "And all your arrows have struck your targets and yet you say you are not a good shot. If all that is true, you are surely the best shot in the kingdom." "Well, sire," gulps the man. "It is all true. But there was one detail I left out." "And what was that?" fumes the King. The archer replies, "I'd been shooting the arrows at the trees, then painting the circles on afterwards."

ARMS

"The right to bear arms is slightly less ludicrous than the right to arm bears."
Chris Addison

ART

☞ A rich old woman goes to Paris to visit the art galleries. She decides to hire the services of a guide to show her around the Louvre. "How wonderful!" she says, looking at a painting, "That's a Monet, isn't it?" "No, madame," says her guide. "It's a Manet." "And that one over there?" says the old lady. "Is that a Pissaro?" "No, madame," says the guide. "That's a Picasso." "I see," says the woman. "But surely that one over there is a Picasso too?" "No, madame," says the guide. "That's a mirror."

"I've been doing a lot of abstract painting lately. Extremely abstract. No brush, no paint, no canvas. I just think about it."
Steven Wright

☞ A woman at an Edinburgh art exhibition is looking at a portrait of three naked black men sitting on a bench. Two of the men have black penises, but the one in the middle has a pink penis. The organiser of the exhibition sees the woman is interested in the painting and goes over to offer his assessment of this curious imagery. He goes on for half an hour explaining how it depicts the sexual emasculation of African-Americans in a predominately white, patriarchal society. After the organiser leaves, an old Scottish man approaches the woman. "Would you like to know what the picture is really about?" he says. "I'm the one that painted it." "Okay," says the woman. "So what is it about?" "They're three Scottish coal-miners," says the old man. "And the one in the middle went home for his lunch."

☞ An art expert is valuing the paintings in a country house. After doing the rounds, the expert approaches the householder and says, "Excuse me, but is that a Constable hanging over the fireplace?" "Yes," replies the householder. "He asked me if he could dry his boots."

☞ He's a modern artist. He throws paint on a canvas, wipes it off with a cloth, then sells the cloth.

☞ Pablo Picasso surprised a burglar in his chateau. The intruder got away, but Picasso told the police he could do a rough portrait of the villain to give them something to go on. On the basis of his drawing, the police arrested a Mother Superior, the Spanish Finance Minister, a washing machine and the Eiffel Tower.

☞ Simon attempted to do a self-portrait the other day. He's one of the very few taxidermists ever to have tried it.

☞ Two old dears, Edith and Edna, are walking through an art museum when they become separated. They eventually meet up again in the canteen. "Here," says Edith. "Did you see that horrible big statue of that naked bloke?" "I did," says Edna. "Disgraceful, it was: with his enormous great thing dangling out for all the world to see. Did you see the size of it?" "Yes," says Edith. "And it was freezing cold, wasn't it..."

BATS

☞ What is the worst enemy of the hibernating bat? Diarrhoea.

BATTLE OF THE SEXES

☞ Men want to be a woman's first love. Women want to be a man's last romance.

"Behind every successful man is a surprised woman."
Maryon Pearson

☞ Men may not be able to experience the miracle of childbirth, but at least we can open all our own jars.

☞ The World's Shortest Fairy Story: Once upon a time a girl went up to a guy and said, "Will you marry me?" The guy said, "No." And the girl lived happily ever after and went shopping, dancing, drank vodka martinis, always had a neat house, never had to cook, stayed skinny and farted whenever she wanted, 'til the end of her days.

"Whatever women must do they must do twice as well as men to be thought half as good. Luckily, this is not difficult."
Charlotte Whitton

☞ There are two times when a man doesn't understand a woman: before marriage and after marriage.

☞ A woman walks up to a man on a beach and says, "You know, your eyes match your swimming trunks." "Oh, yes?" replies the man. "Because they're blue?" "No," says the woman. "Because they're bulging."

☞ Glenda goes to Italy to attend a week-long business conference. Her husband drops her off at the airport. "Is there anything I can get you in Italy?" asks Glenda. Her husband leers and says, "Tell you what: why not pick me up a nice Italian girl?" Glenda is not amused. A week later she returns and is picked up by her husband. "Had a good time?" he asks. "Yes, thanks," says Glenda. Her husband continues, "And did you manage to get me an Italian girl like I asked?" Glenda replies, "Well, I did my best: but you'll have to wait nine months – and it might be a boy!"

☞ Everyone keeps saying that women are smarter than men, but did you ever see a man wearing a shirt that had buttons down the back?

"When women are depressed they either eat or go shopping. Men invade another country."
Elayne Boosler

☞ Only two things are necessary for a man to do to keep his wife happy: to let her think she's having her own way, and to let her have it.

> **"Women reach their sexual peak after the age of 35. Men take about four minutes."**
> *Jimmy Carr*

☞ The average woman would rather have beauty than brains – because the average man can see much better than he can think.

☞ The reason there are so many problems between men and women is that they have such differing views about sex and relationships. Women want a relationship without the complication of unnecessary sex, whereas men want sex without the complication of an unnecessary relationship.

☞ They say that behind every successful man, there stands a woman. Or is it that the woman would be successful if the guy wasn't standing in front of her getting in the way?

☞ Women don't make fools of men; most of them are DIY types.

☞ Women have more imagination than men. They need it to tell men how wonderful they are.

> **"Male menopause is a lot more fun than female menopause. With female menopause you gain weight and get hot flushes. With male menopause, you get to date young girls and drive motorcycles or sports cars."**
> *Rita Rudner*

BATTLE OF THE SEXES – MEN

> **"A male gynaecologist is like an auto mechanic who never owned a car."**
> *Carrie Snow*

☞ All men are animals, but some of them make better pets.

☞ Definition of a bachelor: a man who's missed every opportunity to make some poor woman miserable.

☞ Don't imagine you can change a man – unless he's in nappies.

☞ How many men does it take to change a roll of toilet paper? We don't know; it hasn't happened yet.

☞ If they managed to put a man on the moon, shouldn't they be able to put them all up there?

☞ If you want a committed man, look in a mental hospital.

☞ If you want a man to pay attention to you, wear a full-length black nightgown with buttons all over it. Sure, it's uncomfortable, but it makes you look just like a remote control.

☞ Men aren't interested in what's on TV. They're only interested in what else is on TV.

☞ Remember, having a sense of humour doesn't mean you tell him jokes; it means you have to laugh at his.

☞ Sadly, all men are created equal.

☞ Scientists have finally figured out what's wrong with men. The problem lies in the two halves of their brains – the left half has nothing right in it, and the right half has nothing left in it!

☞ The best way to get a man to do something is to suggest he's too old for it.

☞ The ideal breakfast for the American male; his son's picture is on the packet of Shredded Wheat, his girlfriend's picture is on the back of a box of slimmer's muesli and his wife's picture is on the back of the milk carton.

☞ What are the two reasons why men don't mind their own business? One: no mind. Two: no business.

☞ What do you call the useless piece of skin on the end of a penis? A man!

☞ What do you do if your boyfriend walks out? Shut the door!

☞ What's the difference between getting a divorce and getting circumcised? When you get a divorce, you get rid of the whole prick!

☞ What's the worst part of a man's body? His penis; it has a head with no brains, hangs out with two nuts and lives around the corner from an asshole.

> **"If men can run the world, why can't they stop wearing neckties? How intelligent is it to start the day by tying a little noose around your neck?"**
> *Linda Ellerbee*

☞ Why did God create man? Because a vibrator can't mow the lawn.

☞ Why do men get married? So they can stop holding in their stomachs.

☞ Why do men like falling in love at first sight? It saves them so much time.

☞ Why do men like masturbation? It's sex with someone they love.

☞ Why do men name their penises? Because they want to be on a first-name basis with the one who makes all their decisions.

☞ Why don't men have mid-life crises? So they can stay stuck in adolescence.

> **"Men have higher body temperatures than women.
> If your heating goes out in winter, sleep next to a
> man. Men are like portable heaters that snore."**
> *Rita Rudner*

☞ What do you call a woman without an arsehole? Divorced.

BATTLE OF THE SEXES – MEN (SIMILES)

☞ Men are like chocolate bars. They're sweet, smooth and usually head right for your hips.

☞ Men are like commercials. You can't believe a word they say and they're over in sixty seconds.

☞ Men are like curling irons. They're always hot, and they're always in your hair.

☞ Men are like department stores. Their clothes are always 50 per cent off.

☞ Men are like government bonds. They take so long to mature.

☞ Men are like laxatives. They irritate the crap out of you.

☞ Men are like photocopiers. You need them for reproduction, but that's about it.

☞ Men are like place-mats. They only show up when there's food on the table.

☞ Men are like second-hand cars. They're easy to get hold of, cheap and unreliable.

☞ Men are like snowstorms. You never know when they're coming, how many inches you'll get or how long it'll last.

☞ Men are like trains. They always stop before you get off.

BATTLE OF THE SEXES – WHY IT'S BETTER BEING A WOMAN THAN A MAN

☞ If we forget to shave, no one has to know.

  ☞ If we're dumb, some people will think it's cute.

☞ We can find out everything we need to know about a person by glancing at their shoes.

  ☞ We can get out of speeding fines by crying.

☞ We can talk to people of the opposite sex without having to picture them naked.

  ☞ We don't have to reach down every so often to make sure our privates are still there.

☞ We'll never discover we've been duped by a Wonderbra.

  ☞ We've never lusted forlornly after a cartoon character or the central figure of a computer game.

BATTLE OF THE SEXES – WOMEN

"Bachelors know more about women than married men do. If they didn't, they'd be married too."
HL Mencken

☞ A woman's mind is cleaner than a man's because she changes it more often.

☞ A Woman's Prayer: "Dear Lord. So far today, I am doing very well. I have not gossiped, lost my temper, been greedy, grumpy, nasty, selfish or self-indulgent. I have not whined, cursed or eaten any chocolate. However, I am going to get out of bed in a few minutes and now I will need your help more than ever. Amen."

☞ The seven ages of woman: baby, child, girl, young woman, young woman, young woman and young woman.

☞ Why are hurricanes usually named after women? When they come, they're wild and wet. When they go, they take your house and car.

☞ Why do women rub their eyes when they wake up? Because they don't have any balls to scratch.

☞ Why hasn't there been a woman on the moon? It doesn't need cleaning yet.

☞ Women are unpredictable. Before marriage, she expects a man. After marriage, she suspects him. And after death, she respects him.

BATTLE OF THE SEXES – WOMEN (EXTREME MISOGYNY)

☞ How do you know when it's time to wash dishes and clean the house? Look inside your pants; if you have a penis, it's not time.

☞ How do you turn your washing machine into a snow plough? Buy her a shovel.

☞ How many male chauvinists does it take to change a lightbulb? None – she can do it when she's finished the dishes.

☞ How many men does it take to change a lightbulb? None. She can iron in the dark.

☞ If a motorcyclist runs over a woman, who's to blame? The motorcyclist. He shouldn't have been riding around in the kitchen.

☞ If your wife keeps coming out of the kitchen to nag at you, what have you done wrong? Made her chain too long.

☞ What's worse than a male chauvinistic pig? A woman who won't do what she's told.

☞ Why do women wear make-up and perfume? Because they're ugly and they smell.

BEARS

☞ A bear and a rabbit are having a crap in the woods. The bear says to the rabbit, "When you poop, does crap get stuck to your fur?" "Not really," says the rabbit. So the bear picks him up and wipes his arse with him.

☞ My uncle kept a grizzly bear as a pet once. He had to give it up though; the bastard just wouldn't stop moaning.

☞ What do you called a bear with thinning hair? Fred bear.

BEAUTY TREATMENT

☞ A woman comes back from a week at a beauty spa. She's had the full works and everything is scrubbed, revitalized and glowing. She finds her husband to show off her new look. "So," she says. "If you didn't know me, how old would you think I was?" "Well," says her husband. "From the hair, I'd say 16. From your skin, about 22. From your figure..." "Oh, stop it," giggles the woman. "You're just flattering me." "Well, hang on," says her husband. "I haven't added them up yet..."

☞ Doreen isn't very happy. She paid to have her face lifted last week, but they found another one exactly the same underneath.

**"My friend said to me, 'You must be more American.'
So I went to have botox. The surgeon said to me,
'That's $8,000.' I couldn't even look shocked!"**
Shazia Mirza

☞ My wife was at the beauty shop for two hours – and that was just for the estimate.

☞ My wife's had a facelift, a tummy lift and a buttock lift; now she's two feet off the ground.

**"I don't plan to grow old gracefully. I plan to
have facelifts until my ears meet."**
Rita Rudner

☞ Two women are discussing the merits of cosmetic surgery. "I'm thinking of having my anus bleached," says one. The other woman thinks for a second, then says, "I'm not sure that's such a good idea. I can't imagine your husband as a blond."

"You want to feel really handsome? Go shopping at Asda."
Brendon Burns

BIKERS

☞ A motorcycle cop comes across two bikers. One biker has his index finger up the backside of the other. "What the heck are you boys doing?" asks the cop. "My buddy here's choking," says the biker with the finger. "I'm trying to get him to throw up." "You're meant to stick your finger down his throat, not up his backside," replies the cop. The biker replies, "Yeah, but you get better results if you stick it up his butt first."

☞ Bronco the biker gets into a fight and has all the buttons pulled off his denim jacket. He rides home to nurse his bruises, but is annoyed by the way his open jacket is flapping around in the wind. It's also damned cold. To solve the problem, Bronco pulls over and puts his jacket on back to front. He guns his engine and tears off down the road again. Unfortunately, he hits a patch of oil and skids into a tree. An hour later a team of paramedics is loading Bronco's corpse into an ambulance. One of them interviews the farmer who came across his body. "It's a damned shame," says the farmer. "Apart from his head he didn't look too badly hurt, but when I twisted it the right way round he took a real turn for the worse."

☞ Bronco the biker marries long-time biker chick Charlene. A few weeks after the wedding, Bronco meets his old friend Rex in a bar. "So how's married life treating you?" asks Rex. "Great," says Bronco. "Me and Charlene have our own trailer now." "Bet the sex must be good," says Rex. "I guess so," replies Bronco. "It's the same as before, but it's real handy not having to stand in line any more."

☞ What's the best thing about being the oldest chick in a biker gang? You don't have to pull up your T-shirt so far when you're flashing your tits.

☞ What's the difference between a Harley-Davison and a Hoover? On a Harley the dirtbag sits on the top.

☞ Why do Hell's Angels wear leather? Because chiffon stains too easily.

BITTERNESS

"I don't mean to sound bitter, cold or cruel,
but I am, so that's how it comes out."
Bill Hicks

BLACKSMITHS

☞ The village blacksmith finally found an apprentice willing to work long hours for little money. The blacksmith immediately began instructing the lad: "When I take the shoe out of the fire, I'll lay it on the anvil; and when I nod my head, you hit it with this hammer." The apprentice did just as he was told – and now he's the village blacksmith.

BLONDES – DIM

☞ A beautiful blonde goes to her local pet store in search of an exotic pet. She notices a box full of frogs with a sign saying, "Sex Frogs! Your pleasure guaranteed! Comes with complete instructions." Intrigued, the blonde buys one and takes it home. She reads the instructions and follows them exactly. She takes a shower, puts on perfume, slips into bed and puts the frog between her legs – but nothing happens! The blonde rings the pet shop and complains that her Sex Frog is broken. The man at the shop agrees to come over and fix it. When he arrives, the pet shop man asks the blonde to resume her position on the bed. He then picks up the frog, looks it in the eye and says, "Listen, buddy; I'm only going to show you how to do this one last time!"

☞ A blonde calls up an airline ticket counter and says, "How long are your flights from New York to Atlanta?" The ticket clerk replies, "Just a minute, madame..." "Thank you," says the blonde, and hangs up.

☞ A blonde comes home after a long day at the office. "I feel sick," says the blonde to her flatmate. "On the journey home I was sitting on the train with my back to the engine. I hate travelling backwards. I felt like puking." The flatmate replies, "You should have asked the person sitting opposite you to swap seats." "I couldn't," whines the blonde. "There wasn't anyone there."

☞ A blonde couple are redecorating their house. The blond husband is painting the bedroom ceiling when his blonde wife walks in. "Have you got a good hold of your brush?" she asks. "Yes, dear," replies her husband. "Well, hang on tight," she says, "because I'm taking the ladder."

☞ A blonde decides to try horse-riding. She mounts her steed unassisted and it immediately springs into action. It gallops along at a steady pace, but the blonde begins to slip off the saddle. In terror, she grabs for the horse's mane, but can't seem to get a firm grip. She throws her arms round the horse's neck, but still struggles to stop herself sliding down its flank. While all this is going on the horse still gallops along, seemingly oblivious to the fate of its rider. The blonde panics and attempts to leap away from her steed, desperate to throw herself to safety, despite the risk. At that point, disaster strikes; her foot gets tangled in the stirrup, and she's now at the mercy of the horse's pounding hooves; her head is being struck against the ground over and over again. Things look bad for the blonde, but seconds before she passes out she's saved by the supermarket manager – who comes over and unplugs the ride.

☞ A blonde gets on a plane and finds out it's a Boeing 747. The blonde has never come across this word before. She is delighted at the weird-sounding name and keeps saying it out loud. "Boeing! Boeing! Boeing!" she says, chuckling at the funny, funny word. She turns to her neighbour, a crusty-looking old woman and says, "This plane's name sounds like a big spring, doesn't it? Boeing! Boeing! Boeing! Boeing!..." The old woman has had enough; she turns to the blonde and shouts, "Be silent!" "Oh, wow," says the blonde. "Thanks for telling me. I'd have looked pretty stupid if I'd carried on like that; 'Oeing' sounds even funnier. Oeing! Oeing! Oeing! Oeing!..."

☞ A blonde goes to a clinic to get her baby weighed. "I'm sorry," says the nurse, but the baby scales are broken. However, there is a solution. If we weigh you standing on the adult scales, then weigh you holding the baby, we can subtract the mother's weight and find the baby's weight." The blonde gives the nurse a sharp look. "Well, that's never going to work," she says. "Why not?" asks the nurse. The blonde replies, "Because I'm not the mother; I'm the aunt."

☞ A blonde is being given swimming lessons by a young lifeguard. She turns to him and says, "This isn't very comfortable. Are you sure I'll sink if you take your finger out?"

☞ A blonde is driving down a country road when she sees another blonde sitting in a rowing boat in the middle of a wheat field. The blonde gets out of her car and shouts, "Hey, you! You in the rowing boat! What do you think you're doing? It's doing dumb things like that which gives us blondes a bad name!" The blonde in the boat says, "I can do what I like! And if you don't like it, why don't you come out here and try to stop me?" "I would!" shouts the other blonde, "but I can't swim!"

☞ A blonde is driving down a road when she sees that the lorry in front of her is shedding its load over the highway. She flashes her lights and beeps on her horn and eventually gets the lorry driver to pull over. She climbs out of her car and runs over to the truck. "Mister," she says. "I had to stop you – your truck is losing its load all over the highway." "It's meant to, lady," replies the driver. "This is a gritting truck."

☞ A blonde is pulled over by the police for speeding. The officer asks to see her licence. "Are you for real?" says the blonde. "You guys are so disorganised. Last week you took my licence away and now you want to see it again!"

☞ A blonde is stopped by the police for speeding. As luck would have it, the police officer is also a blonde woman. "Do you have a driving licence?" asks the blonde officer. "I don't know," replies the blonde driver. "What does it look like?" "You big dummy," says the blonde officer. "It's like a square-looking thingy in your handbag with a picture of your face on it." "Oh, yes," replies the blonde driver. "I think I have one of those." With this, she rummages in her bag and pulls out a small, rectangular make-up mirror. She checks her reflection in the mirror and gives it to the blonde officer. The blonde officer looks at the mirror, then hands it back. "Thank you, miss," she says. "That's all in order. But it would have saved us a lot of trouble if you'd told me you were a police lady too."

☞ A blonde is visiting her redhead friend when it starts to rain. The weather gets gradually worse and a full-blown storm eventually whips up, with pelting rain and hail, sheet lightning and ear-shattering thunder. The blonde lives five miles away and neither she nor the redhead has a car, so the redhead suggests that the blonde should stay the night. The blonde agrees and the redhead goes upstairs to get the guestroom ready. When she comes back downstairs, the redhead finds the blonde has disappeared. Puzzled, she looks all over the house, but the blonde is nowhere to be seen. The redhead searches the house again, but the blonde seems to have vanished. The redhead has yet another fruitless search and is about to call the police when she hears a frantic pounding on the front door. The redhead opens the door and the blonde collapses into her arms. The blonde is soaking wet and freezing cold, and her feet and legs are caked in mud. "What happened to you?" asks the redhead. "You asked me to sleep over," replies the blonde weakly. "Yeah," says the redhead. "So?" The blonde replies, "So I went home to get my pyjamas."

☞ A blonde takes a ride in a cab. She's been travelling for five minutes when she realises she's forgotten her purse. "Oh, no!" she cries. "I don't have any money. How much is on the meter?" The cabbie says, "Fifteen dollars. But don't you worry. We'll come to an arrangement. I'll pull into an alley and you take off your bra." 'Well, okay," replies the blonde, "but you'd better ride round the block a few times first; this bra's worth at least twenty."

☞ A blonde, a brunette and a redhead are standing on the roof of a burning building. Suddenly some college students come to their rescue. They hold out a blanket and tell the women to jump. The brunette jumps first, but the students drop the blanket at the last minute and the brunette crashes into the pavement. The students then call out for another to jump. "You bastards!" shouts the redhead. "You'd better not pull that stunt with me!" The redhead jumps but, as before, the blanket is whipped away at the last moment and the redhead has a nasty fall on the pavement. "Come on!" shout the students to the blonde. "Jump! Jump! Jump..!" "Do you think I'm stupid?" shouts the blonde. "You're not getting me with that mean trick. I'm going to jump, but before I do, I want all of you to drop that blanket, step away and put your hands in your pockets..."

☞ A blonde, a brunette and a redhead turn up for a job interview. After filling out their application forms, the interviewer asks them all some simple questions to determine their IQ. The interviewer asks his first question: "How many 'd's are there in 'Dambusters'?" When the redhead hears this question she straightaway answers, "One." When the brunette hears the question, she thinks for a couple of seconds, then says, "One." When the blonde hears the question, she bites her lip and thinks hard. She thinks really hard. After a lot of thinking and mumbling and counting on her fingers and jotting things down on the back of an envelope, she comes up with the answer, "One hundred and thirty-nine." "What?" exclaims the interviewer. "How the hell did you work that out?" "It's easy, dummy," replies the blonde. She then starts counting on her fingers as she sings, "Der, der, dat-a-der-deeer. Dat-a-der-dat-dat-a-der-dat. Der, dat, dat-a-deeer..."

☞ A policeman comes across a blonde wriggling across the road on her belly. "Are you all right, miss?" he asks, thinking she's probably drunk. "I'm fine, thank you," replies the blonde. "What exactly are you doing?" asks the policeman. "I'm crossing the road," answers the blonde. "But why are you wriggling on your front like that?" says the policeman. The blonde replies, "Duuh! Because the sign said, 'Don't Walk'."

☞ A redhead is visiting her blonde friend. She goes to the bathroom and sees a photograph of the blonde taped above the washbasin. When she comes out, the redhead says, "What's up with the picture in the bathroom? It's kind of an odd place to put one." "I suppose," says the blonde, "but last week I broke the mirror and I can't afford to buy a new one."

☞ An airline captain is showing a new blonde stewardess the ropes. The route they're flying has a stay-over in Chicago, so the captain takes the stewardess to the hotel where the flight crew have their reservation. The next morning the crew get back on the plane and go through their pre-flight routines. Suddenly, someone notices that the new blonde stewardess is missing. The captain is concerned she's got lost, so he calls the hotel to find out when she left. The hotel tells him that the young lady in question has still not checked out of her room. The captain is annoyed; it looks as if the stewardess has overslept. He asks to speak to her. The stewardess answers the phone, sobbing, and says she can't get out of her room. "You can't get out?" says the captain. "Is the door jammed? Is it locked?" "No," sobs the stewardess. "There are three doors in here. One goes to the bathroom, one's a closet and the other has a sign on it that says 'Do Not Disturb'!"

☞ An 'Italian stallion' picks up a blonde in a Rome nightclub. He manages to talk her into bed and they spend an hour having energetic sex. Finally the Italian rolls off his conquest and lights a cigarette. "You finish?" he enquires in broken English. "No," replies the blonde. The Italian is determined that his new lady friend should not be left unsatisfied, so he starts his love-making again. After an hour he stops, certain that he's accomplished his mission of love. "You finish?" he says. "No," replies the blonde. Not about to be beaten, the Italian has another go, pulling out all the stops and using every trick in the book. Finally, he collapses beside the blonde and whispers, "Are you finish?" "No," replies the blonde. The Italian moans in dismay, but gives his all in one final effort. Afterwards, shattered by his exertion, the Italian croaks, "You finish?" "No," replies the blonde. "What?" exclaims the beaten lover. "How you can you not be finish?" The blonde replies, "Because I'm Swedish."

☞ How many blondes does it take to make a chocolate-chip cookie? Two: one to hold the cookie and one to squeeze the rabbit.

☞ Three women, a brunette, a redhead and a blonde, are stranded on a desert island. They're running out of food and water, but land is just in sight on the distant horizon, so the women decide to try to swim for it. The redhead jumps into the water, manages to swim a quarter of the way, then collapses and drowns. The brunette has a go. She manages to swim a third of the way, but she too tires and drowns. It's now the blonde's turn. She dives into the water and swims out strongly. After a couple of hours she looks around her and realises she's got half-way. "Jeez," she says. "I had no idea this would be so exhausting. I'm pooped." So she turns round and starts swimming back.

☞ Two blondes are talking. One says, "I took my car for a service yesterday, but I was really worried the mechanic might try to rip me off." "And did he?" asks the second blonde. "No," says the first blonde. "He just charged me £30 for labour and £50 for a can of indicator-light fluid."

☞ Two bowling teams, one of blondes and one of brunettes, charter a double-decker bus for a weekend trip. The brunette team rides on the bottom deck of the bus, and the blonde team rides on the top deck. The brunettes really whoop it up and have a great time, but the blonde team is completely silent. The brunettes suddenly notice the lack of activity from upstairs and send one of their number to investigate. When the brunette reaches the top level, she finds all the blondes sitting in their seats frozen with fear. They're staring straight ahead, clutching their arm-rests with white-knuckled hands. "What's the matter?" asks the brunette. "You all look terrified. We're having a great time downstairs!" One of the blondes looks up at her and says, "Yeah, but you've got a driver!"

☞ What do you call 20 blondes in a freezer? Frosted flakes.

☞ What do you call a blonde behind a steering wheel? An airbag.

☞ What do you call a blonde with two brain cells? Pregnant.

☞ What happens when a blonde gets Alzheimer's? Her IQ goes up.

☞ What's a blonde's idea of natural childbirth? No make-up.

☞ Why can't blondes dial 911? They can't find the eleven.

☞ Why did the blonde creep past the medicine cabinet as quietly as she could? She didn't want to wake the sleeping pills.

☞ Why did the blonde throw away all the brown M&Ms? She's allergic to chocolate.

☞ Why does a blonde have one more brain cell than a horse? So she doesn't poop in the street.

BLONDES – EASY VIRTUE

☞ A blonde is at home with her boyfriend. There's nothing on the TV so the blonde says, "What say we play a game of Hide and Seek? I'll hide, and if you find me I'll give you a blow-job." "Okay," says the boyfriend. "But what if I don't find you?" The blonde replies, "I'll be in the airing cupboard."

☞ A blonde wakes up after surgery. "How long do I have to wait before I can start having sex?" she asks. "You don't have to wait at all," replies the doctor. "It's funny; that's the first time I've been asked that question after taking out someone's tonsils."

☞ A blonde walks into the office of her gynaecologist and asks if she left her knickers there. "Sorry," says the doctor. "We've not come across any." "Damn," says the blonde. "I've tried my bank manager, the dentist and the garage. I guess I must have left them on the bus."

☞ Did you hear about the blonde who went for a day's fishing with the football team? She came home with a red snapper.

☞ How does a blonde part her hair? She does the splits.

☞ Tired of being discriminated against by the education system, a group of blondes forms a campaign group dedicated to creating the 'Blonde Educational Department', a special unit that will cater for their special needs. To highlight their plight, they picket the local university to show they deserve a real education like everyone else. Unfortunately their T-shirt slogan reads, "I belong in BED."

☞ What does a blonde shout after a multiple orgasm? "Way to go, team!"

☞ What's the difference between a blond guy and a blonde girl? The blonde girl's sperm count is higher.

☞ What's the difference between a blonde and a brick? The brick doesn't follow you home after you lay it.

☞ What's the difference between a blonde and a pair of sunglasses? The glasses sit higher on your face.

☞ What's the difference between a blonde and an inflatable doll? About two cans of hairspray.

☞ What's the difference between a blonde and an ironing board? It's difficult to open the legs on an ironing board.

☞ What's the difference between a prostitute, a nymphomaniac and a blonde? The prostitute says, "Aren't you done yet?" The nymphomaniac says, "Are you done already?" The blonde says, "Magnolia... I think I'll paint the ceiling magnolia."

☞ Why are blondes buried in triangular coffins? Because every time their heads hit a pillow, their legs open.

☞ Why are blondes like dog poop? The older they get, the easier they are to pick up.

☞ Why do blondes get confused when they go to the toilet? It's the only room in the house where they have to pull down their own underwear.

☞ Why don't blondes use vibrators? They chip their teeth.

☞ Why was the blonde upset when she got her driving licence? She found they'd only given her an 'F' in sex.

BOOKS AND LITERATURE

"I was reading this book, 'The History of Glue'. I couldn't put it down."
Tim Vine

☞ Did you hear about the pregnant librarian? Her baby was born two weeks overdue and got a 64p fine.

☞ Harry is in his hotel room looking out of the window. He's in town to publicise his new book about his South Sea adventures. Harry had been sailing solo round the world when his boat capsized in a hurricane. After spending four months adrift in a lifeboat he was cast ashore on a desert island where he spent almost a year on the edge of starvation. He was finally picked up by a Japanese whaling boat, but disaster struck again when it hit an iceberg. Harry and a handful of survivors managed to take shelter on the iceberg, living on raw penguin meat. After a month, the iceberg finally melted away to nothing and he was thrown into the sea again. Harry only managed to survive because he'd built a makeshift raft, a craft partly constructed from the bones of his dead companions. After a week in the freezing water he was finally picked up by an Antarctic survey ship and taken home. It's an exciting story and Harry is due to go out to a large department store and do a book-signing. However, Harry picks up the phone and cancels the appointment. Why? Because it's raining!

☞ He is a writer whose books will be read long after the works of Shakespeare, Jane Austen and Dickens are all forgotten – but not until then.

"The last time I was in Spain I got through six Jeffrey Archer novels. I must remember to take enough toilet paper next time."
Bob Monkhouse

BOTTOM, ROCK – YOU KNOW YOU'VE HIT ROCK BOTTOM WHEN...

☞ A dog humps your leg in the street and you try to follow it home.

　☞ The launch of a new type of instant noodle snack gets you so excited you have trouble sleeping.

☞ You work in a burger bar and your uniform doubles up as your 'going out' clothes.

　☞ You decide it *is* worth moving that dog poo so you can pick up the 10p coin underneath it.

☞ You discover you qualify for Oxfam food parcels.

　☞ You give 20p to a tramp and he gives you a pound back.

☞ You try to join a five-a-side football team, and they join a four-a-side league.

　☞ Your apartment is on a Jehovah's Witness 'blacklist'.

☞ The blind date you arrange to meet in a bar turns out to be a 60-year-old amputee with ringworm, and when she goes for a pee she escapes through the toilet window.

　☞ Your parrot asks you to buy it a ladder and a ribbon, then uses them to hang itself while you're at work.

☞ Your most recent erotic encounter was with the photocopying machine at last year's office party.

BOXING

> **"Boxers don't have sex before a fight. Do you know why that is? They don't fancy each other."**
> *Jimmy Carr*

☞ A boxing fan is going abroad for a week and asks his wife to videotape a big match on the TV. When he comes home he asks his wife where she's put the tape. "Oh, I did record the match," says his wife, "but then I taped over it." "Why did you do that?" asks her astonished husband. "You know I wanted to watch it." "There wasn't any point," replies his wife. "It got cancelled. One of the men got knocked out in the fourth round and they had to stop it."

BREASTS

> **"I have no boobs whatsoever. On my wedding night my husband said, 'Let me help you with those buttons.' I told him, 'I'm completely naked'."**
> *Joan Rivers*

☞ A flat-chested woman is visited by her fairy godmother. "My dear," says the godmother, "I have cast a spell that will increase your bust by a cup size every time a man says 'Pardon' to you. Your days of small-breasted misery will soon be over." The woman is delighted. To test out the spell, she takes a walk down the street and accidentally-on-purpose bumps into a man. "Pardon me, miss," says the man, and the woman's boobs instantly put on an inch. The woman is very pleased and tries the trick on another man, bumping into him as he passes her in the street. "Pardon me," says the man, and the boobs grow again. The woman is admiring her new cleavage when she bumps into a man coming out of a restaurant. "I'm so sorry, madam," says the man. "A thousand pardons for my clumsiness." The next day the headline in the local newspaper reads, "Indian Waiter Crushed to Death by Twin Torpedoes!"

☞ Belinda is a very large-breasted girl. She says it's helped her a lot in her career; her bust has opened many doors for her.

☞ Beware of large breasts. Oh, they're fun now, but after twenty years and three kids, you'll be able to make balloon animals with them.

☞ I saw a woman wearing a T-shirt with 'Guess!' written on the front. I said, "Implants?"

☞ Last week, Jordan attended a celebrity wedding at a ski chalet. Unfortunately, she stood too near the fire and toasted the happy couple.

BUFFALO

☞ What did the daddy buffalo say to the little boy buffalo as he was leaving the house? Bison.

BUILDERS AND BUILDING

☞ A builder goes to the doctor with a problem. "I've got terrible constipation," he says. "I haven't been in weeks." The doctor examines him, then asks the builder to drop his trousers and bend over. The builder does so and watches between his legs as the doctor runs to the other end of the room. The doctor then runs back and takes a flying kick at the builder's backside. There's a horrible cracking sound and the builder yelps in pain. "That should fix you," says the doctor, "but the next time you take a dump on a building site, don't wipe your arse with an old concrete sack."

☞ A little boy spends the afternoon watching some builders at work on a neighbour's house. When he goes inside, his mother asks him what he's been doing. "Learning about building," says the little boy. "And what was it you learned?" asks mother. "Well," replies the boy.

"First you put the goddamn door up. Then the son of a bitch doesn't fit, so you have to take the bastard down. Then you have to shave a fanny's hair off each side and put the goddamn bastard back up." "Good God!" exclaims mother. "You go to your room! Just wait 'til your father gets home!" When dad gets home he hears the whole story and goes to the little boy's bedroom. "That was appalling language to use in front of your mother," says dad. "You've got to be punished. Go and get me a switch." The little boy replies, "Screw you; that's the electrician's job."

☞ Ahmed has just finished building a chimney in the middle of the Sahara Desert. He's standing back to admire his work when his boss drops by and points out that he's been holding the plans upside-down; it was supposed to be a well.

☞ The house was a wreck; the only reason it stayed up was because the termites were holding hands.

BULLS

☞ Three bulls overhear a conversation between a rancher and his stockman. It seems that they're buying in another prize bull. This is disturbing news for the other bulls, so they hold a council of war. "When we all arrived at this ranch," says the first bull, "we all agreed to share the cows equally. Right now, we've all got 100 cows each. It doesn't seem right that a new bull is going to take cows away from us. I reckon we've got to get together and keep this new bull off our territory. We'll gang up on him so he'll be too damned scared to make a move on a single cow. With any luck, the rancher'll soon turn him into hamburgers." "I agree," says the second bull. "I'm not giving a single one of my cows to the new guy. If we all pull together, that bull won't know what hit him." "I'm with you," says the third bull. "I ain't giving that bastard even a sniff of one of my cows. By the time we're finished with him, he'll be afraid to step out of the barn." The day comes when the new bull is to arrive and the three bulls line up to greet him. A truck towing an animal trailer comes into sight, but the bulls are disturbed by the fact that it seems to be much larger than a normal trailer. In fact, it's the size of trailer you'd put an elephant in. They also notice that the truck hauling the trailer is really struggling to pull it along the dirt road; the trailer must be pretty heavy. The bulls are further disturbed by the deep snorting sounds coming from the trailer – it sounds like there's a steam train in there! Then comes the moment when the trailer door crashes down and the new bull is revealed. It is the biggest, strongest, meanest-looking bull they have every seen in their lives. It's a giant, bad-tempered, ball-breaking bastard of a bull. The first bull gulps and says, "Y'know, fair's fair. I reckon I could give him a few of my cows: ten, say – no: forty…" "I don't want to be greedy," says the second bull. "I've got a hundred cows. Do you think he'd be happy with eighty of them?" The third bull says nothing; it just snorts and paws the ground, putting on a very masculine display of defiance. "Are you crazy?" says the first bull. "You can't fight that monster. If you don't give him some of your cows, he'll kill you." "He can have *all* my cows," replies the third bull. "I'm just making damned sure he knows I'M a bull."

CAMELS

☞ A man buys a camel from a man he meets in the pub. The camel is tied up in the pub's car park and the man gets on it and rides it home. As he gallops down the street, the man is pleased to see that he's making quite a stir; lots of people point him out as he passes. When he gets home, he proudly shows the camel to his wife. "A camel?" she cries. "What do you know about keeping a camel? You don't know anything about them." "Well, I know a bit," replies her husband. "I know this is a boy-camel." "How did you work that out?" asks his wife. "Well," says the man, "as I was riding down the street, people kept pointing at us and saying, 'Look at the dick on that camel'."

CAMPING

"Canoe plus waterfall equals I don't go camping any more."
Demetri Martin

☞ I went to an outdoor store and said, "I want to buy a tent." The sales assistant replied, "To camp?" I said, "Sorry, mate. I want to buy a bloody tent, don't I?" Then I said, "I also want to buy a caravan." He said, "Camper?" I said, "Make your mind up, ducky."

CANNIBALS

☞ The lone survivor of a plane crash is sitting on a desert island next to a huge pile of human bones. Suddenly he sees a rescue boat and waves to it frantically. The rescue team wades ashore, but their pleasure at finding him evaporates when they see the gruesome pile of human remains. "Don't judge me," sobs the survivor. "I did what I had to. I had to survive. Would you rather I'd starved to death!" "Are you crazy?" exclaims the rescue team leader. "You were travelling with fifteen other people and your plane only went down yesterday!"

  ☞ How do you know if you're really ugly? A cannibal takes one look at you and orders the salad.

☞ I knew this cannibal guy who gave it up to become a vegetarian. He had to stop it up in the end; his diet was so boring – nothing but Swedes.

  ☞ Two starving cannibals capture a missionary. To divide him equally, they agree to start eating him from either end and make their way to the middle. After five minutes of munching, one of the cannibals asks, "How are you doing over there?" The other replies, "I'm having a ball." "Then slow down!" replies the first cannibal, "You're eating too fast."

☞ Three men lost in a jungle are captured by cannibals. The cannibal king tells the prisoners that they can live only if they pass a sacred trial. The first step of the trial is to go to the jungle and collect ten pieces of fruit – all of the same kind. The three men are sent out on their separate ways to gather fruits. An hour later, the first man comes back and says to the king, "I have brought ten apples." The king then explains the second part of the trial. "Now you have your fruit," he says. "You must shove all the fruit up your backside. If you can do this without any expression on your face, you will live. If not, you will die." So the man bends over and stuffs an apple up his rectum. He manages to do this with a straight face, but when the second apple goes up his eyes cross and his mouth puckers up. He is immediately killed. The second man then comes back and shows the king ten small purple berries. The king explains the nature of the trial to the man, and he starts stuffing berries up his backside. This is actually very easy and he manages to get nine up there before disaster strikes – he drops his poker face and bursts into laughter. He too is immediately killed. Up in heaven the second man meets the first man waiting by the Pearly Gates. "I saw what happened to you," says the first man. "Why did you burst out laughing? You almost got away with it." The second man replies, "I couldn't help it; I saw the third guy coming along with a basket of pineapples."

☞ Did you hear about the greedy cannibal? He ordered pizza with everybody on it.

☞ Two cannibals are discussing cooking tips. "I've tried everything with those missionaries," says one. "I've baked them, and I've boiled them. Nothing makes a difference; they're as tough as old boots." "What kind of missionaries are they?" asks the second cannibal. "They're the sort that wear the brown robes and have bald patches on the tops of their heads," replies the first cannibal. "Well, there's your answer," replies the second cannibal. "They're not boilers or bakers; they're friars."

☞ Two missionaries are captured by cannibals in the jungle. Both are stripped naked and thrown in a large cooking pot over the fire. The two are slowly brought to boiling point while the cannibals throw in various vegetables. One of the missionaries notices that the other is smirking.

"What are you laughing about?" he says. "There's nothing funny about this situation. We're both going to be boiled to death, then eaten by a bunch of heathens." The other missionary sniggers, then leans over and whispers, "I just did number twos."

☞ The definition of trust: two cannibals having oral sex.

CARS AND MOTORING

"I had to stop driving my car for a while... the tyres got dizzy."
Steven Wright

☞ What's the difference between a Lada and a sheep? It's slightly less embarrassing getting out of the back of a sheep.

☞ A driving examiner is asking a learner driver some questions. "So," says the examiner. "When driving through fog, what should you use?" The learner thinks for a moment, then says, "A car?"

☞ A cop stops a woman for going 30 miles per hour over the speed limit. "Do you have to give me a ticket?" whines the woman. "Don't you give out warnings?" "We do give out warnings, ma'am," says the cop. "They're posted all along the highway – 'Speed Limit 55mph'."

"I was driving down the highway, and I'm swerving all over, 'cos I'm trying to change the radio. And just as I get the old one taken out, I hear this traffic cop behind me, 'Whee-oo, whee-oo, whee-oo.' Well, I shouldn't make fun of his speech impediment. He asks me to walk in a straight line, so I do. Then he asks me, 'You call that a straight line?' Well, I should have said – I SHOULD have said – 'Yes', but I was nervous and the only thing I could think of was: 'Well, Officer Pythagoras, the closest you'll ever come to a straight line is if they do an electroencephalogram of your own brain-wave'."
Emo Philips

☞ Tom is driving down a country road when his car breaks down. He looks under the bonnet, but can't see what's wrong. At that moment, a voice calls out, and Tom notices a man sitting on the top of a high wall. "I know what's wrong with your car!" calls down the man. "By the sound your engine was making before it stopped, I'd say the fuel-to-air ratio is incorrect." The man then gives Tom very detailed, step-by-step instructions on how to solve the problem. Tom does as he's told and eventually the job is done. Tom starts the car and it runs perfectly. "That's incredible!" shouts up Tom. "Are you a mechanic?" "No," shouts back the man. "I live in the mental home on this side of this wall! They locked me in here although there's absolutely nothing wrong with me!" "Well, I can see that!" says Tom. "You're obviously sane and highly intelligent. When I get to the next town I'll alert the authorities and tell them you've been put in the mental home by mistake!" "Thank you very much!" shouts the man. Tom gets in his car and drives off. He gets a couple of yards when a brick smashes in his rear window. Tom leaps out of the car to see what's happened. The man on the wall waves at Tom and shouts, "You won't forget to tell them, will you?"

☞ A Californian blonde buys a brand-new sports car. She takes it for a spin in the desert and puts it through its paces. She quickly accelerates to 60mph, then climbs to 70, 80, 90, 100, 110, 120. She's just touching 130 when there's a huge explosion and the car's engine bursts through the bonnet. The blonde loses controls and crashes into a cactus patch. An hour later, an air ambulance is on the scene and the blonde is being carried to the helicopter on a stretcher. "Can you remember what happened?" asks the paramedic. "It was all so sudden," says the blonde. "I started in first gear, and that was fine. Then I put it in second, then third, then fourth and then fifth. I was going real fast." "What happened then?" asks the paramedic. "Well," says the blonde. "Then I decided to go flat-out, so I stuck it in 'R', for 'race'."

> **"Yesterday I parked my car in a tow-away zone.**
> **When I came back the entire area was gone."**
> *Steven Wright*

☞ A car is doing 25mph along the outside lane of a motorway. Traffic has backed up for several miles behind it. Eventually, the police catch up with the vehicle and lead it on to the hard shoulder. At the wheel, they find a little old lady. In the passenger seat is another old lady. The passenger is as white as a sheet and is sitting bolt-upright with a grimace of horror frozen on her face. "Do you know what speed you were doing, madam?" asks the policeman. "Is there a problem, officer?" asks the old lady. "I always drive at the speed limit it says on the sign." "And which speed limit would that be?" asks the policeman. "Well, we were just on the A30, so I drove at 30 miles per hour along there. Then we turned on to the M25, so I slowed down to 25 miles per hour. Isn't that right?" The policeman notices that the old lady passenger hasn't moved a muscle since they started talking. He starts to worry she might be dead. "What's the matter with your friend?" asks the policeman. "I'm not sure," says the old lady driver. "She's been like that since we came off the A150."

☞ Fifteen-year-old Billy drives home in a Porsche. His parents are astonished. "Where the hell did you get that car?" asks his father. "Did you steal it?" "No," replies Billy. "I bought it." "What do you mean, you 'bought it'?" asks his mother. "Where does a boy of your age get the money for a car like that?" "Stop worrying," says Billy. "This car only cost me fifteen dollars." "Fifteen dollars?" exclaims dad. "Who'd sell a car like that for fifteen dollars?" "It was Mrs Thompson up the street," replies Billy. "She saw me on my bike and asked if I wanted to buy a Porsche for fifteen dollars." Billy's mother and father storm round to Mrs Thompson's house. "Why did you sell our son a sports car for fifteen dollars?" demands dad. "What exactly is going on?" "It's quite simple," replies Mrs Thompson. "This morning I got a phone call from my husband. He's run off to Hawaii with his secretary. He told me he doesn't intend to come back, so he asked me to sell his new Porsche and send him the money. So I did."

☞ Why do men like women wearing leather? Because they smell like new cars.

☞ A glamorous-looking woman is doing her shopping at the supermarket. When she gets to the checkout she notices that the person bagging up her purchases is an extremely handsome young man. "Could you take my bags to my car?" she says. "Certainly, madam," replies the young man. The woman leans towards him and whispers, "Y'know, I have an itchy fanny." "Well, you'll have to show me," replies the young man. "All these Japanese cars look the same to me."

☞ A man agrees to buy his wife a car, but they can't decide what to get. The husband wants to buy a sensible hatchback, but his wife wants a sports car. In the end, the woman demands that her husband get her something that will go from 0 to 100 as soon as she puts her foot down – so he buys her some bathroom scales.

☞ Why is it that whenever you're driving and you see a police car behind you, you sit up straight? Do you think they're going to flag you down for bad posture?

☞ A woman is taking her driving test when a blind man crosses the road in front of her. The woman ignores him and carries on regardless, nearly running the blind man over. "What's the matter with you?" exclaims the examiner. "You're supposed to slow down and let blind people cross!" "Why, what are they going to do?" says the woman. "Give the cops my registration?"

☞ A man visits a second-hand car dealership and is shown the best cars they have. One car in particular looks very good. "Only had one owner," says the salesman. "An old lady. Must have been eighty-five. Only ever drove it to her sister's house – half a mile every Sunday." The man is impressed. Another customer arrives and the salesman leaves the man to take a closer look at the car. Ten minutes later, the man comes up to the salesman with a question. "Did you say that car had only one owner, an old lady who was eight-five?" "Yeah," replies the salesman. "Why, don't you believe me?" "Of course I believe you," says the man, handing the salesman a plastic bag. "It's just that she left a packet of condoms, a girlie magazine and a bottle of after-shave in the glove compartment and I thought she might want them back."

☞ A policeman gets out of his car to have a word with a kid he's just flagged down for speeding. "I've been waiting for you all day," says the cop. The kid replies, "Yeah? Well, I got here as fast as I could."

☞ A policeman pulls a car over and tells the man driving that he was doing 50 miles per hour in a 40 zone. "But I was only going at 40!" protests the driver. "Not according to my radar," says the policeman. "You were doing at least 50." "I was not!" the man shouts back. "It was probably more like 38!" "Sir! The radar is very accurate," replies the policeman angrily. The man's wife leans toward the window and says, "It's no use, officer. He won't admit he's wrong. My husband gets very pigheaded after he's had a few."

☞ A speeding car goes off the road, hits a piece of sloping ground and is flipped over three times before smashing into a tree. The driver staggers out and a man rushes over to help him. The driver reeks of beer. "Are you drunk?" asks the man. "Of course I bloody am," slurs back the driver. "What do you think I am – a stuntman?"

☞ Why, whenever a car is causing an obstruction, do they think the best thing to do is clamp it so it can't be removed?

☞ A traffic policeman is operating a radar trap on a bridge. He flags over a driver and tells him he was driving at five miles per hour over the limit. "I'm sorry, officer," says the driver, "but my job is very important. I didn't want to be late for work." "Oh, yes?" says the policeman. "And what job's so important that you have to break the law to get there?" "I'm an asshole-stretcher," replies the driver. "You stretch assholes?" says the astonished policeman. "Yes," says the driver. "When I get hold of an asshole, I stick in my thumbs and pull it apart until I can get both hands inside. Then I stretch it, and stretch it, over a week or so, making it bigger and bigger. Eventually I end up with an asshole that's six feet wide." "Wow," says the policeman. "And what do you do with a six-foot asshole?" The driver replies, "Mostly we give them radar guns and tell them to stand on bridges."

☞ An old lady is driving round a busy car park when she spots a space. She's carefully positioning her car so she can back into the gap when a young man in a sports car suddenly come up behind her at speed and expertly swerves into the space. The old lady gets out of her car to complain. "Young man," she says. "I was going into that space. You took it from me." The driver of the sport car shrugs his shoulders and replies, "That's what you can do when you're young and quick." "Oh, really?" says the old lady, "Well, this is what you can do when you're old and rich." Then she starts bashing in the headlights of the sports car with her walking stick.

☞ Barry the clown had to take his new car back to the showroom. One of the doors repeatedly refused to fall off.

☞ Bill and Harry are driving along in Bill's decrepit old car. It's a piece of junk, but Bill refuses to part with it. Disaster strikes when they're going downhill and Bill realises that the brakes have failed. He presses with his foot as hard as he can, but the car's going faster and faster. Bill tries to yank on the handbrake, but it comes off in his hand. He shouts, "Harry! What do I do? How do stop this thing?" Harry shouts back, "Brace yourself! And try to crash into something cheap!"

"The other day I got pulled over for speeding. The officer said, 'Don't you know the speed limit is only 55 miles an hour?' I said, 'Yeah, I know, but I'm not going to be out that long'."
Steven Wright

☞ Clive is looking at a second-hand car. He says to the salesman, "How come this car is covered in dents? I thought you said it had had one careful owner." "It did," replies the salesman, "but the rest of them weren't careful at all."

☞ Driving examiner: "How can you reduce the possibility of you having an accident?" Learner driver: "Get myself so pissed I can't find my keys?"

☞ Driving examiner: "What changes would occur in your lifestyle if you could no longer drive lawfully?" Learner: "I'd be forced to drive unlawfully."

☞ George goes to a garage to complain about a second-hand car he's just bought. "When I purchased this car," says George, "you said it was rust-free. But when I got it home and looked under the chassis I found it was covered with rust." "So?" says the garage man. "We didn't charge you for it, did we?"

☞ Tom bought a second-hand car and it gave him trouble from day one. The most annoying thing about the car was the odd noise it made. Every time he went round a corner, it would make a weird 'thunk' sound. Tom tried everything he could to stop the car making the noise, but he couldn't figure it out. Eventually he got so fed-up, he took it the garage. They soon got to the bottom of it; they took the bowling ball out of the boot.

☞ Harry buys a tiny sports car. He can barely squeeze into it, but it looks great. Harry offers to take his girlfriend Janice out for a spin in the country. The speed and fresh air soon have an effect on Janice and she suggests stopping somewhere quiet to spend half an hour in a haystack. Harry drives up a secluded country lane and parks next to an inviting pile of straw. Janice nips out of the car and starts to undress. Harry, however, stays where he is. "What's the matter?" asks Janice. "Aren't you in the mood?" "Yes," replies Harry. "But until I get out of the mood I can't climb out of this damned seat."

☞ Jim fought for five years against the council's plans to build a by-pass through his kitchen. In the end he was successful; they built it through his living room instead.

☞ Harry is sitting in his brand-new Rolls-Royce waiting to turn right. Suddenly a Mini crashes into the back of him. The Mini's driver is furious. "Why didn't you indicate?" he shouts. "What would have been the point?" asks Harry, "If you can't see a whole Rolls-Royce, how are you going to spot an indicator?"

☞ Harry's rich neighbour, Bill, gives him a lift in his brand-new Rolls-Royce. Harry points to a dial on the dashboard and says, "What's that?" Bill replies, "That's the air-conditioning control." Harry points at a switch and says, "And what does that do?" "That's the control for the champagne cooler," replies Bill. "Oh," says Harry, who then points to a set of buttons. "And what's that for?" Bill chuckles to himself. "That's the satellite TV tuner," he says. "You've obviously never ridden in a Rolls-Royce before, have you." "No," says Harry, "Not in the front seat."

☞ Mavis backed out of her garage and did £1,000 of damage to her car – because her husband had backed it into the garage just a few minutes earlier.

☞ Simon went to the Motor Show this year. He thought it was quite good, but the cars weren't as new as he'd expected. Later, it turned out he'd spent eight hours walking round the car park.

"Never lend your car to anyone to whom you have given birth."
Erma Bombeck

☞ The company I work for has found a way to make sure each of its one hundred employees gets to work in plenty of time. They've reduced the number of spaces in the car park to eighty.

☞ The traffic was really bad this morning; in fact, it was so bad I had to abandon the car and finish my driving test on foot.

☞ There was a rather embarrassing incident last night. My girlfriend and I had parked in a quiet road for a bit of hanky-panky when a policeman caught us at it – he gave me a ticket for doing 69 in a 30mph zone.

☞ Tom is taking his driving test. The examiner says, "When I tap the dashboard, I want you to show me what action you'd take if someone stepped out in front of the car." When he taps on the dashboard, Tom

screeches to a halt. "Very good," says the examiner. "Now carry on."
Tom drives on, but round the next corner a man steps out in front of
them. Tragically, Tom doesn't slow the car down at all and the car
knocks the man flying. "I can't believe it," exclaims the examiner.
"Why didn't you stop the car?" "Well," says Tom, "You didn't tap the
dashboard."

CATS

**"I gave my cat a bath the other day. He just sat there.
Actually, I think he enjoyed it. It wasn't very fun for
me, though. The fur kind of stuck to my tongue."**
Steve Martin

☞ Anything not nailed down is a cat toy.

☞ Bert is reading a paper in the front room when his wife Doris sticks her
head round the door. "Here," she says, "a black cat's just walked into
the kitchen." "That's all right," says Bert. "Black cats are lucky." "Not this
one," replies Doris. "This one's just crapped in your shoes."

☞ Dogs instinctively know what our moods are. So do cats; they just don't give
a damn.

☞ Dogs listen; cats take a message and get back to you.

☞ Dogs won't bite the hand that feed them; cats bite the hand that won't feed
them fast enough.

☞ For many years my wife suffered from a terrible allergic reaction to our cat,
Fifi. We tried everything, but in the end there was no choice. We put an
advert in the paper and, although not many people wanted to take her on
at her age and in her condition, we did eventually manage to rehome my
wife.

"We have a cat called Ben Hur. We called it Ben until it had kittens."
Sally Poplin

☞ George has a tom cat which spends every night in a nearby alley, howling and screeching to attract a mate. Eventually, George decides he's had too many sleepless nights and decides to have the cat castrated. After the cat has had its operation, George is expecting a good sleep, but is astonished to hear his cat howling and screeching as loud as ever. George walks out to the alley and finds his cat sitting on a crate. The cat is surrounded by a group of neighbourhood moggies, all of them yowling their heads off. "I thought we'd had you sorted out," says George. "Why are you still out here? Even if you found a mate you couldn't do anything about it." "I know," says the cat, "but now I'm a consultant."

☞ Jean is boasting about the intelligence of her four cats. Jean's friend Mary doesn't think her cats are that smart, and she says so. Jean decides to prove the intelligence of her pets and asks Mary back next week. The day arrives and Mary sits down on Jean's sofa to witness the proof of the cats' intelligence. Jean puts a tape in her video recorder; it's a film showing one of the cats sitting on the floor licking its paws. After a few moments, Mary leans over and says, "I don't mean to be rude, Jean, but licking your paws is not that smart for a cat. And anyway, where are the other three?" Jean replies, "Mittens is working the camera, Fluffy's on lights and Minky's recording the sound."

"When a dog is watching you put up a shelf, it thinks, 'I don't know what you're doing, but it looks great. I love you.' When a cat watches you put up a shelf, it's thinking, 'Nah; I'd use a three-inch Rawlplug and self-tapping screws on a wall like that...'"
Jack Dee

☞ One day in the Garden of Eden (before Eve came along) Adam said to God, "Oh, Lord, I am lonely. Will you not create a companion for me?" And God replied, "Very well; I will create you a companion who will love you always.

Regardless of how childish, selfish and spiteful you are, your companion will always adore you." So God created a new animal for Adam. And the new animal was pleased to be with Adam and wagged its tail. And Adam called the new animal 'Dog'. All went well at first, but a while later, the serpent called up to God and said, "Lord, that new animal you created is causing problems. It loves Adam so much that Adam believes he must be adored by everyone – even me! Can't you create another animal that will teach Adam humility? So God considered this development, then said, "I will create another companion for Adam: one who will see him as he really is. This new companion will remind Adam of his limitations. So God created 'Cat' and gave him to Adam. And Cat would not obey Adam, but mostly ignored him. And when Adam looked into Cat's eyes, he was reminded that he was not worthy of adoration, and so learned humility. And God was pleased. And Adam found wisdom. And the dog was happy. And the cat really didn't give a crap one way or the other.

☞ There is no snooze button on a cat who wants its breakfast.

☞ What do you call a septic cat? Puss.

"Cats have nine lives. Which makes them ideal for experimentation."
Jimmy Carr

CATTY

☞ Glenda, to Jane: "I wish I had a pound for every boy who's asked me out." Jane: "Yeah – but what does a pound buy you these days?"

☞ Nigella and Fiona are discussing their marriages. "I worry about my husband," says Nigella. "I worry that, as the years take their toll on my face, he will grow to love me less and less." "Well, that's not the case with my husband," replies Fiona. "As I get older, my husband loves me more and more. He told me so." "Yes, darling," replies Nigella, "but remember, he *is* an antiques dealer."

☞ Sandra, to Mary: "My new boyfriend is really clever. He has the brains of two people." Mary: "Wow. You're a perfect match, then."

☞ Two models are at a fashion show preparing for the catwalk. One says to the other, "Do you know, my agent insisted I insure my face for £500,000?" "Really?" says the other model. "So what did you do with the money?"

☞ Two Southern belles are talking on the porch swing of a large, white-pillared mansion. The first woman says, "When my first child was born, my husband built this beautiful mansion for me." The second woman says, "Well, isn't that nice?" The first woman continues, "And when my second child was born, my husband bought me that Cadillac you see parked in the driveway." The second woman replies, "Well, isn't that nice?" The first woman continues, "Then, when my third child was born, my husband bought me this exquisite diamond bracelet." She holds out her arm so the second woman can admire it. Once again the second woman says, "Well, isn't that nice?" "Tell me, my dear," says the first woman, "did your husband give you any gifts when your children were born?" "Oh, yes," replies the second woman. "When my eldest was delivered, my husband sent me to a charm school." "A charm school?" exclaims the first woman. "What on earth did he do that for?" "I was having a little trouble with my vocabulary," replies the second woman. "My language was a little on the coarse side. For example, I used to say things like 'Who gives a flying f***?', whereas now I'll just say 'Well, isn't that nice?'"

☞ Two women meet at a high-class cocktail party. They get talking and one of the women discovers that the other is the daughter of a dustman. "A dustman?" she says. "Really? Well, I'd introduce you to my mother, but I'm afraid she thinks breeding is everything." "Oh, I enjoy it too," replies the other woman, "but I try to find the time for a few outside interests."

CHARITY

"A lady with a clipboard stopped me in the street the other day. She said 'Can you spare a few minutes for Cancer Research?' I said, 'All right, but we won't get much done'."
Jimmy Carr

☞ Tom asks Harry if he would like to run in a charity marathon. "Piss off," says Harry. "I haven't run in years. I get out of breath walking up the stairs." "That's a pity," says Tom. "It's a marathon for handicapped and blind children." "Hang on," says Harry. "I could win this!"

☞ A charity pantomime was staged on behalf of the local paranoid schizophrenic society. Unfortunately the proceedings descended into chaos when someone shouted, "He's behind you!"

☞ A nun receives a letter from her parents. With the letter is a £50 note for the poor. The nun is wondering who to donate the money to when she happens to look out of the window. Outside, she sees a dishevelled man sitting on the wall of the convent garden. The man looks very depressed and in great need, so the nun calls over to him. The man comes to stand under the nun's window and she drops him the £50 together with a note saying, 'Don't despair'. The man looks at the note and the money, and his face suddenly lights up with a smile. He gives the nun a thumbs-up and hurries away. The next day the nun is told she has a visitor. She goes to see who it is and is surprised to find the dishevelled man waiting for her. He hands her a bundle of notes. "What's this?" asks the nun. "That's your winnings, sister," says the man. "'Don't Despair' came in at fifty to one..."

☞ Bono is performing at a U2 concert. The crowd is going wild, but he suddenly asks them to be quiet for a few moments. Bono then starts slowly clicking his fingers over and over again. He speaks into the microphone. "Did you know," he says, "that every time I click my fingers, a child in Africa dies?" A lone voice calls from the balcony, "Well, stop clicking your bloody fingers, then!"

"If you take all the money we in the West spend on food in a day, it would feed the Third World for a year. I can't help feeling we're being overcharged for our groceries."
Jimmy Carr

☞ Four Women's Institute fundraisers are killed in a car crash. Unfortunately, an administrative error means they're sent to hell rather than heaven. Before long, Saint Peter notices that the holy host is four short and starts to make inquiries. He soon finds out where the fundraisers are and picks up the phone to get them transferred. "Hello?" says Saint Peter. "Is that Satan?" "Yes," replies Satan. "It's about the WI fundraisers you were sent," says Saint Peter. "It turns out they should have come to us." "Can't they stay?" asks Satan. "Not really," replies Saint Peter. "And, anyway, I wouldn't have thought they were your sort." "They're not," answers Satan, "but they've only been here a week and they've already raised enough money for an air-conditioning system and a new drinking fountain."

☞ Voluntary work? I wouldn't do that if you paid me.

CHAT-UP LINES

☞ Do you know, I think I could fall madly in bed with you.

☞ Hi; I'm Mister Right. Someone said you were looking for me.

☞ I'd really like to see how you look when I'm naked.

☞ I'd walk a million miles for one of your smiles, and even farther for that thing you do with your tongue.

☞ I'm a birdwatcher and I'm looking for a Big-Breasted Bed-Thrasher; have you seen one?

☞ I'm fighting the urge to make you the happiest woman on earth.

☞ Remember my name. You'll be screaming it later.

☞ Somebody's farted! Quick! Let's get out of here.

☞ Well, it's not going to suck itself, is it?

☞ You might not be the best-looking girl here, but beauty is only a lightswitch away.

CHAT-UP LINES – PUT-DOWNS

☞ Man: "Can I buy you a drink?" Woman: "Actually, I'd rather have the money."

☞ Man: "Can I get you a drink? What are you having?" Woman: "Right now, an attack of nausea."

☞ Man: "Darling, could you ever be happy with a man like me?" Woman: "Why, yes, I suppose I could – if you weren't around so often."

☞ Man: "Can I have your name?" Woman: "Why? Don't you already have one?"

☞ Man: "Do you kiss with your eyes closed?" Woman: "I would if I were kissing you."

☞ Man: "For the sake of the other women here, I think we should leave together – you're making them all look ugly." Woman: "I think we should stay. You're making all the other men look good."

☞ Man: "Go on; don't be shy. Ask me out." Woman: "Okay. Get out."

☞ Man: "Hi. Didn't we go on a date once?" Woman: "It must have been once. I'd never make that mistake twice."

☞ Man: "How about coming back to my apartment for a bit of heavy breathing?" Woman: "Why; is your lift broken?"

☞ Man: "How did you get to be so good-looking?" Woman: "I don't know. Perhaps I got your share too."

☞ Man: "I could fulfil your every sexual fantasy." Woman: "You mean you've got a donkey *and* a Great Dane?"

☞ Man: "I know a great way to burn off a few calories." Woman: "So do I. It involves running away from you."

☞ Man: "If you kiss me, I promise not to turn into a frog." Woman: "So why would I want to kiss you?"

☞ Man: "It's okay; we can be together tonight. I've given my girlfriend the evening off." Woman: "What for: good behaviour?"

☞ Man: "I've bought a couple of tickets for the theatre. Want to come?" Woman: "Sure – but only if you give me both of them."

☞ Man: "My ideal woman has to have a great sense of humour." Woman: "And that'll be the only sense she *does* have."

☞ Man: "What radio station would you like me to switch on in the morning?" Woman: "The one at the hospital."

☞ Man: "What would you say if I asked you to marry me?" Woman: "Nothing. I get hiccups if I try to talk and laugh at the same time."

☞ Man: "What's it like being the most attractive person in the room?" Woman: "You'll never know."

☞ Man: "Where have you been all my life?" Woman: "Where I'll be for the rest of your life – in your wildest dreams."

☞ Man: "Your figure is turning a few heads." Woman: "And your face is turning a few stomachs."

☞ Man: "Whisper those three words that will make me walk on air." Woman: "OK. Go hang yourself."

CHAVS

☞ A businessman is driving through Liverpool when his car splutters to a halt. The man reckons the problem is with his fuel pipe, so he gets out, pops up the hood and takes a look. While he's poking about, he hears a noise from the back of the car. He looks up and sees a chav trying to lever open his boot with a crowbar. "Oi!" shouts the man. "This is my bloody car!" "Keep you hair on, mate," says the chav. "You do the front half, I'll do the back."

☞ A glamorous middle-aged woman goes to Liverpool on a business trip. In the evening, she goes to a nightclub and gets chatting to a couple of good-looking local lads. As the evening goes on, the drink and the music get the woman increasingly turned on, and she decides she's going to give these boys the ride of their lives. She leans over the table – revealing five inches of cleavage – and says to her companions, "Listen, why don't you two sexy young things come back to my hotel and show me what you Liverpool boys do best?" So she takes them back to her room, and they pinch her handbag.

☞ How do you get 100 chavs into a phone box? Paint three stripes on it.

☞ How do you get ten chavs into a Mini? Throw in a giro.

☞ How do you get ten chavs out of a Mini? Throw in a job application.

☞ How do you identify the bride at a chav wedding? She's the most pregnant one.

☞ If you have a car with three chavs on the back seat and no music playing, what do you call the driver? Officer.

　☞ In a recent survey, Britain's chavs were asked if they wanted the pound or the euro as currency. They said neither; they'd prefer to stick with the giro.

☞ What do you call a 30-year-old chavette? Granny.

　☞ What do you call a chav in a box? Innit.

☞ What do you call a chav with an IQ of 160? A housing estate.

　☞ What do you call a chavette wearing a white tracksuit? The bride.

☞ What do you call a group of ugly, shaven-haired gits in shellsuits and baseball caps descending on a pub? A chavalanche.

　☞ What do you say to a chav on a bike? "Stop, thief!"

☞ What's faster than a chav running away with a TV? His mate running away with your DVD player.

　☞ What's the difference between a chav and a park bench? The bench can support a family of four.

☞ What's the difference between a phone battery and a chav just out of prison? The battery will last a couple of days before being charged again.

　☞ What's the difference between Batman and a chav? Batman can go out without Robin.

☞ What's the first question at a chav pub quiz night? What are you looking at?

☞ Why did the chav cross the road? To start a fight with a random stranger for no reason whatsoever.

☞ Why don't chavs like 'Knock, knock' jokes? They keep thinking it's the fuzz.

CHEMISTS

☞ A man walks into a chemist's. He goes up to the feminist assistant and says, "Could I have six condoms, miss?" Indignant, the assistant replies, "Don't you 'miss' me!" "Okay," replies the man. "Make it seven!"

☞ A woman goes into a chemist's with her three young children and starts browsing. "May I help you?" asks the sales assistant. "I need some Vaseline so I can make love with my husband," replies the woman. "After having three children, I wouldn't have thought you'd need Vaseline," replies the assistant. "That's exactly why I need it," she replies. "We put it on the bedroom doorknob so they can't get in."

☞ The difference between the 1950s and today is that now a man walks into a chemist's and says, "I'd like some condoms" then whispers, "...and some cigarettes."

☞ What do you do if you come across a dead chemist? Barium.

CHILDREN AND CHILDHOOD

☞ We had our home completely child-proofed three years ago. It's no good; they're still managing to get in.

"I always wondered why babies spent so much time sucking their thumbs – then I tasted baby food."
Robert Orben

☞ A young woman with a baby boy in her arms goes into a butcher's shop and confronts the owner. "This is your son," she proclaims. "What are you going to do about it?" The butcher is shocked and, to avoid a scandal, agrees to support the mother until the child is 16 years old. In return, the woman must keep quiet about his involvement. So for the next 16 years the butcher supplies the mother and boy with fresh meat every week. After 16 years, the butcher is heartily sick of handing over all this free meat and is delighted when the boy tells him it's his 16th birthday. "And about time!" says the butcher. "Take these sausages. Tell your mother that these are the last she'll ever get from me, and see the look on her face." The boy does as he's told. "Oh, really?" says his mother after hearing the story. "Well, I'm going round to tell him about the free vegetables, milk and groceries we've been getting for the last 16 years and see the look on HIS face."

"I hurt my back the other day. I was playing piggy-back with my six-year-old nephew, and I fell off."
Tommy Cooper

☞ "Mummy, mummy! Why can't we have a waste disposal unit?" "Shut up and keep chewing."

☞ A little boy is tugging harshly on his pet dog's lead. His dad rushes out to stop him being so cruel. "Now, then," says the dad, "do you want to tell me how sorry you are?" "I don't know," says the little boy. "It depends how much you saw."

☞ A little boy runs up to his mother. "Mummy, mummy!" he says. "Why did you name me Leaf?" Mummy replies, "Because when you were a baby, I saw a leaf float down from a tree and land on your head." The next day, Leaf's little sister runs up and says, "Mummy, mummy! Why did you name me Petal?" Mummy replies, "Darling, when you were a baby, a beautiful petal floated down on the breeze and landed on your head." The next day, Leaf's little brother runs up and says, "Meeamth-mewem-wewistsspth..." Mummy says, "Oh, do shut up, Fridge."

☞ A little girl is given a pound coin by her mother. A little while later, the mother asks her daughter if she'll be saving the coin to buy something special. "Oh, I don't have it any more," says the girl. "I gave it to an old lady." "What a kind-hearted child," says mother. "You gave all your money to some poor, suffering old woman. Here's a two-pound coin for being such a good girl." The little girl takes the money and goes off to play. A little while later the girl comes back inside the house. Her mother asks her where she's been. "I went to see the old lady again," replies the girl, "only this time I got a bigger ice-cream."

☞ A mother is showing her small son how to zip up his coat. "The secret," she says, "is to get the left part of the zip to fit into the other side before you try to pull it up." The boy looks at her and says, "So why the hell does that have to be a secret?"

☞ A vicar is greeting some local children at Sunday School when he sees little Suzy. "Why, hello, Suzy," says the reverend. "I understand from your mother that God is sending you a little brother or sister." "Yes, sir," says Suzy. "And God knows where the money's coming from, too. I heard daddy say so."

"My husband and I are either going to buy a dog or have a child. We can't decide whether to ruin our carpet or ruin our lives."
Rita Rudner

☞ A woman sees a group of children playing a game of cricket in the street. She notices that one little boy is sitting in the midst of the players, crying his eyes out. The woman goes over to comfort the boy and picks him up. One of the other children shouts, "Hey! Put him down! He's the wicket!"

☞ Aunt Mildred comes over to dinner. As her nephew and his wife busy themselves in the kitchen, Aunt Mildred is entertained by her great-niece, four-year old Becky. "And what are we having to eat?" asks Aunt Mildred. "Goat," replies Becky. "My, that sounds very exotic," says Mildred. "Are you sure that's what we're having?" "Oh, yes," replies Becky. "Daddy said that tonight is as good as any to have the old goat for dinner."

☞ Grandma is reading little Jenny a bedtime story. Half-way through, Jenny interrupts with a question. "Grandma," she says. "Did God make you?" "Well, yes," replies Grandma. "And did he make me?" asks Jenny. "He made you too, Jenny," replies Grandma. "Then why is your hair white and your skin wrinkly?" asks Jenny. Grandma answers, "Because he made me a long time ago and he made you only a few years ago." "I see," says Jenny. "So he's getting better with practice."

☞ I used to wet the bed when I was little, but mum came up with an instant cure – she bought an electric blanket.

☞ I was very insecure as a child. I once asked my mother if my father loved me. She said, "Of course daddy loves you, darling. He's on Prozac – he loves everyone."

☞ Jill offers to care for the small son of her next-door neighbour. Jill arrives in time to prepare breakfast and makes a generous helping of bacon and eggs. "Mummy always makes me porridge for breakfast," says the boy. Happy to oblige, Jill goes into the kitchen and makes a large bowl of hot porridge. She puts it in front of the boy. He immediately screws up his face and pushes the bowl away, going "Eeeuch!" "What do you mean, 'Eeeuch'?" says Jill. "You said your mother always makes you hot porridge for breakfast!" "She does," replies the boy, "but I never eat it."

☞ Little Billy is a real tearaway. He's always getting into trouble, and his parents are at their wits' end. One day Billy accidentally sets fire to his bedroom, digs up the lawn looking for buried treasure and swaps all his clothes for a video game. His mother has finally had enough; she confronts her husband in the kitchen. "We've tried everything," she says, "and it's just not working. I think we need to buy him a bike." "What?" exclaims her husband. "He wrecks his room and the lawn and sells his clothes, and you want to give him a bike? How is that going to improve his behaviour?" "It won't," replies the mother, "but at least it will spread him over a wider area."

☞ Remember; if you bring your child up to be polite and courteous at all times, he will never be able to change lanes on a motorway when he grows up.

☞ Two grandmothers are babysitting their three-year-old granddaughter, Jane. All three are in the living room, and the old ladies chat while Jane looks at a storybook. "Jane's such a lovely girl," says one. "It's a shame she isn't better l-o-o-k-i-n-g." The other nods in agreement. "You're right," she says. "Bless her heart, but she's not very p-r-e-t-t-y." Little Jane looks up from her book and says, "Hey, I may be no oil painting, but at least I've got b-r-a-i-n-s."

☞ Two primary school girls are discussing their new teacher. "How old is she?" says the first girl. "I don't know," says the second girl, "but she looks pretty old." "We ought to look inside her knickers and find out," says the first girl. "How is that going to tell us how old she is?" asks the second girl. "It'll have it written inside," replies the first girl. "In mine, it says, 'Six to seven years'."

☞ Two small boys are boasting about their fathers, and which is the most important. "Have you ever heard of the Suez Canal?" asks one boy. "Yes, I have," says the other. "Well, my dad's the guy who dug it," says the first boy. "That's nothing," says the second boy. "Have you heard of the Dead Sea?" "Yes," says the first boy. The second boy replies, "Well my dad's the guy who killed it."

☞ Why do children have middle names? So they can tell when they're in *real* trouble.

"My friend has a baby. I'm recording all the noises he makes, so later I can ask him what he meant."
Steven Wright

CHILDREN AND CHILDHOOD – LITTLE JOHNNY

☞ Little Johnny runs up to his mother. "Mummy," he says, "Daddy and I were on the bus and he told me to give up my seat for a blonde lady." "Well, that's very good," replies mummy. "It's polite to give up your seat to a lady." "Yes," replies Johnny, "but I was sitting on daddy's lap."

☞ Little Johnny goes up to his father and says, "Dad, where did I come from?" Father puts down his newspaper and launches into a long talk on love, the birds and the bees and the ins and outs of human reproduction. The last ten minutes of the lecture are devoted to little Johnny's time in his mother's womb and his rather long and messy birth. As the tale continues, Johnny's eyes get wider and wider. Finally father finishes and Johnny whistles in surprise. "Holy cow," he says. "Well, that sure has Mickey Pearson beat; he told me he came from Seattle."

☞ Little Johnny goes up to his mother. "Mummy, mummy," he says. "I found a cat in the street, but it wasn't moving. I think it was dead." "Well, it might not have been dead," replies mother. "Perhaps it was just sleeping." "I think it was dead," says Johnny. "I poked it in the side, and it didn't move; then I clapped my hands and it didn't move. Then I pissed in its ear..." "You did what?" exclaims mother. "That's disgusting!" "What's your problem?" says Johnny. "All I did was lean over and go 'Pssst'."

☞ Little Johnny is at Sunday School where teacher is telling them about Lot. "And God told Lot to take his wife and flee from the city," says the teacher. "But Lot's wife looked back and she was turned into a pillar of salt." "Wow," says Johnny. "So, go on; what happened to the flea?"

☞ Little Johnny is fuming in the playground. His friend, little Sammy, goes over and asks what the problem is. "That Suzie Smith is a real cheat," says Johnny. "She said she'd show me hers if I showed her mine, so I did; then it turns out she don't have one at all!"

☞ Little Johnny is given a homework assignment. He has to write an essay on what he'd do if he won a fortune on the lottery. Next day, he goes up to teacher and gives her a blank piece of paper. "What's this?" says teacher. "Your essay was meant to say what you'd do if you won the lottery." "It does," replies Johnny. "I figured I'd do sod-all."

☞ Little Johnny is in a maths class. "Johnny," says teacher, "if there were four birds sitting on a fence and you shot one with your gun, how many would be left?" "None," replies Johnny. "If I shot one, the rest would fly away." "Well, that's not the answer I was looking for," says teacher, "but I like the way you're thinking." "Now I've got a riddle for you, miss," replies little Johnny. "If you saw three women eating ice-cream cones, and one was licking her cone, and one was biting her cone, and the last one was sucking her cone, how would you know which of the ladies is married?" "Well," says the puzzled teacher, "I guess it would be the lady sucking her cone." "No," says little Johnny, "it would be the one wearing a wedding ring: but I like the way you're thinking."

☞ Little Johnny is standing in front of the class reading out an essay. "I had to write about something I saw that was unusual," begins Johnny, "and yesterday I was walking home from school when I saw these two greyhounds running after each other. One of the dogs stopped suddenly and the one behind was going so fast it rammed its head right up the other's ass..." "Johnny," says the teacher, "we don't use the word 'ass' in the classroom; we say 'rectum'." Johnny replies, "Rectum? Hell, it damn' near killed 'em!"

☞ Teacher asks her pupils to talk about something they think is important. Little Johnny sticks up his hand and is called to the front of the class. Little Johnny draws a tiny dot on the blackboard. "What's that?" asks teacher. "It's a period," replies Johnny. "Well, that's very nice," says teacher, "but is it very important?" "Well, I guess it must be," says Johnny. "This morning my big sister said she'd missed hers, then daddy had a heart attack, Mummy fainted and the man next door shot himself."

☞ Teacher, to little Johnny: "Name six things that contain milk." Johnny: "Ice-cream, custard and four cows."

CHIMPANZEES

☞ A chimp gets into a bath, bares his teeth and goes, "Ahh-ahh-hoo-hoo-eek-eek-eek." His wife says, "Put some cold water in."

CHIN HAIRS

**"I refuse to think of them as chin hairs. I
think of them as stray eyebrows."**
Janette Barber

CHRISTMAS

☞ I love Christmas. At what other time of the year can you sit indoors, in front of a dead tree, eating walnuts out of a big sock?

☞ My dad was really tight. One Christmas, he gave me an empty box and said it was an Action Man deserter kit.

☞ "Mummy, mummy, can I have a dog for Christmas?" "No; you can have turkey like the rest of us!"

**"I bought my brother some gift-wrap for Christmas. I took it
to the gift-wrap department and told them to wrap it, but in
a different print, so he'd know when to stop unwrapping."**
Steven Wright

☞ A small girl visits Santa in a department store grotto. The little tot climbs up on Santa's lap and makes herself comfortable. "Ho, ho, ho," says Santa. "Hello, little girl. And what would you like for Christmas?" "What do you mean, 'What would I like?'" asks the little girl. "Didn't you get my email?"

"I wrapped my Christmas presents early this year, but I used the wrong paper – the paper I used said 'Happy Birthday' on it. I didn't want to waste it. So I added 'Jesus'."
Demetri Martin

☞ A New Yorker is driving past a New Jersey shopping mall when he sees a little boy sitting on the roadside. The boy is holding a $100 bill and crying his eyes out. The New Yorker pulls over to see what the matter is. As he gets closer to the boy, he notices how frayed and dirty his clothing is; he looks very poor and down on his luck. "What's the matter, little fella?" asks the New Yorker. "I had $200," says the little boy, "and half of it got stolen. I came here with the money to wait for my mother so we could go shopping and buy my little brothers and sisters some Christmas presents. We haven't been able to afford presents since my father died, but my mother has been working very hard at three jobs and she'd managed to save $200. I was standing here with two $100 bills when this big boy came by, grabbed one of the notes and ran away." "Didn't you call out when the boy stole your money?" asks the New Yorker. "Yes," replies the boy tearfully, "but nobody took any notice." So the New Yorker looks over both shoulders, grabs the $100 and runs back to his car.

☞ I got a sweater for Christmas, but really what I wanted was a screamer or a moaner.

☞ Little Johnny writes to Santa: "Dear Santa Claus, please send me a baby brother." Santa replies: "Dear Johnny, please send me your mother."

"Those presents the three wise men brought Jesus – were they for Christmas or his birthday?"
Karl Pilkington

CHOCOLATE

☞ Why do they call little chocolate bars 'fun-size'? Wouldn't it be more fun to eat a big one?

☞ A small boy is sitting on a park bench eating chocolate bars. An old man sitting opposite him watches as the boy scoffs down six bars and makes a start on the seventh. "That's a lot of chocolate," says the old man. "So much isn't good for you. It'll rot your teeth, make you fat and give you heart trouble." "Oh, yeah?" replies the small boy. "Well, my granddad lived to be a hundred and ten." "Really?" says the old man. "And did he eat seven chocolate bars at a time?" "No," replies the boy. "Mostly he just minded his own goddamn business."

☞ Five reasons why chocolate is better than sex: you don't get hairs in your mouth; if you bite the nuts, the chocolate doesn't mind; you don't need to fake enjoying it; it won't get you pregnant; and it doesn't keep the neighbours awake.

☞ I have a very healthy diet. Every day I have something from each of the four food groups: the chocolate group, the salty-snack group, the caffeine group and the 'whatever is wrapped in tinfoil in the back of the fridge' group.

CINEMA

"I've been offered a part in a film. It's a very sympathetic part: very sympathetic. I'll give you a rough idea of what it is. The scene opens. It's a thatched cottage, all made of thatch. There's violins going. There's a dear old lady sitting in an armchair, there. And a dear old man sitting in an armchair, there. There's a baby in a cot, and a dog on the mat. And I have this very sympathetic part. I creep in through the door, and hit the old man on the top of the head. Then I stab the old lady in the back. Then I strangle the baby. Now, this is where the sympathetic part comes in. On the way out, I pat the dog."
Tommy Cooper

☞ I hate sex in the movies. I tried it once, but the seat folded up, the drink spilled over my trousers and the ice went down her blouse.

☞ I went to the cinema last night. I had to buy six tickets! There was this girl who kept tearing them up...

☞ Martha was a friendly, but clumsy, cinema usherette. The other day she tripped over, landed on her torch and showed herself up in the circle.

☞ The other day I went to see *Titanic* at the cinema. There was a big queue outside and a sign that said, "Women and children first."

CIRCUMCISION

☞ Harry goes to see his friend Tom in hospital. Harry is surprised at the lavish care and attention that Tom is getting. It seems that every few seconds a nurse is coming round to plump up his pillows, get him a drink, peel an orange for him, adjust the curtains etcetera. Harry is jealous. "When I was in here to have my piles seen to, I was lucky to see a nurse more than twice a day," he complains. "How come you're getting all this special treatment?" "I think it's because of my circumcision," replies Tom. "It seems they've never looked after somebody who needed 32 stitches before."

☞ I believe in circumcision. It's no skin off my nose.

☞ In a hotel toilet two men are peeing at adjacent urinals. One says to the other, "I'll bet you were born in Springfield, Illinois." "Why, yes," says the second man in surprise. "And I bet you were circumcised at the Spring Bank Hospital," continues the first man. "That's incredible," says the second man. "How could you know that?" "And I bet the doctor who circumcised you was called Dillinger," says the first man. "That's astonishing," says the second man. "Doctor Dillinger was our family physician for years. How on earth do you know all that?" "That's easy," replies the first man. "Dillinger was the only doctor I ever heard of who used a 45-degree cut when he did a circumcision. And you're facing forwards while at the same time pissing up my leg."

CLASS

"I'm middle-class, but I'm hard: 'al dente', you might say."
Jimmy Carr

CLEANLINESS

"You know when you put a stick in water and it looks bent? That's why I never take baths."
Steven Wright

☞ A boy decides to wash his sweatshirt, but after a few minutes of staring at the washing machine he goes to find his mother, "What setting should I use?" he asks. "That depends," replies mother. "What does it say on your shirt?" He looks at it and calls back, "FCUK."

☞ A man with terrible body odour walks into a chemist's. He goes up to the counter and says, "I'd like something to get rid of this awful smell." The sales assistant opens a window and says, "Join the club."

☞ If God had meant us to have showers, he would have made our armpits the other way up.

☞ I'm not saying Harry had a problem with personal hygiene, but when he put Odor-Eaters in his shoes, he completely vanished.

☞ Jim was a very dirty man. In fact, he was so unhygienic his clothes were dirtier on the inside than they were on the outside.

☞ My body odour must be worse than I thought. I went to work yesterday and my boss said, "Jeez! What's that stink?" Which wouldn't be so bad, but I work in a sewage farm.

"A good place to meet men is at the dry cleaner's. These men usually have jobs and bathe."
Rita Rudner

☞ Two old men, Bert and Alf, are at the seaside. They have their trousers rolled up and are having a paddle in the sea. Bert looks at Alf's legs and says, "Bleedin' hell, Alf. You're feet ain't half dirty." "I know," says Alf. "We didn't come last year."

CLOTHING AND FASHION

"I base most of my fashion decisions on what doesn't itch."
Gilda Radner

☞ Mary had a little skirt, split right up the sides.
And every time she wore that skirt, the boys could see her thighs.
Mary had another skirt, split right up the front. But she rarely wore that one.

"My wife dresses to kill. She cooks the same way."
Henny Youngman

☞ A young woman is walking down the street swathed in a beautiful leopard-skin fur coat. Suddenly an animal rights activist steps out in front of her. "Murderer!" cries the activist. "What poor dumb creature had to die so you could walk around in those furs?" The woman replies, "My mother-in-law."

☞ A sales assistant in a high-class men's outfitters goes over to the head tailor, Mr Levy, with a problem. "Mister Levy," says the young man, "I have a customer who wants to buy a tie. He also wants to buy one of our 'Gusmann' unshrinkable shirts: the ones that are guaranteed never to shrink: you know – the ones we advertise on the outside of the shop as being the world's most shrink-resistant garments." "So what's the problem?" asks Mr Levy. The assistant says, "He's wearing our smallest Gusmann shirt and it doesn't fit him. It's a little loose." Mr Levy thinks for a second, shrugs and says, "Tell him it'll shrink."

☞ A woman sends her clothing out to a laundry. When the clothes come back, she sees that there are still stains on her knickers. Next week she sends off her dirty clothes again with a note saying, "Please use more soap on underwear." The next week, the same thing happens. She finds stains on her knickers, and writes a note asking the laundry to use more soap on her underwear. Next week the same happens again. This time the woman writes her 'more soap' note and adds that she'll stop using the laundry if her underwear is not washed to her satisfaction. When the clothes next come back she finds a note pinned to a pair of her knickers: "We have been using more soap. Meet us half-way – use more paper on ass!"

☞ Amazing! You hang something in your closet for six months and it shrinks two sizes!

☞ Dick is moaning to Harry about his wife. "She constantly denies how much she's been spending on clothes," says Dick. "That's why I call her 'Narnia'." "Why do you call her that?" asks Harry. "Because," replies Dick, "she's a lying witch with a wardrobe."

☞ George goes into his local dry-cleaners to drop off a suit. The owner takes the suit, then says: "I wish I had ten customers like you." "Really?" says George. "I always thought I was a bit fussy. I'm always complaining about the prices and the standard of work, and the way you never seem to have things ready in time." "I know," says the owner, "but it would be great if I had ten customers like you – the trouble is, I have more than fifty!"

☞ How did Bill Gates become the richest man in the world? By never spending more than $2.50 on a haircut.

☞ I bought my wife a second-hand leopard-skin coat. It was spotless. So I had to send it back.

☞ Julie is passing a clothing store when a dress catches her eye. She goes in and approaches the owner. "Excuse me," she says, "but could I try that dress on in the window?" "That would be fantastic!" says the owner. "What a great way to drum up business!"

"One of my favourite clothing patterns is camouflage, because when you're in the woods it makes you blend in. But when you're not, it does just the opposite. It's like, 'Hey, there's an asshole.' But when you're in the woods, you're like, 'Is there an asshole out here'?"
Demetri Martin

☞ My father used to be a tailor before he gave it up. The money was good, but it was a so-so job.

☞ There are four types of bra: Catholic, Salvation Army, Presbyterian and Jewish. Catholic bras support the masses; Salvation Army bras lift up the fallen; Presbyterian bras keep you upright; and Jewish bras make mountains out of molehills.

☞ You could tell at a glance that his designer-label sweatshirt was a fake; instead of having FCUK written on it, the logo read CNUT.

COLOUR-BLIND

☞ Dick is colour-blind. Last week he got into a fight and got beaten grey and dark grey.

COMEDY

"What is comedy? Comedy is the art of making people laugh without making them puke."
Steve Martin

☞ Tom decides to make a career as a stand-up comedian. To try out his material, he goes to the local hospital and gives some of the patients a free performance. Tom doesn't raise many laughs, but he thinks he's done okay for a first attempt. He finishes his act by saying, "And I hope you all get much better real soon." A voice from the back calls out, "And the same to you!"

> ### "Tragedy is when I cut my finger – comedy is if you fall into a sewer and die."
> *Mel Brooks*

☞ Tom has spent years trying to make it as a stand-up comedian. He started so long ago he can't remember when he got his first laugh; sadly, he can't remember the last one either.

COMMUNICATION DIFFICULTIES

☞ A man gets up one morning and finds his wife in the kitchen. She's standing at the stove, and her husband looks over her shoulder to see what's cooking. He's astonished to see one of his socks sizzling in the frying-pan. "What on earth are you doing?" he asks. "I'm doing what you asked me to do last night," she replies. "I'm not surprised you don't remember; you were very drunk." Puzzled, the man walks away thinking to himself, "I must have been plastered. I don't remember asking her to cook my sock..."

☞ Dick gets a cold and loses his voice. To help him communicate with his wife, he devises an ingenious code based on taps: one tap means 'yes'; two taps mean 'no'; three taps mean 'maybe'; and a hundred taps mean, 'you leave all the housework to me, dear.'

CONFESSIONS

☞ A woman is lying in bed with her boyfriend after a romp under the sheets. "Darling," she says, "that was wonderful, but I have something I must confess to you; when I was young, I worked for a while as a hooker." "Wow!" says the boyfriend. "I appreciate your honesty, but the past is the past. I don't mind about what you did. In fact, I find the idea quite erotic. Tell me about it." "Well," says the woman, "my name used to be Nigel and I played for Hull Kingston Rovers…"

CONSTIPATION, DIARRHOEA AND INCONTINENCE

☞ A man dies and his wife puts a notice in the paper saying he died of gonorrhoea. The man's brother rings up. "Why did you put 'gonorrhoea'?" he exclaims. "You know damn well he died of diarrhoea!" The wife replies, "Yes: but I'd rather people remembered him as a great lover than a big shit."

☞ A man goes to see his doctor. "I've got terrible diarrhoea," says the man. "I just can't seem to stop going." "I see," says the doctor. "And how long have you had this problem?" "I'm not sure," says the man. "I only noticed it when I took my bicycle clips off."

☞ Harry goes to the doctor about his constipation. "I haven't been in weeks," says Harry. "I go to the toilet and sit there for hours, but nothing happens." "Have you taken anything?" asks the doctor. Harry replies, "Only a book."

☞ Uncle Bert had to resign as a local councillor last week. It was so embarrassing; he had gastroenteritis, went to a council meeting anyway, then passed the wrong sort of motion.

CONSULTANTS

☞ A consultant is a man who knows ninety-nine ways to make love, but doesn't know any women.

☞ A consultant is someone who is called in at the last moment and paid enormous amounts of money to assign the blame.

☞ A teacher is asking her young students what their parents do for a living. "Timmy," she says, "what does your daddy do as a job?" Timmy replies, "My daddy's a doctor. He makes sick people well." "That's wonderful," says teacher. "Now, how about you, Jane? What does your daddy do?" Jane replies, "My daddy's a milkman. He delivers milk." "That's very good," replies teacher. "Now you, Jimmy; what does your daddy do?" Little Jimmy replies, "Nothing." Teacher says, "Well, he must do something, Jimmy; he can't just sit in a chair all day." "Yes, he can," replies Jimmy. "He's a consultant."

☞ It takes two things to be a successful consultant: grey hair and haemorrhoids. The grey hair makes you look distinguished and the haemorrhoids make you look concerned.

CONTORTIONISM

"But I'll tell you what I love doing more than anything: trying to pack myself in a small suitcase. I can hardly contain myself."
Tim Vine

COWBOYS

☞ A cowboy walks into a saloon and orders a double whisky for his horse. "Anything for you?" asks the barman. "Better not," says the cowboy. "I'm driving."

☞ A cowboy walks into a store and asks to buy a spur. "You just want one spur?" says the shopkeeper. "We usually sell them in pairs." "Never saw the point," replies the cowboy. "If I get one half of the horse moving the other half usually follows."

☞ A cowboy is riding the range when he comes across a rancher herding some sheep with the help of a dog. "Is that your dog?" asks the cowboy. "Sure is," replies the rancher. "Mind if I have a word with him?" asks the cowboy.

"Sure," laughs the rancher, "but I never heard of a talking dog, and this one's never said a word in my hearing." The cowboy looks down at the dog and says, "Howdy." The dog looks up and says, "Hello, there." The rancher's eyes pop out of his head. The cowboy continues, "Is this your master standing here?" "Yep. Sure is," says the dog. "And does he treat you all right?" asks the cowboy. "He sure does," says the dog. "Every day he takes me for a walk, and he feeds me all kinds of great food. Sometimes he takes me up the mountain to chase rabbits." The rancher is dumbfounded at this. The cowboy turns to him and says, "Is that your horse tied to that there post?" "Well, yes," gulps the rancher. "You mind if I have a word with him?" asks the cowboy. "Well, sure," says the rancher. "I know that dog just spoke to you, but I know for a fact that horses can't talk. It's impossible!" The cowboy goes over to the horse and says, "Howdy." "Hello," says the horse. The rancher's jaw drops. The cowboy points to the rancher and says, "Is that there your owner?" "Yup. He sure is," replies the horse. "He treat you okay?" asks the cowboy. "He's not bad," replies the horse. "He rides me every day, brushes me down in the evening, and gives me lots of hay and oats. I can't complain." "Sounds like a good deal," says the cowboy. The cowboy then looks at the rancher and says, "Say. Are those your sheep over there?" The rancher goes bright red. "Sure them's my sheep: but everyone single one of them is a goddamn liar!"

☞ A religious cowboy loses his copy of the Bible while he's mending fences out on the range. Three weeks later, a cow walks up to him carrying his Bible in its mouth. The cowboy can't believe his eyes. He takes the precious book out of the cow's mouth, raises his eyes to heaven and says, "It's a miracle!" "Not really," says the cow. "You'd written your name inside the cover."

☞ A young gunfighter meets Wyatt Earp in a saloon and asks how he can be a better shot. "I tie my holster to my leg," says Wyatt. "Will that make me a faster shot?" asks the gunfighter. "Should do," replies Wyatt. So the gunfighter ties his holster to his leg and snaps off a shot at the piano-player in the corner, shooting his hat off. "Wow; that's great," says the gunfighter. "You got any other tips?" "Well," says Wyatt. "I file off the sights on my gun." "Will that make me a faster shot?" asks the gunfighter. "Should do," replies Wyatt. So the gunfighter quickly rasps off his gun's sights and snaps off another shot at the piano-player, this time blowing the cigar out of his mouth. "Fantastic!" says the gunfighter. "You got any other tips like that?" "Well," says Wyatt, "if I were you I'd get that gun of yours and cover it all over with grease." "Really?" says the gunfighter. "And will that make me a better shot?" "No," says Wyatt, "but when Wild Bill Hickok finishes playing that piano, it'll hurt less when he stuffs that gun up your ass."

☞ Harry goes on holiday to Texas and visits a rodeo. A huge bull is brought out and a $5,000 prize offered to the man who can ride it for five minutes. Some of the roughest, toughest, most experienced cowboys try to ride the bull, but it's so mean and fierce it shakes them off in seconds. Finally, Harry decides to have a try. The cowboys try to dissuade him, as they're sure he'll kill himself, but Harry will not be put off. He's lowered on to the bull and it's let out of the gate. The bull bucks this way and that, leaping into the air, jumping backwards, rolling from side to side – doing all it can to dislodge Harry, who's hanging on like grim death. Nothing works, and finally, after seven minutes, the exhausted bull slumps to the ground and Harry climbs off. The cowboys gather around him and offer their congratulations. "How in tarnation did you do that?" asks a cowboy. "Do they ride bulls in your part of England?" "No," replies Harry, "but my wife's an epileptic and sex always sets her off."

☞ In an old Wild West town, everyone is going about their business when, all of a sudden, a man runs through the front door of the saloon. "Big Jim's a-comin'!" he yells. In a flash, cowboys and gamblers are knocking over chairs and tables, fighting each other to get out of the door. Some jump out of the windows; poker players are in such a hurry to flee, they leave their money on the table! Hearing the news, the townsfolk go crazy with fear. The undertaker hides in a coffin; old ladies are knocked from their rocking chairs by men running for their lives. The schoolteacher steals a horse and high-tails it for the next state. Even the sheriff locks himself in the town jail and hides under a bed. After a few minutes, the street are deserted. Suddenly, the rumble of thundering hooves can be heard and a huge buffalo comes charging down the main street. The buffalo is being ridden by an enormous man, just under seven foot tall and packed with muscle. He's almost as wide as he is tall. The giant is whipping his buffalo with a rattlesnake, and he has a live mountain lion draped over his shoulders as a coat. The man stops the buffalo in front of the saloon and gets off. "Stay!" he yells, punching the buffalo in the forehead with his fist, knocking it unconscious. He strides into the saloon, hangs the mountain lion on a coat-hook and walks up to the bar. The man slams the bar-top with his fist and shouts, "Service!" The trembling bartender sticks his head out from under the bar and asks what the man would like. "Whiskey!" shouts the man. The bartender takes a bottle of whiskey off the shelf and pours a slug into a glass. "I said give me a drink!" shouts the man. He grabs the bottle, bites off the neck with his teeth and swallows down the whole lot in one gulp. The bartender is terrified. "W...w...w... would you like another one?" he asks. "Are you crazy?" says the man. "I ain't staying here. Ain't you heard? Big Jim's a-comin'!"

☞ In the Wild West, Luke gets a job riding shotgun on a stagecoach. Luke knows his main job is to guard against Indians, but is unsure how to go about it. "If I see an Indian, when do I start shooting?" he asks the stagecoach driver. "Don't shoot too soon," replies the driver. "Wait till they get real close before you blast 'em." The journey starts, and before long Luke hears a war-cry. He looks behind the coach and sees an Indian brave riding after them on a horse. He seems to be catching up on them rather quickly. "Driver," says Luke. "There's an Indian behind us. Should I shoot?" "How far away is he?" asks the driver. Luke holds up his thumb, "About this big", he says. "That's too far away," replies the driver. Luke looks behind the coach again and sees the Indian has got closer. "Should I shoot him now?" he asks. "How far away is he?" asks the driver. Luke hold his hands a foot apart. "Nah," says the driver. "That's not close enough." Luke looks behind the coach for a third time and sees the Indian has got even closer. "Should I shoot him now?" he asks. "How far away is he?" asks the driver. Luke holds his hands four feet apart. "Sure thing," says the driver. "Shoot the son of a bitch." Luke takes aim with his shotgun, but seems reluctant to pull the trigger. "What's up?" asks the driver. "Why ain't you shooting?" Luke puts the gun down. "How can I shoot him?" he says, holding up his thumb. "I've known him since he was this big."

☞ Some Indians capture a cowboy and condemn him to death. Before sentence is carried out, the Indian chief tells the cowboy he can have three wishes. The cowboy asks to see his horse, and the horse is bought to him. The cowboy whispers in the horse's ear and it gallops away. A little while later, the horse returns with a naked redhead on its back. The cowboy looks cross, but he and the redhead go into a tepee for half an hour. The Indians watch this activity with contempt. "Typical behaviour for a white man," they mutter to each other. "Is sex all he can think of at a time like this?" Once the cowboy and the redhead have finished, the cowboy asks for his second wish; he wants to see his horse once more. The horse is brought over and, again, the cowboy whispers in its ear. The horse gallops off and returns an hour later with a naked blonde on its back. Again, the cowboy looks cross, but he and the blonde retire to his wigwam. The Indians again mutter about the depravity of the white man; he must be sex-mad! After an hour, the cowboy comes out of the tepee, waves goodbye to the blonde and asks for his third and final wish; he wants to see his horse again. The horse is led to him, the cowboy whispers in its ear and the horse gallops off. After three hours, the horse returns with a naked brunette on its back. The Indians are astonished. "Is the white man crazy?" they murmur. "Is he some sort of sex-maniac?" The cowboy is furious. He walks over to the horse and shouts, "Are you deaf, you moron? I said 'posse'!"

☞ A doctor is working in a Wild West town when an Indian comes to see him. "You help, please," says the Indian. "Big Chief. No crap." The doctor gives the Indian a couple of pills and tells him to give them to the chief. The next day, the Indian returns. "Big Chief. No crap," he says. The doctor gives the Indian some stronger pills and tells him to give them to the chief. The next day, the Indian returns once more. "Big Chief. No crap," he says. The doctor decides this is a serious case and gets out a bottle of his strongest laxative. "Now mind your chief doesn't drink this all in one go," says the doctor. "Tell him to take a little sip." The Indian appears to understand this instruction and off he goes. The next day, the Indian returns. He sighs and says, "Big crap. No chief."

☞ Three cowboys are in a ranch-house talking about their prowess. One says, "I'm so tough, I wrestled a crazy steer to the ground after it'd gored four men!" The second says, "I'm so tough, I once bit the head off a rattlesnake and drank its poison." The third cowboy sighs and says, "That fire needs a fixing." Then he goes over to the stove, opens the door and starts poking it with his dick.

☞ Two cowboys, Jed and Luke, are in a saloon when they see a man walk in carrying a sack. The man walks over to the bar, pulls an Indian's head out of the sack and gives it to the saloon-keeper. In return, the saloon-keeper gives the man a bag of gold. The man leaves, and Jed and Luke go over to make inquiries. "I hate Indians," the saloon-keeper tells them. "I hate them varmints so much I give $500 for every Indian head I get my hands on." Jed and Luke decide this could be a good line of business, so they leave the saloon, saddle up and go looking for a redskin. They spend the whole day riding, and eventually see an Indian on horseback. They chase the Indian into a valley and, after half an hour's hard riding, Jed snaps off a shot and the Indian falls dead to the ground. Jed and Luke dismount and go to collect the head. They have just reached the Indian's body when Luke taps Jed on the shoulder. "What is it?" says Jed. "You'd better look at this," says Luke. "Can't it wait?" says Jed. "We've got $500 to collect." "You'll want to see this," says Luke. So Jed looks round and sees two hundred Indian braves drawn up on a nearby ridge, watching them. Jed throws his hat in the air. "Yippee!" he cries. "We're millionaires!"

CROSSING THE ROAD

☞ An obese woman is having trouble crossing a busy road. She can't move fast enough to make it over safely without some help. Luckily, she spies a Boy Scout standing on the other side. "Here!" she shouts. "Can you see me across the road?" "Of course I can!" replies the Scout. "I could see you a bloody mile away!"

CULTURE

☞ A Greek and an Italian are discussing culture. "Greece has far superior architecture," says the Greek. "We have the Parthenon." "True," says the Italian. "But we have the Coliseum." The Greek responds, "Of course, you know we gave the world advanced mathematics." The Italian nods. "Yes: but on the other hand," he replies, "we built the Roman Empire." "Yes," says the Greek, "but that can't compare to sex; it was the Greeks who invented it, you know." "Certainly," replies the Italian, "but, then again, it was the Italians who introduced it to women."

CUSTOMER SERVICE

☞ Harry has an appointment to see a urologist. He goes to the doctor's office and finds the waiting room is full of patients. He makes his way to the desk and speaks to the receptionist. She's a large, broad-shouldered woman who looks like a wrestler. Harry gives her his name. "Yeah, I got your name on the list!" bellows the receptionist. "You're the three-thirty who wants to see the doc about impotence, right?" There's absolute silence as the patients in the waiting room digest this information. "No, I'm not here about impotence," replies Harry. "I came to ask about a sex change operation. I'd like the same doctor who did yours!"

DANCING

**"It's ironic that people with club feet tend
not to be very good dancers."**
Jimmy Carr

☞ Definition of an awful dancer: someone who can dance with Dolly Parton and still tread on her toes.

  ☞ I used to go to ballet lessons. The instructor told me there were only two things stopping me from being the world's greatest dancer – my feet.

DATING

☞ When it comes to men, my sister has very high standards; she still hasn't found Doctor Right.

"Burt Reynolds once asked me out. I was in his room."
Phyllis Diller

☞ "I am a single man (35) seeking a female life-partner to share my soul with. I am sensitive, caring and have a deeply loving nature. If you wish to give me your heart, I will give you mine and know that, held within your gentle hands, it will be safe for ever. No fat chicks."

"You have to remember all the trivia that your girlfriend tells you, because eventually you get tested. She'll go, 'What's my favourite flower?' And you murmur to yourself, 'Shit, I wasn't listening...self-raising'?"
Addy Van Der Borgh

☞ A boy is talking to his girlfriend. "Guess what it is I like about you," he says. "Oh, I don't know," she replies. "Is it my appearance?" "No," says the boy. "My intelligence, then?" she says. "No," says the boy. "Do you like my sense of humour?" she says. "No," says the boy. "I give in," she says. "Yes," says the boy. "That's it!"

☞ A simple way to tell a man's sexuality: if he listens to what you tell him, he's gay; if he pretends to listen, he's straight; and if he doesn't listen at all, he's married.

"I can't find a woman anywhere who'll touch me with a shitty stick. Fair enough. It is a bit of an unusual request."
Andrew Lawrence

☞ According to a recent survey, 13 per cent of women have said, "I love you" to a man so they can have sex with him. The other 87 per cent said, "I love you" to get rid of him.

"I first met my wife on Blackpool's 'Golden Mile'. I was a young comic in those days, honing my skills in rough bars and nightclubs, and she was a sweet, innocent country girl. I always remember the first time I saw her; it was in one of the amusement arcades. I was playing the penny slots when I happened to look over and glimpse a young woman standing at the doorway. She was obviously unused to the bright lights, noise and bustle of the raucous town, and I watched as she stood there hesitantly, hardly daring to come in, her small, bright eyes flicking here and there, drinking in the sights, looking, for all the world, like some small, shy forest creature – a weasel."

Les Dawson

☞ A man takes a woman on their first date. The evening is a huge success. At her door, he says, "You look wonderful; you remind me of a beautiful rambling rose. May I call on you tomorrow?" She agrees, and the date is made. The next night he knocks on her door. When she opens it, she slaps him across the face. "What was that for?" asks the man. The woman replies, "I looked up 'rambling rose' in the encyclopaedia last night. It said: 'Not suited to bedding but excellent for rooting up against a garden wall'!"

"You never see a man walking down the street with a woman who has a little potbelly and a bald spot."
Elayne Boosler

☞ A young Italian girl is going on her first date and her grandmother warns her about boys. "They only want one thing," she says, "so don't let him take liberties. Don't let him feel your chest, don't let him touch your legs, don't play with his thingy, and don't ever let him lie on top of you. If you ever let him lie on you, you will bring disgrace on your family." The girl takes in this information and goes off on her date. When she returns, Grandmother asks her how it went. "Well," says the girl. "I didn't let him feel my body and I didn't play with his thingy: but when I wouldn't, he got it out and played with it himself." "Mamma mia!" exclaims Grandmother. "Don't tell me you let him get on top of you and disgrace your family?" "Oh, no," says the girl. "I remembered what you said, so I got on top of him and disgraced *his* family."

☞ A young man is invited to his girlfriend's house for dinner with the family. On the way there, the girlfriend tells him about an odd family custom; the first person to speak after dinner has to do the dishes. They arrive, and the family sits down to eat, chatting normally. However, as soon as dinner is finished, everyone sits at the table in complete silence. The young man starts to get bored; he'd like to go, but just can't get up and leave without saying goodbye. On the other hand, he doesn't want to do the dishes either. The young man decides to try to make somebody else talk first, so he kisses his girlfriend full on the mouth in the hope someone will comment on it. No one says a word, so the young man puts his hands up his girlfriend's blouse. Still no one says a word. The young man then pulls out all the stops; he strips his girlfriend naked and they have sex on the table. Still no one speaks. The young man is not to be beaten. He tries again, but this time he strips his girlfriend's mother and has sex with her. Still no one says a word. The young man sighs. He knows he's beaten and starts to clear the table. He picks up a butter dish and the girlfriend's father jumps out of his chair. "Okay, okay!" shouts Father. "I'll do the damn dishes!"

> **"The only difference between the women I've dated and Charles Manson is that Manson has the decency to look like a nutcase when you first meet him."**
> *Richard Jeni*

☞ Billy is trying to get a girl to go out on a date with him. His mother offers him some advice. "Don't take her dancing or to the cinema," she says. "Every boy does that. Why not try something a little different? Offer to take her back to your flat for a good home-cooked meal." Billy agrees to give it a go. He rings up the girl in question and invites her round. The next day Billy's mother rings up to find how it worked out. "It didn't go very well," says Billy. "I got the wine and all the ingredients for a good meal, but she refused to go anywhere near the oven!"

☞ Bridget goes to see Father O'Leary. "Father," she says, "Brian Murphy and Patrick O'Connor are both in love with me. I like them both, but who should I choose to marry?" "Well," says Father O'Leary. "Brian is a fine, good-looking young man with excellent prospects, but Patrick, though older, has quite a tidy nest-egg tucked away. I would think, knowing you, Bridget, that Patrick would be the one you'd be choosing." "So Patrick is to be the lucky man?" says Bridget. "No," replies Father O'Leary. "Knowing you, Brian Murphy is the lucky man."

> **"I was seeing this girl and she wanted to get more serious. But I wasn't ready to; I'd just gotten out of a difficult relationship before that. So I said to her, 'Listen; you have to understand something. Relationships are like eyebrows. It's better when there's a space between them.' And that's coming from a Greek guy."**
> *Demetri Martin*

☞ Dick walks into his local pub with his arm in a sling. "Been in a fight?" asks the barman. "Yes," says Dick. "I was fighting for my girlfriend's honour." "That must have been quite a bust-up," says the barman. "It was," replies Dick. "She wanted to keep it."

☞ George breaks off his long-standing engagement to Jane. "Is it another woman?" she asks. "It is," replies George. "Is she better-looking than I am?" asks Jane. "No," replies George. "Is she younger than me?" asks Jane. "No," replies George. "Is she rich?" asks Jane. "No," replies George. "So what can she do that I can't?" asks Jane. George replies, "She can sue me for child maintenance."

☞ Glenda spies a good-looking young man at a party and goes over to introduce herself. "Why, hello," she says. "Y'know, you look just like my fourth husband." "Really?" says the man. "How many times have you been married?" Glenda replies, "Three."

"Relationships are hard. It's like a full-time job, and we should treat it like one. If your boyfriend or girlfriend wants to leave you, they should give you two weeks' notice. There should be severance pay, and the day before they leave you, they should have to find you a temp."
Bob Ettinger

☞ I always remember what my mother used to say to me: "Don't pick that up; you don't know where it's been." It always sticks in my mind whenever I walk into a singles bar.

☞ I got a phone call from a gorgeous ex-girlfriend the other day. We chatted about the wild, romantic nights we used to enjoy together and I couldn't believe it when she asked if I'd be interested in meeting up and rekindling a little of that old magic. I told her, "Well, I don't know if I could keep pace with you these days! I'm a few years older and quite a bit balder than when you last saw me!" "That's okay," she said. "I'm sure you'll rise to the challenge." "All right!" I said. "But I hope you won't mind the fact my waistline is quite a few inches bigger than it used to be!" She laughed and told me to stop being so silly. She teased me, saying that tubby, bald men were cute! "And anyway," she giggled, "I've put on a few pounds myself!" So I told her to piss off.

☞ I have a leaning towards redheads. The trouble is they keep pushing me back.

☞ Mary isn't having much luck finding a boyfriend, so her mother suggests putting an ad in a lonely-hearts column. Together they sit down to write a short message describing Mary's charms, her interests and her desire to get married. Then they post the ad and sit back to wait for the replies. A week later, a single letter drops through the letterbox. Mary opens the envelope, reads the letter, then bursts into tears. "What on earth is the matter?" asks her mother. Mary sobs, "It's from daddy!"

"The other day I sent my girlfriend a huge pile of snow. I rang her up. I said, 'Do you get my drift'?"
Tim Vine

☞ My girlfriend returned all my love letters last week. What really hurt was that she'd marked them 'Second-class male'.

☞ What do you call a man who expects to have sex on the third date? Patient.

> **"If a man prepares dinner for you and the salad has more than three ingredients, he's serious."**
> *Rita Rudner*

☞ Suzy goes on a date with Bill. Bill tries to get fresh with the young lady, but she pushes him away. "My mom gave me some advice," says Suzy. "She said I had to say 'no' to everything you suggest." "Really?" replies Bill. "So, er, would you mind if I put my hand down your blouse?" "Well...no," replies Suzy. "And would you object if I put my hand up your skirt?" asks Bill. "Well, no," replies Suzy. "How about if I ask you to strip naked?" says Bill. "Would you mind that?" "Well, no," replies Suzy. Bill starts unbuckling his belt. "Y'know," he says, "tomorrow you've got to remind me to buy your mother a big bunch of flowers."

☞ What did Jack the Ripper's mother keep saying to him? "No wonder you're still single; you never go out with the same girl twice."

☞ For men, New Year's Eve is exactly the same as a date. Both of them involve getting drunk and going to bed making a lot of promises no one has any intention of keeping.

> **"I think, therefore I'm single."**
> *Lizz Winstead*

DATING – BLIND DATES

☞ Two girlfriends are talking. One says, "How was your blind date last night?" "Terrible!" replies her friend. "The guy showed up in a 1932 Rolls-Royce."

"Wow!" says the first girl. "What's so bad about that?" The second replies, "He bought it new."

"I've been on so many blind dates, I should get a free dog."
Wendy Liebman

☞ A man goes out on a blind date and has a terrible time. He really doesn't like the woman, and after being with her for a couple of hours he decides he can't stand another minute in her company. Luckily, the man has secretly arranged to have a friend phone him in case he needs an excuse to leave. The man's mobile rings and the man takes the call. He listens, shakes his head and puts on a grim expression. "I have some bad news," he says. "I'm afraid I have to go; my grandmother has just died." "Well, thank heavens for that," replies his date. "If yours hadn't, mine would have had to."

☞ Three men had been on blind dates the previous evening and were trying to guess the professions of their partners. The first thought his date had been a nurse, because she'd said, "Lie back and relax. This won't hurt a bit." The second decided his date must have been a schoolteacher. She'd said, "Do it again and again until you get it right." The third figured that his date must have been a stewardess. All she'd said was, "Put this over your mouth and nose and continue to breathe normally."

DATING – DATING AGENCIES

"I joined a dating agency and went out on a load of dates that didn't work out. And I went back to the woman who ran the agency and said, 'Have you not got somebody on your books who doesn't care about how I look or what job I have and has a nice big pair of boobs?' And she checked on her computer and said, 'Actually, we do have one, but unfortunately, it's you'."
Karl Spain

☞ I went to a dating agency and the computer picked me out as an ideal boyfriend. But I'm not really into computers.

DEATH

"It's a funny old world. A man's lucky if he gets out of it alive."
WC Fields

☞ A woman goes to church and asks to see the priest. "Something terrible has happened," says the woman. "Last night my husband passed away in bed." "I'm so sorry to hear that," says the priest. "Why, I only saw him last week. He looked so fit and healthy." "He was a very healthy man, father," says the woman. "Was it sudden?" asks the priest. "It was, Father," says the woman, "terribly sudden." The priest continues, "And did you find him dead, or did you have a few final moments together?" "We did have a few final moments, yes, Father," says the woman. "That must be a comfort to you," says the priest. "If you don't mind me asking, what were his last words?" The woman replies, "He said, 'For Christ's sake, Mary, put down that bloody shotgun'."

☞ A funeral procession is going up a steep hill. Suddenly the back door of the hearse flies open and the coffin falls out. It starts to slide down the road, picking up speed as it goes. Soon it's hurtling down the hill like a toboggan. A man finds himself in the path of the coffin but can't jump out of the way; he has to try to outrun it, and pelts down the hill with the coffin bumping along close behind him. People come out of their doorways to watch this gruesome race and the running man notices the pharmacist standing open-mouthed at the door of his shop. "Hey!" shouts the man as he runs past. "You got anything to stop this coffin?!"

☞ A wealthy Indian businessman has spent most of his working life living in Bradford. Suddenly the man is taken very ill and, fearing he will die soon, he asks his sons to take him back to India so he can pass away on his native soil. The sons do as they are asked, and the man is taken by private jet to Delhi. There, the man asks to be taken to the city slum where he was born so he might die amongst his own people. The sons rent a small house in the slum and their father is taken there to prepare for his certain death. Thankfully, a day or two later, the man finds himself feeling much better. He turns to his sons and says, "Get me a taxi to the airport. I want to get out of this dump as quickly as possible." "What do you mean 'this dump'?" says one of the sons. "We spent a fortune getting you here. You said you loved this place so much, you wanted to die here." "That's true," replies the man. "I certainly don't mind dying here, but I'm bloody well not living here."

"I saw that show, 'Fifty Things To Do Before You Die'. I would have thought the obvious one was 'Shout for help'."
Mark Watson and Rhod Gilbert

☞ In a tiny Irish hamlet, the local rogue is lying on his deathbed. The priest is preparing the last rites and asks him: "So, tell me, my son; will you now renounce the devil? Come on now, my son. Do you renounce Satan and all his works?" The rogue opens one eye and says, "Father, to be honest with you, I don't think this is quite the time to be making enemies."

☞ A widow is entertaining her friends and well-wishers after the funeral of her husband. "My dear Harry was very organized," she tells them. "Shortly before he died he gave me three envelopes. The first envelope contained £5,000 so I could buy a decent coffin. The second envelope had £10,000 in it to buy a good plot in the cemetery. And the third envelope had £15,000 to buy a nice stone." She holds up her hand to reveal a huge diamond ring. "So what do you think?"

"I was standing beside the coffin at the funeral home, thinking about my flashlight and its batteries. Then I thought, 'Maybe he's not dead. Maybe he's just in wrong'!"
Steven Wright

☞ A woman goes to view her husband's body at the undertakers and is horrified to find he's been laid out in a brown suit. "He hated brown," complains the woman. "He specifically asked to be buried in a blue suit." The undertaker points out that changing the suit will take time and that the funeral is due to start in ten minutes. However, the woman is adamant that he must be dressed in blue. The assistant undertaker says he'll see what he can do, and wheels the dead man into a back room. A minute later, he's back, with the dearly departed dressed in a blue suit. "That was quick," whispers the undertaker. "How the hell did you do it?" "Easy," whispers the assistant. "We already had a guy in a blue suit. I just swapped heads."

☞ A woman vanishes in a boating accident off the Cornish coast. Next day the police tell her husband they have some bad news, some good news and some more good news. "The bad news is that we pulled your wife's body from the bottom of the sea," says one of the policemen. "Oh, my God!" says the husband. "What's the good news?" "We pulled three big crabs and a king-size lobster off her," replies the policeman. "You call that good news?" exclaims the horrified husband. "What on earth was the other good news?" The policeman says, "We're pulling her up again tomorrow."

☞ Harry is watching a funeral procession go by. He goes up to one of the mourners and asks who's died. The mourner replies, "The fella in the box."

☞ An enormous funeral procession is winding its way through the streets of Chicago. No expense has been spared and the casket is being carried in a huge horse-drawn hearse. A man is watching the procession from a shop doorway. He calls over to the shopkeeper, "Hey! Whose funeral is that? Somebody important?" The shopkeeper replies, "That's the funeral of Tony Viscotti's girlfriend, Angie." "What happened to her?" asks the man. "She died of gonorrhoea," replies the shopkeeper. "Gonorrhoea?" says the man. "But that's impossible. No one dies of gonorrhoea." The shopkeeper replies, "You do when you give it to Tony Viscotti."

☞ My uncle reads the obituaries every day. He can never get over the fact that people always seem to die in alphabetical order.

☞ I've figured out a way of cheating death, I'm going to stay in the living-room.

☞ An old woman dies a virgin and requests the following inscription on her headstone, "Born a virgin, lived a virgin, died a virgin." However, the undertaker economises; he inscribes, "Returned, unopened."

> ## "My dad's dying wish was to have his family around him. I can't help thinking he would have been better off with more oxygen."
> *Jimmy Carr*

☞ An undertaker comes home with a black eye. "What happened to you?" asks his wife. "I had a terrible day," replies the undertaker. "I had to go to a hotel to pick up a man who'd died in his sleep. When I got there, the manager said they couldn't get him into a body bag because he had this huge erection. Anyway, I find the room and, sure enough, there's this big, naked guy lying on the bed with this huge erection. So I did what I always do; I grabbed it with both hands and tried to snap it in half." "I see," says his wife. "But how did you get the black eye?" The undertaker replies, "Wrong room."

☞ Harry wanted to go to his grandmother's funeral. The only way he could get the time off was to tell his boss his football team had just died.

☞ At the crematorium an undertaker is standing next to a grieving widow. The old woman is sobbing her eyes out and the undertaker tries to take her mind off things by striking up a conversation. "How old was your husband?" he asks. "My Jack was ninety-nine," replies the widow, "only a year older than I am." "Really?" says the undertaker. "When you think about it, it's hardly worth you going home, really."

☞ Our local cemetery has just raised its prices for burial plots. Not only that, but they have the gall to blame it on the cost of living!

☞ Beryl is on her deathbed. She calls in her husband, Fred, for a last few words. "Fred," she says. "When you go to the funeral, will you do me a great favour and sit next to my mother?" "Your mother?" exclaims Fred. "I haven't spoken to that old bat in years!" "I know," sniffs Beryl, "but it would make me so happy to think that you might become friends after I'm gone. Will you do it for me, Fred? Will you sit next to her and keep her company?" Fred fumes, but realises he has no choice. "Okay, okay," he snaps. "I'll do it, but I'll tell you this much; it's going to ruin the whole day for me..."

> ## "The dodo died. Then Dodi died, Di died and Dando died...Dido must be shitting herself."
> *Colin and Fergus*

☞ Did you hear about the greengrocer's funeral? There was a huge turnip...

☞ Glenda and Jim are talking. "What would you do if I died before you?" asks Jim. "I hadn't thought about it," replies Glenda, "but I suppose I'd sell this house. It's too big for one person. I might get a flat with an old girlfriend of mine. We'd be able to keep each other company. Yes, that would be nice." She continues, "And what would you do if I died before you?" Jim thinks for a moment, then says, "Same thing."

☞ Glenda is standing at the Pearly Gates while Saint Peter looks at her records. "It says here you were married four times," says Saint Peter, "first to a banker, then to a singer, then a vicar and lastly to an undertaker. That's quite an odd combination." "Not really," replies Glenda. "One for the money, two for the show, three to get ready and four to go."

☞ Harry and George are talking in a bar. They get chatting about their grandparents. "When he was 46, my grandfather fell off a scaffold and died," says Harry. "That's terrible," replies George. "What was he: a builder?" "No," replies Harry. "He was being hanged for murder."

"My uncle's dying wish; he wanted me on his lap. He was in the electric chair."
Rodney Dangerfield

☞ An old man passes away. At the funeral, the preacher talks at length about the fine qualities of the deceased: what an honest man he was, and what a loving husband and kind father he was: how generous and hard-working he was: a paragon of the local community. The man's widow is sitting in the front row with her son. Hearing the preacher, she becomes increasingly concerned. Finally, she can't take it any more; she leans over and whispers in her son's ear, "Go up there and take a look in the coffin. Make sure that's your dad in there."

☞ The wealthiest man in town passes away at a ripe old age. The news of his death makes the front page of the local newspaper. In a bar, one man is particularly upset by the news. He clutches the newspaper to his chest and sobs uncontrollably. "Calm down, buddy," says the bartender. "He wasn't related to you, was he?" "No," sobs the man. "That's the problem."

"I can't afford to die; I'd lose too much money."
George Burns

☞ Two men pass each other in a graveyard. One says, "Morning." The other replies, "No, just walking the dog."

☞ Two old ladies, Ethel and Doris, are enjoying a game in a bingo hall. Ethel looks out of the window and sees a hearse driving past slowly with the name 'Alf' written in flowers on the coffin. Ethel starts to sniff and dab at her eyes. Doris looks over and says, "Don't be so soft, you silly old moo." "I can't help it," replies Ethel. "He was a good husband to me."

"What do I dislike about death? Mostly the hours."
Woody Allen

DEATH – AFTERLIFE

**"Maybe there is no actual place called Hell. Maybe Hell
is just having to listen to our grandparents breathe
through their noses when they're eating sandwiches."**
Jim Carrey

☞ A woman goes to a séance to try to contact the spirit of her dead husband.
The clairvoyant sits the woman down at a small round table and gets
some details. "What was your husband's name and occupation?" asks the
clairvoyant. "His name was Luigi," replies the woman, "and all his life he
worked as a waiter in a restaurant." The clairvoyant puts her hands to her
brow, closes her eyes and points her face upward. "Luigi. Luigi," she cries.
"If you can hear me, make yourself known." A distant voice calls out. "I can't.
It's not my table."

☞ Murphy dies and goes to heaven. One day, he's walking through a
heavenly park when he sees his old priest, Father Mulroony, sitting on a
bench. Murphy is shocked to see that the Father has a busty blonde girl
sitting on his lap. "Father Mulroony," gasps Murphy, "this is a terrible
thing to see. In life you were the most strict, staunch, upright priest in the
country: and yet I find you here in heaven sitting with a blonde floozy in
your lap. The shame of it!" "Don't jump to conclusions," replies Father
Mulroony. "She's not my reward; I'm her punishment."

☞ On their way to get married, a young couple are involved in a fatal car crash.
After drifting up towards the light, the couple find themselves sitting outside
the Pearly Gates, waiting for Saint Peter to let them into heaven. While they
wait, they start to wonder if they could possibly get married in heaven.
When Saint Peter arrives, they ask him. Saint Peter looks puzzled, strokes
his beard thoughtfully and says, "I really don't know. This is the first time
anyone's asked. Let me go and find out." So the couple sit outside the Pearly
Gates and wait for an answer. They have to wait a long time, and as the days
and weeks pass they discuss the pros and cons of a marriage in heaven.
They think it might be nice and romantic, but if they were stuck together

for eternity what would happen if they decided they didn't like each other? Eventually Saint Peter finally returns. "Yes," he says. "I've looked into it and you can get married in heaven." "Great!" says the couple. "But we were just wondering – what if things don't work out? Could we also get a divorce in heaven?" Saint Peter blows his top. "Are you crazy?" he shouts. "It's just taken me three months to find a priest up here! Do you have any idea how long it would take to find a lawyer?"

☞ Saint Peter is at his station by the Pearly Gates when he sees Jesus walking by. He calls out, "Jesus! Could you mind the gate while I do an errand?" Jesus agrees and waits by the gate while Saint Peter goes about his business. While he's waiting, a wrinkled old man walks up to the gates. Jesus asks him the standard questions, "So what did you do for a living?" he asks. The old man replies, "I was a carpenter." "That's interesting," says Jesus. "My dad was a carpenter. Did you have any family?" "Oh yes," replies the old man. "I had just one son, but I lost him." "You lost your son?" says Jesus. "Can you tell me about him?" "Well, he wasn't really my son, but I raised him." "Wow," says Jesus. "I was lost, too: and I was adopted. Anything else you can tell me?" "Well," replies the old man, "my boy had holes in his hands and feet: and he died, but a spirit brought him back to life and people all over the world tell his story to this very day!" "But that's me!" cries Jesus. "You're my daddy!" So saying, he grabs the old man in a hug and shouts, "Father!" The old man hugs Jesus and shouts, "Pinocchio!"

☞ The difference between heaven and hell. In Heaven: the cooks are French, the policemen are English, the mechanics are German, the lovers are Italian and the bankers are Swiss. In Hell: the cooks are English, the policemen are German, the mechanics are French, the lovers are Swiss and the bankers are Italian.

DEATH – THREATS

"I've had death threats. Well, okay, a petition."
Jack Dee

DEFINITIONS

☞ An Australian aristocrat: a bloke who can trace his ancestry back to his father.

☞ Bagel: a doughnut with rigor mortis.

"Another word for 'balloon' is: bad breath holder."
Demetri Martin

☞ Barbecue: a line of people waiting for a haircut.

☞ A bargain: something you can't use at a price you can't resist.

☞ Being logical: the art of being wrong with confidence.

☞ B-negative: pessimist's blood type.

☞ Cannibal: a man who walks into a restaurant and orders the waiter.

☞ Chef: a cook who swears in French.

☞ Cholera: the fear of lapels.

☞ Committee: a cul-de-sac down which ideas are lured and then quietly strangled.

☞ A conference is a gathering of people who, singly, can do nothing but, together, can decide nothing can be done.

☞ Cynics: a word invented by optimists to describe realists.

☞ Desk: a square dustbin with drawers.

☞ Diet: a system of starving yourself to death because you think it will help you live a bit longer.

☞ A diplomat: someone who can tell you to go to hell in such a way that you look forward to the trip.

☞ Drawing pin: an aroused smartie.

☞ Egghead: what Mrs Dumpty gives her husband.

☞ Experience: the thing that causes a person to make new mistakes instead of old ones.

☞ Expert: someone who knows more and more about less and less, until he knows absolutely everything about nothing.

☞ Guru: someone who knows more jargon than you.

☞ An intellectual: someone who can listen to the William Tell Overture and not think of The Lone Ranger.

"Countryside: To murder Piers Morgan."
Stephen Fry

☞ Jack of all trades: someone unemployed in all trades.

☞ Jury: twelve people appointed to determine which client has the better lawyer.

☞ A lady: someone who only shows her underwear intentionally.

☞ Laziness: resting before you get tired.

☞ Making love: what a woman does while a man's screwing her.

☞ Mallzheimer's disease: when you go shopping, then forget where you parked the car.

☞ Misfortune: the kind of fortune that never misses.

"Navy: an army entirely surrounded by water."
Spike Milligan

☞ Parachute: a double-barrelled shotgun.

☞ A pay rise: something just large enough to increase your taxes, but small enough to have no effect on your take-home pay.

☞ Pedestrian: a motorist with two or more children over 17.

☞ Possum: a member of a posse.

☞ Rugged: the act of sitting on a mat.

☞ Semi-conductor: a part-time band leader.

☞ Shingles: a bar Sean Connery used to frequent in his youth.

☞ Spouse: someone who will stand by you through all the trouble you wouldn't have had if you'd stayed single in the first place.

☞ Transistor: a man who likes to cross-dress as a nun.

DENTISTS

☞ A dentist goes up to a woman in his waiting room and says, "I'm really sorry, but I'm going to have to charge two hundred pounds for doing your little boy's filling." "Two hundred pounds!" squeals the woman. "I thought the treatment was going to be on the NHS?" "It was," replies the dentist, "but the little bastard screamed so loudly, he's frightened all my other patients out of the surgery."

☞ A woman with an enormous mouth goes to the dentist for a check-up. He asks her to open up and is confronted by her huge, cavernous gob.

"I don't mean to be rude," says the dentist, "but this has to be the biggest mouth I've ever seem. The biggest mouth I've ever seen. The biggest mouth I've seen." "Okay!" snaps the woman. "So it's a big mouth! Stop going on about it!" "I'm not," replies the dentist. "I only said it once."

☞ Did you hear about the judge who went to the dentist's? He told the dentist to 'pull my tooth, the whole tooth and nothing but the tooth'.

☞ A man goes to a dentist with a painful abscess. The dentist takes a look and announces that it needs a lot of work: so much in fact, that he will need to anaesthetise the man and put him to sleep. Hearing this, the man takes out his wallet and starts flicking through the notes. "It's all right," says the dentist. "There's no need to pay me now. I'll bill you for it." "I wasn't going to pay you now," replies the man. "No offence, doc, but if you're putting me under, I'm counting my money first."

☞ Laura falls for her dentist and pretty soon the pair are enjoying passionate encounters whenever she visits his clinic. One day, the dentist breaks some bad news. "We have to stop seeing each other," he says. "I'm worried your husband will find us out. He's bound to get suspicious." "No, he won't," says Laura. "He's really stupid. We've been messing around for six months now and he doesn't suspect a thing." "That's true," says the dentist, "but now you're down to one tooth!"

☞ Somehow, Bill managed to get cavities in his dentures. It turned out he'd been eating too many artificial sweeteners.

☞ What do you get if you win 'Dentist of the Year'? A little plaque.

DEVIL-WORSHIP

☞ If you're a devil-worshipper, but are really lousy at it, where do go when you die? Heaven?

DICTIONARIES

☞ Why is the word 'dictionary' in the dictionary? If someone doesn't know what a dictionary was, how the hell would they know to look it up in a dictionary?

DIETING

☞ My mother was trying to lose weight, so I taped a picture of a supermodel in a skimpy bikini to the fridge door. It sort of worked; Mum lost half a stone, but dad put on two and three-quarters.

☞ Rose is discussing her daughter's failing marriage with her friend Paula. "She's so unhappy," says Rose. "The stress is affecting her appetite. She lost two stones in two months." "That's terrible," says Paula, "but if she's that unhappy, why doesn't she just leave him?" Rose replies, "She wants to lose two and a half."

DINOSAURS

☞ Harry is a palaeontologist and he's just discovered the biggest, most complete set of teeth from a Tyrannosaurus Rex ever found: not only that, but he found them in the world's biggest glass of water.

DISABILITY

☞ A deaf-mute man goes into a pharmacy to buy a pack of condoms. The man tries explaining what he wants to the pharmacist in sign language, but the pharmacist can't understand. Eventually the deaf-mute resorts to a demonstration. He unzips his fly, pulls his penis out, drops it on to the counter and lays a five-pound note next to it. "Ah!" exclaims the pharmacist, who then unzips his own fly, flops his penis on the counter and pockets the deaf-mute's money. The deaf-mute is furious and starts banging the counter. "Hey!" says the pharmacist. "If you can't afford to lose, don't gamble!"

☞ A nervous father is waiting outside the delivery room. The midwife comes out and says, "I'm sorry, but your son has a serious birth defect." She then takes him into the delivery room and shows him his son lying on a blanket. The boy has no head or body; he's just a pair of blinking eyes. The father says, "I don't care what wrong with him. We'll look after him the best we can." The father then gives his son a little wave. The nurse says, "There's not much point doing that; he's blind."

☞ A year after their wedding, the Smiths have a baby boy they name Chris. Sadly, the little fellow is born without arms or legs. Chris doesn't even have a torso; he's just a head. Despite this handicap, the Smiths love and care for their baby boy and buy him everything he could possibly want. Time passes. It is now 25 years since Chris was born and his parents are having a meeting with a famous surgeon. The surgeon is convinced that he has the skills to graft Chris's head on to a body. All he needs to do is find a suitable donor, but he's sure that one will come along within the year. The future looks bright for Chris, and his parents hurry home to tell him the good news. When they get to their house, they run upstairs to Chris' room. They find him sitting on a pillow watching TV. "Chris," says Mrs Smith, "we have the most wonderful birthday surprise for you." Chris rolls his eyes and says, "Oh, crap! Not another frigging hat!"

☞ Two men are approaching each other on the sidewalk. Both are dragging their right foot as they walk. As they meet, one man looks at the other knowingly, points at his foot and says, "Vietnam, 1969." The other points behind him and says, "Dog crap."

☞ Three brothers, Tom, Dick and Harry, are sharing a house. One day, their new cross-eyed neighbour comes round to say hello. The neighbour says to Tom, "What's your name?" "Dick," replies Dick. "I wasn't talking to you," says the neighbour. Harry replies, "But I didn't say anything."

☞ Three men enter a disabled swimming contest. The first has no arms, the second no legs, and the third has no body – just a head. The whistle blows and they jump in the pool. The head sinks straight to the bottom. The head is fished from the bottom of the pool and resuscitated. "Damn it!" he shouts. "Three years I've spent learning to swim with my f***ing ears, and two seconds before the whistle, some bastard puts a swimming cap on me!"

☞ What do you do if you see a person having a fit in the bath? Throw in your laundry!

DISABILITY – BLINDNESS

"I wonder what the word for 'dots' looks like in braille."
Demetri Martin

☞ A blind man goes into a restaurant, but instead of having the menu read out to him he asks for a used fork from a previous customer, "I can smell it and order from that," he says to the manager. The manager brings him a fork and the man sniffs it. "Aaah," he says, "my favourite: spaghetti and meatballs. I'll have that." The manager is impressed by this display and brings the blind man his meal. This goes on for weeks. Every day the blind man comes in, sniffs a fork and orders exactly what the previous customer had. Eventually the manager tries to catch him out. The blind man comes in and asks for a fork, and the manager asks his wife Mary to rub it between her boobs. He then hands the fork to the blind man. The man sniffs it and says, "Hey! I didn't know Mary worked here!"

☞ A blind man is travelling on his private jet. He has a nap, but wakes up with a start; he suddenly realises that something is seriously wrong with the aircraft. The blind man makes his way to the cockpit and finds that both the pilot and co-pilot have collapsed unconscious. The blind man tries to take control of the aircraft, then finds the radio and starts calling the nearest airfield. "Help! Help!" he shouts. "I'm blind. My pilot and co-pilot have passed out, and now we're flying upside-down!" The airfield replies, "If you're blind, how do you know you're upside-down?" The blind man replies, "Because I'm strapped in the pilot's seat and the pee's running up my back!"

☞ I always thought that the braille writing on bottles of bleach was a safety warning for blind people, but really it's a nasty trick. Apparently it says, "Drink me".

☞ What's the definition of endless love? Ray Charles and Stevie Wonder playing each other at tennis.

DISABILITY – DEAFNESS

"You can say what you like about deaf people."
Jimmy Carr

☞ A man goes into a bar and sees a group of deaf people talking using sign language. The man also notices that the barman can talk in sign language and is using it to take a drinks order. The barman asks the man what he wants. "A beer, please," says the man. "That's pretty cool, being able to speak in sign language. Do you have a deaf relative or friend or something?" "No," says the barman, "but there's a deaf college up the road and since so many of my customers have bad hearing, I thought I ought to learn how they talk." "Well, I'm very impressed," says the man. At that point the barman notices the deaf group waving their arms in the air. He rapidly gestures at them and the deaf people put their arms down again. "Goddamn bastards," says the barman. "I must have told them a dozen times – no singing!"

☞ Dick and his wife are in the theatre. Dick's stomach is playing up and he lets out a huge, evil-smelling fart. He leans over to his wife and says, "Can I borrow your programme? I did a silent fart and I need to waft it about a bit before anyone notices." Dick's wife hands over the programme, and a small silver disc. "What's this thing?" says Dick. His wife replies, "It's a new battery for your hearing aid."

☞ Fred and Bill are both a little hard of hearing. They're walking down the street when Fred says, "Windy, isn't it?" Bill replies, "No, it's Thursday." Fred says, "So am I. Let's go to the pub."

☞ Fred gets a new hearing aid and shows it off to his friend Albert. "That's very impressive," says Albert, admiring the tiny device. "You can hardly see it. Does it work?" "Like a charm," replies Fred. "I can hear as clear as a bell now." "That's good," says Albert. "You've been deaf as a post for years. Your family must notice the difference." "Nah," says Fred. "I haven't told them about it. I like to sit there and listen to them talking. Since I bought it, I've changed my will five times."

☞ Fred's hearing is getting worse and worse, so he goes into a pharmacy to buy a hearing aid. The sales assistant shows him some models. "This is our best one," she says, holding up a tiny ear-piece. "It's almost invisible once it's inside your ear and one battery will last for three years. It uses the latest digital technology to give excellent results." "How much is it?" asks Fred. "£500," replies the assistant. "Blimey," exclaims Fred, "bit pricey for me. Got anything cheaper?" The sales assistant shows him a larger earpiece; this one is the size of a matchbox. "This one's larger than the other hearing aid and the battery will only last a year. It'll work just as well as the first appliance in most conditions, but doesn't work very well over the phone." "How much is it?" asks Fred. "£150," replies the sales assistant. "Still too much for me," says Fred. "What's the cheapest hearing aid you've got?" The sales assistant reaches under the counter and lifts out a large device the size of a shoe-box. "You strap this round your waist," says the assistant, "then you plug this ear-piece into it." The assistant holds up a large plastic disc with a rubber nozzle, attached to a thick length of wire. "How much?" asks Fred. The assistant replies, "It's £3.50." "That's reasonable," says Fred. "What does it do?" "Nothing," replies the assistant, "but when people see you wearing it, they start talking louder."

☞ Harry is showing off his new hearing aid to Tom. "It cost £1,000," says Harry. "That's a lot for a hearing aid," says Tom. "They're the best you can get," says Harry. "So what make is it?" asks Tom. Harry replies, "Half past four."

☞ It's spring, and a young grizzly bear stumbles out of his cave into the sunshine. The young bear looks terrible. He's all skin and bone, he shakes uncontrollably and he has huge bags under his bloodshot eyes. Father Grizzly sees the state of his son and comes over for a few words. "Son," he says, "answer me truthfully. Did you hibernate all winter like you promised me you would?" "Hibernate?" says the young bear tearfully. "God damn it; I thought you said 'masturbate'!"

☞ Matthew is deaf but has learnt to communicate using sign language. Now he has to wear boxing gloves in bed in case he puts an eye out talking in his sleep.

☞ Murphy and O'Leary are chatting. "I come from a big family," says Murphy. "Sixteen children. I blame it on my mam being a bit deaf." "A bit deaf?" says O'Leary. "How do you work that out?" "When my mam and my daddy went to bed," says Murphy, "he'd always roll over to her and say, 'Do you want to go to sleep or what?' and she'd say, 'What'?"

☞ My wife and I are both deaf so we communicate using pre-arranged signals. For example, if we're in bed and the lights are off, I'll reach over and grab her right boob if I want sex. If she also wants to have sex, she pulls on my dick once: and if she doesn't, she pulls on it fifty times.

☞ There's one huge advantage in being a married deaf person; if you ever get tired of the nagging, you can just turn out the light.

DISABILITY – LOSS OF LIMBS ETC

☞ A woman is walking along the beach when she sees a man with no arms and legs lying in the sand, crying. She asks him what's wrong and he says he's upset because he's never been kissed before. She kisses him and carries on walking. An hour later, she walks back up the beach and finds the man crying again. The man says he's upset because no one's ever given him oral sex. Feeling sorry for him, the woman obliges, then goes up the beach again. Later on, she strolls back the same way and finds the man still crying his eyes out. "So what's wrong this time?" she asks him. "I'm crying because I've never been screwed before," replies the armless, legless man. "Well, you are now," replies the woman. "The tide's coming in."

☞ After a whirlwind romance, Harry gets married. However, he has a big secret he's been keeping from his fiancée; his right leg has been amputated below the knee. Harry is very nervous about revealing this secret, but on the day of the wedding he tells his bride that he's got a big surprise for her later. That evening, in the honeymoon suite, Harry gets into bed and slips off his false limb. His bride then comes in, strips off and climbs into bed. "Now," she says, "what was that big surprise you said I had coming?" Harry gulps and guides her hand under the bed-covers to rest on the end of his stump. "My!" she exclaims, "that is a big one. But don't worry; hand over the Vaseline and I'll see what I can do."

☞ An armless man walks into a bar. The place is empty except for the bartender. The armless man orders a beer and asks the bartender if he'd mind getting the money to pay for it out of his wallet. The bartender obliges, reaching into the man's jacket and pulling out the right money. The armless man then asks if the bartender if he'd hold the glass to his mouth. The bartender does so, and the man quickly gulps down his beer. The man then asks the bartender if he'd mind getting a napkin and wiping the foam off his mouth. The bartender picks up a paper napkin and starts wiping. "Must be kind of difficult managing without arms," says the barman. "Yup," says the man. "It causes all sorts of problems. It can be a little embarrassing sometimes. By the way: where's the nearest gents'?" The barman replies, "Half a mile up the road at the gas station."

DISNEYLAND

☞ When you have your picture taken with Mickey Mouse at Disneyland, do you ever wonder what face the guy inside the costume is pulling?

DODGY ACCENTS

☞ A Japanese tourist goes to a bank in London and exchanges 10,000 Yen for £100. Next week, he goes back, but this time he only gets £95 for his 10,000 Yen. "Why I get less this time?" asks the tourist. The cashier replies, "Fluctuations." The Japanese tourist gives her the finger and says, "Yeah? Well, fluck yu Blitish too."

☞ A woman goes to Chinese sex therapist Dr Chong to see if he can solve her difficulty in finding sex partners. Dr Chong invites the woman into his office, then says: "Take off all yo' clothes and crawl real fass away from me across the froor." She does so and crawls to the other side of the room. Dr Chong then says, "Now yo' crawl real fass back to me." She does this too. Dr Chong shakes his head and says, "You haf real bad case of Ed Zachary syndrome. Worse case I ever seen! No wonder you never get a date." The woman is baffled by this diagnosis. "So what the hell is Ed Zachary syndrome?" she asks. Dr Chong replies, "You musta heard of Ed Zachary Syndrome; that's when your face look Ed Zachary rike your ass!"

☞ Sean Connery is out of work. He's had no movie offers in weeks and he's stuck at home watching the TV. Suddenly the phone rings. It's Sean's agent. "Sean," says the agent, "I got a great deal lined up. Are you free tomorrow?" "Sure I'm free," says Sean. "Then get over to Paramount Studios," says the agent, "but make it early. Get there for ten-ish". "Ten-ish?" says Sean, frowning. "What do you mean ten-ish? I don't even have a bloody racket."

DOGS

☞ What do you get if you cross a Rottweiler with a Labrador puppy? A dog that bites your head off, then nicks your toilet roll.

☞ The sex shop in the high street has branched out into sex aids for dogs. So far, the only thing they have is an inflatable human leg.

☞ Two dogs are walking down the street. One dog says to the other, "Wait a minute. I'll be right back." The dog then walks across the street and sniffs a fire hydrant for a few seconds. When he comes back, the other dog says, "What were you were doing?" The first dog replies, "Just checking my messages."

☞ I finally managed to teach my dog to beg. Last night he came home with £30.

☞ A man loses a rare and valuable dog. He advertises in the local paper offering a reward of £25,000 for its return. The man is sure this huge reward will get results, but after a few days he's heard nothing. He rings the paper to see if the advert has gone in, but gets no answer. Annoyed, he pulls on his coat and goes to the newspaper office in person. He gets to the office and speaks to the receptionist. "Could I see the advertising manager?" he says. "I'm sorry, sir," says the receptionist, "but he's out." "Very well," says the man, "what about his secretary?" "I'm sorry, sir," says the receptionist, "but she's out as well." "Well, how about the editor?" asks the man. "He's out too," replies the secretary. "What?" exclaims the man. "Have you no staff working here at all? Where on earth are they?" The secretary replies, "They're all out looking for your bloody dog."

"I got a new dog. He's a paranoid retriever. He brings back everything because he's not sure what I threw him."
Steven Wright

☞ Every day, Harry used to take his dog to school with him. Unfortunately, the school authorities decided a dog was too much of a distraction and had them separated. The dog was the one who eventually graduated.

☞ A little girl is out with her grandmother when they come across a couple of dogs mating. "What are they doing, grandma?" asks the little girl. Grandmother says, "Well, the dog on top has hurt his paw, so the one underneath is carrying him to the doctor." "They're just like people, aren't they, grandma?" says the girl. "How do you mean?" asks the grandmother.

The girl replies, "Offer someone a helping hand and they screw you every time!"

☞ A man goes to his doctor and complains of tiredness. "It's the dogs in my street," complains the man. "When one starts barking, the others start up too and their noise keeps me up all night." The doctor sympathises and prescribes the man some sleeping pills. The next week, the man returns. He's looking even more tired than last time and now he has some nasty scratches and bite-marks on his arms and face. "Did you try the sleeping pills?" asks the doctor. "Excuse me for speaking my mind," replies the man. "But those pills were the stupidest thing I ever heard of. Have you any idea how hard it is to make a dog swallow one of those things?"

☞ A woman gets on a bus and sits next to a man holding a handsome border collie on a leash. "What a lovely dog," says the woman. "What's his name?" The man replies, "Roger Bacon." "How interesting," replies the woman. "Wasn't Roger Bacon a famous scientist?" "Yes," replies the man. "So you called your dog Roger Bacon because he's clever?" asks the woman. "No," replies the man. "I called him Roger Bacon because he's fond of pigs."

"A dog is not intelligent. Never trust an animal that's surprised by its own farts."
Frank Skinner

☞ A woman goes to buy a dog. The woman lives alone and she wants a dog that will offer her some protection. The pet shop owner shows her a large mastiff. "You have to be careful with this one," says the owner. "He doesn't like men at all." "That's perfect," says the woman. She pays for the dog, puts it on a lead and takes it into the street. On the way home, the woman comes across a man coming out of a bar. Worried her dog might attack the man, the woman keeps a tight hold on the dog's lead. But the dog proves the pet shop owner wasn't kidding; he barks, breaks free, runs off and hides under a car.

☞ When you pat a dog on its head he will usually wag his tail. What will a goose do? Make him bark.

☞ Harry goes over to Dick's house and finds he has a new pet: a dog that was left to him by a recently deceased aunt. "That looks like a nice, friendly animal," says Harry. "He is," says Dick, "and he can do tricks, too. Auntie taught him lots of things. Watch this." Dick gives a whistle, and the dog immediately starts doing a routine; it juggles four balls using its front paws, dances an Irish jig on its back legs, plays a ragtime medley on the piano and finishes off with a selection of card tricks. "Wow," exclaims Harry. "That was fantastic. If you got that dog on the television you could earn a fortune." "That's what I keep trying to tell him," replies Dick, "but he wants to go to medical school."

☞ Women just don't understand me; that's why I bought a dog. This dog is like my dream date. As soon as I get her in the house, she's all over me, rubbing against my leg, licking me. I can't get a girl to do that; I can't even get a girl to crap on my carpet!

☞ Harry mated a bulldog with a shitzu. He ended up with a bullshit.

☞ How many dogs does it take to change a lightbulb?
Border Collie: one. Then he'll rewire the house.
Rottweiler: Go on – make me.
Cocker Spaniel: Why bother? Darkness does not affect my ability to leave wet patches on the carpet.
Poodle: Let the collie do it.
Old English Sheepdog: Lightbulb? Sorry, I think I just ate the new one.

☞ A little girl goes out to play after a rainstorm and comes across three puppies. "Hello," says the little girl. "What are your names?" One of the puppies replies, "I'm Jasper." "Hi, Jasper," says the little girl. "And what have you been doing all day?" "I've been having a great time," replies Jasper. "I've been in and out of puddles all day long." "And how about you?" says the little girl to the second puppy. "My name is Simon," says the second puppy. "I've been having a great time too. I've been in and out of puddles all day long." "And what about you, little feller?" says the little girl to the third puppy. "I've had a really crappy day," replies the puppy. "My name's Puddles."

☞ I've got a border collie. I only have to look after him during the school holidays.

☞ Little Suzie wants to take Patty the pooch for a walk round the block. "It's not a good idea to take Patty out today," says mom. "Patty's on heat." "What does that mean?" asks Suzie. "Well, it sort of means she smells," replies mom. "It's a smell other dogs, especially boy-dogs, like a lot. If they smell it, they'll come round bothering her." "But I really want to take Patty for a walk," whines Suzie. "Can I please take her? Can I pleeeease..?" Suzie continues like this for so long that mom asks grandma if she has any ideas. "I know a trick that might work," says grandma. "If you put some gasoline on a rag and rub that on Patty's back legs, that might hide her scent." Mom follows this advice and daubs the back of Patty the pooch's legs with gasoline. Little Suzie then takes the dog for a walk round the block. After ten minutes Suzie comes back by herself. "Where's Patty?" asks mom. "Just my luck," says Suzie. "Patty ran out of gas half a block away. Now another dog's pushing her home."

"We've begun to long for the pitter-patter of little feet – so we bought a dog. Well, it's cheaper, and you get more feet."
Rita Rudner

☞ Nature always provides a cure. If you sting yourself on some nettles you'll always find a soothing dock leaf growing nearby. And if you need to wipe dog crap off your shoe, you're never far from a small, fluffy, highly absorbent dog.

☞ What did the vet say to the dog who kept licking his balls? "Good boy!"

☞ Two men are walking down the street when one grabs the other's arm. "Stop!" he says. "That looks like a pile of dog crap. Be careful not to step in it." The other man bends over and scoops up some of the offending substance on the end of his finger. "I think you're right," he says, peering at the brown mess. "It certainly looks like dog crap. And it feels like dog crap. Phew. It certainly smells like dog crap. Yeeeuh! It even tastes like dog crap. Y'know I'm pretty sure this *is* dog crap...Lucky we didn't step in it."

☞ Two men in a pub are arguing about who has the fiercest dog. One has a rottweiler with him and the other a pit-bull. Both dogs look extremely dangerous and are spoiling for a fight. The pub landlord decides to join in the conversation. "Those dogs are both as soft as butter. My Rover could beat both of those pooches easy." "Want to bet?" says the owner of the pit-bull. "My dog can slaughter any mutt alive. I'll bet you £50 my dog will reduce yours to bloody scraps." "And if his dog can't do it," says the owner of the rottweiler, "then my dog will. I'll bet you £50 as well." So the landlord puts £100 on the bar and calls out, "Rover! Here, boy!" A snuffling sound can be heard; then a horrid-looking animal covered in black spots puts its head round the side of the bar. It sees the pit-bull and snaps it up, gulping it down in two mouthfuls; then it turns on the horrified rottweiler and eats it head-first in about a minute. "Oh, my God!" cries the appalled owner of the pit-bull. "What kind of dog is that?" "Well, I never said it was a dog, did I?" replies the landlord. "Before I docked its tail and painted spots on it, it was an alligator."

"If the dog's tail is still wagging, then how can that be rape?"
Marek Larwood

☞ We used to have this very intelligent dog. When little Jimmy fell down a mineshaft, the dog came running up to us and started barking and running around, and eventually we got the message that Jimmy was hurt, so we followed the dog and found Jimmy in the mine. A week later, little Billy got swept downstream in a storm and became stranded on a rock in the middle of the river. Same as before, the dog ran up to us and barked and ran around and even pulled on my leg with his teeth to get me to the river. And eventually we figured out that little Billy was in trouble, so we followed the dog and rescued him. A week after that, the dog came bounding up to us again. He was barking and running around and making whining noises, but we couldn't figure out what the matter was. Both little Jimmy and little Billy were safe in the house, and so were Ma and Pa and grandma; all the neighbours were fine too, and there were no signs of tornadoes or floods or anything that could harm us, but that dog keep on yapping and whining until, a week later, it dropped dead. We finally figured out it had most likely wanted something to eat.

"If you think dogs can't count, try putting three dog biscuits in your pocket, then giving Fido only two of them."
Phil Pastoret

DREAMS

☞ I have friends who swear they dream in colour. They don't, of course. It's just a pigment of their imagination.

☞ Bad weather causes the cancellation of lots of flights and the airport hotel starts to fill up. In fact, it gets so overcrowded that three men find themselves sleeping in the same bed. When they wake up the next morning, the man on the right-hand side of the bed says, "I had a great dream last night. I dreamed that a beautiful woman was jacking me off all night long." "Hey," says the man on the left-hand side of the bed, "I had exactly the same dream. I dreamed that a beautiful woman was jacking me off all night long as well." "What a couple of perverts," says the man in the middle. "You're both disgusting. I had a lovely dream – all about skiing."

☞ Colin comes home drunk from the pub late one evening. He creeps into bed beside his sleeping wife, gives her a peck on the cheek and falls asleep. Suddenly he awakes, and finds a white-robed man standing at the end of his bed. "Who the hell are you?" demands Colin. "I am Saint Peter," says the man. "You died in your sleep." Colin is stunned "You mean I'm going to heaven?" he says. "No," replies Saint Peter. "You'd be going to purgatory. Or you could be reincarnated. However, there is a catch. Since you haven't lived your life very well, you can only go back as a dog or a hen." Colin is devastated, but knowing there's a farm nearby, he asks to come back as a hen; at least that way he might get to see his family once in a while. There's a flash of light, and Colin finds himself covered in feathers and clucking around, pecking the ground. "This isn't so bad," he thinks. Then he feels a strange sensation welling up inside himself and, after a few uncomfortable seconds, an egg pops out from under his tail. An immense feeling of relief sweeps over him. Then he lays a second egg, with an overwhelming feeling of happiness. Then comes a third, and Colin feels someone hitting the back of his head. He wakes up in bed and his wife shouts, "You dirty, drunken bastard! You're crapping in the bed again!"

☞ I daydreamed that I was falling and, just before I hit the ground, I fell asleep.

DRINK, DRINKING AND DRUNKENNESS

☞ A man walks into a bar and says, "Have people been talking about me?"

> **"I made wine out of raisins so I wouldn't have to wait for it to age."**
> *Steven Wright*

☞ Murphy decides to boost business at his pub by having a special offer. He puts a sign over a keg of beer saying, 'All you can drink for £5!' When O'Leary comes in the pub, he sees the sign and immediately asks for a drink from the keg. He hands over a £5 note and Murphy hands him a pint of ale. The beer is fantastic and O'Leary soon drains the glass. He hands the glass back for a refill, but Murphy shakes his head. "Sorry," he says, "That'll be another £5." "What?" exclaims O'Leary. "But that sign says, 'All you can drink for £5'." "I know," says Murphy. "And you see that glass I just gave you?" "Yes," replies O'Leary. Murphy continues, "Well that *is* all you can drink for £5."

☞ A bunch of rowdy drunks are making a racket in the street in the small hours of the morning. A woman flings open an upstairs window and shouts at them to keep quiet. "Is this where Frank lives?!" asks one of the drunks. "Yes, it is!" shouts back the woman. "Well, could you come and pick him out?" replies the drunk. "Then the rest of us can go home!"

☞ Before a night of heavy drinking you should do the following: eat one banana, two pieces of broccoli, an orange, some red jelly and a chocolate bar. It doesn't keep you from getting sick; it just makes it more colourful.

☞ Paddy goes to a nightclub and makes the acquaintance of a gorgeous-looking young woman. As the night progresses, they have more and more to drink and get friendlier and friendlier. Eventually, the girl leans over and says, "Would you like to take me home and sleep with me?" Paddy looks at his watch. "Thanks for the offer," he says, "but it's still a bit early for me to get my head down."

☞ Scientists have developed a pill for heavy drinkers that will restore any alcohol-related memory loss. Of course, if you're married, you won't need a pill; your wife's always there to remind you of every stupid thing you've ever done.

☞ What's the best thing for a hangover? Lots to drink the night before.

☞ A cop pulls over a drunk driver. "I believe you've been drinking, sir," says the cop. "Drinking?" exclaims the man. "That's a ludicrous suggestion. The very idea! I haven't touched a single drop all evening: swear to God." "Can I see your licence?" asks the cop. "Sure," replies the driver, fumbling in his pockets. "Here, would you hold this beer for a second?"

"I told my girlfriend last night how much I loved her, and she said that I must have been out drinking again. I asked her why she'd say that, and she said, 'Because I'm your father'."
Dave George

☞ A cowboy walks into a saloon. He goes up to the bartender and says, "You see that horse tied up in front of the saloon? I'll bet you a bottle of whisky I can make it laugh." The bartender agrees and watches as the cowboy walks out of the door and goes over to the horse. He whispers something in the horse's ear and it starts laughing like a hyena. The bartender is impressed, and gives the cowboy his bottle of whisky. The next day, the cowboy comes back. He goes over to the bartender and says, "Y'know that horse outside? Well, I'll bet you a crate of whisky I can make that horse cry." The bartender accepts the bet and watches as the cowboy walks out to the horse, stands in front of it and drops his trousers. The horse starts crying, big tears rolling down its cheeks. The barman is astonished, "How in tarnation did you make the horse do that?" The cowboy replies, "Well, to make him laugh, I told him I had a bigger dick than him: and to make him cry, I showed him."

☞ A drunk is out looking for a brothel, but takes a wrong turn and ends up in a chiropodist's. The receptionist shows him to a couch in a curtained cubicle and tells him to get ready. The drunk strips off and playfully sticks his erection through the gap in the curtains. He hears someone scream, "Oh, my God! That's not a foot!" "Bloody hell," replies the drunk. "I didn't know you had a minimum!"

☞ A friend of mine bought a DIY breathalyser: a bag that tells him exactly how much he's had to drink. I don't need to buy one; I married one.

☞ A drunk is thrown out of a bar, but soon staggers back using the back door. The drunk is expelled again, but a few minute later manages to stumbles back inside via the fire exit. Again the drunk is shown the door, but once more he manages to find his way back in, this time using the kitchen door. The barman prepares to throw out the drunk for a fourth time. The drunk looks at him blearily and says, "Christ! You again? Do you own ALL the bars round here?"

☞ A drunk rolls up at a fairground rifle range and pays for three shots. The drunk aims unsteadily at the target, then lets off his three shots in quick succession. Astonishingly, the drunk manages to score three bullseyes. The star prize is a bottle of bourbon, but the booth operator figures the man has had enough to drink, so he fobs him off with a consolation prize: a small turtle. The drunk wanders off, but an hour later he's back. He's even more drunk than before, but he insists on having another go on the rifle range. He pays for his three shots and lets them off one after another. Again, the drunk manages to get three bullseyes and, again, the booth operator manages to fob off the inebriated gent with a turtle. An hour later, the same thing happens again; the drunk rolls up, insists on having another go and scores another three bullseyes. Unlike the last two times, there's a small crowd at the rifle range and they insist that the drunk should get the star prize. The booth holder reluctantly hands over the bottle of bourbon. The drunk looks at it and says, "Gee, thanks, but I couldn't drink another drop. What I'd really like is another one of those delicious crusty meat pies."

☞ A pair of glasses walk into a bar. The barman says, "I'm not serving you. You're off your face."

☞ A drunk staggers into a bar and shouts, "A beer for me! A beer for the bartender! And a beer for everyone here!" The bartender lines up all the drinks, then asks for the money to pay for them. The drunk pulls out his pockets. "I ain't got none," he hiccups. The bartender reaches over, grabs the drunk's lapels and beats his head on the bar, then has the doorman throw him out. The next evening, the drunk is back. "A beer for me!" he shouts. "A beer for the bartender! And a beer for everyone here!" The bartender figures the drunk can't be crazy enough to pull the same stunt twice, so he lines up drinks for everyone. "So where's the money?" asks the bartender. "Don't have any," replies the drunk, emptying his pockets. The bartender is furious; he grabs the drunk by the ankles, holds him upside-down and bangs his head on the floor for a minute before having him thrown out. The next evening, the drunk comes back a third time. The drunk is holding a huge wad of notes in his hand. "It's me!" he cries. "A beer for me! And a beer for everyone here!" "Oh, yeah?" says the bartender. "And what about a beer for the bartender?" "Nah," says the drunk. "That's not such a good idea. You get violent when you've had a drink."

"I was at a bar nursing a beer. My nipple was getting quite soggy."
Emo Philips

☞ I'm starting to think that I drink too much. The last time I gave a urine sample, there was an olive floating in it.

☞ A drunk staggers into the back of a cab. He leans towards the driver and says, "Here; have you got room for a lobster and a bottle of wine on your front seat?" "I think so," says the driver. "Good," replies the drunk, and throws up.

☞ A drunk stumbles out of a pub. He really needs a pee, so he makes his way into a nearby cemetery. He walks right to the edge of a freshly-dug grave, unzips his fly, then loses his balance and falls in. There's a puddle of water in the hole, and the drunk – being too short to climb out – spends the next few hours shouting for help. "I'm cold!" he cries. "Someone help me! It's freezing in here!" At closing time, another drunk staggers out of the pub to have a pee in the cemetery. He hears the racket the other drunk is making and goes to investigate. The first drunk looks up and says, "Give us a hand, mate. It's freezing in here." The second drunks peers down at him, and says, "No wonder you're cold, you stupid bastard. You've gone and kicked all the dirt off!"

"When I read about the evils of drinking, I gave up reading."
Henny Youngman

☞ A girl comes across a drunken Scotsman lying in a ditch. The Scotsman is fast asleep and the girl decides to take a peek up his kilt to see if the stories are true. She looks, and discovers that the stories *are* true and that the Scotsman is hauling a whopper. As a joke, she takes a blue ribbon out of her hair and ties it round the Scotsman's todger. A few hours later, the Scotsman wakes up with a hangover and a full bladder. He hitches up his kilt to have a pee and is surprised to see the blue ribbon tied round it. "Well, laddie," he says. "I don't know where you've been, but I'm mightily pleased to see you won first prize."

☞ A group of young men are in the pub when a drunk shuffles in and starts shouting. He points to one of the men and says, "Here. I've shagged your mum, I have!" The man ignores him. "Yeah!" shouts the drunk. "I've done it loads of times!" Again the man does his best to ignore the drunk. The drunk gets his penis out and waves it around. "See this?" he shouts. "That's been in your mum's gob!" Finally the man can't contain himself any more: "Give it a rest, Dad! Go home! You're pissed!"

☞ A man approaches an attractive woman in a bar. "Can I buy you a drink?" he says. The woman sighs and says, "Sorry; you can't. Drink's bad for my legs." "That's a shame," says the man. "Do they swell up?" The woman replies, "No, they open."

☞ A man goes into a bar and orders a pint of beer. "That's two pounds," says the barman. "Two?" exclaims the customer, "When I came in here yesterday it was one pound." "New pricing policy," replies the barman. "Now you pay a pound for the beer and a pound to hire the glass it comes it." The man mutters to himself, but he's very thirsty, so he hands over two pounds. The barman hands back one of the pounds, gives him an empty glass and says, "We're out of beer."

☞ A man rushes into a bar and orders a double martini. The man downs it in one swallow, puts a five-dollar bill on the bar, then runs out again. The bartender picks up the five-dollar bill and surreptitiously tucks it into his shirt pocket. Suddenly he realises that his boss is standing right behind him. He does a bit of quick thinking. "Hi, boss," he says. "Can you believe that guy? He came in here, ordered a double martini, gave me a five-dollar tip, then ran out without paying!"

☞ A man walks into a bar and is astonished to see that everything is golden. The floor, the walls, the ceiling, the table, the chairs, the pool table, the bar: everything has the rich sheen of solid gold. Amazed, the man goes to the bathroom and discovers that there, too, everything is made of gold. Before leaving, the man has a pee in an ornate golden urinal, then goes and orders a drink. Next day, the man returns to the bar with his wife. The wife doesn't believe the story about the golden bar, but once inside she looks around in amazement. They go and sit at the bar and order a couple of beers. "Gee," says the wife. "And you say even the bathroom is made of gold?" "It sure is," replies the man. "I had a pee in a golden urinal." The bartender overhears this remark and grabs the man by his lapels. "Did I hear you right?" he says. "Did you go into the bathroom yesterday and pee in a golden urinal?" "Y-yes," stammers the man. "Well I got news for you, buddy," says the bartender. "We don't *have* a golden urinal!" He calls over to a man at the pool table. "Hey, Eddie! I found the bastard who pissed in your saxophone!"

☞ A man walks into a bar and orders a martini: then another one, and another. Martini follows martini. Each time his drink is served, the man takes out the olive and drops it in a jar. Three hours later, the jar is full and the man is very much the worse for wear. He gets up and staggers to the door. "What's with the jar?" asks the curious barman. "My wife sent me out for some olives," slurs the man, "and the damned grocery store's shut."

☞ A man walks into a bar with a snake and orders two pints of beer. The beer is poured and the man starts happily sipping his drink. The snake is less happy; it has trouble getting a grip on the glass with its tail and soon drops it. The man orders a second pint but, as before, the snake finds it very difficult to get a grip on the slippery glass; it just about manages to lift the glass from the bar top, then suddenly drops it. The man orders a third pint for the snake. The snake tries very hard to pick up the glass, concentrating as hard as it can, but again, it soon loses control and the glass slips out of its grasp and smashes on the floor. The man orders a fourth pint. "I'm sorry, sir," says the barman. "But I can't serve you." "Why not?" asks the man. "It's the snake, sir," replies the barman. "He just can't hold his drink."

☞ A man walks into a pub and does a triple hand-flip that turns into a double somersault and ends with him doing a hand-stand on a bar-stool. The man then pushes off with his hands and does a roll in the air before landing on his feet in front of the bar. The barman is impressed. "I don't see many

customers doing that," he says. "I'm not surprised," replies the customer. "I work for the circus. We're setting up a show in the local park." At that moment, another man enters the pub. As he steps over the threshold, he leaps forward and does a triple roll into the side of the bar, then pushes away with his feet to do a reverse somersault and land heavily in a chair. "Don't tell me," says the barman, "you work for the circus as well." "No," says the man, gasping for breath. "I'm an accountant. Your doormat's loose."

> **Sam: "What'll you have, Normie?" Norm: "Well, I'm in a gambling mood, Sammy. I'll take a glass of whatever comes out of that tap." Sam: "Looks like beer, Norm." Norm: "Call me Mister Lucky."**
>
> *Cheers*

☞ A man walks out of a bar somewhat the worse for wear. Outside, he sees a nun. He walks over to her and slaps her in the face, then punches her on the nose and knocks her flat on her back. Then he bends down and says, "So! Not so tough tonight, are you, Batman?"

☞ A Mother Superior is dying and her nuns are gathered around her bed trying to make her comfortable. The doctor has told them that the Mother Superior ought to be given lots of fluids, so they offer her a glass of water. The Mother Superior takes a small sip, then shakes her head. The nuns offer her some tea. Again, the Mother Superior takes a small sip, then shakes her head. The nuns then offer the Mother Superior some milk with a tot of whisky in it. The Mother Superior tries a little, then has a little more, then drains the whole glass. A nun goes off to get some more milk and adds another generous tot of whisky. The Mother Superior drains this glass as well, and asks for another. The nuns give the Mother Superior another glass of milk and whisky and she drains it to the last drop. Then the Mother Superior lies back on her pillows and shuts her eyes. "Mother Superior," pleads one of the nuns. "Do you not have some words of wisdom to give us before you pass away?" The Mother Superior looks at her and, in a slightly slurred voice, says, "My child, whatever you do, don't ever sell that feckin' cow."

☞ A policeman pulls over a driver on the motorway. The man has been swerving all over the road and the policeman suspects he's had a few too many. He gets out his drunk kit and says, "Can you breathe into this breathalyser, sir?" "No," says the man. "I'm very sorry, but I can't do that, officer. I'm asthmatic. If I blow into that tube it could bring on an attack." "All right, sir," says the policeman. "We'll take you to the station for a urine sample." "I'm sorry, officer," says the man. "I can't do that either. I'm diabetic. If I pee in a cup it could disturb my sugar levels." "I see," says the policeman. "Well, then, we can take a blood sample instead." "I'm sorry, officer," says the man. "I can't do that either. I'm a haemophiliac. If I give blood, I could die." "Very well, sir," says the policeman. "Then could you get out of your vehicle and walk along the straight white line running down the side of the road?" "I'm sorry, officer," says the man, "I can't do that either." "Oh," says the policeman. "And why is that?" The man replies, "Because I'm pissed out of my head."

☞ A policeman watches as a man unsteadily weaves his way across a busy road, narrowly avoiding getting squashed. The policeman goes over to apprehend the dangerous jaywalker. "Drinking?" asks the policeman. "Depends," slurs the man. "You buying?"

☞ A tourist up from Mississippi is sitting with his drink in a Las Vegas bar. He beckons a pretty young waitress over and says, "Miss, can ah possibly persuade y'all to give me a piece of ass?" "Why, that's a very direct proposition!" gasps the girl. Then she looks the tourist up and down and says, "Okay. Why not? You're a nice-lookin' fella and it's pretty slow here right now. Let's slip away to my room." The pair return half an hour later and the exhausted tourist collapses into his seat. The waitress winks and says, "I hope that was to your satisfaction, sir. Will there be anything else?" "Why yes," replies the Southern gentleman. "Ah sure appreciate what y'all just did for me, miss. That was right neighbourly, but I do like my Bourbon real cold, so I'll still be requirin' that piece of ass."

☞ A woman is always complaining that her husband neglects her, never takes her anywhere and spends all his time in the pub. One night, he decides to takes her along with him to try to shut her up. When they get to the pub, he asks her what she wants to drink. "The same as you, I suppose," she says. The man orders a couple of double vodkas and swallows his in one go. His wife watches him, then takes a sip from her glass. Immediately she spits it out. "Euuch! That's horrible!" she cries. "How can you drink this stuff?" "Well, there you go," says her husband. "And there's you thinking I went out every night enjoying myself!"

☞ After a night of heavy drinking, Bill wakes to find that his penis now has two rings round it, one is red and one is brown. Unable to remember how he acquired these rings, he goes to the doctor for a check-up. The doctor does some tests, then says, "I have good news and bad news. The good news is that the red ring's lipstick." "Okay," says Bill. "So what's the bad news?" The doctor replies, "The brown ring appears to be chewing tobacco."

"Would you describe yourself as a binge drinker? Have you ever downed a bottle of binge in one go?"
Paul Merton

☞ Sister Anne goes into an off-licence and asks for a bottle of vodka. "It's for the Mother Superior," she explains. "It's to relieve her constipation." An hour later, the shopkeeper is closing up for the night when he hears noises coming from a nearby alley. He looks in and sees Sister Anne sitting dead drunk in a pool of vomit and urine. "Sister Anne!" he exclaims. "You said that drink was to help the reverend mother's constipation!" "It is," slurs the nun. "When she hears about this, she's going to crap herself."

☞ An angry drunk staggers into a pub and shouts, "I can lick every guy in this place!" "Sweetie, don't be in such a hurry," says the barman. "Is this your first time in a gay bar?"

☞ An attractive policewoman is in her patrol car when she sees a vehicle swerving all over the road. The driver is obviously drunk, so she pulls him over. The driver falls out of his car, gets to his feet and makes his way unsteadily to the police car. "You're staggering," says the policewoman, sternly. The driver slurs, "You're not so bad yourself, love."

☞ Why is American beer like making love in a boat? They're both f***ing close to water.

☞ Father Murphy crashes his car into a tree. A police officer is nearby and runs over to help. "Are you okay, Father?" says the policeman. "Sure, I'm right enough. Hic!" replies Father Murphy. "Father, have you been drinking?" asks the policeman. "No," says Father Murphy. "Never in a million years. Nothing but water has passed my lips this evening." "I see, Father," says the policeman. "Well, in that case, can you explain the half-empty bottle of wine you have on your front passenger seat?" Father Murphy looks at the bottle, then at the crucifix dangling from his mirror. "Ah, would you believe it?" he exclaims. "He's only gone and done it again!"

☞ George and his wife Beryl are sitting in a pub. As they enjoy their drinks, George notices that Beryl is staring at a drunk slumped at the bar. "Do you know him?" asks George. "Yes," replies Beryl. "He's my ex-husband." "Is he a boozer?" asks George. "Not when I was married to him," replies Beryl, "but he's been like that ever since our divorce. That was six years ago now." "That's incredible," says George. "I didn't think anybody could celebrate for that long."

☞ George comes home drunk after spending all night at the office Christmas party. His fuming wife meets him at the door. "I know what you've been up to," she growls. "You've been canoodling with your secretary." "No, I haven't," protests George. "Then how do you explain the lipstick on your collar?" asks his wife. George looks down at the bright pink stain on his white shirt. "I have no idea," he confesses. "I thought I'd taken the bloody thing off..."

☞ What's the difference between an alcoholic and a drunk? The alcoholic has to go to meetings.

☞ Hamish and Jamie are sitting in a bar. "I had a terrible row with my wife last night," says Hamish. "I came home drunk, and my wife wouldn't let me in the house. She opened the door, took one look at me and slammed it in my face. I had to spend the night on a park bench." "You ought to do what I do," says Jamie. "If I come home dead drunk, I strip off on my doorstep, then throw my clothes through the front door when my wife opens it. She always lets me in; she's too embarrassed to see me run about naked outside the house." "That's a great idea," says Hamish. "I'll try that the next time I go for a drink." A month later, Jamie bumps into Hamish again. "I haven't seen you for a while," says Jamie. "What have you been up to?" Hamish replies, "I tried that stripping-off trick you told me about, but I got charged with indecent exposure and spent two weeks in prison." "Oh, no," says Jamie. "What went wrong?" "Well, I got completely bladdered one night, but I got myself home, stood outside my front door and stripped off. Then when the door opened I chucked all my clothes through." "And your wife didn't let you in?" says Jamie. "No," says Hamish. "The door shut, a voice said 'Edinburgh Central, next stop' and I realised I was still on the bloody train!"

☞ Harry goes to his doctor with an embarrassing problem. He thinks his privates are too small to satisfy his wife. His doctor sympathises, but short of surgery there's not a lot he can do. Then he remembers an interesting folk-cure he heard about recently. "Do you drink beer?" asks the doctor. "Sometimes," replies Harry. "Well, in future, always drink real ale. I've heard that thin, gassy beers shrink the private parts, but rich, full-bodied beers will make them expand." Harry agrees to give this a go and goes home to try it out. Two weeks later the doctor meets Harry in the street. "How's your problem?" asks the doctor. "It's solved," replies Harry. "I've no more worries in that department." "So you've been drinking the real ale, have you?" asks the doctor. "No," replies Harry. "I don't really like it. But I've put the wife on lager."

☞ I'm on a whisky diet. I've lost three days already.

☞ Looking to earn some extra money, a Native American enters a tea-drinking competition with a top prize of $5,000. The man joins the contest and drinks cup after cup of hot tea. After three hours there are only two contestants left, the Native American and another man. They both down five gallons of tea, then six, then seven and eight. At nine gallons the other man drops out, and the Native American is proclaimed the victor with a total score of ten gallons. He celebrates with a final cup of tea, then retires to his tent with the prize money. His future as a champion tea-drinker looks bright: but tragically, that night, he drowned in his own teepee.

☞ Old Bert shuffles into his local pub and orders half a pint of stout. After nursing his drink for an hour, Bert watches as a well-dressed man comes in and speaks to the barman. "Can I have four crates of bottled ale, two crates of mild and two crates of bitter?" says the man. Old Bert starts rapping on the bar with his knuckles. The man continues, "Also, I'll need a keg of lager, three bottles of whisky, two bottles of gin, a bottle of tequila, three litres of tonic water, four litres of coke and fifty packets of assorted crisps." Bert continues to rap his knuckles on the bar; he's now looking quite angry. The barman calculates the bill, hands over the goods and takes the man's money. As this goes on, Bert continues to rap on the bar. The barman finishes the transaction and turns to Bert. "So, then; what can I do for you?" he asks. "About bloody time," says old Bert. "I'll have half a pint of stout. You ought to watch it, you know. You'll go broke if you carry on like that." "What do you mean?" asks the barman. "Ignoring your regular customers like that. You'll lose business. I'm in here every evening; that other sod only comes in once a week!"

Sam: "What's the story, Norm?"
Norm: "Thirsty guy walks into a bar. You finish it."
Cheers

☞ Since I first started sampling and collecting white wines I've become enchanted by the rich palette of experiences they offer. Who could fail to be charmed by the elegance and superlative balance of a bottle of Swartz-Bass Gewurzt – the 1987, of course – or the individuality of a Chateau Marusann Pinot – so complex, but with a rich bouquet, buttery taste and a cheeky effervescence? I've tasted so many delightful white wines that I'm heartbroken I didn't start years ago. I used to drink nothing but red wine, you see, but I had to stop; it was giving me the squits.

☞ Three men are discussing a night out. One says, "I was so pissed last night, I got home and wet the bed." "That's nothing," says the second, "I was so pissed last night, I woke up naked in the front garden." "I can beat that," says the third man, "I was so pissed last night I spent the whole night blowing chunks." "Well, there's nothing unusual in that," says the second man. "I threw up too." "No," replies the third man. "Chunks is the name of my dog."

☞ Two drunks are standing outside a seedy whorehouse. The first drunk says, "I heard half the whores in here have the clap, and the other half have got crabs: and none of them would think twice about cutting our throats and stealing every penny we've got!" "Shhhhh!" says the second drunk. "Not so loud, or they won't let us in."

☞ Two drunks, Tom and Dick, are in a bar. Tom gets up to go to the toilet. Tom's only been gone a minute when the sound of screaming starts coming from the bathroom. Dick rushes in to see what's wrong and finds Tom sobbing on the floor. "It was terrible," he says. "I sat down and had a crap, but every time I tried to flush the toilet something reached up and squeezed my balls." Dick looks in the toilet stall. "You moron," he says. "You were sitting on the mop bucket!"

☞ Two fat blokes are in a pub. One says to the other, "Your round." The other one says, "So are you, you fat bastard!"

☞ Two guys walk into a pub and ask the landlord to settle an argument. "Are there two pints in a quart, or four?" asks one. "There are two pints in a quart," confirms the landlord. "Okay. Thank you very much," says the man. The pair move along the bar to where a barmaid is standing. "Two pints please, miss," says one of the men, "and they're on the house." "On the house?" says the barmaid. "I've worked here for five years and the landlord's never given away a glass of water, let alone two pints of beer." One of the men calls over to the landlord, "You did say two pints, didn't you?" "That's right," calls back the landlord. "Two pints!"

☞ Two old drunks are sitting in a bar. One says, "Y'know, when I was 30 and got a hard-on, I couldn't bend it with both my hands. By the time I was 40, I could perhaps bend it a little if I tried really hard. But by the time I was 50, I could bend it over with no problem at all. And you know what? Now I'm almost 60 I can pretty much bend it in half with just one hand." "So what's your point?" asks the second drunk. "Nothing," replies the first. "I was just wondering how much stronger I'm going to get."

☞ Zeke walks into town holding a shotgun and a bottle of moonshine. He comes across Billy-Bob standing outside the general store. "Here," says Zeke, holding out the bottle. "Have a draw on that. That be the best moonshine I ever made." "No, thanks," replies Billy-Bob. "I like moonshine, but that there stuff outta your still is rotgut. It'll make me sick." Zeke holds the shotgun to Billy-Bob's head. "I'll ask you again, real polite," says Zeke. "Now you drink up." Billy-Bob gulps, then puts the bottle to his mouth and takes a long pull. The moonshine hits the back of his throat like a shot of hot acid and he has a coughing fit that makes his eyes water. "Jeez," says Billy-Bob. "That is just awful." "I'll be the judge of that," replies Zeke. He hands the shotgun to Billy-Bob and says, "Now you make ME drink some."

"You're not drunk if you can lie on the floor without holding on."
Dean Martin

☞ Of course, the trendiest cocktails today are the ones with bits of food in them, such as blue cheese, cucumbers, and pieces of ham. Hang on! Didn't alcohol with food in it just used to be called vomit?

DRUGS

"The main problem with heroin is that it's very moreish."
Harry Hill

☞ I don't do drugs now I'm middle-aged. These days I get the same effect just by standing up too quickly.

☞ Last week I caught my son taking drugs. I wouldn't have minded so much, but they were mine!

☞ A new study says that Ecstasy can damage key areas of the brain. So which parts of the brain aren't 'key'?

☞ Last week my brother was put in prison for selling drugs. He got seven years; four years for the possession of 50 one-ounce packets of heroin, and three years for retailing using non-metric weights and measures.

"Tranquilizers work only if you follow the advice on the bottle; keep away from children."
Phyllis Diller

DUCKS

☞ A male duck and a female duck decide to get together. However, they think they're a cut above the other ducks on the pond, so they decide to book into a local motel. The ducks book in and the male rings up room service. "I'd like a couple of sandwiches sent to our room," says the duck, "a morning paper, coffee for two – oh: and a packet of condoms." "Yes, sir," says room service. "Would you like that on your bill?" The duck replies, "Why? Do you think I'm some sort of pervert?"

DUDES

> **"I wonder what the most intelligent thing ever said
> was that started with the word 'dude.' 'Dude, these are
> isotopes.' 'Dude, we removed your kidney. You're gonna
> be fine.' 'Dude, I am so stoked to win this Nobel Prize. I
> just wanna thank Kevin, and Turtle, and all my homies'."**
> *Demetri Martin*

DYSLEXIA

☞ A dyslexic pervert goes into an S&M shop – and buys a nice pair of socks.

> **"I realised I was dyslexic when I went to
> a toga party dressed as a goat."**
> *Marcus Brigstocke*

☞ Did you hear about Hank Nasty, the dyslexic punk rocker? He choked to death on his own Vimto.

☞ I went to a dyslexic rave. There were lots of people taking F and this bloke in the corner was trying to inject a heron.

EAGLES

☞ How do you identify a bald eagle? All his feathers are combed over to one side.

ECONOMICS

☞ Bert is talking to Harry. "I'm a walking economy," says Bert. "How come?" says Harry. Bert replies, "My hairline's in recession, my stomach's a victim of inflation and both of these are putting me into a deep depression!"

ECONOMISTS

☞ A chemist, a mathematician, a physicist and an economist are shipwrecked on a desert island. The only food they can find is a crate full of tins of baked beans. Unfortunately, they don't have a tin-opener. The chemist says, "If we heat a tin to the correct temperature it will explode, and we can feast on the hot beans that are released." "What an excellent idea," says the mathematician. "I'll calculate how much wood we'll need for each can." "I can help, too," says the physicist. "I can calculate the force and direction of the explosion so we lose as few beans as possible during the explosive event." The economist shakes his head in pity, "Guys, guys," he says. "You're making life way too difficult for yourselves. Let's just *assume* we have a tin-opener and work from there…"

　☞ An economist is a man who takes longer strides to save his £30 shoes, and splits his £150 trousers.

☞ Economists of the world, unite – you have nothing to lose but your Keynes.

EDUCATION

☞ A college student is delivering a pizza to an old man's house. "I suppose you'll be wanting a tip," says the old man grumpily. "That would be much appreciated," replies the student, "but they warned me about you at the pizzeria. They said not to expect much from you. They said I'd be lucky to get a quarter." The old man is offended by the accusation of meanness. "I'll prove them bastards wrong," says the old man. "Here you go, sonny: a five-dollar tip." "Why, thank you, sir," says the student. "I'll put this in my college fund." "What are you studying?" asks the old man. The student replies, "Applied psychology."

　☞ A boy comes home from school and tells his father that he was knocked out of the class spelling competition in the first round. "What word did they give you?" asks dad. The boy replies, "Posse." Father laughs, "I'm not surprised you can't spell it; you can't even pronounce it."

"I live near a remedial school. There's a sign on the road that says, 'Slow. Children'. That can't be good for their self-esteem: but, to look on the positive side, they can't read it."
Jimmy Carr

☞ A high school is having trouble with lipstick stains in the girls' washroom. Some of the girls have got into the habit of putting on their make-up, then pressing their lips to the washroom mirror to leave behind lip-prints. Sometimes there are dozens of prints, and every night the caretaker has to clean them off. Finally, the headteacher decides that something has to be done. She calls all the girls to the washroom and explains that the lip-prints are causing the caretaker a big problem because they're really difficult to clean off. To demonstrate, the caretaker takes out his faithful long-handled mop, dips it in a toilet bowl and wipes it over the mirror. He has to give it a few goes, and spits on a couple of the more stubborn marks to loosen them up, but the demonstration works! From that day on, no one ever kisses a washroom mirror again.

☞ A lecturer is giving his medical class a lesson in observation. He holds up a jar of stale urine. "To be a doctor, you have to be observant," he explains. "You must observe colour, smell, sight and taste." The lecturer then dips a finger into the jar and puts his finger in his mouth. His students watch in disgust but, when the jar is passed round, they all do the same and grimace at the horrible taste. When the jar is back on his desk, the lecturer says, "I hope this will teach you a valuable lesson; the observant amongst you will have noticed that I put my second finger into the jar and put my index finger in my mouth."

"I remember once I was walking through campus and my instructor grabs me and yells, 'It's been six weeks since I saw you in camouflage class!' I said, 'I'm getting good'!"
Emo Philips

☞ A teacher is explaining the definition of the word 'definitely' to her class, and asks them to make up a sentence using the word. A pupil raises her hand

and says, "The sky is definitely blue." The teacher replies, "That's good, but sometimes the sky can be grey." Another pupil says, "Grass is definitely green." The teacher says, "That's good too, but grass can also go brown." Little Johnny sticks up his hand and says, "Miss, do farts definitely have lumps?" The teacher, annoyed, says, "No: and just for that, you're not leaving this classroom until you use 'definitely' correctly." Little Johnny replies, "Well, in that case, I definitely just crapped my pants."

☞ A teacher is giving a lesson on the circulation of the blood. "Now, class," she says, "if I stood on my head, the blood would run into it, and I would turn red in the face. Do you agree?" "Yes, miss," replies the class. The teacher continues, "Then why is it that while I'm standing upright, the blood doesn't run into my feet and make them red?" From the back, little Jimmy shouts: "Because your feet aren't empty!"

"You don't appreciate a lot of stuff in school until you get older: little things like being spanked every day by a middle-aged woman: stuff you pay good money for in later life."
Emo Philips

☞ Teacher reminds her pupils about an important exam that's taking place the next day. "Listen, class," she says, "Apart from a nuclear attack, a serious injury or the death of a member of your immediate family, I will not tolerate any excuses for your non-attendance tomorrow." Brian, the class clown, raises his hand to ask a question. "Miss," he says, "so what would you say if I rang in tomorrow saying I was suffering from complete and utter sexual exhaustion?" The class chuckles. Teacher replies, "In that case, Brian, I'd expect you to come into school and do the test with your other hand."

☞ College is like a woman. You work incredibly hard to get in, but nine months later you wish you'd never come.

☞ Did you hear about the public school where all the pupils stank to high heaven? You had to be filthy rich to go there.

☞ How do you stop a media studies graduate from ringing your doorbell? Pay for the pizza.

☞ I was bullied at school. The other kids used to call me all kinds of horrible names. But one day I turned to my bullies and said, "Sticks and stones may break my bones, but names will never hurt me!" And it worked! From then on, it was sticks and stones all the way.

☞ Last week, our English teacher set us an assignment. She said we had to describe ourselves in ten words or less. I wrote, 'Succinct.'

☞ Little Jimmy puts up his hand to ask teacher a question. "Sir," says little Jimmy. "Do you have holes in your underpants?" "I most certainly do not," says teacher. Little Jimmy replies, "Then how the hell do you get your legs through them?"

☞ Little Johnny is in class and needs to go to the bathroom. He yells out, "Miss, I need to take a piss!" Teacher replies, "Johnny, the word you want to use is 'urinate.' Use the word 'urinate' in a sentence correctly, and I will allow you to go." Little Johnny thinks for a second, then says, "Miss, you're an eight, but if you had bigger tits, you'd be a ten!"

☞ My son has degrees in psychology and philosophy. He can't get a job, but at least he knows why.

☞ School reports cards – what those phrases really mean:
A born leader – runs a protection racket.
Easy-going – bone-idle.
Making good progress – slightly less awful than last year.
Friendly – never shuts up.
Helpful – a creep.
Reliable – informs on his friends.
Expresses himself confidently – a rude bastard.
Enjoys physical education – a bully.

Does not accept authority easily – Dad is in prison.
Often appears tired – insomniac telly addict.
A rather solitary child – he stinks.
Popular in the playground – sells pornography.

☞ Teacher asks her class for a sentence with the word 'beautiful' in it twice. First, she calls on little Suzy, who responds with, "My father bought my mother a beautiful dress and she looked beautiful in it." "Very good, Suzy," replies teacher. She then calls on little Michael. "My mummy planned a beautiful banquet and it turned out beautifully," he says. "Excellent, Michael!" says teacher. She then calls on little Johnny. Little Johnny says, "Last night my sister told my father that she was pregnant, and he said, 'Beautiful: f***ing beautiful'!"

☞ Teacher asks her class some questions, telling them that the first pupils to answer can go home early. "Who said, 'Four score and seven years ago'?" asks the teacher. Little Johnny sticks his hand up, but little Pattie beats him to it, "Abraham Lincoln," she says. "Very good," replies the teacher. "You can go home. Now who said, 'I have a dream'?" Little Johnny puts his hand up, but is beaten by little Mary. "Martin Luther King," she says. "Very good," replies Teacher. "You can go home. Now who said, 'Think not what your country can do for you'?" Little Johnny's hand shoots up, but he's beaten by little Susie. "President Kennedy," she says. "Very good," replies teacher. "Jesus!" says little Johnny. "I wish these f***ing bitches would keep their mouths shut." "Who said that?!" demands teacher. "President Clinton," replies little Johnny. "Can I go home now?"

☞ Teacher asks her class to come up with a sentence with the word 'contagious' in it. Little Johnny sticks his hand up, "Miss, me and my dad were driving down to the zoo the other day when we saw a lorry that had turned over and spilt pineapples all over the road. The lorry driver was trying to clean up the mess, and my dad said it would take that contagious to pick them all up."

☞ Teacher asks her pupils what their fathers do for a living. "My father's a lawyer," says little Mary. "He puts bad men into prison." "My daddy's a doctor," says little Tommy. "He makes sick people feel better." "And what about your father, little Johnny?" asks the teacher. "My daddy's dead," says little Johnny. "Oh, dear," says the teacher. "That's very sad: but tell us what your daddy did before he died." "Well," says little Johnny, "first he turned blue, and then he fell over and crapped on the carpet."

☞ Teacher gets little Johnny to read out the answer he wrote down in his test. "Sdjah tagow ghlk nmgp sfgha whlowfgh astyu inhaa bbbxxxpqzz," reads Johnny. "That's absolute nonsense," says the teacher. "I know," says Johnny, "but the question said to answer using my own words."

☞ Teacher is handing out marked homework assignments to her students. Last night's assignment was to define a list of words. She calls little Johnny over to her desk. "You did very well, Johnny," she says. "You defined all the words correctly apart from one. For bachelor, you've written 'blissfully happy man'. You should have written that a bachelor is an unmarried man." "You don't say?" replies Johnny. "I'd better tell Dad; he was helping me with my homework last night."

☞ Teacher is telling her class about syllables. "Now, children," she says, "syllables are the sounds that make up words. 'Cow' has one syllable but 'roo-ster' has two. Can anyone think of a word with three syllables?" Little Johnny sticks his hand up. "Miss! I know a word, miss!" "What is it Johnny?" asks Teacher. Johnny says, "It's 'masturbate'. Mas-tur-bate." "Well, yes," says Teacher, blushing. "But that's a bit of a mouthful, isn't it?" "Oh, no, miss," says Johnny. "That would be a blow-job."

☞ Teacher, to little Billy: "Your handwriting is terrible!" Billy: "Yes, but if I made it any clearer you'd realise I can't spell."

☞ The class is learning about nature when little Johnny sticks his hand up. "Miss," he says. "Is it true that baby birds have spare parts?" "No," replies Teacher. "Whatever gave you that idea?" Johnny replies, "I heard my Dad and Uncle Billy talking, and Uncle Billy said he'd like to screw the ass off the chick next door."

☞ Three students are studying at university. They're doing well in their coursework, and to celebrate they hire a car and go for a wild weekend party with friends. They have a great time, but enjoy themselves so much they forget they have an important exam on Monday. When Monday arrives, they remember the exam and realise they have no chance of getting back in time. To avoid punishment, they decide to make up a story about getting a flat tyre on the motorway. When they get back to college, they tell this story to their tutor. The tutor nods understandingly and tells them they can take the exam on the following day. Tuesday arrives, and the three students sit down to take their test. The first question, for five per cent, turns out to be fairly easy. After completing the simple question, the students turn the page and see the next question; it reads, 'For 95 per cent – which tyre?'

☞ Two fathers are talking. "My son's at medical school," says one. "Oh, yes?" says the other. "What's he studying?" "He isn't," says the first. "They're studying him."

☞ What's rectangular, pink and takes about an hour to drink? A student's grant cheque.

EDUCATION – DUMB EXAM ANSWERS

☞ Can you name a major disease associated with cigarettes? Premature death.

☞ Charles Darwin was a naturalist who wrote the organ of the species.

☞ How do lungs work? When you breath, you inspire. When you do not breath, you expire.

☞ How does blood circulate in the human body? Blood flows down one leg and up the other.

☞ How does genetics affect your appearance? Genetics explains why you look like your father, and if you don't, why you should.

☞ How is dew formed? The sun shines down on the leaves and makes them perspire.

☞ Name the three kinds of blood vessels. Arteries, vanes and caterpillars.

☞ What causes the tides in the oceans? The tides are a fight between the Earth and the Moon. All water tends to flow towards the moon, because there is no water on the moon, and nature abhors a vacuum. I forget where the sun joins in this fight.

☞ What happens to a boy when he reaches puberty? He says goodbye to his boyhood and looks forward to his adultery.

☞ What happens to your body as you age? When you get old, so do your bowels and you get intercontinental.

☞ What is a fossil? A fossil is an extinct animal. The older it is, the more extinct it is.

☞ What is a planet? A body of earth surrounded by sky.

☞ What is a right angle? A right angle is 90 degrees Fahrenheit.

☞ What is a skeleton? It's what's left after the insides have been taken out and the outsides have been taken off.

☞ What is 'momentum'? Momentum is what you give a person when they are going away.

☞ What is rhubarb? A kind of celery gone bloodshot.

☞ What is the composition of water? Water is composed of two gins, oxygin and hydrogin. Oxygin is pure gin. Hydrogin is gin and water.

☞ What is the most common form of birth control? Most people prevent contraception by wearing a condominium.

☞ What is water? Melted steam.

☞ Where would you find the world's largest mammals, and why? The largest mammals are to be found in the sea, because there is nowhere else to put them.

EDUCATION – EXTRACTS FROM SUPPOSEDLY GENUINE LETTERS FROM PARENTS

☞ Carlos was absent yesterday because he was playing football. He was hurt in the growing part.

☞ Excuse Roland from PE for a few days. Yesterday he fell out of tree and misplaced his hip.

☞ My son is under a doctor's care and should not take PE today. Please execute him.

☞ Please excuse Gloria from Jim today. She is administrating.

☞ Please excuse Jennifer for missing school yesterday. We forgot to get the Sunday paper off the porch, and when we found it on Monday, we thought it was Sunday.

☞ Please excuse Jimmy for being. It was his father's fault.

☞ Please excuse Tommy for being absent yesterday. He had diarrhoea and his boots leak.

☞ Sally won't be in school a week from Friday. We have to attend her funeral.

ELECTRICITY AND ELECTRICAL EQUIPMENT

"Electricity is really just organised lightning."
George Carlin

☞ Harry installed solar panels on his house. At the end of the year he got an electricity bill from the Meteorological Office.

"I have a switch in my apartment; it doesn't do anything. Every once in a while, I turn it on and off. One day I got a call; it was from a woman in France. She said, 'Cut it out'."
Steven Wright

☞ How do they fit all that hot air into blow-dryers? What's more, why don't they ever run out?

☞ If electrical stores are always cutting their prices, why aren't any of their things free yet?

"I invented the cordless extension cord."
Steven Wright

ELEPHANTS

☞ "Knock, knock." "Who's there?" "Elephants." "Elephants who?" "Ella Fitzgerald!"

☞ A female elephant is walking through the jungle when she steps on a thorn. The thorn is sharp and becomes embedded so deeply that the elephant can't get it out. As she hobbles home, the elephant is accosted by a mouse. "I can pull out that thorn for you," says the mouse. "I'll be able to get a good hold of it with my teeth and yank it free." "Why, thank you," says the elephant. "But I'll want a favour in return," continues the mouse. "I want to have sex with you." The elephant pauses for a moment, trying not to laugh. "Well, okay," she says. "You get that thorn out and you can do what you like." So the mouse pulls out the thorn, then climbs on a large tree stump to collect his reward. The elephant backs into position. "Let me know when you're done!" calls out the elephant. The mouse prepares to get to it. At this moment, an eagle happens to be flying past holding a tortoise. Suddenly, the eagle loses its grip and the tortoise plummets downwards, landing with some force on the elephant's head. "Ouch!" she says. "Oh yeah, baby," says the mouse. "Yeah. You like that, don't you, bitch?"

☞ A man is on safari in Africa when he comes across a distressed elephant lying on the ground. The man investigates, and finds a thorn stuck deep in the elephant's foot. He manages to pull it out, and the elephant gets to its feet and trots merrily away. Twenty years later, the man is standing in a London street watching a circus procession pass by. A performing elephant walks past, but when it gets level with the man, it stops and looks him straight in the eye. The elephant then reaches out with its trunk, lifts the man high into the air and smashes him down on the ground. Then the elephant leaps over the barrier and jumps up and down on the man until he's squashed flat. It was a completely different elephant.

☞ George the elephant-tracker was buried today. Serves him right for being so close behind the elephant.

☞ How do you know when a female elephant is having her period? There's a quarter on your dresser and your mattress is missing.

☞ Two elephants fall off a cliff. Boom, boom.

☞ Two old ladies go to the zoo and see an angry male elephant with a huge erection. The elephant is rampaging round the enclosure, stamping its feet and trumpeting through its trunk. One of the old ladies turns to the other and says, "Gracious; d'you think he'll charge?" The other old lady looks at the erection and says, "Well, yes. I think he'd be entitled to!"

☞ What do you get if you take an elephant into work? Sole use of the lift.

☞ What has two tails, two trunks and five feet? An elephant with spare parts.

☞ What's grey and not there? No elephants.

☞ What was the name of the girl who lost her herd of elephants? Big Bo Peep.

☞ What's grey, yellow, grey, yellow, grey, yellow, grey, yellow, grey, yellow, grey, yellow? An elephant rolling down a hill with a daisy in its mouth!

☞ What's the difference between an African elephant and an Indian elephant? About 5,000 kilometres.

☞ Why are elephants wrinkled? Ever tried to iron one?

☞ Why did the elephant cross the road? It was the chicken's day off.

☞ Why do elephants drink so much? To try to forget.

ENCOUNTERS WITH EXTRA-TERRESTRIALS

☞ Larry and Jean are kidnapped by aliens. The aliens turn out to be quite friendly, but they want to know how Earth people have sex. They decide that the easiest way to find out is if Larry has sex with a female alien and Jean has sex with a male alien. Once this is agreed, Jean and the male alien go to a bedroom and strip. It turns out the male has got a tiny penis, about half an inch long and a quarter of an inch thick. "I don't think this is going to work," says Jean. "That's not long enough." "No problem," says the alien, and he starts to slap his forehead with his hand. With each slap, his penis grows three inches. Next, the alien starts pulling his ears. With each pull, his penis grows an inch wider. The alien pulls and slaps until his penis is big enough to satisfy Jean; then they get into bed and make mad, passionate love. Next day, the aliens drop off Larry and

Jean at their house. "Well, was it any good?" says Larry. "I had a great time," replies Jean. "How about you?" "It was horrible," says Larry "All I got was a terrible headache. All night long she was slapping my forehead and pulling my ears..."

☞ Last week, I woke up feeling really muzzy-headed and peculiar. As my head cleared, I remembered that I'd been lying down, surrounded by weird flashing lights, while strange, unearthly figures bent over me, doing things. All the time, there had been this horrible repetitive, pounding noise in the background. What's more, my body felt like every orifice had been thoroughly probed. It really worried me; these were all classic signs of an alien abduction. Then my friend confessed he'd got me drunk and dumped me in a gay disco.

END OF THE WORLD

☞ Harry and Bill are in a bar. "What would you do if you knew the world was going to end in the next half-hour?" asks Harry. Bill says, "I'd run around and have sex with anything that moved. Why, what would you do?" Harry replies, "I'd stand very, very still."

ENTERTAINMENT

"I love to sing, and I love to drink scotch. Most people would rather hear me drink scotch."
George Burns

ENVIRONMENT

☞ The reason the rainforest is called the 'Brazilian' is because deforestation will soon leave it almost completely bare, with just a thin strip of trees running up the middle of it.

ESCALATORS

"If I have to move up in a building, I choose the elevator over the escalator, because one time I was riding the escalator and I tripped. I fell down the stairs for an hour and a half."
Demetri Martin

ETHNIC

☞ An American, a Russian, a Chinese man and a German are standing at a bus stop when they are approached by an opinion pollster. "Excuse me," says the pollster, "but what's your opinion of the current meat shortage?" The American says, "What's a shortage?" The Russian says, "What's meat?" The Chinese man says, "What's an opinion?" The German says, "What's 'Excuse me'?"

☞ An Englishman, a Welshman and a West Indian are in hospital, waiting for their wives to give birth. After a lot of pacing up and down, the nurse comes out and announces that all three are the fathers of bouncing baby boys. "There's just one problem," she says. "We got the tags mixed up and don't know which baby is which. Would you mind coming to identify them?" The men agree and walk into the delivery room to take a look at the babies. Immediately, the Englishman stoops down and picks up the black baby. "Yes, this is definitely my baby," he says. "Um... excuse me," says the West Indian, "but I think it's fairly obviously that baby is my son." The Englishman pulls him aside and says, "I can see where you're coming from, mate, but one of these babies is Welsh, and that's simply not a risk I'm prepared to take."

☞ An Englishman, Irishman and Scotsman go for a round of golf and take their wives along as caddies. While walking around the course, the Englishman's wife catches her foot in a rabbit hole. She trips up and lands in a heap on the ground. Her skirt flies over her head and reveals that she isn't wearing any knickers. The Englishman storms over and demands the reason for her state of undress. "Well, darling," she explains, "you give me so little housekeeping money I have to make sacrifices. Usually no one notices." The Englishman hands his wife some money. "Here's twenty pounds," he says. "Go to Marks and Spencer and buy yourself some underwear." Two holes further along, the Irishman's wife catches her foot on a molehill. She trips up and, like the Englishwoman, her skirt flies over her head, revealing that she isn't wearing any knickers. The Irishman is livid. He demands a reason for the lack of undergarments. "I can't afford to wear any," she explains, "You don't give me enough money to buy knickers." So the Irishman gives his wife a handful of coins, "Here's four pounds," he says. "Go to Woolworth's and buy yourself some underwear." Three holes further on, the Scotsman's wife trips over an exposed root. She too takes a tumble and lands with her skirt over her head. Like the other wives, she is also revealed to be without knickers. "Ye should be ashamed of yourself!" fumes her husband. "Look at the state of you!" "But I can't afford underwear," complains his wife. "You're too tight-fisted to pay for them." "I'll no waste money on fripperies like that!" says the Scotsman. "Now here's a comb, woman. Tidy yourself up a bit!"

☞ Did you hear about the Native American who married a Scottish lady? They named their son Hawkeye-the-Noo.

☞ How can you tell if a Scotsman is well-balanced? He has a chip on each shoulder.

☞ How do all ethnic jokes start? With a look over both shoulders.

☞ Why do Greek men wear gold neck-chains? So they know when to stop shaving.

ETHNIC – AFGHAN

☞ A journalist goes to Afghanistan and is surprised to see that the local men allow their wives to walk in front of them. The journalist approaches a local and says, "I thought the custom in Islamic countries was for wives to walk ten paces behind their husbands?" "It was," replies the local, "but that all changed with the war." "How did the war change things?" asks the journalist. The local replies, "Landmines."

ETHNIC – AUSTRALIAN

☞ A middle-aged spinster wants to get married, but will only consider a gentleman who's never made love with a woman. A man like this proves hard to find, but eventually she tracks down a willing partner who's lived all his life in the Australian outback. They get married, but on their wedding night the woman is surprised to find her husband standing naked in the living room. What's more, the carpets have been rolled back and the furniture piled in the corner. "What are you doing?" asks the woman. "Well, I've never made love to a woman," says her husband, "but if it's anything like screwing a kangaroo, I'm going to need all the room I can get."

☞ A tourist is driving through the Australian bush when he sees a man having sex with a kangaroo. Appalled, he heads back towards town to report this incident, but on the way he's shocked to see another man having sex with a kangaroo, and then another. Disgusted, he drives into town, only to see a man with a wooden leg masturbating outside a pub. The tourist pulls up outside the police station and accosts a sergeant. "I was out in the bush when I saw three men having sex with kangaroos!" "Did you?" says the sergeant. "Yes. And then I saw a man with a wooden leg masturbating in the street. How can you tolerate such filthy behaviour?" "Well, be fair, mate," replies the sergeant. "How's the poor bastard going to catch a kangaroo in his condition?"

☞ An Aussie is wandering around the outback when he comes across a remote farmhouse. A pretty girl meets him at the gate. "D'yer root?" he asks. "Not normally," she replies, "but yer talked me into it, yer silver-tongued bastard!"

☞ An English tourist is visiting the Australian outback. He's walking through some farmland when he notices a farmer in a field going at it with a sheep. The Englishman is taken aback by this. He climbs the fence, walks over to the farmer, taps him on the shoulder and says, "You know, mate, back home, we shear those!" The Aussie farmer looks round and says, "Find your own."

☞ The Australian Prime Minister is having tea with the Queen when he suggests it might be an idea to make Australia an independent kingdom. "Ah, but you'd need a king to do that, and you haven't got one," replies Her Majesty. "Then how about making it an empire?" says the Prime Minister. "You'd need an emperor," replies Her Majesty. "Well, what about a dukedom?" asks the Prime Minister. "Same problem," replies Her Majesty. "You'd need a duke." "Well, then: any suggestions?" asks the Prime Minister. The Queen replies, "To be honest, after meeting you I think it would be more suitable to keep Australia as a country."

☞ Two drovers are standing in a bar. One asks, "What are you up to, Bruce?" "Ahh, I'm takin' a mob of six thousand from Goondiwindi to Gympie." "Oh, yeah? What route are you takin'?" "Prob'ly the missus. After all, she stuck by me durin' the drought."

ETHNIC – COCKNEYS

☞ How much are Cockneys prepared to pay for shampoo? Pantene.

ETHNIC – FRENCH

☞ A Canadian wants to pass himself off as a Newfoundlander, so he goes to a surgeon to have a third of his brain cut out. He wakes up after the operation and sees the surgeon looking down at him. "I made a terrible mistake," says the surgeon. "I cut out three quarters of your brain by accident." The Canadian replies, "Pardon, monsieur. Je ne parle pas Anglais."

☞ A man walks into a cannibal restaurant and looks at the menu. "Excuse me," he says to the waiter, "but if an Englishman costs 50 beads, and a German costs 50 beads, and an Italian costs 50 beads, why on earth does a Frenchman cost 600 beads?" The waiter replies, "Have you ever tried to clean a Frenchman?"

☞ During a test of the rocket Ariane, a Frenchman is sent into orbit with a monkey. Each is given an envelope prior to launch. When they finally leave the Earth's atmosphere, the monkey opens his envelope and reads the instructions, 'Adjust trim, jettison fuel pods, check matter/anti-matter readings, correct course to 110 degrees and ease back on throttle controls'. The Frenchman then reads *his* instructions: 'Feed the monkey'.

☞ France's military capacity was put into jeopardy last week when a fire broke out in the country's largest white flag factory.

"Going to war without France is like going deer-hunting without your accordion."
Norman Schwartzkopf

☞ How can you recognize a French war veteran? Sunburned armpits.

☞ How do you stop a French tank? Shoot the guy pushing it.

☞ How many Frenchman does it take to defend Paris? We don't know; it's never been tried.

☞ How many gears does a French tank have? Five: four in reverse and one forward (in case of attack from the rear).

☞ It seems that this year's French Tennis Open has been cancelled due to a national crisis; they have plenty of racquets, but no balls.

☞ Next time there's a war in Europe, the loser has to keep France.

☞ Scientists tell President Bush that they have discovered a meteor heading towards the earth. The scientists have calculated that it will strike France at approximately two o'clock in the morning. The meteorite is large enough to completely wipe France from the face of the earth, for ever. President Bush is faced with a terrible dilemma. Should he stay up late and watch it live on TV, or tape it and watch it after breakfast?

☞ We can count on the French to be there when they need us.

"There is no hell. There is only France."
Frank Zappa

☞ What did the mayor of Paris say to the German Army as they entered the city in 1940? "Table for 200,000, m'sieur?"

☞ What's the most useful thing in a French tank? The rear-view mirror; it lets them watch the fighting.

☞ What's the first thing the French army teaches at basic training? How to surrender in at least ten languages.

☞ What's the first thing the French did when they heard Germany was reunified? They installed speed bumps at the border to slow down the panzers.

☞ Why are the streets of French cities lined with trees? So German soldiers can march in the shade.

☞ Why don't they have fireworks at EuroDisney? Because every time they set them off, the French try to surrender.

ETHNIC – GERMAN

☞ A Dutch farmer is working near his barn when he sees a distant figure leaning over a horse trough. The figure is a hiker and it looks as if he's going to slake his thirst with a long, cool drink of water out of the trough. The alarmed farmer shouts, "Don't drink the water! It's full of pesticides!" The figure shouts back, "Ich verstehe nicht! Was sagen Sie?" The farmer calls out, "Help yourself!"

☞ How do you make a Black Forest Gateau? First you occupy the kitchen...

☞ Tom tried out the German restaurant that had opened on the high street. The food was great, but an hour after he'd finished he was hungry again – for power!

☞ Why do Germans have such large heads? So they have somewhere to put their big mouths.

ETHNIC – GREEK

☞ What does a Greek bride get on her wedding night that's long and hard? A new surname.

ETHNIC – IRISH

☞ A woman goes to a police station and says, "Officer, I've been molested by an Irishman." The desk sergeant says, "How do you know it was an Irishman?" The woman replies, "I had to help him."

> **"Irish people love Muslims. They've taken a lot of heat off us. Before, we were 'the terrorists', but now we're 'the Riverdance people'."**
> *Andrew Maxwell*

☞ An Irishman and an Apache are walking through the Navajo desert when they hear a 'Woo! Woo!' sound coming from a nearby cave. The Apache tears off his clothes and runs towards the cave, shouting "Woo! Woo!" in return. "Why are you making that sound?" calls out the Irishman. "And why have you stripped stark naked?" The Apache shouts back over his shoulder, "It's a mating call. There's a woman in that cave who needs a good seeing-to! Woo! Woo!" With that, the

Apache runs over to the cave and disappears inside. Suddenly the Irishman hears another 'Woo! Woo!' coming from over the hill. He runs to the top of the hill and sees a large cave in the next valley. The 'Woo! Woo!' noise comes from the cave once more. "Hang on, me darlin'!" shouts the Irishman. "I'm coming!" The Irishman runs down the slope tearing off his clothes. "Woo! Woo!" he shouts, and runs into the cave. Next day the newspaper headline reads, 'Naked Irishman run over by freight train.'

☞ An Irishman goes to a funfair, where he sees an unusual act. A trainer claims that his elephant can tell a person's age just by looking at them. To demonstrate this talent, the trainer shows the elephant a small boy. The elephant stares at the lad, then stamps its foot nine times. "Is that your age?" asks the trainer. "Yes, sir," says the boy. "I'm nine years old." The Irishman reckons this is some sort of trick and bets the trainer that the elephant won't be able to guess his age. The trainer takes the bet and the elephant has a close look at the Irishman. The animal then raises its tail, lets out a huge bottom-burp and stamps its foot twice. The Irishman goes pale and says, "Begob: he's right. Farty-two!"

☞ How does an Irishman count apples? "One, two, three, four, five, another apple, and another, there's another, and another..."

ETHNIC – ISRAELIS

☞ An Israeli arrives at Heathrow airport. The customs officer says to him, "Occupation?" "No," replies the Israeli, "just visiting."

ETHNIC – ITALIANS

☞ Did you hear about the Mafia version of the Nativity play? Jesus was visited by three shepherds and 20 wise guys.

☞ The students at an Italian university decide to form a rowing team, so they choose their strongest athletes and start practising. Unfortunately, they discover they aren't very good. They're due to race an Austrian team the next month and their best time is always at least four minutes behind their opponents'. In desperation, they decide to send a spy over to Austria to see if he can pick up any tips. The spy is dispatched, and a week later he comes back with good news; he's been able to see the Austrians practising and has discovered their secret. "So what *is* their secret?" asks one of the Italians. "It's so simple," replies the spy. "They have eight men rowing and only one man shouting and waving his arms."

ETHNIC – JEWISH

☞ A brief summary of Jewish holidays: they tried to kill us, we won, let's eat.

☞ A Chinese man is sitting is a restaurant when a Jewish veteran comes and punches him in the nose. "That's for Pearl Harbor," says the veteran. "But that was the Japanese," protests the Chinese man. "Japanese, Chinese – they're all the same," says the veteran. Hearing this, the Chinese man gets up and punches the veteran on the nose. "That's for the Titanic!" he shouts. "Are you crazy?" says the Jewish man. "The Titanic was sunk by an iceberg." The Chinese man replies, "Iceberg, Goldberg – they're all the same."

☞ A German exchange student comes to stay with the Cohen family in London. On his first morning, the student comes down to breakfast and is given a toasted bagel. "Mmmm, delicious," says the student. "Ve are not having bagels like this in Germany." Grandma Cohen stands up and yells, "And whose fault is that, y'bastard?"

☞ A Jewish curse: may all your hairs fall out except for one – and it should have dandruff!

☞ Another Jewish curse: may all your teeth fall out – except one, so you can have a toothache.

☞ A Jewish grandmother takes a call from her newly-married grandson, Maurice. It turns out that Maurice wants to bring his new bride over for a visit. "That's wonderful," says grandma. "You'll love my new apartment. It's on the fifth floor: very nice views. You want to come to the north end of Bekerman Street. My block is half-way down, opposite the park. Just come up to the front door and use your elbow to press on the button for number 56. Then, when I buzz you in, get in the elevator and elbow the button for the fifth floor." "That sounds easy enough," says Maurice, "but why am I hitting buttons with my elbow?" There's a pause; then Grandmother replies, "You're coming empty-handed?"

☞ A Jewish man goes to his psychiatrist. "I had this really weird dream last night," he says. "I saw my mother, but then I noticed that she had your face and your voice. I found that really disturbing. I couldn't get back to sleep at all. I just lay there until it was time to get up and have breakfast. So I had a slice of toast and a cup of coffee and came straight over here. What on earth do you think the dream was about?" The psychiatrist shakes his head. "One slice of toast and a cup of coffee?" he says. "And you call that a breakfast?"

☞ A Jewish man is talking to his friend and starts to tell a joke, "Levy and Abraham were going to this Bar Mitzvah when…" "Stop it, already," says his friend. "Always with the Jewish jokes. Levy this, and Abraham that. Why not tell a different kind of joke for a change? Know any Irish jokes?" "Sure," says his friend. "O'Leary and Seamus were going to this Bar Mitzvah…"

☞ A Jewish woman becomes President of the USA and eventually persuades her mother to attend the swearing-in ceremony. The old lady is given a seat in the stands between the Chief of Staff and an Admiral. As the ceremony reaches its climax, she nudges the Admiral in the ribs. "See her, holding the Bible?" she says. "Her brother's a doctor."

☞ A man is walking down a street when he comes across a tailors' shop called 'Cohen and O'Leary'. The man is intrigued and goes inside to have a look around. He checks out the off-the-peg suits then goes over to have a chat with a little old Jewish man standing behind the counter. "That's quite an odd combination: Cohen and O'Leary," says the man. "Is it?" replies the little old Jewish man. "Well, yes," says the man. "It's not often you see a Jew and an Irishman in business together." "This surprises you?" exclaims the old man. "Certainly it does," says the man. The Jewish man replies, "Well, if that surprised you, this one will give you a heart attack – I'm O'Leary."

☞ A young Jewish man goes to his father and tells him that he's fallen in love with a girl down the road. "What's her name?" asks dad. "Rachel Jones," replies the boy. "Jones?" says dad. "What sort of name is that? Why don't you find a nice Jewish girl?" A few weeks later, the boy comes back to his father and tells him he's fallen in love again, this time with a girl called Mary McGregor. "McGregor?" cries dad. "What sort of stupid name is that? Find a nice Cohen, or a Levy, why don't you?" A few weeks later, the son returns to announce that he's engaged to be married. "Married?" exclaims dad. "Don't tell me; her name is Bacon, perhaps, or Murphy?" "No," replies the son. "Her name is Goldberg." "Thank God!" exclaim dad. "A good, respectable Jewish name. You've made me very proud. So, tell me; what's her first name?" The son replies, "Whoopi."

☞ According to Jewish doctrine, when does a foetus become human? When it gets a place at medical school.

☞ An athletics tournament is under way in Israel. While they're waiting for the starting gun, an American sprinter turns to his Israeli opponent and says," So what's your best time for the 100 metres?" The Israeli replies, "Just over nine seconds." "Nine seconds?" says the American. "But that's crazy. The world record is over ten seconds." "Yeah," says the Israeli, "but I know a short cut."

☞ An old Jewish couple are sent an invitation to a wedding. At the bottom of the card it says 'RSVP', but for the life of them they can't figure out what it could stand for. At last, the old man has a brain-wave, "Of course," he shouts. "It means 'Remember Send Vedding Present'!"

☞ An old Jewish lady goes to a travel agency and books a flight to Calcutta. The travel agent tries to dissuade her, as he knows Calcutta isn't very touristy, but the old lady doesn't want to go on a cruise, or go to Florida, or to a nice country hotel; she wants to go to Calcutta – so he sells her a ticket. Once she gets to Calcutta, the old lady gets on a rickety old bus going out into the hot and dusty interior of India. The bus driver tries to recommend a luxurious hotel on the coast, but the old lady wants to go to a remote Indian town, out on the hot dry plain with the dust and the flies. After a day and a half of bouncing around in a creaky old bus, the old lady gets to the town. She climbs off the bus and joins a queue outside a temple; it's a queue of people wanting to see a famous guru. One of the temple priests explains to the old lady that the queue is very long. He suggests that she'd be better off seeing the temple from the outside, perhaps from the comfortable shade of a nearby restaurant: but no; the old lady wants to queue in the hot afternoon sun to see the guru. Four hours later, the old lady is at the head of the queue. The priest warns her that tradition demands she only speaks five words to the guru. The old lady assures him that the guru will only hear five words from her. The moment arrives and the old lady finds herself standing in front of the loin-clothed guru who is sitting cross-legged on a platform. The old lady locks eyes with the mystic, folds her arms and says, "Morris. Come home this instant!"

☞ Aunt Ruth went on holiday in Australia. She had a nice time, but almost died of heatstroke on Bondi Beach; thankfully the lifeguards managed to take off her mink coat in the nick of time.

☞ Did you hear about Solly Yakamoto, the Jewish kamikaze pilot? He crashed his plane into his brother's scrap-yard.

☞ Did you hear about the Jewish detective? He had a tip off.

☞ Did you hear about the Jewish mother who was thrown off jury service? They sent her home because she kept insisting *she* was guilty.

☞ Father Mahoney goes to a barber and has a haircut. When it's time to pay, the barber refuses to take any money. "Father," he says, "you're a man of the cloth; I couldn't charge you anything. The haircut is on the house." Father Mahoney is touched by this gesture and the next day, when the barber opens his shop for business, he finds 12 gold coins on his doorstep. The next week, the Reverend Smith pays a visit to the barber. He has a trim and a shave and, just as before, the barber refuses to take any payment from a man of God. The Reverend Smith is also very touched by this gesture and, next day, when the barber opens his shop for business, he once again finds 12 gold coins on his doorstep. The next week, Rabbi Cohen goes into the barber's for a trim. Once more, the barber refuses to take any payment from a holy man. Rabbi Cohen is most impressed for this consideration and, next morning, when the barber opens his shop for business, he finds 12 rabbis standing on his doorstep.

☞ God approaches a German and offers him a set of commandments. "What sort of commandments are they?" asks the German. God replies, "Well, for example, 'Thou shall not kill'." The German shakes his head, "Sorry. Not interested." God then approaches an Italian and offers him a set of commandments. "You got any samples?" asks the Italian. "Well, one of them is, 'Thou shall not steal'." says God. The Italian throws up his hands. "That'll not go down well in Italia," he says. "No, thanks." God then approaches a Frenchman and offers him some commandments. "Commandments like what?" asks the Frenchman. "How about, 'Thou shall not covet thy neighbour's wife'?" says God. The Frenchman shrugs his shoulders, "Sorry. That's not very good for me. I will decline." God then approaches Moses and offers him some commandments. "So how much are you charging for these things?" asks Moses. "Charging?" says God. "I'm not charging anything. They're free." "Free?" says Moses. "I'll take ten!"

☞ How can you tell if a Jewish wedding is Reform, Orthodox or Liberal? In a Reform wedding, the bride's pregnant. In an Orthodox wedding, the bride's mother is pregnant. In a Liberal wedding, the rabbi is pregnant!

☞ How do Jewish mothers get the kids ready for dinner? They put them in the car.

☞ Hymie and Saul run a Jewish deli. One day, a new customer comes in and is surprised to see a Chinese man walk out of the storeroom. The Chinese man come up to Hymie and Saul and speaks to them in perfect Yiddish. Once the Chinese man has gone back to the storeroom, the customer goes up to Hymie and Saul to investigate. "That's very unusual," says the customer. "I don't think I've heard a Chinese man speaking Yiddish before: and he speaks it so well." Hymie leans over and whispers, "Not so loud. He thinks we're teaching him English."

☞ It's snowing, and Hymie struggles to walk down the street in the teeth of a howling storm. He staggers onwards, occasionally falling into a deep snowdrift, until he reaches the door of an all-night delicatessen. He pushes the door open and falls inside on to the wet floor, his hands and face blue with cold. The shopkeeper helps him to his feet. "It's filthy weather outside," he says. "You're my first customer this evening." "I can believe it," says Hymie, his teeth chattering. "What would you like?" asks the shopkeeper. "Two bagels," says Hymie. "And what else?" asks the shopkeeper. "Just the bagels," replies Hymie. "You came out on a day like today for just two bagels?" says the shopkeeper. "Yes," says Hymie, "one for me and one for Miriam." "Is Miriam your wife?" asks the shopkeeper. "Of course," replies Hymie. "Do you think my mother would send me out on a night like this?"

☞ Jewish telegram: 'Start worrying. Details to follow.'

☞ Mr and Mrs Cohen strike it rich and buy a big house. Since they have such a fine home, they decide to get a butler to go with it. After lot of searching they discover James, a top-notch butler who has served some of the most blue-blooded families in the country. That weekend, the Cohens decide to have their old friends the Levys over for a meal. They tell James there will be four for dinner. However, when they come home that evening, they discover the table is laid for six. "Why six?" asks Mr Cohen. "There's only the Levys and us." "Yes, sir," replies James, "but when Mr Levy rang, he said he would be bringing the Bagels with him."

☞ Mrs Cohen is telling her husband off. "You're a schmuck!" she shouts. "You always were a schmuck and you always will be a schmuck! You look, you act and you dress like a schmuck! You'll be a schmuck until the day you drop dead! And if they ran a competition to find the world's biggest schmuck, you'd be the world's second-biggest schmuck!" "What?" says Mr Cohen. "Why would I only get second place?" Mrs Cohen yells, "Because you're a schmuck!"

☞ Harry meets his friend Solomon in the high street. Solomon, who is very Orthodox, is all dressed up for a trip to the synagogue. "It's only Thursday," says Harry. "Why are you dressed in your Sabbath clothes with your prayer tools?" "To be honest," says Solomon, "I'm on my way to a brothel. I've never been to one before." "So what?" says Harry. "How does that explain the clothes?" "Well," replies Solomon. "If I like it, I thought I might stay for the weekend."

☞ Solly goes out to get a paper. On the way back, he doesn't look both ways crossing the road and gets hit by a car. He's knocked flying and loses consciousness. A few minutes later, he comes round to find a Catholic priest administering the Last Rites. Solly doesn't want to embarrass the priest by admitting that he's Jewish, so he lets him continue as he's loaded into the ambulance. "So I've got a bit of Catholic in me now," he thinks to himself. "How can it hurt?" At the hospital it turns out that, apart from a nasty bang on the head, all Solly's injuries are superficial, so they bandage his head and send him home. As Solly turns the key of his front door, his wife Ruth barges past him. "Ruth," he says, "you'll never believe me when I tell you what happened." By this time, Ruth is hurrying down the street. She calls back over her shoulder, "Tell me tomorrow. I'm late for my bridge night." Solly sighs and goes indoors. He sees his daughter Judith climbing the stairs. "Judith," he says, "you'll never guess what happened to your old dad." "Whatever it was, I bet it was boring," she says. "I'm going upstairs to take a bath, so take my calls. If David rings, say I'll call him right back." "All right, sweetie," sighs Solly. At this moment Solly's son Benjamin comes out of the front room. "Benjy," says Solly. "You'll never guess what happened. I was walking across the road when

– " "Not now, dad," says Benjamin. "I'm going out. By the way, I found your wallet and borrowed £50." With that, Benjamin is out of the front door and away. Solly's shoulders slump. He goes to the front room and sits in his favourite chair. "This anti-Semitism is a terrible thing," he sighs. "I've only been a gentile for a couple of hours and already I hate three Jews."

☞ Solomon has been trying to get into the local tennis club for years, but it's very exclusive and he has no luck at all. One day, a rich relative dies and leaves him some money, so Solomon uses it to improve his chances. He gets elocution lessons to help improve his speech, hires a private tennis coach to improve his game and changes his name from Solomon Goldbaum to Simon Golding. Eventually it works, and he gets into the club. On his first day, he's drinking at the bar when the waiter spills a Bloody Mary over his brand-new tennis shoes. Solomon leaps up and shouts, "Oy vey!" He looks around at his startled companions and continues, "Whatever that might mean…"

☞ Two Jewish men go to a Chinese restaurant. While they're talking, one of them wonders how many Jewish people there are in China. They both agree there must be some, but neither is sure how many. When the waiter comes over, they ask him if there are any Chinese Jews. "I don't know," replies the waiter. "I ask in kitchen. They will know." So the waiter goes to the kitchen, then comes back. "Sorry. No Chinese Jews," he says. "What?" says one of the men. "No Chinese Jews at all?" "Sorry," repeats the waiter. "We got orange Jews, apple Jews and grape Jews, but no Chinese Jews."

☞ Two Jewish men, Simon and Daniel, are walking down the road when they pass a Catholic church. Outside the church, a sign says, '£50 for each convert to the Catholic faith'. Simon reads the sign thoughtfully. "What are you doing?" asks Daniel. "You're not thinking of going in there, are you?" "Well," says Simon, "£50 doesn't grow on trees." So saying, he walks into the church. Half an hour later, Simon walks out again and finds Daniel waiting for him. "Did you do it?" asks Daniel. "Did you convert?" "Yes," says Simon. "So what was it like?" asks Daniel. "Not too bad," replies Simon. "Did you get your money?" asks Daniel. Simon replies, "Is that all you people ever think about?"

☞ Two tramps are sitting on a pavement in Dublin. One tramp is holding a large crucifix and the other is holding a large Star of David. Both are holding hats to collect coins. A lot of people walk past, but they all ignore the tramp holding the Star of David. However, nearly all the passers-by drop money in the hat of the tramp with the cross: so much, in fact, that it's soon overflowing with coins. A priest happens to walk past and stops to offer advice. "Do you not know that this is a Christian country?" says the priest to the tramp holding the star. "No man will give you money for holding up a Star of David." The tramp holding the star turns to the tramp with the cross and says. "Hey, Hymie; look who's trying to teach us marketing."

☞ What would Superman say if he was Jewish? "Up, up and oy vey!"

☞ What's the definition of a Jewish threesome? A hard-on and two headaches.

☞ What's the definition of genius? An average student with a Jewish mother.

☞ What's the name of the Jewish fairytale about an uncircumcised troll? Rumpled Foreskin.

☞ What's the technical term for a divorced Jewish woman? The plaintiff.

☞ Which is the most popular Internet provider in Israel? Netan-Yahoo.

☞ Why do Jewish divorces cost so much? Because they're worth it!

☞ Why don't Jews drink? It interferes with their suffering.

ETHNIC – MANCUNIANS

☞ What do you call 20 Mancunians sitting in a filing cabinet? Sorted!

☞ Why do couples from Manchester like making love doggy-style? They both get to watch Coronation Street.

ETHNIC – MEXICAN

☞ What do you call a black man driving a Jaguar? Black power. What do you call a white man driving a Jaguar? White power. What do you call a Mexican man driving a Jaguar? Grand theft auto.

☞ What do you call a Mexican who's had a vasectomy? A dry Martinez.

☞ When does a Mexican turn into a Spaniard? When he marries your daughter.

☞ Which words start most recipes in a Mexican cookbook? "First, steal a chicken…"

☞ Why do Mexican cars have such small steering wheels? So they can drive while they're wearing handcuffs.

☞ Little Johnny comes home and says to his mother, "Am I Jewish or Mexican?" "Well, you're neither," replies mother. "Why on earth are you asking a question like that?" "Because part of me feels Jewish and part of me feels Mexican," replies little Johnny. "What a strange thing to say," says mother. "What brought this on?" "It's Pete down the road," explains Johnny. "He's offered to sell me his bike for $40, but half of me thinks I can haggle him down to $20, and half of me thinks I ought to wait until it's dark and steal it."

ETHNIC – NATIVE AMERICANS

☞ A man goes to a fair and sees a sign saying, "Meet Big Chief Laughing Crow, the man with the best memory in the world. Will answer any question for $5 or give you $100." Intrigued, the man goes into the tent and meets

Chief Laughing Crow, who is sitting cross-legged on a blanket. He hands over his $5 and says, "Who won the Californian Pro-Am tennis tournament in 1938?" Straight away the Chief says, "Bill Ankerman." The man is impressed; he hands over another five-dollar bill and says, "Who did he play?" Without hesitation the Chief says, "George Hubbins." The man tries another question, this time slightly harder: "Who did Bill beat in the quarter-final?" The chief answers, "Rod Smith." The man is beaten; these are the most obscure questions he can think of. Twenty years later, the man is on holiday with his wife when he comes across Big Chief Laughing Crow's tent at another fair. "This guy's incredible," says the man to his wife. "We've got to go in and see him. You won't believe what a great memory he has." The pair enter the tent and find the chief sitting on his blanket. The man's wife puts up her hand Indian-style and says, "How." The chief replies, "Straight sets."

☞ A man is visiting a Native American reservation when he comes across a man making smoke signals. "Why are you doing that?" asks the visitor. The man replies, "We have no water." "Really?" says the visitor. "And this is part of a ceremony that'll make it rain?" "No," replies the man, "I'm calling for a plumber."

☞ NASA is preparing for another flight to the moon. As part of their preparation, some astronauts are sent on a training mission to a Navajo reservation. The reservation land is remarkably like the lunar surface and a good place to try out the new space-suits. One day, an old Navajo man is herding sheep when he comes across some astronauts putting their suits through their paces. The old man gets talking to the astronauts and asks if he might be allowed to send a message into space. The astronauts think this is a great idea. They produce a dictation machine and the old man records his message to the stars in the Navajo tongue. However, before this message is broadcast, the officials at NASA decide they ought to get a translation and find out exactly what the old man said. Eventually they find a college linguist who is able to decipher the words. It turns out the old man said, "Watch out for these guys – they have come to steal your land."

ETHNIC – POLISH

☞ Mr Slatisvlaski is convinced his wife is trying to kill him. Yesterday he went home and found she'd bought a bottle of Polish Remover.

ETHNIC – RUSSIAN

☞ Boris saves his roubles for twenty years to buy a new car from the state car factory. After taking his money, the salesman tells Boris his car can be picked up in two years' time. "I see," says Boris. "And do you know what week that will be?" "Yes," says the salesman. "The car will be here in the second week of May." "I see," says Boris. "And do you know what day of the week it will be?" The salesman consults a document and replies. "We will have it ready for collection on Tuesday. Almost exactly in two years' time from now." "Oh dear," says Boris. "You don't know if that's morning or afternoon, do you?" The salesman sighs and consults another document. "Yes. It will be the morning, before 11am." "Thank goodness for that," replies Boris. "It's just that I've booked a plumber to come round that afternoon."

☞ What's 30 feet long and lives on potatoes? A Russian meat queue.

ETHNIC – SCOTTISH

☞ A Scotsman, his wife and their three children have just finished shopping and decide to get a taxi home. The Scotsman hails a cab. He says to the driver, "Here, laddie. If you turn your meter off, how much will ye charge to drive us back to Morningside?" "I'll charge £12 for you and your wife," replies the cabby, "and I'll take the three kiddies for free." The Scotsman turns to his children and says, "Right, you lot; jump in the taxi and this nice man will drive you home. Your mother and I are catching the bus."

☞ How do you disperse a mob of angry Scotsmen? Charge at them with a collection box.

☞ Hamish comes home from work early and finds a plumber's van parked in the drive of his house. He turns pale and gulps. "Christ," he says. "I hope that's her bloody boyfriend."

☞ How do you take a census in a Scottish town? Throw a handful of change into the main square.

☞ Hamish's wife dies. At her funeral, he unveils her tombstone. It reads, 'Morag McDonald. Loving wife of Hamish, certified tree surgeon. No job too small!' Hamish stands at the graveside, tears streaming down his face. The chaplain looks at him sternly. "I'm noo surprised you're crying, Hamish," he says. "Tears of remorse, nee doubt, for turning your poor wife's grave into a cheap advertisement!" "It's not that," sniffs Hamish. "They left off the bloody telephone number..."

☞ It's very easy to catch Scotsmen who make obscene phone calls; they always try to reverse the charges.

"There are two seasons in Scotland – June and Winter."
Billy Connolly

☞ Angus contacted the authorities in Scotland to tell them he'd just seen a UFO hovering over his house. It turned out it was the sun.

☞ A Glaswegian dies in a car accident. He wakes up and finds himself lying on a litter-strewn street. A man wearing a Rangers scarf helps him to his feet. "What's goin' on?" asks the Glaswegian. "You got run over by a car," replies the man. "You're dead." "Christ Almighty," says the Glaswegian. "This place is a right dump. It looks like the Gorbals. I expected Heaven to be all white and glittery." The man replies, "So who told you this was Heaven?"

☞ A Scottish sailor is taking shore leave in Cuba. He's sitting in a bar when a man with a huge bushy beard walks in and orders a whisky. The man gulps it down and then heads for the door. "Hey!" calls out the barman. "You haven't paid." The man points at his beard and says, "I'm in the army." The barman waves him away, saying, "For you, it's free." Another man with a huge bushy beard comes in and orders a whisky; he too gulps it down and heads for the door. "Hey!" calls out the barman. "You haven't paid." The man points at his beard and says, "I'm in the navy." The barman waves him away, saying, "For you, it's free." The Scotsman decides he might as well have a go at this and orders a whisky for himself. He knocks it back and heads for the door. "Hey!" calls out the barman. "You haven't paid. And I know you're not in the Cuban army or the Cuban navy because you don't have a bushy beard." "You're right," says the Scotsman. "I'm not in the army *or* the navy." He lifts up his kilt and says, "I'm in the Secret Service."

☞ An Irishman is having sex with a Scottish girl. Neither of them is enjoying it very much. "I thought all Irishmen were supposed to be big and thick," says the girl. The Irishman replies, "And I thought all Scots were meant to be tight."

☞ Frazier and Hamish are using a public lavatory when Frazier accidentally drops a £1 coin down the toilet. "Och, Frazier," says Hamish "It's no worth getting your hands dirty for a pound." "You're right," says Frazier, throwing in a £10 note. "But it is for £11."

☞ Hamish comes to London and never tires of telling people how marvellous Scotland is. One day one of his work-mates decides he's had enough and asks the obvious question. "All right," he says, "if Scotland is so bloody great, why did you come down here?" "I had no choice," sighs Hamish. "I'm not so bright and they're all so damned clever up there, England's the only place I had a chance of making a living."

☞ Hamish has just washed his kilt; now he can't do a fling with it.

☞ Old Jock walks into a pub and orders a pint of bitter. The barman pushes over a pint of beer and Jock peers at it. "Excuse me," he says, "but do ye think you could squeeze a dram o'whisky into this pint?" "Aye," says the barman. "I'm sure I could." Jock replies, "Then would ye mind topping it up with beer?"

☞ They're remaking 'Silence of the Lambs' for a Scottish audience. It's being called, 'Shut Up Ewes Two'.

☞ Two Scotsmen are walking through the woods when one ducks into the bushes to have a crap. After much grunting, he calls out to his friend, "Hey, have you got a piece of paper?" His friend replies, "Don't be so tight-fisted, Hamish; leave it where it is."

☞ What do you call a Scotsman at a World Cup final? A linesman.

☞ What does a Scottish football team have in common with a three-pin plug? They're both useless in Europe.

☞ Why did the Scotsman die of a heart attack when he tossed a £1 coin into the blind beggar's cup? The string broke.

☞ Why do Scotsmen march when they play the bagpipes? Because it's harder to hit a moving target.

☞ Why is a traditional Scottish church round? So no one can hide in a corner when the collection plate comes round.

☞ The Queen visits a Scottish hospital, and takes a tour of the wards. In one of the wards, a patient sits up in bed and shouts, "In this strange land, this uncouth clime. A land unknown to prose or rhyme!" The patient in the next bed says, "Wee, sleekit, cow'rin, tim'rous beastie, O, what a panic's in thy breastie!" Another patient exclaims, "Ae fond kiss, and then we sever; Ae fareweel, alas, for ever!" "Good heavens," says the Queen. "I hadn't realised this was the Psychiatric Ward". It's not," replies the doctor. "It's the Serious Burns Unit."

ETHNIC – SCOUSERS

☞ A huge, rough-looking Scouser is sitting in a bar when a prim little gay man sits next to him. The gay man likes a bit of rough, so he leans over to the scouser and whispers, "Would you like a blow-job?" The scouser turns round and punches the man in the face, knocking him to the floor. "Blimey," says the barman. "What did he say to make you do that?" "Dunno," says the Scouser. "Something about a job."

☞ A new teacher decides to make friends with her class in a Manchester school. "I support Manchester United," says the teacher. "Hands up who supports them too." All the children put their hands up except one little girl. "And who do you support?" asks the teacher. "I support Manchester City," replies the little girl. "I support them because my mum supports City and so does my dad and so does my brother." "You don't have to support a team just because your family does," says the teacher. "I like my dad, my mum and my brother," replies the little girl, "so I support the same team." "Well, what if you didn't like them so much?" asks the teacher. "What would happen if your family wasn't very nice? What if your mother was a street-walker, your father was a drunk and your brother was a criminal? What team would you be supporting then?" The girls thinks for a moment, then says, "Everton."

☞ Two Scousers are browsing in a clothes store when one holds up a shirt and says, "There's the one I'd get." And a passing cyclops smacks him in the face.

☞ What do you call a Brummie surrounded by 200 Scousers? A prison warder.

ETHNIC – SPANISH

☞ A fire truck arrives at a burning building in a small Spanish town. On the roof, a man is prancing around dressed in a matador's costume. Four of the firemen hold out a safety-net and urge him to jump. The man refuses and loudly proclaims, "I'm Fearless Jose, the bullfighter who fears nothing, not even fire!" The firemen beg and plead, but to no avail. The man keeps prancing around while shouting the same phrase over and over again, until the firemen are really sick of hearing it. Finally, when the flames begin to scorch his backside, the man announces he's changed his mind. He stands on the edge of the roof, shouts, "I'm Fearless Jose, the bullfighter who fears nothing, not even fire!", then leaps. A second before he hits the safety-net, the four firemen shout, "Olé!" and whisk it away.

☞ Why don't the Spanish have driving lessons and sex education classes on the same day? Because it tires out the donkey.

ETHNIC – USA

☞ An American, a Mexican and a Puerto Rican are walking along a Florida beach when they come across an old bottle. The American picks up the bottle and rubs the sand off it. As you might expect, a genie pops out and gives each of them a wish. The Mexican says, "I wish I could return to my homeland with all my compatriots and live in peace and prosperity." The genie claps his hands and the Mexican disappears. The Puerto Rican says, "I wish I and all my fellow-Puerto Ricans could go back to our island home and live in peace and prosperity." The genie claps his hands and the Puerto Rican disappears. The genie turns to the American and says, "And what is your wish?" The American says, "Let's see if I've got this right. All the Mexicans have gone home?" "All of them," replies the genie. "And all the Puerto Ricans have gone home too?" continues the American. "Yes," says the genie. "All are gone." "Gee," says the American. "Then I guess I'll just have a beer."

☞ Two families move from Pakistan to America and the fathers make a bet to see which of them can become the most American in twelve months. A year later they meet up, and the first man says, "Look at me. My son is playing quarterback, I am having a McDonald's for breakfast, and I am now on the way to the ballpark to root for my team. How about you?" The other man looks at him and says, "F*** you, towel-head."

ETHNIC – WELSH

☞ What do you call a sheep tied to a Welsh lamp-post? A leisure centre.

"In the Bible, God made it rain for 40 days and 40 nights. That's a pretty good summer for us in Wales. I was eight before I realised you could take a Kagoul off."
Rhod Gilbert

ETHNIC – YORKSHIRE

☞ Alfred Othelthwaite dies and goes to heaven. He knocks on the Pearly Gates and Saint Peter comes out to see who's there. "Where are you from?" asks Saint Peter. Alfred proudly says, "Yorkshire." "Piss off," replies the saint. "We're not cooking Yorkshire Pudding for one."

☞ Never ask an English person where he comes from. If he's from Yorkshire, he'll tell you; if he's from anywhere else, it's unfair to embarrass him.

ETIQUETTE

"At a formal dinner party, the person nearest death should always be seated closest to the bathroom."
George Carlin

☞ Why don't polite people like having group sex? Writing all the thank-you letters afterwards gives them cramp.

EYES

☞ My aunt is very short-sighted; she can't see past the end of her nose, though admittedly that is quite a distance.

"I have such poor vision I can date anyone."
Gary Shandling

☞ A man is dining in a fancy restaurant when he notices a gorgeous woman sitting alone at the next table. The man checks her out, but doesn't have the nerve to introduce himself. Suddenly the woman sneezes, and her glass eye comes flying out of its socket. It hits a light fitting, then bounces off the man's table. By reflex, he grabs it in mid-air. The man wraps the eye in a napkin and gives it back to the woman. "I'm so sorry," says the woman, as she pops the eye back into place. "That always happens when I sneeze. Can I buy you dinner as a reward for getting it back to me?" The man is delighted to accept this invitation and the pair enjoy a wonderful dinner together. Afterwards they decide to make a night of it and go to the cinema, followed by drinks. One thing leads to another and they end up spending the night at the woman's apartment. Next morning, the man awakes after a night of incredible lovemaking. He turns to the woman and says, "Last evening was fantastic. Are you this nice to every guy you meet?" "Not every guy," replies the woman. "Only those who catch my eye."

FAME AND CELEBRITIES

☞ A woman goes to a tattooist to have a picture of Lennox Lewis tattooed on her right inner thigh, and a picture of Mike Tyson tattooed on her left inner thigh. However, when the tattooist is finished the woman is appalled at the quality of his handiwork. She goes into the manager's office, sits on his desk and opens her legs. "Excuse me," she says. "But do you really think that looks like Lennox Lewis or that looks like Mike Tyson?" "No," replies the manager, "but that one in the middle definitely looks like Don King."

☞ Harry saw Elvis last week! He swears it's absolutely true. He says he sat right between him and the Loch Ness Monster on the UFO.

> **"If life were fair, Elvis would be alive and all**
> **the impersonators would be dead."**
> *Johnny Carson*

☞ In an interview about his failed marriage, Paul McCartney was asked if he would ever go down on one knee again – or, as she prefers to be known, Heather.

☞ Michael Jackson is in a hotel just before his trial. He's bored and decides to send his bodyguard out to get a Disney DVD for him to watch. The bodyguard says, "Shall I get Aladdin?" "Are you crazy?" says Jacko. "Don't you think I'm in enough trouble?"

"People say Callum Best is only famous because of who his dad was. But then you could say the same thing about Jesus."
Karl Pilkington

☞ We've had our front room done in paint that's white with a tiny hint of colour. Now all we need is Michael Douglas and Catherine Zeta Jones to come round so we can have guests with a tiny hint of personality to match.

☞ What do people say when Woody Allen hits town? "Look out! It's Woody Allen! Lock up his daughters!"

☞ What do you call five dogs with no balls? The Spice Girls.

☞ What do you get when you cross Billy Ray Cyrus with thrush? An Itchy Twitchy Twat.

"Someone once came up to me and asked, 'If you could sleep with anyone living or dead, who would it be?' And I said, 'Anyone living'."
Jimmy Carr

☞ What's got four legs and goes 'Shhhhhhhhh...'? Rod Hull's TV.

☞ What's stiff and excites women? Elvis Presley.

"Nobody thought Mel Gibson could play a Scot, but look at him now! Alcoholic and a racist!"
Frankie Boyle

☞ Why did the journalist think Oprah Winfrey had been arrested for drug-smuggling at the airport? He heard she bent over and someone saw fifty pounds of crack.

☞ Which celebrity recently had 40DD breast implants, two months of electrolysis, hormone therapy and a blonde dye-job? Osama Bin Laden.

FAMILIES

"I came from a very big family. There were so many wet nappies in the kitchen there was a rainbow in the lobby."
Les Dawson

☞ A mother cooks some deer for dinner and she and her family sit down to eat. The little boy asks if it's beef they're eating. "No," replies father. The little girl asks if they're eating pork. "No," replies father. "So what are we eating?" asks the little boy. "I'll give you a clue," says father, "It's what your mother sometimes calls me." The children spit out their food. "Christ!" shouts the little boy. "They're feeding us assholes!"

☞ Fred sees his old friend Jim and asks about his family. "The kids are doing fine," says Jim. "My son John's an artist. He paints watercolours. He's had a lot of very good reviews: and my daughter, Jane, is doing very well with her harp. Plays all round the country, she does." Fred says, "So how about your other boy, Jake?" "Oh, him?" says Jim. "He's still the same: still selling second-hand clothes from his tatty old market stall. Mind you, if it wasn't for him, the rest of us would be starving."

☞ Little Johnny goes up to his sister's boyfriend and says, "If you don't give me some money, I'll tell mum and dad that you and my sister have been having sex. I know you have, because I saw you." "Okay, okay," says the boyfriend. "Here's a pound; now keep your mouth shut." "It'll cost you a tenner," says Johnny. "What!" exclaims the boyfriend. "I'm not giving you that much." "Why not?" says Johnny. "It's what all your friends have been giving me."

☞ My relatives are in the iron and steel business. My mother irons and my father steals.

☞ What's the difference between in-laws and outlaws? Outlaws are wanted.

FAMILIES – MOTHERS-IN-LAW

> **"I was going to the mother-in-law's funeral
> tomorrow, but she's cancelled it."**
> *Les Dawson*

☞ A man comes home from the night shift and goes straight to bed. He finds his wife under the sheets and makes love to her. After this activity, he fancies a snack and goes downstairs to the kitchen. There, he's amazed to see his wife reading a magazine. "What are you doing down here?" he asks. "We were just upstairs having sex!" "Oh, my God," gasps his wife. "That was my mother in our bed! She came over and said she was feeling ill." The wife runs upstairs to the bedroom. "Mother," she says. "I can't believe this. Why didn't you say something?" Mother snorts. "What!" she says. "I haven't spoken to that idiot in ten years; I wasn't about to start now!"

☞ I just got back from a pleasure trip. I took my mother-in-law to the airport.

> **"I can always tell when the mother-in-law's coming to
> stay; the mice throw themselves on the traps."**
> *Les Dawson*

☞ A man goes on holiday to Jerusalem with his wife and her mother. Sadly, the mother is taken ill and dies suddenly. A local undertaker speaks to the man and outlines the options. "We could have your mother-in-law buried locally," explains the undertaker, "or have her transported home. A local burial is $350, but transportation is very expensive; it would be around $2,000." The man thinks for a moment, then opts for transportation. "Won't you reconsider?" asks the undertaker. "I'd hate to see you put to so much expense, and the paperwork's very complicated and time-consuming." "Thank you," replies the man, "but I have to have her shipped back home. Two thousand years ago they buried a poor guy here, and three days later he came back from the dead. I just can't take that chance."

☞ A young man excitedly tells his mother he's fallen in love and is going to get married. "I've invited her over to meet you," says the man. "She's coming over this afternoon with two of her girlfriends. Tell you what; instead of me introducing her, why don't you see if you can tell which of the gals is the one I want to marry?" A few hours later there's a knock at the door and the young man shows in three beautiful young women, a blonde, a brunette and a redhead. He sits the girls down on the couch and says, "Okay, Ma. Guess which one of these beauties I'm going to marry." Ma looks the girls over, then says, "Her. The redhead in the middle." The young man and the redhead are delighted. Ma picked the right one! "That's amazing, Ma," says the young man. "You're right. However did you know?" Ma walks over and whispers in her son's ear, "I don't like her."

"I said to my mother-in-law, 'My house is your house.' She said, 'Then get the hell off my property'."
Joan Rivers

☞ Harry is sitting in the pub looking depressed. George comes in and asks him what's wrong. Harry sighs and says, "I've got a problem with my mother-in-law." "No need to be glum," says George. "Every man has problems with his wife's mother." "I know," says Harry, "but I've got mine pregnant."

"I took my mother-in-law to the Chamber of Horrors at Madame Tussaud's. One of the attendants said, 'Keep her moving, sir; we're stocktaking'."
Les Dawson

☞ I went out Christmas shopping last week. I was looking for something cheap and nasty for my mother-in-law; then I realised she'd already married him.

☞ I've figured out the ideal weight for my mother-in-law: about one kilogram, excluding the urn.

☞ When are a mother-in-law and a beer both at their best? When they're cold, on a table and opened up.

"The wife's mother said, 'When you're dead, I'll dance on your grave.' I said, 'Good; I'm being buried at sea'."
Les Dawson

FAMILIES – MUM AND DAD

☞ A little girl asks her mummy, "Do all fairy tales begin 'Once upon a time'?" "No," says mummy. "Your father's usually begin, 'The train was late again...'"

☞ A mother knows all about her children. She knows about dentist appointments, romances, best friends, favourite foods, secret fears and hopes and dreams. A father, on the other hand, is vaguely aware that there are some short people living in the house.

"We spend the first twelve months of our children's lives teaching them to walk and talk and the next twelve telling them to sit down and shut up."
Phyllis Diller

☞ At the age of six I was left an orphan. What kind of idiot gives an orphan to a six-year-old?

**"Most children threaten at times to run away from home.
This is the only thing that keeps some parents going."**
Phyllis Diller

☞ Four men are chatting on the golf course. One says, "My son's made quite a name for himself in the building industry. He began as a carpenter, and now owns his own design and construction firm. He's very successful. In fact, last year he was able to give a friend of his a brand-new home as a gift." The second man says, "Well, my son began his career as a car salesman, but now owns a multi-line dealership. He's so successful, he recently gave a friend of his two brand-new cars as a gift." The third man says, "My son has worked his way up through a stock brokerage firm. He's so successful, he just gave a good friend of his a $25,000 stock portfolio as a gift." The fourth man says, "Well, my son's a gay hairdresser." The other three recoil in horror. The man continues, "But on the bright side, he must be good at it. His last three boyfriends gave him a new house, two new cars and a $25,000 stock portfolio."

**"My dad's Irish and my mum's Iranian, which meant that
we spent most of our family holidays in Customs."**
Patrick Monahan

☞ Jane, a harassed mother, answers the phone. A voice on the other end says, "Hello, darling. It's mummy." Jane says, "Thank God you rang, mother. I'm having a terrible day. The baby spilled prune juice all over the carpet and now he won't have his afternoon nap. The washing machine's broken and the repairman's three hours late. The fridge is empty, there's nothing for tea and I have a terrible migraine." "Calm down," says mum.

"I'll sort it out. I'll come over, and on the way I'll buy some food for dinner and some painkillers for your headache. I know a very easy way of getting rid of prune juice stains, and I'm sure I can send our little precious one asleep with a lullaby. When that's done, I'll make dinner while I wait for the repairman to arrive. While that's going on, you can have a nice sit down and put your feet up until Jeffrey gets home." "Jeffrey?" says Jane. "Who's Jeffrey?" "Your husband, of course," says mum. "My husband's name is Paul," replies Jane. "Did you dial 457 889?" "No," says mum. "I dialled 347 889." There's a second's pause, then Jane says, "Does this mean you're not coming over?"

☞ Tom's mother was a clairvoyant and his father was a contortionist; as a result he was able to foresee his own end.

> **"I want my children to have all the things I couldn't afford. Then I want to move in with them."**
> *Phyllis Diller*

FANCY DRESS

☞ A bald man with a wooden leg turns up at a fancy dress party. On the doorstep, he pours a tin of treacle over his head. "What have you come as?" asks the host. The man replies, "A toffee apple."

☞ A man goes to a fancy dress party stark naked with his privates stuffed in a jam jar. "What sort of outfit is that?" asks the host. "I'm a firefighter," replies the man. "In case of emergency, break the glass, pull the red knob and I'll come as quickly as I can."

☞ A man turns up at a fancy dress party wearing only a pair of trousers. "And what are you?" asks the host. "A premature ejaculation," replies the man. "I just came in my pants."

FARMERS

☞ A farmer is wondering how many sheep he has in his field, so he asks his sheepdog to count them. The dog runs into the field, counts them, and then runs back to his master. "So," says the farmer. "How many sheep are there?" "Forty," replies the dog. "How can there be forty?" exclaims the farmer. "I only bought thirty-eight!" "I know," says the dog, "but I rounded them up for you."

☞ A farmer orders a large amount of animal feed from a supplier. The supplier checks his books and notices that the farmer still hasn't paid for his last lot of feed, or the one before that. He rings up the farmer and tells him he can't send out the current order until the first two have been paid for. "Are you crazy?" says the farmer. "How do you expect me to wait that long?"

☞ Henri, a French exchange student, gets work on a sheep farm in Nevada. One of Henri's jobs is to castrate the young rams and, although squeamish at first, he soon gets the hang of it. That evening, the farmer and his wife and Henri sit down to dinner. The wife dishes up a plate of what looks like deep-fried eggs. "What eez this?" asks Henri. "Them's fried rams' testicles," says the farmer. "They're real tasty. We call them Sheep Fries." "Sacré bleu," thinks Henri. "Ah, well; how bad can zey be?" So Henri tries some, and to his surprise finds the Sheep Fries are very good indeed. The next evening, Henri asks what's for dinner and the farmer's wife tells him, "Sheep Fries." The same thing happens the next day, and the next, and Henri is delighted; he's really developed a taste for the delicious Sheep Fries. However, the next evening, the farmer is washing his hands before dinner when he hears a scream. He hears the front door burst open and looks out of the window to see Henri running down the road as fast as his legs will carry him. The farmer goes down to the kitchen to see his wife. "What the hell happened to Henri?" asks the farmer. "I don't know," replies the wife. "He asked if we was having Sheep Fries for dinner, and I said, no, we was having French Fries."

☞ A Kansas farmer owns some land near a reservation. One autumn day, the air turns colder than usual and the farmer builds up a large haystack to prepare for a hard winter. The farmer is unsure how bad the weather will get, but he's heard that the local Indian chief is a good judge of these things, so he visits the reservation to ask his advice. The man meets the chief and tells him his problem. The chief is happy to help; he scans the horizon and says, "Bad winter. Much snow." Hearing this, the farmer goes back to his farm and adds another few feet to his haystack, ensuring that his cattle will have enough winter feed. A week later, he goes back to the reservation to see if the outlook has changed. As before, the chief scans the horizon and says, "Very bad winter. There will be much snow on the plain." The farmer hurries back to his haystack and adds more hay, almost doubling its size. A week later, he returns to the reservation to ask if the chief can tell him when the bad weather will arrive. The chief scans the horizon and says, "I do not know when the snows will come. All I know is that this will be a bad, bad winter: one of worst we have seen." "Tell me, chief," says the farmer. "How do you predict how bad the weather will be?" The chief replies, "I look at the size of white man's haystacks."

☞ I know a man in Fort Worth with 100,000 head of cattle. No bodies: just heads.

☞ A man falls in love with a farmer's daughter. Unfortunately, the farmer doesn't think much of the man, so he sets him some 'impossible' tasks to perform before he will grant him his daughter's hand in marriage. The farmer says, "Before you can marry my daughter you must first jump the barbed-wire fence; then you must swim the river; then you must go and have sex with the cow in the barn." The man is surprised at these requests but manages to complete the tasks with ease. The farmer is astonished. "Actually, there are some more tests you have to do as well," he says. "To marry my daughter, you must harvest a field of potatoes in one night. Fix my rusty old tractor, and then go and have sex with the cow in the barn." The young man has more trouble this time, but eventually the tasks are completed. The farmer still can't believe it, so he sets more tasks. This time the young man must divert the river, put up 100 miles of fencing, build a new farmhouse and then go and have sex with the cow in the barn. The man struggles to complete the tasks, but eventually he prevails. "Hell!" says the farmer. "If you can do all that, I'd be glad to have you as a son-in-law. Of course you can marry my daughter." To which the man replies, "Screw your daughter; how much for the cow?"

☞ A townie decides to leave the rat-race and buy a farm. He moves on to a smallholding in Dorset, then goes out to buy some livestock. He finds a poultry supplier selling chicks and decides it might be an idea to raise chickens, and perhaps sell some eggs. The man buys 50 chicks and takes them back to the farm. A week later, the man returns and buys another 50 chicks. The next week, the man returns and again buys 50 chicks. "You seem to be doing well," says the poultryman. "No, I'm not," replies the townie. "I keep buying new chicks because the old ones keep dying on me." "That's unusual," says the poultry man. "You must be very unlucky to have all your chicks die on you like that." "I know," says the townie, "but I think I know what the problem is; I'm either planting them too deep or too close together."

☞ A Yorkshire farmer goes to his doctor and says, "I'm reet worried about me wife. Yesterday morning she got up at four and fed t'chickens and milked t'cows. Then she ploughed three fields, mek me breakfast and spent an hour repairing t'pigsty. After that, she got in two ton of potatoes and mended t'fence on t'bottom field. Then she come in, lies on t'bed, and says she's too tired to do 'owt else! Have you got a tonic I could give her?"

☞ A woman hiker is walking down a country lane when she comes across a tractor and a trailer. The trailer has shed its load of muck on the road and a young farm worker is sweating away, shovelling it all back on. The woman takes pity on the exhausted farmhand and offers him a drink from her water bottle. "Can't stop," says the farmhand. "Dad wouldn't like it." "Well, at least take a break," says the woman. "Why don't you sit down and I'll rub your shoulders?" "Sorry," says the farmhand, "Dad wouldn't like it." "But you'll do yourself an injury, shifting all that by yourself," says the woman. "Why not come to the pub and I'll buy you some lunch?" "Sorry," says the farmhand, "Dad wouldn't like it." "Well, I must say," exclaims the woman, "your father's a real slave-driver. I'd like to meet him and give him a piece of my mind. Where is he?" The farmhand nods at the pile of manure and says, "He's buried under this muck."

☞ Dick is out walking in the countryside when he comes across a farmer waiting by a gate. "Hello!" calls Dick. "Do you have the time?" The farmer doesn't respond. "Do you have the time, please?" asks Dick. The farmer ignores him. "Did you hear me?" asks Dick. "I asked if you had the time." The farmer looks at him and says, "You'll not get the time from me, young man." "Why not?" asks Dick. "Because if I did give you the time we might start talking and get friendly," says the farmer, "and I might get to inviting you to my house for a bite to eat, and there – you being a handsome young devil – you might steal the heart of my only daughter. You might even come to marry her." "Well, what's wrong with that?" asks Dick. "I'll tell you what's wrong with that," says the farmer. "When my girl gets married, it'll be to a man of substance – not to some poor sod who can't even afford a bloody watch!"

☞ Harry goes to see his friend who lives on a farm. One morning, Harry gets up early and decides to fix breakfast. Later, the farmer comes downstairs and finds Harry covered in white liquid, holding a milk jug. "Look," says Harry. "I milked the cow for you." "We don't have a cow," replies the farmer. "It's a bull!"

☞ Old Tom is a farmer. Apart from his land and his house, he has two things in his life: an old mule called Sarah, and a horrible old wife who does nothing but nag. One day, Old Tom is brushing down Sarah when his wife comes along to give him a good tongue-lashing about some forgotten chores. Suddenly, Sarah kicks up her back legs, hitting the wife in the head and killing her stone dead. At the funeral, the vicar is conducting the service at the graveside. When it's over, he notices a queue of people waiting to offer Old Tom their condolences. The vicar is curious, because when Tom speaks to a woman he says a few words and nods, but when he speaks to a man, he says a few words and shakes his head. After the last wellwisher has gone, the vicar goes over and asks about the unusual behaviour. "So, Tom," says the vicar, "I couldn't help noticing you agreeing with all the ladies and disagreeing with the gentlemen. What was that about?" "It's nothing, Reverend," replies Tom. "The ladies were saying how nice the missus looked in her funeral clothes, and I was agreeing with them." "What about the men?" asks the vicar. Tom replies, "They were asking if Sarah was for sale."

☞ Our local farmer isn't that bright. He heard Express Dairies were popular, so he taught his cow to use a skateboard.

☞ A government inspector visits a farm. The inspector introduces himself to the farmer and says, "I've come to do a spot-check on your farming practices. I want to make sure you're obeying all the rules, so I must have access to all your property." "Well, all right," says the farmer, "but you can't go into the bottom field at the moment." The inspector is incensed. "How dare you?" he says, pulling a piece of paper from his briefcase. "You see this document? This gives me permission to go anywhere I like on your farm – and you don't have any say in the matter!" "I still wouldn't go in the bottom field if I were you," says the farmer. The inspector fumes, "This piece of paper means I can visit any property without let or hindrance – and your bottom field is the first place I'm going to go." The inspector storms off towards the bottom field and the farmer makes himself a cup of tea. Fifteen minutes later, the farmer ambles down to the bottom field and finds the mud-spattered inspector being chased round and round the paddock by an enraged bull. "Help!" cries the exhausted inspector. "Quick!" shouts back the farmer. "Show him your bit of paper!"

☞ Three prostitutes are comparing clients. "Last night I had a construction worker," says the first. "He kept his boots and hard hat on all the time he was with me." "Well, I had a stockbroker," says the second girl. "I could tell he was a stockbroker because the whole time he was with me he talked on a mobile phone about share prices." The third girl pipes up. "Well, I had a farmer last night," she says. "Did he wear rubber boots?" ask the first girl. "No," says the third girl. "Did he smell of cows?" asks the second girl. "No," replies the third girl. "Then how did you know he was a farmer?" asks the first girl. "It was easy," replies the third girl. "First he moaned that it was too dry; then he moaned that it was too wet; and then he asked if he could pay in the spring."

☞ Zeke is watching Billy-Bob plough a field. "You sure do that good," says Zeke. "You gettin' all those straight lines an'all. I can never plough straight. No matter how hard I watch the plough, it always goes bendy." "Well, that's your problem," says Billy-Bob. "The last thing you want to watch is the plough. What you want to watch is something way off on the other side of the field. That way your ploughlines will be as straight as arrows." "Gee," says Zeke. "Can I try that out?" "Sure you can," says Billy-Bob. "Get up on the tractor and have a go." So Zeke climbs into the tractor's driving seat, stares at a scarecrow on the far side of the field and ploughs a line as straight as a ruler. "That's the business," says Billy-Bob. "Tell you what; to give you some practise, why don't you plough this whole field while I get something to eat?" So Zeke ploughs the field while Billy-Bob goes to have his lunch. Forty-minutes later, Billy-Bob comes back and finds the field is a complete mess. Some of the ploughlines are zigzagged, others wriggle all over the place and lots of the ploughlines go around in giant wavy circles. "Dammit," says Billy-Bob. "What the hell happened?" "I did what you said," says Zeke. "First I stared at that scarecrow and I got a real straight line, but then it fell over and I started looking at a jackrabbit – the little bastard wouldn't stay still!"

FAT

☞ Inside every fat person is a thin person crying to get out – but you can usually shut the bastard up with biscuits.

Sam: "Whatcha up to, Norm?" Norm: "My ideal weight, if I were 11 feet tall."
Cheers

☞ A man is about to have sex with a hugely obese woman. As he climbs on top of her, he says, "Do you mind if I turn the ceiling light off?" "Why?" says the fat woman. "Are you feeling shy?" "No," replies the man. "It's just that the bulb's burning my ass."

☞ What do you call a 40-stone stripper? Unemployed.

"It's easy to distract fat people – it's a piece of cake."
Chris Addison

☞ Big Larry the comedian walks out on stage. A heckler calls out, "Oi, mate! Why are you so fat?" Larry replies, "Because every time I sleep with your mother, she gives me a biscuit."

☞ Little Johnny and his mother are standing in a queue at the supermarket checkout. Standing in front of them is a hugely fat lady. Suddenly a mobile phone starts bleeping in the fat lady's handbag. "Watch out, mum," says Johnny. "She's about to reverse."

"'Chubby-chasers' – how much chasing is actually going on there? A little bit of waddling and wheezing, then 'Gotcha'!"
Jimmy Carr

☞ Bill is walking down the road when he sees Harry, dressed in a tracksuit and trainers, sitting in a café eating a huge pile of chips. Bill goes in to confront him. "Here," he says, "I thought you said you were going to try and get into shape?" "I am," says Harry. "I've decided to go for pear-shaped."

☞ Two larger ladies, Hilda and Annie, went running last week: one in short bursts and the other in burst shorts.

"If you have a pear-shaped body, you should not wear pear-coloured clothes, or act juicy."
Demetri Martin

☞ The Government has proposed a new set of food labels: 'No fat', 'Low fat', 'Reduced fat' and 'Fat – but a great personality'.

"When I was a child, I was so fat I was chosen to play Bethlehem in the school nativity play."
Jo Brand

☞ The older you get, the tougher it is to lose weight; by then, your skeleton and your fat cells are really good friends.

☞ When fat people go skinny-dipping, shouldn't it be called 'chunky-dunking'?

**"You know you're getting fat when you can
pinch an inch on your forehead."**
John Mendoz

☞ Becoming overweight is something that just sort of snacks up on you.

☞ Harriet was a big-hearted girl. Not only that; she had hips to match.

☞ Now that food has replaced sex in my life, I can't even get into my OWN pants.

☞ One of women's biggest fears is getting fat. That's also one of men's biggest fears – that their wives are going to get fat.

FAT – YO MOMMA...

☞ Yo momma's so fat, the last time she went to Sea World the killer whale got a hard-on.

☞ Yo momma's so fat, when I have sex with her I have to slap her ass and ride the wave in.

☞ Yo momma's so fat, after we had sex, I rolled over nine times and I was still on her.

☞ Yo momma's so fat, if you want to have sex with her, you roll her ass in flour and look for the wet spot.

☞ Yo momma's so fat, when I get on top of her my ears pop.

FIRE

☞ Why is it that you can throw a burnt match out of the window of your car and start a forest fire, but you can use two boxes of matches and a whole edition of a Sunday paper and still not be able to start a fire under the logs in your fireplace?

"I was in a bar, minding my own business, and this guy came up to me and said, 'You're gonna have to move; you're blocking a fire exit.' As though if there was a fire, I wasn't gonna run. If you're flammable and have legs, you are never blocking a fire exit!"
Mitch Hedberg

☞ Last week, Harry pulled three men out of a burning building. He got six months. It turned out they were firemen.

"You know those trick candles that you blow out and a couple of seconds later they come alight again? Well, the other day there was a fire at the factory that makes them..."
Tim Vine

FIREARMS

"They say that guns don't kill people; people kill people. But I think the guns help."
Eddie Izzard

"When I was crossing the border into Canada, they asked if I had any firearms with me. I said, 'Well, what do you need?'"
Steven Wright

FISH

☞ A policeman sees a man fishing by the river and goes over to have a word. "You need a permit to fish here," he says. "No, thanks," replies the fisherman. "I'm doing okay with the worm."

☞ An aquarium is just interactive television for cats.

☞ Which day of the week do fish hate? Fry-Day.

☞ Harry walks into a pet shop. "I'd like to buy a goldfish," he says. The pet-shop owner replies, "Do you want an aquarium?" "No," says Harry. "I'm not bothered what star sign it is."

☞ Jim is walking through a park when he sees an old man with a fishing rod in his hand. The poor old fellow seems to be mad, as he has the end of the rod dangling over a bed of roses. "What are you doing?" asks Jim. "Fishing," replies the old man. "I'm trying to catch my lunch. I'm starving." Jim takes pity on the old geezer and offers to buy him a meal in a nearby cafe. The old man accepts eagerly and goes with Jim to have a huge plate of steak and eggs. After the old man has finished stuffing himself, Jim makes conversation. "So; do you go fishing in the park very often?" he asks. "Oh, yes," replies the old man. "Every day." "And do you catch much?" asks Jim. "Sure," says the old man. "You're the sixth today."

FLATULENCE

"I went to my doctor and asked for something for persistent wind. He gave me a kite."
Les Dawson

☞ Fred and Bert are sitting on a park bench. Fred says, "I've been sitting here too long; my backside has fallen asleep." "I thought so," replies Bert. "I could hear it snoring."

☞ How do you produce home-made tear gas? Eat a tin of beans and an onion.

☞ Why do farts smell? So that deaf people can enjoy them as well.

FOOD

☞ A man goes into a butcher's shop. "Do you keep dripping?" he says. The butcher replies, "Yes. It's really embarrassing."

☞ A man storms into a baker's shop. "I bought a currant bun here yesterday," he fumes, "and when I got it home, I discovered that one of the currents was a dead fly." "Fair enough," says the baker. "Bring in the fly and I'll give you a currant."

> **"So I went down the local supermarket; I said, 'I want to make a complaint; this vinegar's got lumps in it'. He said, 'Those are pickled onions'."**
> *Tim Vine*

☞ I have a self-cleaning refrigerator. If I leave food in there for long enough, it eventually crawls out under its own steam.

☞ Why do they put expiry dates on preservatives? Couldn't they just add a bit more preservative?

> **"I'm at the age where food has taken the place of sex in my life. In fact, I've just had a mirror put over my kitchen table."**
> *Rodney Dangerfield*

☞ A man comes home from work and complains about the packed lunch his wife made for him. "It was disgusting," he says. "It was the most revolting sandwich I ever tasted. What on earth was in it?" "Crab paste," replies his wife. "It must have been off," says the husband. "How long ago did you buy it?" "It was only a day old," replies his wife. "I got it yesterday. The pharmacy was having a sale."

☞ What's the Native American word meaning 'crappy hunter'? Vegetarian.

☞ A man goes into a butcher's shop and says, "I saw your sign saying you had a special on pissoles." "That's not a 'P'," says the butcher, "That's an 'R'." "Oh," replies the man. "Then I'll have two pounds of arseholes, please."

> **"When you eat a lot of spicy food, you can lose your taste. When I was in Mexico last summer, I was listening to a lot of Michael Bolton."**
> *Jimmy Carr*

☞ To hell with health foods! At my age I need all the preservatives I can get!

☞ A man walks into a delicatessen and asks for a tub of vanilla ice-cream, a tub of strawberry ice-cream and a tub of chocolate ice-cream. "Sorry," says the woman at the counter, "We're out of chocolate ice-cream." "In that case," says the man, "I'll have a tub of tutti frutti, a tub of coffee and a tub of chocolate." "I just told you we don't have any chocolate ice cream," says the woman "Okay," says the man. "Then I'll have a tub of Rocky Road, a tub of mango and a tub of chocolate." The woman is getting annoyed. "Listen," she says. "What does the v-a-n in vanilla spell?" "Van," says the man. "And what does the s-t-r-a-w in strawberry spell?" asks the woman. "Straw," says the man. "Okay, so what does the f-u-c-k in chocolate spell?" asks the woman. "There's no f*** in chocolate," replies the man. "That's what I've been trying to tell you!" says the woman.

☞ What do ghosts serve for dessert? Ice scream.

> **"I went down my local ice-cream shop, and said I wanted to buy an ice-cream. The man behind the counter said, 'Hundreds and thousands?' I said, 'We'll start with one.' He said, 'Knickerbocker glory?' I said, 'I do get a certain amount of freedom in these trousers, yes'."**
> *Tim Vine*

☞ If we're not supposed to eat late-night snacks, why is there a light inside the refrigerator?

☞ The Japanese eat very little fat and have fewer heart problems than the British or Americans. However, the French eat lots of fat and also have fewer heart problems than the British or Americans. The Japanese drink very little red wine and have fewer heart problems than the British or Americans, but Italians drink excessive amounts of red wine and also have fewer heart problems than the British or Americans. From this we can conclude that you can eat and drink what you like; it's speaking English that kills you!

☞ The opera house is packed solid, but seconds before the curtain is due to rise the house manager goes onstage and makes an announcement, "I'm sorry to break this tragic news," he says, "but tonight's performance has been cancelled due to the sudden demise of our leading tenor, Mr Viscotti." A voice calls out from the back of the house, "Give him some chicken soup!" The stage manager replies, "I'm sorry if I have not made myself clear, but our leading tenor, Mr Viscotti is dead. The performance is cancelled." Once again, the voice calls out, "Give him some chicken soup!" The manager, annoyed, shouts back, "Mr Viscotti is dead. He has passed away. Giving him chicken soup could not possibly help." There's a pause. Then the voice calls back, "It couldn't hurt!"

☞ I'm in a great mood today; last week I entered a competition and today I found out I've won a year's supply of Marmite – one jar.

FOOD – COOKERY

☞ My wife's a terrible cook; the last time she made a cottage pie, it was condemned.

> **"I've got Gordon Ramsay's new book,**
> **'Take Two Eggs and F*** Off'."**
> *Jack Dee*

☞ Tom is standing over his wife, Jane, while she makes a cake in the kitchen. "Not too much flour, now. That's too much – never mind. Now pour in the eggs: slowly, slowly. That's too fast! Now the raisins. Not all at once. Take your time. Be careful. Now get the spoon ready. Not that spoon: the other one..." Jane turns to Tom and says, "What exactly do you think you're doing?" Tom replies, "Showing you what it's like listening to you when I'm driving."

☞ A mother asks her son if he'd like a frozen pizza for his dinner. "No," he replies. "I'd prefer mine warmed up a bit."

☞ Harry bought himself a wood stove last week. He used it once and it burnt to cinders.

"I bought my girlfriend a cookbook called 'The Quick and Easy Vegetarian', because not only is she a vegetarian..."
Jimmy Carr

☞ Jim goes to his mother-in-law's house for dinner. As usual, the meal is terrible. Jim leans over to his wife and whispers, "This food's like manure." His wife whispers back. "No, it's not. Take that back." Jim thought for a second, then says, "You're right. I will take it back. Manure's usually warm."

☞ A husband comes home to find he's being given a slice of fruit pie for his dinner. "Where's the rest of it?" he says to his wife. "When you rang me at work, you said we were having a three-course roast dinner." "I know," replies his wife, "but mother rang and she wouldn't get off the phone. By the time I could get away, the roast had caught fire, the flames had spread to the vegetables and I had to douse the whole lot with the soup!"

"For a long time, I thought 'coq au vin' meant love in a lorry."
Victoria Wood

☞ My wife's a terrible cook. Last night she cooked me a casserole. After I'd forced it down, she asked me what I wanted for dessert. I said, "The antidote."

☞ My wife woke me up the other night and told me there was a burglar in the kitchen eating some of her left-over risotto. I didn't know who to call first: the police or an ambulance.

☞ Some people can cook, but don't. My wife is the exact opposite.

"Men like to barbecue. Men will cook if danger is involved."
Rita Rudner

☞ They say that most accidents happen in the kitchen; unfortunately I usually end up eating them.

FOOTBALL

"The reason women don't play football is because 11 of them would never wear the same outfit in public."
Phyllis Diller

☞ A Chelsea player is transferred to Tottenham but his first match doesn't get off to a good start; in fact a substitute comes on and tells him that the manager's going to pull him off at half-time. "Fantastic," says the player. "At Chelsea we only got half an orange and a bottle of water."

☞ A man from Manchester dies and goes to Hell. After a week or so the Devil notices that the new Manchester inmate doesn't suffer from the heat as much as the other damned souls. The Devil turns the thermostat from 50 to 70 degrees and asks the man how he's feeling. "Not bad," says the man. "It's a nice change from the foundry where I used to work. That was boiling hot." The Devil goes over to the thermostat and turns up the heat to 80 degrees. He lets the Mancunian stew a bit before going over to ask how he's feeling. "It's a little warm," replies the man, "but not as bad as my old mum's flat. She always had three bars on the electric fire turned on, even in summer. I hated going round there, I can tell you – I used to sweat cobs." The Devil is rather annoyed by this, so he turns the thermostat up to 90 degrees. Later, the Devil goes to see the man and is pleased to see that he's finally taken his jumper off. "Bit warmer now, isn't it?" says the Mancunian, "but not as bad as that holiday I had in Majorca: terrible, that was. Talk about a heatwave." The Devil is stumped. The thermostat only goes up to 90. He can't make it any hotter, so he decides to try another tack. He turns the thermostat down to minus 10 degrees. Immediately, Hell starts to cool down, and within the hour large snowflakes start drifting down. The Devil cackles in anticipation as he goes to see how the heat-loving Mancunian is reacting to the cold. The Devil is expecting to find the man a shivering wreck, but is horrified to see the Mancunian and a group of other men holding hands and dancing round in a big circle. "Hooray!" they cry, as the snow swirls around them. "City have won the FA Cup!"

☞ A Manchester United fan dies and go to heaven. He's greeted at the Pearly Gates by Saint Peter, who's wearing a Manchester City scarf. "We don't want your sort in here!" shouts Saint Peter. "Go away!" "But I've been a good man," complains the United fan. "You have to let me in." "Okay; so what were your last three good deeds?" asks Saint Peter. "Er... I gave £10 to a children's charity," says the fan. "And before that, I gave £10 to a cancer charity. And before that I gave £10 to an animal charity." "Hang on," says Saint Peter. "I'll go and ask the boss." Ten minutes later, Saint Peter returns holding a wad of money. "I had a word with God, and he agrees with me. Here's your thirty quid back. Now sod off!"

☞ At the start of the second half of a football match, the men of one team drop their shorts and start masturbating. The coach runs on to the pitch and yells, "What the hell do you think you're doing?" The centre-forward says, "But you told us to come out here and pull ourselves together!"

☞ Did you hear about the footballer who was given a six-match ban after committing a vicious foul? He got a four-match ban for the original foul and two more for the action replay.

☞ Gavin was a huge fan of Arsenal. When he died, he put in his will that he wanted to be cremated – and his ashes scattered over a Chelsea supporter.

☞ How can you tell ET is a Manchester United fan? He looks like one.

☞ In last Saturday's match between Celtic and Rangers, fighting in the stands had to be postponed after football broke out on the pitch.

☞ Our local football teams are rubbish. It's a wonder they have any fans at all. Last week a groundsman saw three kids trying to climb the boundary wall – he told them to get back inside and watch the match.

☞ The attendance at our local football ground is very bad. It's got to the point where the Tannoy announces changes in the crowd's line-up to the players.

☞ The manager of Everton rings up the manager of Liverpool for some training tips. "I'm trying to improve my players' ball-handling skills," says the Everton manager. "I know it's a cheek, but do you have any advice you could give me?" The Liverpool manager replies, "Well, it's not much, but what I do is put twelve traffic cones on the pitch and tell my lads to pretend they're the opposing players. They then have to use their ball skills to get past different formations." The Everton manager thanks the Liverpool manager and says he'll give it a go. A couple of week later the two managers bump into each other in a bar. "Did you try the traffic cones idea?" asks the Liverpool manager. "I did," replies the Everton manager, "but it didn't work out very well. We put out twelve traffic cones and sent the boys to get the ball past them, but the orange bastards beat us 3-1."

☞ Two third-division Scottish football teams are playing in a small town. It's an important match, as the losers will be relegated into oblivion. A fan hurries up the street from the railway station trying to find the football ground. He sees an old man out walking his dog and asks for directions. "Will ye be wanting to see the big match, then?" asks the old man. "Aye," replies the fan. "Well, you've plenty of time," says the old fellow. "I walked past the ground a few minutes ago and they were still queuing at the entrance." "Where is it?" asks the fan. "At the top of the hill and turn left," replies the old man. The fan thanks him and hurries off. The old man calls after him, "But mind you don't join the *long* queue!" he shouts. "That's fer the chip shop!"

FORTUNE-TELLERS

☞ Bill goes to an old gypsy fortune-teller to see what life has in store for him. The old gypsy takes one look at him and gasps in shock. "Oh, dear," says Bill "Is it bad news?" "Put it this way," says the fortune-teller, "I want the money in advance."

FRUIT

☞ I used to work in an orange juice factory. They had to sack me in the end; I just couldn't concentrate.

☞ Why did the banana go to the doctor? He wasn't peeling well.

> **"I like fruit baskets because it gives you the ability to mail someone a piece of fruit without appearing insane. Like, if someone just mailed you an apple you'd be like, 'Huh? What the hell is this?' but if it's in a fruit basket you're like, 'This is nice'!"**
> *Demetri Martin*

☞ Why did the orange stop rolling down the hill? Because it didn't have any juice left.

FUN THINGS TO DO

☞ At home: Sit outside your house in your car with sunglasses on and point a hairdryer at passing cars. In the memo field of all your cheques, write 'For smuggling diamonds'. Repeatedly specify that your drive-through order is 'to go'. Tell your friends that you can't go to their party because you're not in the mood; do this five days in advance. When the money comes out of the ATM, scream "I won! I won!" Take your kids to the zoo; when you leave, start running towards the parking lot, yelling, "They're loose! They're loose!" Over dinner, tell your children, "Due to the economy, we're going to have to let one of you go."

☞ In a lift: Give name badges to everyone getting on (wear yours upside-down). Occasionally make a mewing sound. Wear toy X-ray specs and leer suggestively at other passengers. Suck your thumb while holding a comfort blanket to your head. Make 'missile-launch' noises whenever anyone presses a button. Draw a square on the floor with chalk and tell the other passengers that this is your 'personal space'. Repeat nursery rhymes while continually pushing buttons. Stand motionless in the corner, facing the wall, without getting off. Give a warm handshake to anyone who gets on and introduce yourself as 'Iron-Balls Bradley'. When arriving at your floor, strain to lever the doors open, then pretend to be embarrassed when they open by themselves. Shout "Lordy! We all gonna die!" every time the lift starts to descend. Carry a box with 'Human Organs' written on the side. Try to start a sing-along. Say goodbye to anyone who gets off.

☞ In the office: Page yourself over the intercom – don't disguise your voice. Every time someone asks you to do something, ask if they want fries with that. Put your garbage can on your desk and label it 'In', Put decaf in the coffee-maker for three weeks; once everyone has got over their caffeine addictions, switch to espresso. Finish all your sentences with the words, "In accordance with the prophecy". Skip rather than walk. Order 'diet water' when you go to the cafeteria; complain loudly if they don't have any. Put mosquito-netting around your work area and play tropical jungle sounds all day. Insist that your co-workers address you by your wrestling name, 'Rock Bottom'.

FURNITURE

☞ A little boy arrives home dragging an armchair with one hand and a settee with the other. His father says to him, "What have I told you about accepting suites from strangers?"

FUTURE

☞ The future is that time when you'll wish you'd done what you aren't doing now.

GALLEY CREWS

☞ The captain of a Roman galley assembles his crew. His officers and oarsmen gather round. "Men," he shouts. "I have good news and bad news. The good news is that our galley has been selected to row the Emperor to his new Sicilian palace!" The officers and oarsmen cheer. The captain continues, "The bad news is, he also wants to go water-skiing."

GAMBLING

☞ A man walks into a pub and goes up to the barman. "I bet you £100 that if you put a glass at the other end of the bar, I can stand at this end and pee into it," says the man. The bar must be 20 feet long, so the barman reckons this is an easy way to make £100. He agrees to take the bet and places an empty glass at the other end of the bar. The man climbs up on the bar-top, drops his trousers and tries to pee in the glass. He fails miserable. He barely gets the stream to go four feet and it sprays all over the place; it even splashes the barman. The barman doesn't care, though. He's just won £100. The man climbs down and hands the barman his money. The barman takes the cash with a big smile – then notices that the man doesn't seem to be sorry to lose the bet. In fact, the man seems delighted, and he's even happier when another man gives him a big bundle of notes. "Why did that guy give you all that money?" asks the barman. "It was a bet," replies the man. "I bet him £500 that I could pee all over your bar and you'd be happy about it."

☞ A young boy and his granddad are watching the horse-racing on television. The boy asks his granddad if he can place a bet. Granddad says, "That depends. Can you touch your arsehole with the end of your dick?" "No," replies the boy. "Then you're not old enough to gamble," replies granddad. "Now go and get me a copy of the Racing Post." The boy hurries to the newsagents to get the paper. While he's there, he buys a scratchcard that wins him £50,000. Excitedly, he runs home and tells his granddad the good news. "Y'know what?" says granddad. "Seeing as you bought that card with my money, we ought to split the prize." "Granddad," says the boy. "Can you touch your arsehole with the end of your dick?" "Why, of course I can," replies granddad. "Good," says the boy. "Then go screw yourself."

☞ George is playing poker with his friend Tom and some cronies. The betting is getting quite heavy and Tom has just wagered £1,000 on the turn of a card. The card is turned and Tom loses. The shock is too much. Tom clutches his chest and falls to the floor, stone dead. Tom's friends discuss how to break the news to his wife and select George as the right man to do the job. George goes off to perform the deed, but doesn't know what to say. He rings on Tom's doorbell and Tom's wife, Glenda, opens the door. "I've come about Tom," says George. "What's the idiot been up to now?" snaps Glenda. "Well it's difficult to tell you this, but he lost £1,000 at cards and…" "What?!" shouts Glenda. "He lost £1,000? You go back and tell that bastard to drop dead!" "Okay…" says George. "I'll do that."

☞ Harry comes home and finds his wife kissing a strange man. "How dare you, sir?" says Harry. "Who the devil are you?" The stranger replies, "I'm the man your wife's going to marry after she divorces you." "Rubbish," says Harry. "I'll never divorce her." "I'll throw down a gauntlet," says the stranger. "I've heard you're a sporting gentleman, so I suggest we gamble for you wife's affections. What say you to a game of gin rummy? If you win, I will leave for ever: but if I win, you get a divorce." "Agreed," says Harry. "And to make it interesting, how about playing for a pound a point?"

☞ How do you make a group of old ladies all shout, "F***!" at once? Say, "Bingo!"

☞ One morning, Harry wakes up and goes downstairs into the kitchen. It's his birthday. It's the third day of the third month and Harry is 33 years old. Harry notices that the kitchen clock has broken and stopped at 3.33am. On the radio, the weather announces that the temperature is 33 degrees. Opening the sporting section of his newspaper, he turns to page three; he sees that a horse called 'Triple Chance' is running in the 3.30. He rings up a bookmaker and puts £333 on it to win. It comes in third.

☞ What's black and white and sticks two fingers up at the Pope? A nun who's just won the lottery.

GAMES

"I failed to make the chess team because of my height."
Woody Allen

☞ Harry and Jim are at the pub and decide to have a game of darts. Harry and Jim take their places in front of the dart-board. Harry says, "Nearest to the bull starts." Jim says, "Baa!" Harry says, "Moo!" Jim says, "Go on; you're closest."

☞ Have you ever played Jockey's Knock? It's like Postman's Knock, but with more horseplay.

☞ How do you get 200 cows into a barn? Put up a sign that says 'Bingo'.

> **"I like video games, but they're really violent.**
> **I'd like to play a video game where you help the**
> **people who were shot in all the other games."**
> *Demetri Martin*

☞ I once had dinner with a chess grandmaster at a table with a checked tablecloth. It took him two hours to pass me the salt.

☞ I was playing patience last night when my wife walked by and said, "Why don't you go and play cards with John? You always used to be round at his house. I thought you liked playing cards with him." "I did," I replied, "but would you enjoy playing cards with a habitual cheat who'd pull any low-down, dishonest, devious trick to win a game?" "I suppose not," said my wife. I said, "Well, John feels the same way."

☞ Two children are trying to decide what to play. "Let's plays doctor," says one." "Okay," says the other. "You operate and I'll sue."

> **"Stone, papers, scissors – to most of us it's a**
> **game, but to Australians it's a wedding list."**
> *Angus Deayton*

GARDENING

☞ A man goes into a flower shop and asks for a potted geranium. "Sorry; we don't have geraniums," says the florist. "We've got some nice African violets. Would you like one of those?" "No," replies the man sadly. "It was definitely a geranium my wife asked me to water while she was away."

☞ My granddad died over the weekend. He was out on his allotment when he got caught in a terrible blizzard. When they eventually dug him out they found him frozen to the marrow.

☞ Steve is a keen gardener who managed to give himself a hernia lifting his huge champion marrow. Now he's switched to pumpkins and has developed two new strains.

**"I planted some bird seed. A bird came up.
Now I don't know what to feed it."**
Steven Wright

GAYS AND LESBIANS

☞ After years of avoiding the subject, Ricardo decides it's time to come out to his Italian mamma. He finds her in the kitchen and tells her he's a homosexual. "You mean you're gay?" says mother. "Yes, mamma," says Ricardo. "You mean you do all those dirty sex things with other men?" "I do, mamma," says Ricardo. "You mean you even put other men's 'things' in your mouth?" asks mother. "Yes, mamma," says Ricardo. "I see," says mother. She wipes a tear from her eye, then suddenly starts hitting Ricardo with a wooden spoon. "So you do all that, and you still have the nerve to complain about the taste of my lasagne?!"

**"As of last month we have gay bishops: official.
I wonder if this will filter down into the game
of chess? Those bishops can make all the same
moves, but can only be taken from behind."**
Jason Wood

☞ Did you hear what happened to the gay Arab with a heart condition? They found him dead up an Ali.

☞ How can you tell when you enter a gay church? Only half the congregation are on their knees.

☞ How do you get four gay men on a barstool? Turn it upside-down.

☞ How do you know when you're in a lesbian bar? Not even the pool table has balls.

"I was asked to judge Mr Gay UK. I said it's against man, against nature and against God. You're going to hell."
Jimmy Carr

☞ Mrs Cohen is heartbroken. Her son has declared he's gay and intends to move in with his male lover. Mrs Goldblum comes round to comfort her. "Look on the bright side," she says. "He might be sleeping with another man, but at least he's a doctor..."

☞ Two men are playing a round of golf. Unfortunately, one of the men takes a swing at the ball, slices it and sends it flying towards a gay couple walking on a nearby path. The ball hits one of the gay men on the head and he falls to the ground. His partner drops to his knees and starts wailing. "Nigel!" he shouts. "Nigel! Wake up! Can you hear me?" The two guys come over. "Sorry about that," says the man who took the shot. "It was an accident." "Accident my ass," says the gay man. "You did it on purpose!" "I did not," says the man. "Did too!" replies the gay man. "And we're going to sue the pants off you!" "Sue me?" shouts the enraged man. "You bastard! You can suck my dick!" The gay man shouts at his friend. "Nigel! Wake up, wake up! They're going to settle out of court!"

☞ What's the difference between a heterosexual man and a homosexual man? About three beers.

☞ What's the motto of the US Marines? Never leave your buddies behind. What's the motto of the Greek army? Never leave your buddy's behind.

GENEALOGY

☞ What's the difference between a genealogist and a gynaecologist? One looks up the family tree, the other up the family bush.

GENIES AND WISHES

☞ A civil servant is sitting in his office. Out of boredom, he decides to see what's in an old filing cabinet in the corner of the room. At the back of the cabinet he finds an old brass lamp. He takes it out to have a look, and gives it a rub. Poof! A genie appears and grants him three wishes. "I wish I had a more interesting job," says the man. Poof! The civil servant finds himself in downtown Los Angeles, directing a movie. "This is great," says the man, "but I wish I was in a more glamorous location, surrounded by nymphomaniacs." Poof! The civil servant finds himself directing a high-class porno film on a tropical island." "Wow," says the civil servant. "This is fantastic, but directing is a bit of a drag. I want to spend more time enjoying all these beautiful girls. I wish I never had to work again!" Poof! He's back in his office.

☞ A cowboy, Earl, is out riding the range when he comes across a rattlesnake sunning itself on top of a boulder. The boulder is right next to the trail, so Earl decides not to take any chances. He lifts up his rifle and takes aim. Suddenly, the snake sees Earl and calls out, "Stop! Don't shoot!" Earl is astonished; he's never heard of a talking snake before, and puts down the rifle. The snake continues, "I'm a magic snake. If you spare my life I'll grant you three wishes." "Okay," says Earl. "I can see you're a talking snake, but I ain't so sure you're a magic snake. How are you going to prove it to me?" "It's easy," says the snake. "Just make three wishes – whatever you want." "Okay," says Earl. "How about you fix it for me to be the best damned shot in the world?" "It's done," says the snake. "You see that ant, standing on that cactus way over there? You can shoot that ant right between the eyes." Earl looks at the cactus and find he now has superhuman sight; he can clearly see the ant, and when he raises his rifle it is as steady as a rock in his hands. He pulls the trigger and Blam! The ant gets it in the middle of the forehead. "Damn!" exclaims Earl. "I *am* the best shot!" "What else would you like?" asks the snake. "You've got two wishes left." "Well," says Earl. "I've always wanted to be one of them handsome dudes that gets all the girls. Tell you what; make me as good-looking as that there Robert Redford, and give me a package like this here horse I'm sitting on, and I reckon we're quits." "It's done," says the snake and it quickly slithers away. Earl heads back to the ranch-house as fast as his horse will carry him. When he gets there he leaps out of the saddle and runs inside to find a mirror. He stands in front of it and, sure enough, he looks like a handsome movie-star. Another cowboy, Jeb, walks in and comments on the difference. "You been to a beauty parlour, Earl?" he asks. "You sure are better-looking now than when you rode out." "That's nothing," replies Earl. "Just wait till you see the size of the dick I'm hauling inside these jeans." With this, Earl drops his pants and looks down to admire his new equipment. There's a pause, then Earl lets out a sigh, pulls his pants up and heads for the door. "What's up?" asks Jed. "Where you goin'?" "Gotta find a snake," replies Earl. "Turns out I was riding the goddamn mare."

☞ A man walks into an expensive restaurant with four beautiful women and a chicken in a cage. He then orders a sumptuous meal for himself and his female companions and two gallons of rice pudding for the chicken. The courses arrive and the man and the women tuck in, as does the chicken, which proceeds to devour the rice pudding at an alarming rate. The meal continues, and the waiter is asked to bring a tub of ice-cream for the chicken, then a roast piglet, then a bucket of oats. The chicken eats non-stop while the man watches it with a depressed look on his face. Finally, the head waiter comes to present the bill. "I can't help asking, sir," he says, "but where did you acquire such an extraordinary chicken? It's eaten non-stop for the last three hours and still appears to be hungry." "The bird's my fault," sighs the man. "One day I was polishing an old lamp when a genie flew out and granted me three wishes. I asked for a limitless supply of money, all the women I could ever want and an insatiable cock."

☞ A man walks into a bar. The man has a normal body but his head is tiny: roughly the size of a satsuma. The man orders a drink and the barman decides to ask him about his curious noggin. "So: is that some kind of medical condition?" he asks. "Nah," says the man. "It was like this. I was walking along the beach when I stumbled across a magic lantern. I rubbed it, and out came this stunningly beautiful female genie. She says, 'I will grant you one wish. I will do anything you ask except for one thing;

I cannot sleep with you.' So I said to her, 'Okay, so I can't have sex with you – but is a little head out of the question'?"

☞ A woman buys a mirror at an antique shop, and hangs it on her bathroom door. One evening, she playfully says, "Mirror, mirror, on my door, make my bust-size forty-four." There's a brilliant flash of light, and her boobs grow to enormous proportions. She runs to tell her husband what's happened. He takes a look at her huge bust, then runs into the bathroom and says, "Mirror, mirror on the door, make my dick touch the floor!" There's a brilliant flash of light – and both his legs fall off.

☞ An Englishman, an Irishman and a Scotsman are trapped on the top of a cliff by a landslide. There's no way down, and it's a 100-foot drop. The Englishman spots an old lamp lying on the ground. He picks it up and rubs it. Poof! Out comes a genie. The Englishman explains their predicament and the genie promises to help. "I cannot make you and your friends fly," says the genie, "but I can help you jump off the cliff. Choose something soft and I will ensure that when you leap from the cliff's edge you will land in it." The Englishman jumps off the edge of the cliff and shouts, "Pillows!" He lands safely on a huge pile of pillows. The Scotsman takes a running jump and shouts, "Heather!" He lands safely on a huge heap of heather. The Irish guy takes a running jump, trips on a stone, falls over the edge and shouts, "Crap..!"

☞ Feeling in a good mood, a genie makes two statues in a park come to life. The statues are of a nude man and a woman which have stood opposite each other for centuries. "I think you two deserve to have some fun," says the genie, "For the next fifteen minutes you can do whatever you like, but when your time is up you'll be turned back into stone." The man and woman look at each other, then run into the bushes. There's a lot of rustling and some shrieks of pleasure, and after a few minutes the couple stagger back out into the open. The male statue asks the genie how long they have left. "You have six minutes," says the genie." "Want to do that again?" says the male statue to the female, "Okay," she replies, "but this time you hold down the pigeon and I'll crap on it."

☞ Harry and Dick are in the gym, getting changed after a game of squash. As Dick is getting dressed, he can't help but notice a large cork lodged up Harry's backside. "I don't mean to pry," says Dick, "but you seem to have a cork up your anus." "Yeah," sighs Harry. "It's stuck up there. They can't get it out." "But how did it get up there in the first place?" asks Dick. "It's a weird story," says Harry. "I was walking on the beach when I found an old bottle. I picked it up and brushed off some sand, and then this genie popped out. Then this genie says, 'Ask anything you want of me. Your wish is my command.' And I said, 'No shit'!"

☞ A homeless man finds an old tin can on the beach. He picks it up and a genie pops out. "Your wish is my command," says the genie. "You're an answer to my prayers," says the man. "What I really want is a nice house." "Are you kidding?" says the genie. "D'you think I'd be living in an old can if I could magic up houses?"

GENIUS

**"A genius is a man who can rewrap a new
shirt and not have any pins left over."**
Dino Levi

☞ If genius is one per cent inspiration and ninety-nine per cent perspiration, then you really *do* smell like a genius.

☞ They say the man who invented the wheel was a genius. He wasn't. He was an idiot. The guy who invented the next three wheels – he was the genius.

GEOGRAPHY

**"I was born in Slough in the 1970s. If you want to know
what Slough was like in the 1970s, go there now."**
Jimmy Carr

☞ Where are the Seychelles? On the sey shore.

GEORDIES

☞ General Custer is standing on a hill overlooking the Little Big Horn. In the distance he can hear Sitting Bull's braves pounding on their drums. He turns to a little Geordie soldier in his ranks, "Listen," he says. "They have war drums." The Geordie replies, "Why, man! The thievin' bastards!"

GERBILS

☞ What's the hardest part of milking a gerbil? Getting the damned bucket underneath it.

GHOSTS, GHOULIES ETC

☞ How did the headless horseman know where he was going?

☞ If vampires can't see their reflections, how come their hair is always so neat?

GIFTS

☞ A girl is talking to her friend, "My boyfriend bought me flowers for Valentine's Day; I guess that means he'll want my legs in the air." Her friend says, "Why? Don't you have a vase?"

☞ A man orders a bouquet of flowers for his wife and they're delivered to her that same afternoon. As she's putting the bouquet in water, the wife notices that a message has been included with the flowers. She opens the card to read a single word, 'No'. The wife puzzles over what this could mean, but can't imagine what her husband is trying to tell her. That evening, she confronts him about the ambiguous note. The man denies sending any message. "But it's here in black and white," says the woman. "I don't understand it," replies the husband. "When the shop asked me if I wanted to include a message I said, 'No'."

☞ A man walks into a fancy department store. "I want something my wife would never think of buying for herself," he says, "and that eliminates almost everything."

☞ I said to my wife, "What do you want for your birthday?" She said, "Surprise me." So I said, "Boo!"

☞ Tom is standing in his garden when an angel appears before him. "Thomas," says the angel, "for all the good works you have done in your lifetime you shall be rewarded. Will you have infinite health, infinite wealth or infinite wisdom?" "I will choose wisdom," says Tom. The angel raises its arms and Tom is surrounded by a glowing light. Then the light and the angel vanish. Tom is left standing alone. Suddenly he slaps his forehead. "Oh, crap!" he says. "I should've taken the money."

GIRAFFES

"Why didn't evolution give giraffes genes to make them good at carpentry? Then they could build a ladder instead of growing long necks."
Karl Pilkington

GOLF

☞ A golfer turns to his caddy and says, "This green is terrible. This must be the worst golf course I've ever played on." "What do you mean, 'course'?" replies the caddy. "We left the course half an hour ago."

☞ A husband and wife are out playing golf. They're on the sixth hole when the wife has a heart-attack and collapses to the ground. "Go and get help!" she cries, then passes out. Her husband dutifully trots off to get assistance. A short while later, the woman comes round and finds her husband lining up a putt. "What are you doing?" she asks. "Did you go and find a doctor?" "Yes, dear," replies the man. "Right now he's on the fourth hole." "The fourth hole?" says the astonished wife. "Oh, it's all right," says her husband. "The people on the fifth are letting him play through."

> **"Give me my golf clubs, fresh air and a beautiful partner, and you can keep my golf clubs and fresh air."**
> *Jack Benny*

☞ A man and his wife consult a golf pro to try and improve their game. The pro examines the man's technique and says, "Your grip's too tight. Imagine you're holding the club like you'd hold your wife's breast." The man does so, and hits the ball right on to the green. Next, the pro looks at the technique of the man's wife. "I can see your problem," says the pro. "Your grip's too tight. Handle the club as if it was your husband's penis." The woman does so, but only manages to knock the ball a few feet from the tee. "Okay," says the pro, "Not to worry. Now, the first thing you have to do is take the club out of your mouth."

☞ A man is playing in a golf tournament on an Irish course. He's doing very badly. Suddenly, a leprechaun pops out of a rabbit-hole and offers to help the man out. "I'll give you a hand every time you get in trouble," says the little green man, "but every time I do, you have to pay a price; you lose one year of your sex life." The man agrees and the leprechaun gets the man out of trouble ten times. At the end of the tournament, the man is the winner. After the man has picked up his trophy, the leprechaun accosts him in the car park. The little green fellow chortles and rubs his hands with glee. "Well, you big idiot," he cackles. "That's ten years off your sex life. I hope you think it was worth it." "Well, yes," says the man. "I think it was." "Then more fool you!" laughs the leprechaun, pulling out a notebook. "Now, what's your name?" The man replies, "Father Murphy."

☞ An avid golfer is preparing for his normal weekend outing to the local golf club. His angry wife accosts him at the door. "Y'know," she snaps, "If you offered to spend a Sunday with me instead of going golfing, I'd probably drop dead with shock." Her husband replies, "If you'd said 'definitely', I'd probably have asked you."

☞ Golf scores are directly proportional to the number of witnesses.

> ☞ Harry is at his golf club when he meets up with a new lady member. They get chatting and arrange to play a round. The lady turns out to be an excellent player and roundly beats Harry. There are no hard feelings, however, and Harry takes his new friend out for dinner. Harry then drives her home. One thing leads to another and they end up smooching in Harry's car. The same happens on four Sundays in a row until Harry suggests they go away for a dirty weekend; at this point the woman bursts into tears and confesses that she's a transvestite. "What?" shouts Harry, "You rotten cheat! You've been playing off the ladies' tee for a whole month!"

☞ Tom gets a kidnap note saying, 'Bring £15,000 to the 17th hole of the Redbridge Golf Club by midday tomorrow, or you'll never see you wife again.' The next day, Tom takes the money to the golf club but he doesn't turn up at the 17th hole until two in the afternoon. When Tom does eventually arrive, the masked kidnapper leaps out from behind a bush. "You're two hours late!" he says. "I ought to cut your wife's ears off for that!" "Oh, come on," says Tom. "Give me a break. My favourite driver broke on the second hole, and I lost a ball on the 15th…"

GOOD ADVICE

☞ Someone told me the way to inner peace is to finish all the things you've started. It really works; yesterday I finished a six-pack of beer, a bottle of brandy, a bottle of vodka and a chocolate cake.

> ☞ The next time you have to fill out a form and write down an emergency contact, don't put down the name of your wife or mother; write, 'A good doctor!'

GREETINGS CARDS

☞ A woman in a card shop spends twenty minutes browsing the shelves but can't find what she wants. Eventually she goes to the till and says to the assistant. "Excuse me, but do you have any 'Sorry I laughed at your penis' cards?"

> **"I see cards that say 'Get Well Soon'.
> F*** that! Get well now!"**
> *Demetri Martin*

☞ Glenda goes into a stationery shop and looks at their selection of Valentine's Day cards. She can't see anything she likes and asks the shop assistant if he has any more. "We have a few in the storeroom," he says. "What sort of card do you want?" Glenda replies, "I want one that says, 'You are my one true love' or something like that." The assistant has a look in the storeroom and comes back with a card that reads, 'Yours is the only heart I crave'. "That'll do," says Glenda. "Give me a dozen."

HAIR AND/OR THE LACK OF IT

> **"I'm not actually bald. It's just that I'm
> taller than my hair."**
> *Clive Anderson*

☞ Do bald people have bad head days?

☞ It's always a bad hair day when you're bald.

☞ Linda is a natural redhead. She's completely bald and badly sunburnt.

HAIR AND/OR THE LACK OF IT – YOU KNOW YOU'RE HAVING A BAD HAIR DAY WHEN...

☞ Birds start weaving twigs into it.

☞ Children point at your head and ask the name of your kitty.

☞ Cinema ushers ask you to take off your hat.

☞ People ask you what it's like to get electrocuted.

☞ People stop you on the street and ask if you do children's parties.

HAPPINESS

☞ A new army recruit is on parade. The Colonel stops in front of him to ask a few questions. "Private Johnson, isn't it?" "Yes, sir," replies the recruit. "Are you happy in the army?" asks the Colonel. "Yes, sir," replies the recruit "I'm quite happy." "And what were you before you joined the army?" asks the Colonel. The recruit replies, "Oh, sir, I was very happy."

> **"Cloud 9 gets all the publicity: but Cloud 8 is actually cheaper, less crowded and has a better view."**
> *George Carlin*

☞ Happiness is having a large, loving, caring, close-knit family in another city.

☞ When I'm feeling down, I like to give a little whistle; it makes my neighbour's annoying dog run to the end of its chain and gag itself.

HEALTH AND DOCTORS

☞ A friend of mine said, "You want to go to Margate. It's great for rheumatism." So I did, and I got it.

☞ A brief history of medicine. 2000 BC: you got a pain in your head? Here, eat this root. 1000 AD: that root is heathen; say this prayer. 1850 AD: that prayer is superstition; drink this potion. 1940 AD: that potion is snake-oil; swallow this pill. 1985 AD: that pill is ineffective; take this antibiotic. 2000 AD: that antibiotic is artificial. Here, eat this root!

☞ A doctor and his wife have a huge argument over breakfast. It ends with the doctor yelling at his wife, telling her she's rubbish in bed. He then storms off to work. A couple of hours later, the doctor is feeling sorry about the row, so he phones his wife. After twenty rings, his wife eventually answers the phone. "What took you so long?" asks the doctor. "I was in bed," replies his wife. "In bed?" says the doctor. "What are you doing in bed at this time of day?" His wife replies, "Getting a second opinion."

☞ Two women are talking. One says to the other, "My husband is so ill, I have to watch him night and day." "Why haven't you hired a nurse?" asks the second. "I have," says the first. "That's why I have to watch him."

☞ I got some bad news from my doctor; then I got some *really* bad news. The bad news was that I have to go on pills for the rest of my life. The *really* bad news was written on the pill bottle's label – it said, 'No repeat prescriptions'.

☞ A doctor is at a garage picking up his car. He's just had the bill and can't believe his eyes. "This is an extraordinary amount you're charging for servicing my car," he says. "It's more per hour then I get paid as a doctor." "Well, that's fair enough," says the mechanic. "I mean, I have to keep up with new types of car coming out all the time. You doctors get to work on the same old model year after year."

☞ A doctor is doing a tour of the wards with a nurse. They come to a bed where a man's lying half-dead under the sheets. "Has this man been given the correct medication?" asks the doctor. "I told you to give him two tablets every eight hours." "Oh, no!" says the nurse. "I'm sorry. I gave him eight tablets every two hours!" The doctor tuts and shakes his head. At the next bed, another patient is also found to be close to death. "Nurse," says the doctor. "I asked you to give this man one tablet every twelve hours. Is that the dose he's been receiving?" "Oh, no!" says the nurse. "I thought you said to give him twelve tablets every one hour." The doctor groans and shakes his head. At the next bed, the doctor and nurse find a man lying down with a very pained look on his face. "Nurse," asks the doctor. "Did you prick this patient's boil?" The nurse slaps her forehead and says, "Oh, crap!"

☞ I have a very good doctor. Last year, I couldn't afford an operation, so he touched up the X-rays.

☞ Two old-timers are chatting on a porch. One says to the other, "Y'know what? With my bad back, bad legs and bad heart, this year I reckon I must've spent over $5,000 on medical bills." "Dang!" says the second old-timer. "I remember a time when you could be ill for five years on that kind of money."

☞ A nurse is paying for her groceries at a supermarket checkout. She takes a biro out of her pocket to write a cheque, but finds she's holding a rectal thermometer. "Well, that's great," she says. "Some asshole's got my pen."

☞ Yesterday, Harry accidentally ate a bowlful of mini Brillo pads which he'd mistaken for Shredded Wheat. The news from the hospital is good, however; they expect him to scrape through.

☞ A man goes to the doctor with a patch of water on his cheek. Nothing will get rid of it. The doctor is baffled and tells the man to come back next week. When the man returns, the doctor discovers that the patch of water is now surrounded by reeds and grass and tiny trees. The doctor is astonished, but he can't suggest a solution and asks the man to come back in a week's time. The man comes back a third time. The patch of water is now revealed to be a lake surrounded by flowery fields and green woods. Tiny little ducks are splashing in the water, and on the grass tiny people are setting out a picnic. "Ah, yes. I can see what this is now," says the doctor. "This is a beauty spot."

☞ A man has been conscripted into the army and is having his medical. The man is confident he won't pass, as an accident has left him with one leg three inches shorter than the other. After a rigorous medical examination, the man is passed fit for service. "What?" exclaims the man. "You must be crazy. Didn't you see my legs? One is three inches shorter than the other." "That's all right," replies the doctor. "We'll make sure you get to fight on a slope."

☞ There's a clinic which says they can cure snoring and haemorrhoids with laser surgery. They're very busy; apparently they're burning the candle at both ends.

☞ A man walks into a doctor's surgery. The receptionist asks the man what he has. "Shingles," he replies. The receptionist then notes down his height, weight and medical history and tells him to take a seat. A few minutes later, a nurse comes out and asks the man what he has. "Shingles," replies the man, so the nurse takes a blood and urine sample and tells him to wait in the examination room. Ten minutes later, another nurse comes in and asks him what he has. Again, the man replies, "Shingles", so the nurse gives him a blood pressure test and an electrocardiogram. She then tells the man to take all his clothes off and wait for the doctor. Fifteen minutes later, the doctor comes in and asks the man what he's got. "Shingles", says the man. "Oh, yes?" says the doctor. "Whereabouts?" "Outside in my truck," says the man. "Where do you want me to put them?"

☞ If tennis players get tennis elbow, and squash players get squash knees, what do gynaecologists get? Tunnel vision.

☞ A nurse dies and goes straight to hell – it takes her two weeks before she realises she's not at work any more.

☞ A patient is complaining to his doctor, "That rectal examination you just gave me hurt like anything," says the patient. "I'm sorry," says the doctor, "but I had to use two fingers." "Two fingers?" says the patient. "What the hell for?" The doctor replies, "I needed a second opinion."

☞ An apple a day keeps the doctor away – but you have to throw it quite hard.

"An apple a day keeps the doctor away, but in my experience so does an air rifle in the top bedroom window."
Harry Hill

☞ An old man shuffles into an arthritis clinic. The poor old soul is almost bent double and staggers along with great difficulty, even with the help of his walking stick. The old man takes a seat and, before long, his name is called. The old man grasps his stick, totters to his feet and shuffles to the doctor's consulting room. Ten minutes later, the old man strides out of the room with his back as straight as a ram-rod. "That's incredible," says one of the waiting patients. "Did he give you some sort of miracle cure?" "No," replies the old man. "He gave me a longer stick."

☞ Harry goes to his doctor complaining about a pain in his right arm. "Don't worry about it," says the doctor. "It's just old age." "What d'you mean, 'old age'?" says Harry. "I've had my left arm for just as long and there's nothing wrong with that."

☞ Barry and Janet are sitting on the sofa watching a medical documentary about people in comas. Barry leans over to Janet and says, "Just so you know, I never want to end up like that. I'd hate to be lying there endlessly dependent on some machine, getting fluids out of a bottle. If I ever end up like that, just pull the plug." So Janet gets up, unplugs the television and throws Barry's beer out of the window.

☞ Harry tells Tom his wife is terribly sick. "Oh dear," says Tom. "Is there any danger?" "Oh, no," says Harry. "She's too weak to be dangerous any more."

☞ Dick tells Harry he's just visited Tom, who's sick at the moment. "Oh, dear," says Harry. "What's the matter with him?" "I don't know," says Dick. "He was too sick to tell me."

☞ Bill has worked in the same noisy factory thirty years. He likes his job but is concerned that he's damaged his hearing by working near the loud machinery for so long. He goes to his doctor and tells him about his concerns. "It's my ears, doc," says Bill. "I reckon my hearing's getting so bad I can't even hear myself fart." The doctor examines him, then writes out a prescription for some pills. "Thank you, doc," says Bill. "So will these pills help me hear better?" "No," replies the doctor, "but they should make you fart a lot louder."

☞ Do paediatricians take Wednesdays off to play miniature golf?

☞ George goes to the doctor with an upset stomach. The doctor examines him and announces that George has a tapeworm. "A tapeworm?" exclaims George. "Can you get rid of it?" "Yes," says the doctor, "but we're out of the regular medication, so I'm going to try an old country cure." "Whatever," says George, "just get rid of the damned thing." The doctor asks George to come back the next day and bring a sausage and a banana. Next day, George turns up with his sausage and banana and the doctor asks him to drop his trousers and bend over a chair. George does as he's asked, and the doctor sticks the sausage up George's backside. After five minutes, the doctor takes out the sausage and sticks up the banana. "Is the tapeworm gone yet, doctor?" asks George. "Not yet," replies the doctor. "Come back tomorrow with another sausage and another banana." George does as he's asked and the doctor repeats the performance, first sticking the sausage up George's backside, then sticking up the banana. At the end of every session George asks if the tapeworm is gone and the doctor always tells him to come back tomorrow. After six days of this, the doctor changes his tune. "When you come in tomorrow," he says, "bring a sausage and a hammer." George does as he's asked and, as before, the doctor gets him to drop his pants and bend over for the sausage. After five minutes, the doctor removes the sausage and picks up the hammer. A minute passes, then another, and another. Then George hears a little voice pipe up, "Hey! Where the hell's my banana?" And the doctor brings down the hammer – Wham!

☞ My father always thought that fresh air and laughter were the best medicine, which is probably the reason all my brothers and sisters died of pneumonia.

☞ Harry goes to his doctor with a streaming cold. The doctor pokes and prods him, then says, "I'm sorry, but there's nothing I can do. You'll have to get some rest and wait for it to get better." Harry protests, "But I'm going on holiday next week; this cold will ruin it. Isn't there anything you can do?" The doctor replies, "All I can suggest is standing in the middle of your lawn on a cold night pouring cold water over yourself." "What?" exclaims Harry. "If I do that I'll get pneumonia!" "I know," replies the doctor, "but I can cure pneumonia."

"I do a lot of charity gigs. I did one in this very room – for a charity I now know is called Laugh FOR Leukaemia."
Jimmy Carr

☞ Harry is on the first night of his honeymoon. He starts to undress and his new bride notices that Harry's toes are bent out of shape. "I suffered from tolio when I was a child," explains Harry. "Don't you mean polio?" asks his bride. "No: tolio," says Harry. "It only affects the toes." Harry's bride then notices Harry's pockmarked knees. "They were scarred by a bad bout of the kneasles," explains Harry. "Don't you mean measles?" asks his bride. "No, kneasles," says Harry. "It only affects the knees." Harry then steps out of his underpants. His bride looks at him and cries out, "Oh, you poor man! Not smallcox as well?"

☞ Oddly enough, my father's medical practice really got popular after he developed Parkinson's – he was a gynaecologist.

☞ Hilda comes back from the doctor with a little plastic bottle and shows it to her husband, Fred. "What's that for?" asks Fred. "I'm not sure," replies Hilda. "The doctor said he needed a sample. He didn't say what of." "Why didn't you ask him?" says Fred. "I didn't like to," says Hilda. "He'd think I was stupid." "I know," says Fred, "go and ask your sister Florence. She's always down at the doctor's. She'll know what sort of sample they want." So Hilda pops down the road to see Florence. Half an hour later, Hilda comes back – only now she has a black eye, a split lip and a torn dress. "Blimey!" exclaims Fred. "Did you get run over?" "No," says Hilda. "I asked Florence what a sample was, and she told me to piss in a bottle; then I called her a rude old cow, and we started knocking seven bells out of each other."

☞ My neighbour was bitten by a rabid dog. I found him lying on the ground scribbling on a piece of paper. "There's no need for that," I said. "They can cure rabies these days. You don't have to write a will." "Will?" says my neighbour. "What will? I'm making a list of all the people I want to bite."

☞ O'Malley has been feeling unwell for quite some time. Eventually he gives in to his wife's nagging and goes to see a doctor. After a thorough examination, the doctor gives him some awful news. That evening, O'Malley takes all his friends down to the pub. He buys them a round of drinks and tells them what the doctor has discovered, "Lads," he says, "it's terrible news, to be sure. It turns out I've only got a few weeks to live. The doctor has diagnosed me with the AIDS." O'Malley's friends gasp in shock and offer their condolences. They then drown their sorrows with beer and whiskey. After the evening's drinking is over, O'Malley walks home with his teenage son. "Dad," says the boy. "I didn't like to say anything in the pub, but I thought the doctor said you were dying of cancer?" "I am, son," says O'Malley. "I just don't want any of them bastards sleeping with your mother after I'm gone."

☞ Three old men, Fred, Bill and Bert, go for their annual check-up. Fred goes first. Ten minutes later he comes out of the doctor's room and says, "I'm very healthy for an eighty-year-old. The doctor says I could live another twenty years." Bill goes in next. After twenty minutes he comes out and says, "I'm very healthy for a ninety-year-old. The doctor says I could live another ten years." Bert goes in last. After an hour, he comes out with a grim look on his face. "What happened?" asks Fred. "Well, he examined me," says Bert, "then he asked me how old I was – so I told him I was a hundred." "And what happened then?" asks Bill. Bert replies, "He told me to have a nice day."

☞ Two medical students are sitting outside a café when they see an old man shuffling towards them up the road. The old man has one hand supporting his back and is dragging one leg behind him. One of the students says, "Typical stroke patient." The other disagrees: "No; I think he has a trapped nerve." The first student says, "See how he keeps grimacing, as if he had a bad smell under his nose? That sort of facial tic's very symptomatic of stroke damage." "Yes," agrees the second student, "but also notice that he keeps shaking the leg he's dragging. That kind of behaviour's typical of a patient with a trapped nerve." Unable to agree, the students wait until the old man is walking past their table. They then ask him about his problem; has he had a stroke, or does he have a trapped nerve? "Neither," says the old man. "Five minutes ago I tried to fart and crapped in my trousers."

HEALTH AND DOCTORS – BIRD FLU

☞ A lion, a bear and a chicken are arguing about which is the most feared animal in the world. The bear says, "When I roar, the whole forest shakes". The lion says, "That's nothing. When I growl, the whole jungle shudders." And the chicken says, "You pussies. When I cough, the whole world craps itself."

☞ Following the death of a parrot from a deadly strain of bird flu, the government has issued the following warning: "If you hear someone go 'Ah-tishoo', just says 'Bless you'; if you hear them go 'Ah-tishoo's-a-pretty-boy-then', turn round and run like hell!"

☞ President Bush is very concerned about the threat that bird flu poses to the US. In fact, he's so worried he's decided to take pre-emptive action by launching a nuclear attack on Turkey. The Canary Islands are next.

HEALTH AND DOCTORS – DOCTOR, DOCTOR...

☞ "Doctor, doctor! I keep thinking I'm a cowboy." "How long have you felt like that?" "About a yeeeehaaah!"

☞ "Doctor, doctor! I'm still seeing spots before my eyes." "Didn't the new glasses help?" "Yes; now I can see the spots much more clearly."

☞ "Doctor, doctor! I keep thinking I'm a lady who delivers babies!" "It's all right; you're just going through a midwife crisis."

☞ "Doctor, doctor! I feel like a small bucket." "Yes, you do look a little pail."

☞ "Doctor, doctor! I keep thinking I'm a burglar!" "Have you taken anything for it?"

☞ "Doctor, doctor! I keep thinking I'm a fruitcake." "Oh? So what do you think's got into you?" "Flour, butter, raisins..."

☞ "Doctor, doctor! I swallowed a pound coin last week." "Oh, yes? So still no change, then?"

☞ "Doctor, doctor! I think I've broken my neck" "Don't worry; keep your chin up!"

☞ "Doctor, doctor! I'm manic-depressive." "Calm down. Cheer up. Calm down. Cheer up. Calm..."

☞ "Doctor, doctor! I've only got 59 seconds to live." "Just wait a minute, please."

☞ "Doctor, doctor! Nobody understands me." "What do you mean by that?"

☞ "Doctor, doctor! People tell me I'm a wheelbarrow." "Well, don't let them push you around."

HEALTH AND DOCTORS – EXAMINATIONS

☞ A doctor is examining a man. "I'm sorry," says the doctor, "but I can't determine the cause of your bad breath. It could be drink." The man replies, "Shall I come back when you're sober?"

☞ A vet is feeling under the weather and goes to see his doctor. The doctor starts asking a series of questions about symptoms and how long they've been occurring. The vet interrupts him. "Hey, look," he says bad-temperedly. "I'm a vet. I don't get to ask my patients any of these stupid questions. I have to look at them and work out what's wrong. Can't you do the same with me?" "Well, I suppose so," says the doctor, who then looks him over briefly and scribbles a note. "Here's a prescription for you. But I should warn you; if this doesn't work, we may have to put you down."

☞ A woman goes to her doctor for a check-up. The doctor asks her to strip off, do a handstand and open her legs. The woman is mystified by this, but follows the doctor's instructions. The woman is further mystified when the doctor props his chin between her legs and stares into the mirror. "What exactly are you doing?" asks the woman. "Oh, nothing," replies the doctor. "I just wondered what I'd look like with a goatee."

☞ Fred goes to the doctor and asks him to take a look at his privates. The doctor tells Fred to drop his trousers and spends ten minutes examining Fred's impressively-sized todger. Eventually the doctor finishes. "Well, I've had a good look," says the doctor, "and I can find nothing wrong with it at all." "I know," says Fred. "Ain't he a beauty?"

☞ George goes to the doctor with a number of aches and pains. The doctor examines him and says, "Well, I can see you have some problems, but they're all down to old age. You're sixty-five; I'm afraid I can't make you any younger." "I'm not interested in getting younger," replies George. "I just want you to make sure I get a bit older."

☞ Glenda goes to the doctor for a check-up. "How tall are you?" asks the doctor. "I think I'm five foot eight," says Glenda. The doctor checks. "You're actually five foot three," he says. "How much do you weigh?" Glenda replies, "Um... I think around six and a half stone." The doctor puts her on the scales. "You've put on a bit," he says. "You're actually a little over eight stone." The doctor takes Glenda's blood pressure. "That's not good," says the doctor. "Your blood pressure is quite high. "Are you surprised?" exclaims Glenda. "When I came in here I was tall and willowy. Now I'm short and fat!"

☞ Harry is feeling a little under the weather. He goes to the doctor for a check-up and is given the all-clear. "But what about my migraines?" asks Harry. "They're not serious," replies the doctor. "I wouldn't worry about them." "That's not the point," replies Harry. "If you had my headaches I wouldn't worry about them either."

☞ One of Harry's eyes gets sore, so he goes to his doctor for an examination. As the doctor examines Harry's eyes, he says, "You need to stop masturbating so often." "Why, doctor?" asks Harry. "Am I going blind?" "No," replies the doctor, "but it upsets the other patients in the waiting room."

HEALTH AND DOCTORS – HEALTH REGIMES AND EXERCISE

☞ I do 20 sit-ups every morning. It may not sound like much, but there are only so many times you can hit the snooze button!

☞ Fred is about to celebrate his 110th birthday and a TV crew have come round to interview him. "How have you managed to live so long?" asks the reporter. "It's not been easy," replies Fred. "I've followed a rigorous exercise regime. I have cold showers every morning and a hot shower in the evening. I only eat fresh fruit and fish, and I never touch alcohol or tobacco." "I see," says the reporter. "But I understand that your twin brother followed exactly the same routine and he died when he was 65." "That's right," says Fred. "He didn't keep it up long enough."

☞ I bought myself a treadmill, but it's quite hard work. At the moment I'm just doing widths.

  ☞ George goes for a check-up. "You're in incredible shape," says the doctor. "For a man in his seventies, you look like you're in your mid-fifties. What's your secret?" George replies, "My wife and I made a pact when we got married. Whenever we had an argument, my wife would go to the kitchen and cool down, and I'd go outside to cool down." "Well, that's a very sensible idea," says the doctor, "but how does that explain you excellent health?" George replies, "I put it down to fresh air and sunshine. Ever since I got married, I've been pretty much living outdoors."

☞ I used to fight my sexual urges by taking cold showers; now I get an erection every time it rains.

  ☞ If walking is good for you, why does my postman look like Jabba the Hutt?

☞ Last week I signed up for an exercise class. They asked me to bring some loose-fitting clothing. I told them that if I had any loose-fitting clothing, I wouldn't have signed up in the first place!

  ☞ The average woman burns more calories walking round the shops than walking around a track. That makes sense; at the shopping mall the women are dragging along their husbands.

☞ I get enough exercise just pushing my luck!

  ☞ Good diet and exercise can add years to your life. Unfortunately, they're always added on to the end.

☞ My mother-in-law told me that doing exercise helps her burn off the calories. I told her a flamethrower might do the job a bit quicker.

  ☞ Now Fred is in his seventies, he says he gets all the exercise he needs being a pallbearer for his friends who died doing exercise.

☞ Tom doesn't drink, smoke, gamble or chase loose women. Yesterday it was his birthday, but he had no idea how to celebrate it.

☞ I had to give up jogging for health reasons; my thighs were rubbing together and setting my underwear on fire.

☞ At which machine in a health club would you be most likely to meet a supermodel? The ATM.

HEALTH AND DOCTORS – HYPOCHONDRIA

☞ A Frenchman, an Englishman and a hypochondriac are lost in the desert. The Frenchman says, "I'm tired and thirsty. I must have wine." The Englishman says, "I'm tired and thirsty. I must have beer." The hypochondriac says, "I'm tired and thirsty. I must have diabetes."

☞ How do you cheer up a hypochondriac? Tell him he looks terrible.

HEALTH AND DOCTORS – INAPPROPRIATE INVOLVEMENT WITH PATIENTS

☞ A doctor is in his surgery having sex with a woman patient. Suddenly, the woman's husband bursts in on them, brandishing a shotgun. The doctor panics and shouts, "It's not what it looks like. I was only taking her temperature!" "Oh, yes?" replies the husband, aiming his gun. "Then when you take it out, you'd better hope it's got numbers on it."

HEALTH AND DOCTORS – OPERATIONS

☞ Cissy and Flo are talking about their health. "I've got to have some bits out," says Cissy, "only I can't get it done on the National Health and I can't afford to have it done private. It'll take me twelve months to save up for it." "Well, never mind," says Flo. "We'll just have to talk about your old operation for another year."

243

☞ A man is lying in a hospital bed with an oxygen mask over his face. A young nurse arrives to wash his face. "Nurse," mumbles the man from behind the mask, "Are my testicles black?" Embarrassed, the young nurse replies, "I don't know; I'm only here to wash your face." The man asks again, "Nurse, are my testicles black?" "I really don't know," stammers the nurse. The man asks again, "But nurse; are my testicles black?" The nurse gives in. She pulls back the covers, raises the man's gown and takes a close look. "No," she says. "There's nothing wrong with them." The man pulls off his oxygen mask, "I said, 'Are my test results back'?"

☞ My nephew was very ill; they rushed him to hospital and operated on him just in time. Two days later and he would have got better without it.

☞ Two doctors are chatting in a bar. "I operated on Mr Smith yesterday," says the first doctor. "What for?" asks the second. "Just over $10,000," replies the first doctor. "What did he have?" asks the second. The first doctor replies, "Just over $10,000."

☞ What's the worst part about getting a lung transplant? The first couple of times you cough, it's not your phlegm.

HEALTH AND DOCTORS – STDs

☞ A man goes to the doctor's and says his penis feels like it's burning. "Well, you know what that means," says the doctor. "Somebody, somewhere, is talking about it."

☞ An old couple totter into their doctor's surgery and ask to be tested for HIV. "I don't think you're in any danger of catching AIDs," says the doctor. "You've told me that you're both monogamous and haven't had different partners in over forty years." "That's true," says the old man. "But a woman on the telly said you ought to have a test after annual sex."

☞ If a case of the clap spreads, is it considered a case of the applause?

☞ It seems you *can* catch AIDS from a toilet seat, but you have to sit down before the last guy has got up.

HEALTH AND DOCTORS – SUPPOSITORIES

☞ A man goes to the doctor with a bowel problem and is prescribed a course of suppositories. The doctor inserts the first suppository, then sends the man home to continue the course of treatment – one suppository every six hours. The time comes for the next suppository, and the man tries to stick the lozenge up his arse. It's very tricky, so the man calls in his wife to help. She grabs hold of his arm to keep him steady and pushes the pill inside using an index finger. Suddenly the man lets out a yelp. "What's the matter?" asks his wife. "Did I push too hard?" "No," replies her husband. "I've just realised something; when the doctor did it, he had both his hands on my shoulders."

HEALTH AND DOCTORS – THINGS YOU DON'T WANT TO HEAR DURING SURGERY

☞ "Accept this sacrifice, oh Great Lord of Darkness!"

☞ "Anyone know what this is doing in here?"

☞ "Better save that; we'll need it for the autopsy."

☞ "Could you stop that thing from beating? I'm trying to concentrate here."

☞ "Damn it! There go the lights again..."

☞ "Did this patient sign the organ donation card?"

☞ "Don't worry; I'm sure it'll be sharp enough."

☞ "Dylan! Dylan! Come back with that! Bad dog!"

☞ "Hand me that... uh... that... uh... whatdyoucallit."

☞ "Now, if I could just remember how they did this on ER the other week..."

☞ "Now, then... did anyone see where I left that scalpel?"

☞ "Okay! Everyone stand back! I've just lost a contact lens!"

☞ "Oops!"

☞ "So has anyone ever survived 500 millilitres of this stuff before?"

☞ "Someone call the janitor and get us a mop in here."

☞ "That's all I need! Page 47 of the manual's gone missing!"

☞ "This is very difficult. I really wish I hadn't forgotten my glasses this morning."

☞ "Wait a minute; if *that's* his spleen, then what the hell's this?"

☞ "Well, folks, we're all going to learn something today."

☞ "What do you mean, he wasn't in for a sex change?"

HIGH SOCIETY

☞ Lady Edgemont is greeting her dinner guests at a banquet. She's saying hello to a bishop when she suddenly lets out a huge bubbling fart. Embarrassed, she looks around, sees her butler and decides to shift the blame on him. "Jenkins!" she cries. "Stop that at once." "Certainly, madam," replies Jenkins. "Which way did it go?"

HILARIOUS MATHS JOKES

☞ 1 + 1 = 3, for large values of 1.

☞ Five out of four people don't understand fractions.

☞ What is 'pi'? Mathematician's answer: "Pi is the number expressing the relationship between the circumference of a circle and its diameter." Physicist's answer: "Pi is 3.1415927 plus or minus 0.00000005." Engineer's answer: "Pi is around about 3."

HISTORY

☞ After you've heard two eyewitness accounts of the same car crash it makes you wonder about history.

> **"All castles had one major weakness. The enemy used to get in through the gift shop."**
> *Bill Bailey*

☞ It's the olden days and a Scottish army is invading northern England. The Scottish army is camped in a valley when a lone Yorkshireman strides to the top of a hill and shouts, "One Yorkshireman can beat fifty Scotsmen!" To prove him wrong, fifty Scotsmen immediately run over the hill to teach the Yorkshireman a lesson. Half an hour later, the Yorkshireman reappears and shouts, "One Yorkshireman can beat a hundred Scotsmen!" This time, one hundred Scotsmen get together and run over the hill to teach the Yorkshireman a lesson. An hour later the Yorkshireman reappears and shouts, "One Yorkshireman can beat two hundred Scotsmen!" Enraged, a group of two hundred Scotsmen rush over the hill after the Yorkshireman. Two hours later, a single bloodied and battered Scotsman runs back over the hill. "Run fer it, lads!" he cries. "It's a trap! There's two o'them!"

"My wife is a very ignorant woman. For years she thought the Charge of the Light Brigade was an electricity bill."
Les Dawson

☞ Dick went on a history tour of England. He was taken to Runnymede, where the barons made King John sign the Magna Carta. Dick asked the guide when it had happened, and the guide told him 1215. Dick couldn't believe his bad luck; he'd missed it by half an hour!

"People always ask me, 'Where were you when Kennedy was shot?' Well, I don't actually <u>have</u> an alibi."
Emo Philips

HOLIDAYS

☞ A secretary comes back from holiday and raves about the great time she had at her resort. "They had loads going on: all sort of activities. While I was there, I even won the beauty contest. You ought to go." "It's not for me," says her colleague. "I'd prefer somewhere with more people."

"Honolulu; it's got everything: sand for the children, sun for the wife, sharks for the wife's mother."
Ken Dodd

☞ I am a traveller; you are a tourist; they are trippers.

"It's all very well going on a round-the-world trip for your holiday, but where are you going to go next year?"
Jimmy Carr

☞ My wife was very excited when we went to the Grand Canyon, but when she eventually saw it her face dropped a mile. It was my fault, really; I pushed her over the edge.

☞ The Spanish hotel I stayed in was good in one respect; it overlooked the sea. Unfortunately it also overlooked hygiene, good service and edible meals.

"Some National Parks have long waiting lists for camping reservations. When you have to wait a year to sleep next to a tree, something is wrong."
George Carlin

HOME IMPROVEMENTS

☞ Harry is having his house painted. One evening, he comes home from work and accidentally puts his hand on a freshly-painted door. As he peels it away, he leaves a big palm print on the woodwork. Harry's wife says she'll speak to the painter the next day and ask him to give the door another coat. The next morning, Harry's wife goes up to the painter and says, "Can I show you where my husband put his hand last night?" The painter rolls his eyes and says, "Thanks, lady, but I've got a long day ahead of me; can't you make me a cup of tea instead?"

☞ Tom goes round to Dick's house to borrow a hammer. "Sorry," says Dick, "I lent it to my son to do some DIY." "You should never lend things to your children," says Tom. "You'll never see that hammer again." "It doesn't matter," says Dick. "It was my dad's."

HOMELESSNESS

☞ A beggar goes up to Tom and asks for £3 for a cup of tea. "£3?" says Tom. "You don't need £3 to buy a cup of tea." The beggar says, "I'm a big tipper."

☞ What did the slug say to the snail? "Big Issue?"

> ## "No matter how much you give a homeless person for tea, you never get that tea."
> *Jimmy Carr*

☞ What's the best part of having a homeless girlfriend? You can drop her off wherever you like!

HONESTY

☞ A man goes to see his boss on his first day at work. "There are only two things we insist on here," says the boss, "cleanliness and honesty. Now; did you wipe your feet on the mat when you came in?" "Yes, sir," says the man. "You're fired," replies the boss. "We don't have a mat."

☞ A man is walking out of a shop when he is stopped by a youngster carrying a wallet. "You dropped this inside," explains the youngster. "Why, thank you," says the man. "You've restored my faith in human nature. But... that's odd..." he says, checking the contents of the wallet. "I had a £50 note in here, but now there are three tenners and four fivers." "I got you some smaller notes," explains the youngster. "The man who owned the last wallet I returned didn't have any change to give me a reward."

☞ Bill goes to his doctor and tells him he's dating a much younger woman. "I'm 65," says Bill, "and she's only 30. I'm worried I won't be able to perform in bed like I used to. Can you give me anything? Perhaps some Viagra?" "I'm sorry," says the doctor, "but at 65, there's not much anyone can do. "Bill protests, "But my friend Harry's 67 and he says he can do it twice a night." "Okay," replies the doctor. "So you say it too."

HONOURS

☞ The man who invented the zip fastener is to be honoured with a peerage; he's going to be known as the Lord of the Flies.

HORSES

"Horse sense is the good judgement that prevents horses from betting on people."
WC Fields

☞ Billy-Bob is having a yard sale at his farm. Two of the items on offer are a horse and a saddle. Zeke has a look at the animal, then asks how much it is. "That there horse is $250," says Billy-Bob, "but he don't look so good." Zeke is surprised; the horse looks fine to him, and $250 sounds like a bargain. "I'll take him," says Zeke, handing over the money, "and here's another $50 for the saddle." "Well, okay," says Billy-Bob, "but only if you're sure you don't mind him not looking so good." "He looks pretty good to me," says Zeke. "Reckon I'll take him for a canter." Zeke then saddles up his new horse and takes it for a gallop. All goes well until they come to a bend in the road. The horse ignores the bend, carries on going forward and crashes head-first into a tree. The horse is knocked senseless and Zeke is thrown into the next field. Next day, Zeke staggers over to Billy-Bob's farm on a pair of crutches. He finds Billy-Bob feeding the chickens. "You cheating bastard!" shouts Zeke. "I had a vet take a look at that horse you sold me – it's completely blind!" "I know," says Billy-Bob. "I told you he didn't look so good."

☞ We had to cancel the steeplechase; the horses kept falling off.

☞ I don't mind when my horse is left at the post. I don't mind when my horse comes up to me in the stands and asks, "Which way do I go?" But when my horse is at the $2 window, betting on another horse in the same race...

☞ My horse was so late getting home, he tiptoed into the stable.

☞ Not a good day at the race once again. It was the first time I saw a horse start from a kneeling position!

☞ Harry buys a horse from an old man. "She's a good horse," says the old-timer, "but something I have to warn you about is watermelons. She loves to sit on watermelons: can't get enough of it. If she sees a watermelon, she'll sit right on it: won't get off." Harry admits this behaviour is quite unusual, but decides to buy the horse anyway. He pays the old-timer, saddles up the horse and rides her home. There's a melon patch near his normal route, so Harry takes a detour on a path that crosses a stream. However, half-way across the stream the horse sits down in the water and won't budge. Harry tries everything he can think of, but the horse won't shift an inch. Baffled, Harry goes back to find the old-timer and tells him what's happened. "I went out of my way to avoid going past watermelons," says Harry. "Then she got half-way across the stream and just sat down in the water. You did say she liked sitting on 'watermelons' didn't you? Perhaps I misheard you and you just said 'water'?" "Oh, no; you heard right," replies the old-timer. "I sure did say watermelons. Loves sitting on watermelons, does that horse: just loves it. But she sure does like sitting on fish, too. Can't get enough of it..."

☞ To prevent rude names being given to racehorses, a committee was set up to vet all new ones. One of the first names to be rejected was 'Norfolk And Chance'.

☞ What does a horse say when it steps out of the fridge? Brrrrrrrrrrrrrrrr.

HOTELS

**"A hotel is a place that keeps the manufacturers
of 25-watt bulbs in business."**
Shelley Berman

☞ "Room Service? Can you send up a towel?" "Can you wait, sir? Someone else is using it."

☞ Fred books into a small hotel, but finds that every room is taken. "I have one bed left," says the manager. "It's a twin bedroom and the guy who's already in there has agreed to share. There's only one problem; this guy snores like a warthog with adenoids. I've got to warn you; you probably won't get a wink of sleep." Fred isn't worried. He takes the keys and finds his room. Next day in the breakfast lounge, the manager sees Fred sitting at a table while his snoring room-mate sits on the other side of the room. Fred looks fine, but his room-mate is a wreck and has huge bags under his eyes. The manager goes up to Fred and says, "How did you get on last night?" "No problem," replies Fred. "He didn't make a sound." "What did you do?" asks the manager, "stuff his nose with cotton wool?" "No," replies Fred. "When I went into the room, I kissed him on the cheek and said, 'Goodnight, darling'. He stayed up all night watching me."

☞ It used to be the case that you needed to speak four foreign languages to get a job in a London hotel. Nowadays you need four languages just to be a guest in a London hotel.

"A hotel mini-bar allows you to see into the future, and what a can of Pepsi will cost in 2020."
Rich Hall

☞ A big hotel chain has just launched a new promotion; they let guests keep their pillow. They figure if you stuff a pillow in your suitcase, you won't have room for bedsheets, towels, bathrobes, the shower curtain, toilet rolls...

☞ Harry went to a hotel and booked a room with a shower. He said they were both great, but it was a little inconvenient; they were in two separate buildings!

☞ Harry booked into another hotel. He said his room was so small, the mice were hunchbacks.

☞ Jack books into a country guest-house for the night. The next morning, he's getting packed when he finds he's desperate for a crap. Unfortunately, his room doesn't have an ensuite toilet and the bathrooms in the hallway are occupied. Jack's bowels won't wait, so he's forced to crouch on the floor and do his business on a sheet of newspaper. Now Jack has the problem of hiding the evidence. He looks around and notices a large pot plant in the corner of his room. He lifts the plant out of the pot, drops in the poop and pushes the plant down on top of it. "Phew," thinks Jack. "I'm in the clear." A week later, Jack is back home when he gets a letter from the guest-house. The letter reads, 'We know what you did. All is forgiven. But PLEASE, PLEASE tell us where you hid it!'

☞ Harry's just booked into another hotel. He said it was absolutely fantastic. The towels were so fluffy, he could hardly close his suitcase.

HOUSES

☞ An old man is forced to give up his country cottage after living in it for ninety years. He puts the cottage on the market and prepares to show round prospective buyers. The first people to arrive are a young couple from London looking to buy a weekend retreat. They love the old cottage, its gardens and the views of the countryside, but they are a bit concerned by the lack of amenities. The cottage has no gas supply and the only water source is a well. They get an even bigger shock when they ask to see the toilet and are shown to a privy in the corner of the garden. They peer into the dank interior and look at each other. "It's a bit grim," says the husband to his wife. "It's horrible," she replies. She turns to the old man and says, "This nasty shack doesn't even have a lock on the door." "Oh, don't worry about that, miss," replies the old man. "I've lived here for ninety years and I've not had a single turd stolen yet."

☞ My mother was very houseproud; in fact, she divorced her first husband because he clashed with the curtains.

"I had a great business plan; I was going to build bungalows for dwarfs. There was only one tiny flaw..."
Justin Edwards

☞ My next house will have no kitchen: just vending machines and a large trash can.

☞ Our house is so small we have to clean the windows with Optrex.

HOUSEWORK

"Housework can't kill you, but why take a chance?"
Phyllis Diller

☞ A man comes home from work and is surprised to find toys spread all over the living-room floor. He looks into the kitchen and sees that the sink is piled high with dirty dishes, and there's a big pile of unwashed laundry sitting in the corner. The man looks for his wife and finds her swinging in a hammock in the garden. "What's going on?" he asks. "Why is the house in such a mess?" His wife replies, "Well, you know when you come home and ask me what I've been doing all day?" "Yes," replies the husband. His wife replies, "Well, today I didn't do it."

☞ In the past, Jenny was not what you'd call a good housekeeper; however, an incident made her change her ways. One evening her husband called up from the living room and said, "Sweetheart, what happened to the dust on the dining-table? I had a phone number written in it..."

☞ My wife's a real neat-freak. Last night I got up at three in the morning to go to the bathroom. When I got back, she'd changed the sheets and made the bed.

> **"Cleaning your house while your kids are still growing
> is like shovelling the walk before it stops snowing."**
> *Phyllis Diller*

☞ My wife is a lazy, lazy woman. It would kill her to do any cleaning or housework. It seems every time I go to pee in the sink, it's full of dirty dishes!

☞ Why do children stop wanting to help you with the housework just at the age they might be some good at it?

☞ Why is it that when people find a bit of carpet fluff their vacuum cleaner refuses to pick up, they pick it up, examine it and then – rather than put it the bin – they put it back on the carpet and go over it with the vacuum cleaner again?

☞ Woman to husband: "When are you thinking about mowing the lawn?"
Husband: "After I've thought about putting up those shelves."

HOUSING – EXTRACTS FROM (SUPPOSEDLY GENUINE) LETTERS TO LANDLORDS

☞ Can you please tell me when our repairs are going to be done, as my wife is about to become an expectant mother?

☞ Could you please send someone to fix our bath tap? My wife got her toe stuck in it and it is very uncomfortable for us.

☞ I am writing on behalf of my sink, which is running away from the wall.

☞ I request your permission to remove my drawers in the kitchen.

☞ I want some repairs done to my stove, as it has backfired and burnt my knob off.

☞ I want to complain about the farmer across the road. Every morning at 5.30 his cock wakes me up, and it is getting too much.

☞ Our kitchen floor is very damp; we have two children and would like a third, so will you please send someone to do something about it?

☞ Our lavatory seat is broken in half and is now in three pieces.

☞ The lavatory is blocked; this is caused by the boys next door throwing their balls on the roof.

☞ The man next door has a large erection in his back garden, which is unsightly and dangerous.

☞ The toilet is blocked and we cannot bathe the children until it is cleared.

☞ The toilet seat is cracked; where do I stand?

☞ This is to let you know that there is a smell coming from the man next door.

☞ When the workmen were here they put their tools in my wife's new drawers and made a mess. Please send men with clean tools to finish the job and keep my wife happy.

> **"If your house is really a mess and a stranger comes to the door, greet him with, 'Who could have done this? We have no enemies'."**
> *Phyllis Diller*

☞ Will you please send a man to look at my water? It is a funny colour and not fit to drink.

☞ Will you please send someone to mend our cracked sidewalk? Yesterday my wife tripped on it and is now pregnant.

☞ Would you please send a man to repair my downspout? I am an old age pensioner and need it straight away.

HUNCHBACKS

☞ Quasimodo walks into a gentleman's' outfitters. "Have you got an off-the-peg suit that will fit me?" he asks. The manager replies, "If we do, our tailor's getting the sack."

☞ Quasimodo walks into a pub and orders a whisky. "Certainly, sir," says the barman. "Bells all right?" Quasimodo says, "Mind your own bloody business!"

☞ Two men are looking at a photo of a hunchback. "That's Quasimodo," says one. "Do you know him?" "No..." says the other, "but his face rings a bell!"

☞ What's got four wheels, runs on petrol and zooms around a cathedral in Paris? The Hatchback of Notre Dame.

☞ What's made of plastic, contains sandwiches and crisps and goes up and down a bell-rope? The lunch pack of Notre Dame.

☞ Where does Quasimodo keep his pet rabbit? In a hutch back in Notre Dame.

☞ Quasimodo is running along the street being chased by a pack of children. He stops, turns around and shouts, "Will you get lost? I haven't got your bloody ball!"

HUNTING

☞ A hunter goes out looking for buffalo and hires an Indian scout to help him. After a while the Indian gets off his horse, puts his ear to the ground and says, "Buffalo come." The hunter scans the area with his binoculars. "I can't see anything," says the hunter. "How can you tell?" The Indian replies, "Ear sticky."

☞ Bill, Fred and Harry decide to go on a weekend moose-hunt and hire a small plane to fly them to the wilderness of northern Canada. Before they set off, the pilot turns to them and says, "Remember, this is a very small plane, so you'll only be able to bring one moose back." As luck would have it, the three hunters are very lucky indeed and each manages to bag a moose. However, each refuses to leave his moose behind; they all want to take their trophies home with them. The pilot argues with them: "I told you before you went: one moose only. Two of you have to leave your moose behind." "We heard you," says Bill. "It's the same story every year. Every time we come on a hunt you tell us it's one moose only and every year we hand over $500 for each extra moose we lug on board." So saying, he tucks $1,000 into the pilot's top pocket. The pilot sighs and helps the boys carry on their moose. When they're all on board, the pilot guns the engine and the small craft slowly takes to the sky. However, it's carrying too much weight and the undercarriage clips a pine tree, sending the plane crashing to the ground. Fred and Harry pull themselves out of the wreckage. There's no sign of Bill and the pilot. "Where the hell are we?" asks Fred. Harry replies, "Oh, I reckon we're about a hundred yards west of the place we crashed last year."

☞ Colonel Carruthers is at his club telling some of the younger members about his African hunting exploits. "I remember one occasion when I was hunting a man-eating lion," he says. "It had grabbed two of my bearers and we were waiting for it to come back for more that night. I'd made myself a hide using some thorn bushes and I positioned myself so I had a clear shot down the jungle path. I was certain the lion would use the path to get to our camp, so I was pretty confident of an easy kill: a little too confident, I should say, because that lion outwitted us all. While I was intent on the path, the black-hearted animal skirted right round our encampment and came at us from the other side. I was sitting on a log wondering when the beast would make an appearance when I heard a twig snap behind me. I turned round and there he was: an enormous brute, twelve foot from nose to tail. He prepared to leap, opened his frightful maw and let out a terrible roar, 'Grrwoooawwr!' he went. Good Lord. I just messed my pants." "I don't blame you, sir," says one of the listeners. "I would probably have done the same." "I don't mean then," replies the Colonel. "I mean just now."

☞ Harry goes into the hills to hunt bears. He sees a huge grizzly, takes aim and misses. The bear runs up to him and says, "Were you trying to kill me?" Harry nods. "Okay," says the bear. "This is how it works. If you try to kill me and fail, then I have the right to have sex with you. Now bend over and drop your pants." Harry does so and, half an hour later, shuffles home with a sore bottom. Next day, he returns with his gun, sees a grizzly, shoots and misses. The bear runs over and says, "Weren't you here yesterday?" Harry nods. The bear says, "Well, you know the drill. Bend over." Next day, Harry returns, sees a grizzly, shoots and misses. The bear comes over and says, "You again?" Harry nods. "Y'know," says the bear, "I don't think you're really here for the hunting, are you?"

☞ Lord Mountfast, the famous hunter, is showing a guest round his stately home. His Lordship points to a stuffed lion standing by the fireplace. "This trophy has particular sentimental value," says Lord Mountfast. "I bagged it when I was honeymooning with my late wife." "It's huge," says the guest. "What do you stuff those things with?" "Ordinarily we'd use cotton wadding," says his Lordship, "but in this case it's stuffed with Lady Mountfast."

☞ Zeke and Billy-Bob take their wives on a hunting trip. On the first morning, Zeke and Billy-Bob go off with their rifles, while the ladies fix breakfast. Two hours later, Billy-Bob returns to camp with a huge buck slung over his shoulders. "But where's Zeke?" asks Zeke's wife. "His heart gave up on him when he shot this here deer," replies Billy-Bob. "I left him two miles back. Flat on his back, gasping like a fish outta water." "So you lug this goddam deer over here and leave Zeke in the goddam woods!?" yells Zeke's wife. "Well, sure," replies Billy-Bob. "I figured no one was going to steal ol' Zeke."

HYENAS

☞ Did you hear about the hyena who ate an Oxo cube? He made himself a laughing stock.

IMMUTABLE LAWS OF THE UNIVERSE

> **"All tapes left in a car for more than about a fortnight metamorphose into 'Best of Queen' albums."**
> *Terry Pratchett and Neil Gaiman*

☞ An object in motion will head in the wrong direction. An object at rest will be in the wrong place.

☞ How long a minute is depends on which side of the bathroom door you're on.

☞ In order for something to become clean, something else must become dirty; but you can get everything dirty without getting anything clean.

☞ People will believe anything if you whisper it.

☞ The older a man gets, the farther he had to walk to school as a boy.

IMPATIENCE

> **"When someone is impatient and says, 'I haven't got all day,' I always wonder: how can that be? How can you not have all day?"**
> *George Carlin*

IMPONDERABLES

☞ At sporting events, why do we sit in stands?

☞ Do geese get person bumps?

☞ Do the workers at tea factories get coffee breaks?

☞ Does condensed milk come from small cows?

☞ During the winter, why do we set our central heating to make the house as warm as it was during the summer, when we complained about the heat?

☞ God is love, love is blind and Stevie Wonder is blind. So does that mean that Stevie Wonder is God?

☞ How can they force criminals to do volunteer work? If they're forced, they aren't volunteers.

☞ How can you tell when sour cream has gone bad?

☞ How come Bugs Bunny walks around naked all the time, but puts on a bathing suit when he goes swimming?

☞ How come quicksand works so slowly?

☞ How come the word 'verb' is a noun?

☞ How did they measure hail before golf balls were invented?

☞ How did waiters get their name? It's the customers who have to wait.

☞ How is it possible to act natural? If it's acting, it isn't natural; if it's natural, it isn't acting.

☞ How is it possible to 'draw a blank'?

☞ If a slightly overweight woman sings, does that mean it's half-over?

☞ If a tree falls in the forest, and no one is around to hear it, do the other trees laugh at him?

☞ If carrots are so good for your eyes, why are there so many dead rabbits on the road?

☞ If electricity comes from electrons, does that mean that morality comes from morons?

　☞ If honesty is the best policy, does that mean dishonesty is the second-best policy?

☞ If Jimmy cracks corn, and no one cares, why the hell does he carry on doing it?

　☞ If Milli Vanilli fell over in a wood, would someone else make a sound?

☞ If rhino horn is such an aphrodisiac, how come rhinos are virtually extinct?

　☞ If it's true that "Early to bed and early to rise makes you healthy, wealthy and wise", why are so many chickens sick, poor and stupid?

☞ If vegetarians eat vegetables, what do humanitarians eat?

　☞ If Wile E. Coyote had enough money to buy all that Acme crap, why didn't he just buy himself some dinner?

☞ If you ate solidified helium, would you get heavier or lighter?

　☞ If you have 50 odds and ends on a shelf, and you break 49 of them, are you left with an odd or an end?

☞ If you have dyslexia and develop cross-eyes, does your reading improve?

　☞ If you had X-ray vision, and could see through anything, wouldn't you see through everything and see nothing?

☞ If you put a chameleon in a mirrored box, what colour would it turn? See-through?

　☞ If you wear four 3D glasses at once, would you be able to see in 12D?

☞ Is there ever a day that mattresses aren't on sale?

☞ They say that for every rule, there's an exception. So is there an exception to that rule?

☞ What was Captain Hook's name before he got the hook?

☞ What would the speed of lightning be if it didn't zigzag?

☞ Whatever happened to Preparations A through G?

☞ What's the opposite of opposite?

☞ When James Bond started out, did he have to buy a provisional licence to kill from the Post Office?

☞ When you're standing at the end of a long queue, why do you feel so much better when somebody comes and stands behind you?

☞ When you've lost something, and ask somebody else if they've seen it, why do they always say, "Where did you last see it?" If you knew that, it wouldn't be lost!

☞ Where do you send someone who has become addicted to counselling?

☞ Which disease was it that cured ham used to have?

☞ Whom do male ladybirds dance with? Female daddy-long-legs?

☞ Why are living *the* good life and living *a* good life more or less opposite in meaning?

☞ Why are 'Save the trees' signs always made of wood?

☞ Why aren't moustaches called 'mouthbrows'?

☞ Why do AM radio stations keep broadcasting in the afternoon?

☞ Why do radio stations always interrupt '60 minutes of uninterrupted music' to tell you that you're listening to 60 minutes of uninterrupted music?

☞ Why do the words 'loosen' and 'unloosen' mean exactly the same thing?

☞ Why do they call a women's prison a penal colony?

☞ Why do we put suits in garment bags and garments in a suitcase?

☞ Why do you always have to whisper the names of diseases?

☞ Why does no one ever have bulletproof pants?

☞ Why does the sun come up and go down, when everything else goes up and comes down?

☞ Why doesn't the fattest man in the world become a goalkeeper?

☞ Why don't birds get tickled by their own feathers?

☞ Why hasn't someone invented a solar-powered air-conditioner?

☞ Why is common sense so rare?

☞ Why is it called a TV set when you only get one?

☞ Why is it called 'after dark' when it's really 'after light'?

☞ Why is it called an escalator even when it's going down?

☞ Why is it that most nudists are people you really don't want to see naked?

☞ Why is it that people who tell you to have an open mind always want you to agree with them?

☞ Why is Mickey Mouse, who is a mouse, bigger than his dog Pluto, who is a dog?

☞ Why is the Lone Ranger called the 'Lone' Ranger, when he always has Tonto with him?

☞ Why is there only one company that makes the game Monopoly? Or is the clue in the name? In which case, why is there more than one version of the game Monopoly available?

☞ Why, when you throw a soft drink can away, will it last for ever, but a £15,000 car will start to rust in a couple of years?

INBREEDING

☞ There's been a lot of inbreeding in my family. I have a cousin who can count to 13 on his fingers.

INDUSTRIAL ESPIONAGE

☞ A man applies for a job as an industrial spy. Together with several other applicants, he's given a sealed envelope and told to take it to the fifth floor. As soon as he's alone, the man steps into an empty hallway and opens the envelope. Inside he finds a message saying, "Congratulations! You're our kind of person. Report to the Personnel Office on the sixth floor."

INQUISITIVENESS

☞ A man is walking past a tall wooden fence surrounding an insane asylum when he hears some inmates chanting, "Thirteen! Thirteen! Thirteen..!" Curious about this, he finds a hole in the fence, and looks in. Immediately he gets poked in the eye with a stick. The chanting changes to, "Fourteen! Fourteen! Fourteen..!"

INSECTS

☞ An ant has a one-night stand with an elephant. When the ant wakes up the next morning he finds the elephant lying dead at his side. It seems to have had a heart attack in the night. "Great," says the ant. "One night of romance and now a whole lifetime digging a grave."

☞ I got stung by a bee yesterday. I couldn't believe it: twenty quid for a jar of honey.

☞ Murphy runs into a doctor's surgery. "Help me, doctor," he says. "I got stung by a bee. The pain's terrible." "Don't worry," says the doctor. "I'll put some cream on it." "You'll never find it," replies Murphy. "That bee must be miles away by now." "No," says the doctor, "I won't put it on the bee; I'll put some cream on the place where you were stung." "I see," says Murphy. "Well, I was stung in my back garden" "No," says the doctor, through gritted teeth, "I'll put it on the part of your body that was stung." "Ah," says Murphy. "Well, that bee stung me on a finger." "Which one?" exclaims the doctor. "How should I know?" says Murphy. "All them bees look the bloody same to me."

☞ It's just like life, isn't it? The caterpillar does all the work and the butterfly gets all the publicity.

☞ My uncle has invented a new fly-spray. The secret ingredient is an aphrodisiac; it doesn't actually kill the flies, but it does mean you can swat two at the same time.

☞ What lies on the ground, 100 feet in the air, and smells? A dead centipede.

"Did you know that if a stick insect laid its eggs in a jar of Bovril, it will give birth to a litter of Twiglets?"
Tim Vine

INSOMNIA

☞ Jim had a bad case of insomnia. In the end there was nothing for it; he just had to try and sleep it off.

INSULTS

☞ A half-wit gave you a piece of his mind, and you held on to it.

☞ A hard-on doesn't count as personal growth.

☞ All that you are you owe to your parents. Why don't you send them a penny and square the account?

☞ And which dwarf are you..?

☞ Are you an experiment in Artificial Stupidity.

☞ Brains aren't everything. In fact, in your case they're nothing!

☞ Can I borrow your face for a few days? My ass is going on vacation.

☞ Did your parents ever ask you to run away from home?

☞ Do you ever wonder what life would be like if you'd had enough oxygen at birth?

☞ Don't feel too bad. A lot of people have no talent!

☞ Don't thank me for insulting you. It was my pleasure.

☞ Don't you have a terrible, empty feeling – in your skull?

☞ Every girl has the right to be ugly, but you seem to have abused that privilege!

☞ Everyone is gifted, but some open the parcel sooner.

☞ For two cents I'd give you a piece of my mind – and all of yours.

☞ Have you thought about donating your brain to science? I hear they're trying to come up with the perfect vacuum.

☞ He comes from a long line of estate agents – they're a vacant lot.

☞ He fell out of the ugly tree and hit every branch on the way down.

☞ He has a mind like a steel trap – always closed!

☞ He has one brain cell, and it's fighting for dominance.

☞ He hasn't got enough brains to give himself a headache.

"He's as useless as rubber lips on a woodpecker."
Earl Pitts

☞ He's the kind of a man you'd use as a blueprint to build an idiot.

☞ He was a man of many parts, but badly assembled.

☞ He'd steal the blanket from his own mother's kennel.

☞ He's as useful as a condom machine in the Vatican.

☞ He's as useful as a one-legged man at an arse-kicking contest.

☞ He's as useful as a screen door in a submarine.

☞ He's as useful as a trap-door on a lifeboat.

☞ He's as useful as dental floss at a Willie Nelson concert.

☞ He's got a face like a bulldog chewing a wasp.

☞ He's got a face like a cat licking piss off a thistle.

☞ He's reached rock-bottom and is now starting to dig.

☞ He's so fat, he has the only car in town with stretchmarks.

☞ He's so short he can sit on a piece of toilet paper and dangle his feet.

"His finest hour lasted a minute and a half."
Phyllis Diller

☞ His origins are so low, you'd have to limbo under his family tree.

☞ How did you get here? Did someone leave your cage open?

☞ I can't talk to you right now; tell me, where will you be in ten years' time?

☞ I don't mind you talking, so long as you don't mind me not listening.

☞ I don't want you to turn the other cheek – it's just as ugly.

☞ I hear you changed your mind. What did you do with the diaper?

☞ I know you're not as stupid as you look. Nobody could be!

☞ I like you, but I wouldn't want to see you working with sub-atomic particles.

☞ I like you. People say I've no taste, but I like you.

☞ I see you have a speech impediment – your foot.

☞ I see you've set aside this special time to humiliate yourself in public.

☞ I think, therefore... we have nothing in common.

☞ I will always cherish the initial misconceptions I had about you.

☞ I wish your dad had settled for a blow-job.

☞ I worship the ground that awaits you.

☞ I would ask you how old you are, but I'll guess you can't count that high.

☞ I'd hate to see you go, but I'd love to watch you leave!

☞ I'd insult you, but you're not bright enough to notice.

☞ I'd love to go out with you, but my favourite breakfast cereal commercial is on TV this evening.

☞ I'd slap you senseless, only I can't spare the three seconds!

☞ If I had a dog that looked like you I'd shave its arse and make it walk backwards.

☞ If I had a face like yours, I'd sue my parents!

☞ If I had a head like yours, I'd get it circumcised.

☞ If I promise to miss you, will you go away?

☞ If manure were music, you'd be a brass band.

☞ If things get any worse, I'll have to ask you to stop helping me.

☞ If you ever tax your brain, you'll find you're due for a rebate.

☞ If you had another brain like the one you've got, you'd still be a half-wit.

☞ If you really are what you eat, you must be cheap, fast and easy.

☞ If you had your life to live over again, do it overseas.

☞ If you were twice as smart, you'd still be stupid.

☞ If your brain were chocolate, there wouldn't be enough to fill an M&M.

☞ I'm blonde; what's your excuse?

☞ I'm not your type. I'm not inflatable.

☞ It's been lovely, but I have to go and scream now.

☞ It's hard for you to get the bigger picture when you have such a small screen.

☞ I've had many cases of love that were just infatuation, but this hate I feel for you is the real thing.

☞ Let's play horsey. I'll be the front end and you... you be yourself.

☞ Make a mental note of that – oh, I see you're out of paper!

☞ Make somebody happy. Mind your own business.

☞ My business partner died yesterday; would you like to replace him? You would? Good. I'll arrange it with the undertaker.

☞ My friend said you're not fit to sleep with a pig, but I stuck up for you. I think you are.

☞ People clap when they see you – mostly their hands over their eyes.

☞ People say you're outspoken, but not by anyone that I know of.

☞ Pull your lip over your head and swallow!

☞ She liked her first chin so much, she added a couple more.

☞ Shouldn't you have a licence for being that ugly?

☞ Some people are has-beens. You're a never-was.

☞ Some people don't hesitate to speak their minds because they have nothing to lose.

☞ Some people say that you're a perfect idiot. I don't reckon you're perfect, but you're doing okay.

☞ Some day you'll go far; you just have to catch the right train.

☞ The closest you'll ever get to a brainstorm is a slight drizzle.

☞ The fact that no one understands you doesn't mean you're an artist.

☞ The next time you shave, could you stand a little closer to the razor?

☞ The thing that terrifies me the most is that someone might hate me as much as I loathe you.

☞ The twinkle in his eyes is actually the sun shining between his ears.

☞ There are several people in this world I find obnoxious and you are all of them.

☞ They said you were a great asset. I told them they were off by two letters.

☞ They say that two brains are better than one. In your case, one would have been better than none.

☞ Thinking isn't your strong suit, is it?

☞ This is an excellent time for you to become a missing person.

☞ When shall we meet up next? How about never? Is never good for you?

☞ Who am I calling stupid? I don't know. What's your name?

☞ You have a striking face. Tell me, how many times were you struck there?

☞ You must be the only living brain donor.

☞ You possess a mind not merely twisted, but actually sprained.

☞ You started at the bottom – and it's been downhill ever since.

☞ Your mind works like lightning. One brilliant flash and it's gone.

☞ Your viewpoint sounds very reasonable: must be time to up my medication.

☞ You're acquitting yourself in a way that no jury ever would.

☞ You're like a Happy Meal: small, cheap and greasy!

☞ You're like a toilet; you're fat, white and smell like crap.

☞ You're so fat, when you wear a yellow raincoat in the street people shout, "Taxi!"

☞ You're so slow, it takes you an hour and a half to watch 'Sixty Minutes'.

☞ You're the kind of person who, when you first meet them, you don't like them, but when you get to know them a little better, you absolutely hate them.

☞ Yours is a prima facie case of ugliness: and your body's pretty nasty too.

INSURANCE

☞ A woman goes into a car showroom and speaks to the salesman. "You know that car you sold me last week?" she asks. "It *is* under guarantee for breakages, isn't it?" "Yes, madam," replies the salesman. "It's fully covered in that respect for a whole year." "Oh, good," says the woman. "In that case I'd like to claim for a garage door, a bicycle, a garden wall and three other cars."

☞ An insurance salesman is trying to convince a young wife to take out a policy on her husband. The woman can't make up her mind up, so the salesman tries being blunt. "Be honest with me," he says. "If your husband died tomorrow, what do you think you'd get?" The woman thinks for a moment, then says, "I suppose I'd get a budgie."

"Every two minutes, someone phones Admiral Insurance for a quote. What a nutter."
Jimmy Carr

☞ I've taken out insurance that will look after all my family's needs if I die. Now their only worry is what'll happen to them if I live.

☞ Larry is trying to sell life insurance to an old man. The old geezer's ninety years old and is proving to be a difficult customer. "I know it's more than you wanted to spend," says Larry, "but you don't have to decide now. Go home and sleep on it. If you wake up, give me a call."

☞ These days you can take insurance out on everything. I've just taken out insurance against all my other insurance letting me down.

☞ Two old ladies are at the airport, booking a flight. One of them says, "Do you think we should take out insurance?" "No," replies the other. "I used to, but it never seemed to make any difference."

☞ I used to be bothered by a really persistent insurance salesman, but he doesn't call me any more: not since I took out a $100,000 life insurance policy – on him.

INTOLERANCE

☞ You know who I can't stand? Intolerant people. The bastards!

INVENTIONS

☞ My uncle has invented a way of making instant butter; he's strapped a cow into a rocking chair.

☞ Sidney's a brilliant inventor. He's just developed a truss-cum-calculator. It means that, at last, you can count on your own support.

JEALOUSY

"I'm very, very jealous. Sometimes I walk down the street and I see a beautiful woman and I think to myself: 'I'll bet my boyfriend would like to sleep with her.' And I get so angry, I run right home and smack him. And he says, 'How much more of this do you think I can take'?"
Denise Munro

JEWELLERY

☞ A elderly woman goes to a portrait artist to have her picture painted. Before the artist starts, the woman reaches into her bag and pulls out a huge emerald necklace, ruby earrings and a number of large diamond rings. "That's a very impressive set," says the artist. "It must have cost a fortune." "Not really," replies the woman. "These are costume gems I rented for this sitting. I don't actually care for this kind of adornment myself; it's too showy." "Then why have yourself painted wearing it?" asks the painter. The woman replies, "Because if I die before my husband, he'll probably remarry, and if he does, I want her to go crazy trying to find the jewellery."

☞ A woman arrives home from work and her husband notices she's wearing a diamond necklace. "Where did you get that necklace?" he asks. She replies, "I won it in a raffle at work. Now go and get my bath ready while I start supper." The next day, the woman arrives home from work wearing a diamond bracelet. "Where did you get the bracelet?" asks the husband. The woman replies, "I won it in a raffle at work. Now go and get my bath ready while I start supper." The next day, the woman arrives home wearing a mink coat. "I suppose you won that in a raffle at work?" says the husband. The woman replies, "Yes, I did! How did you guess? Now go and get my bath ready while I start supper." After supper, the woman goes to take her bath and finds there's only half an inch of water in the tub. She yells down to her husband, "Hey, there's hardly any water in the bath!" "I know!" shouts back her husband. "I didn't want you to get your raffle ticket wet."

☞ A woman is looking at the display of diamond necklaces in a jeweller's shop. She picks up one and holds it against her neck. "Do you like that one, madam?" asks the manager. "Certainly," replies the woman, "but if my husband didn't, would you refuse to take it back?"

"My husband gave me a necklace. It's fake. I requested fake. Maybe I'm paranoid, but in this day and age, I don't want something around my neck that's worth more than my head."
Rita Rudner

JOKES

☞ Did you hear about the bass drum and cymbal that fell out of the tree? Ba dum dum CHING!

☞ Did you hear the one about the three holes in the ground? Well, well, well...

☞ I was going to tell you a joke about a blunt pencil...then I thought, "No, it's pointless."

☞ Why are some people no good at telling jokes timing?

KITCHEN

☞ How do you keep flies out of your kitchen? Use your living room as a toilet.

KNOCK, KNOCK

☞ "Knock, knock." "Who's there?" "Dana." "Dana who?" "Dana talk with your mouth full!"

☞ "Knock, knock." "Who's there?" "Wanda." "Wanda who?" "Wanda have another guess?"

☞ "Knock, knock." "Who's there?" "Control freak; now *you* say 'Control freak who'?"

☞ "Knock, knock." "Who's there?" "Few." "Few who?" "Yeah, it stinks. Have you farted?"

☞ "Knock, knock." "Who's there?" "Biggish." "Biggish who?" "No, thanks; I just bought one."

LANGUAGE AND LINGUISTICS

☞ A creative writing class is asked to write an essay containing four elements: religion, royalty, sex and mystery. The winning essay reads: "My God," said the Queen. "I'm pregnant. I wonder who did it?"

☞ A linguistics professor is lecturing his class. "In English," he says, "a double negative forms a positive. In some languages, such as Russian, a double negative remains negative. However, there isn't a single language in the world in which a double positive can express a negative." A voice from the back of the room shouts out, "Yeah: right."

☞ A tourist goes into a Bulgarian shop and, being unable to speak Bulgarian, asks in English if they sell bread. The shopkeeper and his wife look at the man blankly; they obviously don't have a clue what he's saying. The tourist then has another go, this time in French. The shopkeeper shrugs; he still can't understand. The tourist then asks the question in German. Again, the shopkeeper and his wife don't understand and shake their heads. The tourist has a smattering of Russian and does his best to ask for bread for a fourth time. The Bulgarian shopkeeper shakes his head apologetically. The frustrated tourist sighs and walks out of the shop. The shopkeeper turns to his wife and says, "Y'know, it might be useful if we spoke another language." His wife replies, "What do you mean, useful? It didn't do that guy any good at all."

☞ A truck carrying copies of Roget's Thesaurus crashed on the motorway. The local newspaper reported that the onlookers were 'stunned, overwhelmed, astonished, bewildered and dumbfounded'.

☞ An Italian woman marries an Englishman. She can't speak much English, so she gets on as best as she can with sign language. One day, she goes to the butcher to buy some meat. She wants a leg of ham, but can't remember the words; instead, she slaps her leg and goes, "Oink, oink." The butcher understands and gives her a leg of ham. The woman then wants to buy some chicken breasts. Again, she can't remember the words, so she points to her breasts while holding up four fingers and going, "Cluck, cluck." The butcher understands and gives her four chicken breasts. Next, the woman has to buy some sausages. She struggles to think of a sign that she can give the butcher. Then she has a brainwave; she goes outside and, a few moments later, drags in her husband. She lines her husband up in front of the butcher and... he asks for some sausages.

☞ Learn Chinese in ten minutes: That's not right – Sum Ting Wong. Small horse – Tai Ni Po Ni. Did you go to the beach? – Wai Yu So Tan. I ran into that table – Ai Bang Mai Ni. You need a facelift – Chin Tu Fat. How come it's so dark in here? Wao So Dim. Aren't you on a diet? – Wai Yu Mun Ching. Double yellow lines – No Pah King. Our meeting is next week – Wai Yu Kum Nao. I'm hiding – Lei Ying Lo. I'm cleaning my hatchback – Wa Shing Ka. When did you last have a bath? – Yu Stin Ki Pu. Fantastic! – Fa Kin Su Pah. Will you lend me £50? – No Fu Kin Wai!

☞ There was a pregnant silence, followed by a lot of little silences.

LAW AND ORDER

☞ It's okay to love sausages and to respect the law, but you should never watch either of them being made.

> **"It is no secret that organised crime in America takes in over forty billion dollars a year. This is quite a profitable sum, especially when one considers that the Mafia spends very little on office supplies."**
> *Woody Allen*

☞ A man who posed as a woman during a three-year marriage was sentenced to a long jail term. The judge warned the man that his career as a female impersonator was probably not over just yet.

☞ A man from Seattle is offered a job in Chicago but is worried about the level of crime in the city. He remembers that his neighbour used to live in Chicago and goes to ask what the place is really like. "I loved Chicago," says the neighbour. "The people were great and there was lots to see and do; it's a great town for shopping." "Was there a lot of crime?" asks the man. "I never suffered myself," says the neighbour. "In ten years I was never robbed once." "Well, it sound pretty nice," says the man. "Perhaps I should take up that job offer after all. By the way, what kind of work did you do in Chicago?" The neighbour replies, "I was the rear gunner on a bread truck."

> **"When being chased by a police dog, try not to go through a tunnel, then on to a little seesaw, then jump through a hoop of fire. They're trained for that."**
> *Milton Jones*

☞ A policeman came up to me with a pencil and a piece of see-through paper. He said, "I'd like you to help me to trace someone."

☞ A politician has just finished an evening's pleasure with a call-girl. He presses a $100 bill into her hand and adds another. "Here's the hundred dollars we agreed on," he says, "and here's another hundred as a tip." "Oh, that's okay," says the girl, handing back the extra hundred. "I don't really need it." "You don't need it?" says the politician. "How do you live on a hundred dollars a trick?" "I don't," replies the call-girl, "but I have a nice sideline in blackmail."

☞ A shoplifter is caught red-handed in a jeweller's shop. "Don't call the police," pleads the shoplifter. "If I pay for what I tried to steal, will you let me go?" "Well, all right," says the jeweller, "if it'll teach you a lesson. That necklace you tried to pinch costs £500." "£500?" exclaims the shoplifter. "That was a bit more than I wanted to spend. Have you got anything cheaper?"

☞ A woman and a psychopath are walking through some deep, dark woods. "I'm scared!" exclaims the woman. "These woods are really creepy." "How do you think I feel?" replies the psychopath. "I've got to walk back all by myself!"

☞ Before my dad was sent to prison, he earned over a million a year as a sports repairman. He fixed football matches, boxing matches, horse races...

☞ Dick was the world's most unsuccessful forger. He used to file the corners off 50p pieces, then try and pass them off as 10p coins.

☞ Even crime wouldn't pay if the government ran it.

"Capital punishment would be more effective as a preventive measure if it were administered prior to the crime."
Woody Allen

☞ Harry goes into a police station to report a theft. "My wallet was stolen," says Harry. "A couple of girls did it. I was coming out of the supermarket when these two blondes jumped out of a van wearing bikinis. They said I was the store's 1,000th customer that day and I'd won a special prize. Then they started kissing me and rubbing up against me, and then they said they were going to take me to where my prize was, but it was a secret and they'd have to blindfold me. So they did, and all the time they were kissing and fondling me. And then they stopped, and when I took off my blindfold they'd gone. I realised they must have pinched my wallet, because it was missing." "I see," says the desk sergeant. "And when exactly did this take place?" Harry replies, "Last Thursday, twice on Friday and again this Saturday."

☞ Harry is the world's only cross-eyed burglar. If you ever see him peering in your front window, warn the people next door.

☞ Harry was arrested for walking out of a department store carrying a cast-iron oven he hadn't paid for. He said he did it in a moment of weakness.

☞ Harry was the world's only one-fingered pickpocket. He didn't make a very good living, though; all he could steal was Polo mints.

☞ How many cops does it take to throw a man down the stairs? None. He fell.

☞ I had a fantastic job last year; I was making big money. That was the trouble; people started noticing the notes were 5mm too wide and they put me in jail.

☞ I listen to the police band on my CB radio. Once I dialled 911 and dedicated a crime to my girlfriend.

☞ I opened a jeweller's shop last year. It wasn't a success; he called the police.

☞ If a criminal turns himself in, does he get the reward money?

☞ I'm an apathetic psychopath; I'd kill you, if I could be bothered.

☞ In the USA, everything that is not prohibited by law is permitted. In Germany, everything that is not permitted by law is prohibited. In Russia, everything is prohibited, even if permitted by law. In France, everything is permitted, even if prohibited by law. In Switzerland, everything that is not prohibited by law is obligatory.

☞ Last week, Harry was arrested for stealing a violin. I always knew he'd get into treble one of these days.

☞ Mabel is caught shoplifting and sent to court. "And what did you steal?" asks the magistrate. Mabel says, "A bunch of bananas, Your Honour." "How many bananas was that?" asks the magistrate. Mabel replies, "There were five bananas in the bunch." "I see," says the magistrate. "In that case, I think a sentence of five months would be appropriate." Mabel's husband calls out from the back of the court, "She also stole a bunch of grapes..."

☞ The police were called to a robbery in progress at a large grocery store. The police covered all the exits, but the robber was too clever for them; he left by the entrance.

☞ There's been a triple killing in a house. A detective inspector visits the crime scene and is shown around by his sergeant. "There are two men and a woman," says the sergeant, "and they've all been shot. We found the dead woman and one of the dead men lying in bed together, and the second dead man on the floor by the door." "Any idea what happened?" asks the inspector. "Yes, sir," says the sergeant. "We think the woman and the man by the door were husband and wife. The wife was having an affair with the second man. The husband came home unexpectedly and found them in bed. He shot them both and then shot himself." "Ah, well," says the inspector. "It could be worse." "Worse?" says the sergeant. "There are three people dead. How could it be any worse?" The inspector replies, "If the husband had come home unexpectedly yesterday, it would have been me dead in the bed."

☞ Two Alabama state troopers are chasing a car east towards the Georgia border. The troopers are just about to overtake the fugitive when he crosses the state line. The sergeant slams on the brakes. "Hell, Sarge," says the trooper. "Why did you stop? We almost had him." "You idiot," says the sergeant. "Georgia's an hour ahead of us. We'd never have caught him."

☞ When I left the house this morning I found a man stealing my gate. I didn't like to say anything in case he took a fence.

LAW AND ORDER – COURT

☞ The longest ever swearing-in of a witness lasted for six and a half weeks. Instead of holding the Bible and reading what it said on the card, the witness held the card and read out the Bible.

☞ A defendant takes the stand in court. The prosecuting lawyer approaches him and says, "You have asked if you can present your evidence in a written statement. However, that is not acceptable to the prosecution. All your responses to the questions I ask must be oral. Do you understand?"

The defendant nods. "Very well," says the lawyer. "What school did you attend in the fall of 1995?" The defendant says, "Oral..."

☞ The clerk of the court addresses the prisoner standing in the dock. "Do you wish to challenge the jury?" he says. "Not all at once," says the prisoner, "but I reckon I could go a few rounds with the little fat guy at the back."

☞ Harry is in court as a defence witness. The prosecuting counsel asks a question, "Where were you on the eleventh of May between three and four in the afternoon?" The defending counsel raises an objection: "The whereabouts of the witness are immaterial, Your Honour." "I'm happy to answer the question," says Harry. "I will repeat the question," says the prosecuting counsel. "Where were you on the eleventh of May between three and four in the afternoon?" "I must protest," says the defending council. "The question is immaterial." "I'm happy to answer the question," says Harry. "Then I will repeat the question once more," says the prosecuting counsel. "Where were you on the eleventh of May between three and four in the afternoon?" "I object most strenuously," says the defending counsel. "The answer to that question can have no possible bearing on the outcome of this case." "I'm happy to answer the question," says Harry. The judge makes a decision. "The objections of the defence are noted," he says, "but the question is a simple one, and whereas I can see no reason why it should be asked and what possible outcome the answer could have on the proceedings, it appears that the witness is quite happy to answer it. Bearing this in mind, I will allow the prosecuting counsel to ask the question." "Thank you, Your Honour," says the prosecuting council. "I repeat. Where were you on the eleventh of May between three and four in the afternoon?" Harry says, "I don't know."

☞ A judge addresses Mr Jones the defendant in a court case. "Mr Jones, do you understand that you have sworn to tell the truth, the whole truth and nothing but the truth?" says the judge. "I do," says Mr Jones. "Good," says the judge, "Now, what have you got to say in your defence?" "Well," says Mr Jones, "under those limitations, nothing at all."

☞ A judge admonishes a witness, "Do you understand that you have sworn to tell the truth?" "I do," says the witness. The judge continues, "And do you understand what will happen if you are not truthful?" "Yes," replies the witness. "My side will win."

☞ A judge asks a defendant, "Have you anything to offer to this court before I pass sentence?" "Sorry," says the defendant. "My lawyer's already cleaned me out."

☞ A judge asks a surly defendant if he has anything to say for himself. The defendant mutters, "F*** all." "What did you say?" asks the judge. The court clerk turns to the judge and says, "The defendant said 'F*** all', Your Honour." "Really?" replies the judge. "I could have sworn I saw his lips move."

☞ Jenkins Smyth, the well-known big game hunter and suspected poacher, is in court facing a charge of illegally shooting a cheetah. "It was a matter of self-preservation," argues Smyth. "I was on the edge of the desert and hadn't seen any game in days. All my food had run out. If I hadn't shot and eaten that cheetah, I would have starved before the rescue party found me." "I see," says the judge. "Pardon my curiosity, but what exactly does a cheetah taste of?" Smyth replies, "A bit like panda."

LAW AND ORDER – LAWYERS

☞ Why did God create the devil? So people wouldn't blame everything on him. Why did God create lawyers? So people wouldn't blame everything on the devil.

☞ What's the difference between a lawyer and a vulture? One collects frequent flyer miles.

☞ Harry is beginning to think his lawyer is charging too much. He just received a bill that reads, 'For waking up at night and thinking about your case: £25.'

☞ A big guy walks into a bar, slams his fist down on the bar and shouts, "All lawyers are assholes!" There is a stunned silence. Then a small, weedy man from the far end of the room pipes up and says, "Hey! I take exception to that remark!" "You do, do you!" shouts the big guy. "So are you a goddam lawyer?" "No," says the man. "I'm an asshole!"

☞ What's the difference between a good lawyer and a bad lawyer? A bad lawyer can let a case drag on and on for several years. A good lawyer can make it last MUCH longer than that.

☞ Arguing with a lawyer is a bit like mud-wrestling with a pig. After a while, you start to realise that the pig actually enjoys it.

☞ A businessman decides his firm needs to employ a lawyer, so he advertises for a young law graduate. The businessman, being an upright sort, also specifies that the lawyer must be able to prove his or her integrity and honesty. Many people apply for the job but no one makes a very good impression. At the end of the day, there's one young lawyer left to see. The young man sits down in front of the businessman and makes a very good case for himself. Eventually it's time for the two most important questions. "Now," says the businessman. "How can you prove your integrity and honesty?" "Well, sir," says the young man, "I suppose an example of my integrity would be the fact that I borrowed £20,000 from my cousin to see me through law school, and I paid it all back after my very first case." "That's impressive," says the businessman, "but how honest are you?" "Oh, I'm very honest," says the young man. "If I wasn't honest, I wouldn't tell you that my cousin is also a lawyer and he had to sue me for the £20,000."

☞ The funeral of my uncle Lenny, the lawyer, was very poorly attended. In fact, he only had two pallbearers; mind you, the dustbin only had two handles.

☞ A man goes into a lawyer's office with a tatty old suitcase. He puts it on the lawyer's desk and says, "I want to sue an airline for damaging my luggage." The lawyer looks at the tatty bag and pokes it with a ruler. "I'm sorry," he says, "but your case simply isn't strong enough."

☞ Dick says he's a criminal lawyer – so at least he's honest about describing himself.

☞ A team of research scientists has announced a major innovation; from now on they will be using lawyers instead of rats to perform their experiments on. Apparently it's a lot easier to perform experiments on lawyers, as the scientists used to get quite fond of the rats.

☞ Did you hear about the two Native Americans who formed a legal partnership? Their firm was called Cachem and Sioux.

☞ George hires Brenda as his new secretary. Brenda is a very good-looking girl and when they go on a business trip together, George eventually manages to charm her into bed. This happens a few times and the relationship seems to be going well: that is, until Brenda starts neglecting her work; she comes in late, spends most of her time talking to friends on the phone and takes three-hour lunch-breaks. George decides to have a word with her, "Brenda," he says, "I know we've had a bit of fun together, but I'm still your boss. Who said you could start coming in late and ignoring your work?" Brenda looks at him and says, "My lawyer."

☞ What's the difference between a lawyer and a leech? The leech will let go when its victim dies.

☞ How many lawyers does it take to change a light-bulb? Whereas the party of the first part, hereafter known as 'Lawyer', and the party of the second part, hereafter known as 'Light-bulb', do hereby and forthwith agree to a transaction, wherein the 'Light-bulb' shall be removed from the current position as a result of its failure to perform previously agreed upon duties, ie. the lighting, elucidation and otherwise illumination of the area ranging from the front (north) door, through the entryway, terminating at an area just inside the primary living area, this area being demarcated by the beginning of the floor covering. Any spillover illumination is additional to this agreement and provided at the discretion of the 'Light-bulb'. The aforementioned removal transaction shall include, but not be limited to, the following steps: 1) The 'Lawyer' shall, with or without elevation, by means of a chair, stepstool, ladder or any other means of elevation, grasp the 'Light-bulb' and rotate the 'Light-bulb' in a counter-clockwise direction, this point being non-negotiable, except if it is found that the 'Light-bulb' has a non-rotary bayonet fitting, in which case, refer to the stipulations of transaction paper 34b. 2) Assuming the successful completion of step (1) the 'Lawyer', upon reaching a point where the 'Light-bulb' becomes separated from the party of the third part, hereafter known as the 'Receptacle', shall have the option of disposing of the 'Light-bulb' in a manner consistent with all applicable state, local and federal statutes. 3) Once separation and disposal have been achieved, the 'Lawyer' shall have the option of beginning installation of the party of the fourth part, hereafter known as the 'New Light-bulb'. This installation shall occur in a manner consistent with the reverse of the procedure described in step (1) of this document, being careful to note that the rotation should occur in a clockwise direction, this point also being non-negotiable, except as previously stated where a non-rotary bayonet fitting is identified (in this case refer to the stipulations of transaction paper 34c.) Note: The above-described steps may be performed, at the option of the 'Lawyer', by any or all persons authorised by him, the objective being to produce the most possible revenue for the party of the fifth part, hereafter known as the 'Partnership'.

☞ If you're driving along and see a lawyer on a bicycle, why shouldn't you swerve to hit him? It might be your bicycle.

☞ Mervin gets onto a flight and takes an aisle seat next to a couple of men. They all get chatting and Mervin discovers that the men are doctors; in turn, they discover that Mervin is a lawyer who specialises in medical malpractice. As the flight gets under way, Mervin makes himself comfortable and takes off his shoes. One of the doctors then asks to get past so he can get a Coke. "Stay where you are," says Mervin "I'll get it for you." So saying, he gets up and goes to find a stewardess. While he's gone, one of the doctors wads up some paper and stuffs in into the toe of one of Mervin's shoes as a practical joke. Mervin comes back, hands over the Coke and settles back to watch the movie. A short while later, the other doctor also asks to get past; he wants a Coke too. As before, Mervin offers to get the drink. While he's gone, the second doctor stuffs Mervin's other shoe with wadded paper. Mervin comes back and hands over the Coke. A few minutes later, Mervin decides to visit the toilet and decides he'd better put his shoes on for the journey. He finds he can't get his feet into the shoes and soon discovers the practical joke that's been played on him. He wags his finger at the two doctors. "We should end this bickering between the professions," he says. "These pointless tricks: the paper in shoes, the pissing in Cokes…"

☞ Only a lawyer could write a 10,000-word document and call it a 'brief'.

☞ The day after a verdict has been entered against his client, a lawyer rushes into the judge's chambers and demands that the case be reopened. "New evidence has just come to light," says the lawyer. "I've made a discovery that could make a huge difference to my client." "And what is this discovery?" asks the judge. The lawyer replies, "I've just heard that he's got an extra £10,000 in his bank account that I didn't know about!"

☞ What's the difference between a lawyer and a cockerel? When a cockerel wakes up in the morning it has a primal urge to cluck defiance.

LAW AND ORDER – PRISON

☞ A new guy arrives in prison and is put in a cell with an old-timer called Jones. Jones greets the new arrival. "I'm in here for fraud," he says. "Made quite a good living at it for a while. I wintered in the south of France on a yacht: had fast cars, beautiful women, and ate in all the best restaurants. I tell you, I used to live the life of Riley. Then one day, it all came to a stop." "What happened?" asks the new guy. Jones replies, "Riley found out his credit cards were missing."

☞ After his arrest, Bill was incarcerated on a prison ship. A week later he tried to tunnel his way out and drowned.

☞ Paddy and Michael are sent to prison. Desperate to stay in touch with each other, they invent a code and tap messages to each other by banging on the hot water pipes with a spoon. The system worked perfectly for a time, but sadly it soon broke down after they were transferred to separate cells.

☞ There's been a prison riot and the Governor is interviewing one of the convicts involved. "I understand that your main complaint was about the quality of the food," says the Governor. "That's right," replies the convict. The Governor continues, "But what I don't understand is how you escaped from your cell. What did you use to lever open the door?" The convict replies, "A rice pudding."

LAZINESS

"I am so lazy, I married a pregnant woman."
Steven Wright

☞ Dad always wanted to be a procrastinator, but he never got around to it.

☞ It might look like I'm doing nothing, but at a cellular level I'm really rather busy.

☞ Mary comes into work late one morning and apologises to her boss for her tardiness. "I'm sorry I'm late," she says, "but my husband left the house early this morning and I had to shift some furniture." "Your husband's a big, strong fellow," says the boss. "Couldn't you have waited until he got home to do that?" "I could have," replies Mary, "but the sofa's easier to move when he's not sitting on it."

"The very existence of flamethrowers proves that some time, somewhere, someone said to themselves, 'You know, I want to set those people over there on fire, but I'm just not close enough to get the job done'."
George Carlin

LEPERS

☞ Did you hear about the rent boy who got leprosy? He did okay for a while, but then his business dropped off.

☞ How can you tell if your Valentine is a leper? His tongue is still in the envelope.

LETTERS

"I wrote my friend a letter using a highlighting pen, but he couldn't read it; he thought I was just trying to show him certain parts of a piece of paper."
Mitch Hedberg

LIFE

Sam: "How's life, Norm?" Norm: "Ask a man who's got one."
Cheers

☞ After years of trying, I figured I was finally winning the rat race. Then along came a bunch of faster rats.

Sam: "Hey, Norm. How's the world been treating you?" Norm: "Like a baby treats a diaper."
Cheers

☞ Despite the high cost of living, it remains popular.

Sam: "How's life treating you Norm?" Norm: "Like it caught me sleeping with its wife."
Cheers

Woody: "How's it going, Mr Peterson?" Norm: "It's a dog-eat-dog world, Woody, and I'm wearing Milk Bone underwear."
Cheers

☞ Why do people long for eternal life when they don't even know what to do on a rainy Sunday afternoon?

"Life is something that happens when you can't get to sleep."
Fran Lebowitz

LIGHT-BULB

☞ How does it change many dyslexics to take a light-bulb?

☞ How many amoebas does it take to change a light-bulb? One – no, two – no, four – no, eight – no, sixteen – no, thirty-two...

☞ How many anarchists does it take to change a light-bulb? All of them.

☞ How many auto mechanics does it take to change a light-bulb? Six: one to force it in with a hammer and five to go out for more bulbs.

☞ How many bankers does it take to change a light-bulb? Four: one to hold the bulb, and three to try to remember the combination.

☞ How many blues musicians does it take to change a light-bulb? Two: one to change the light-bulb, and another to look at him and say, "Oh, yeah!"

☞ How many bureaucrats does it take to screw in a light-bulb? Two: one to assure everyone that everything possible is being done, while the other screws the bulb into the water faucet.

☞ How many children with ADHD does it take to change a light-bulb? Let's build sandcastles!

☞ How many circus performers does it take to change a light-bulb? Four: one to change the bulb and three to go, "Ta-daaaah!"

☞ How many consultants does it take to change a light-bulb? Five: one to change the bulb and four to tell him how much better they could have done it.

☞ How many consultants does it take to change a light-bulb? No one knows. They never get past the feasibility study.

☞ How many consultants does it take to change a light-bulb? Three: one to change the bulb and two to write the standards and tell him what he did wrong.

☞ How many cops does it take to change a light-bulb? Only one, but he's never around when you need him.

☞ How many drummers does it take to change a light-bulb? Ah one. Ah two. Ah one, two, three, four...

☞ How many drummers does it take to change a light-bulb? None. They have machines to do that now.

☞ How many electricians does it take to screw in a light-bulb? One: they're quite good at that sort of thing.

☞ How many film directors does it take to change a light-bulb? Just one, but he wants to do it thirty-two times, and when he's done, everyone says that his last light-bulb was much better.

☞ How many fishermen does it take to change a light-bulb? Only one, but you should have seen the bulb; it must have been THIS big.

☞ How many idiots does it take to change a light-bulb? Two: one to hold the light-bulb and one to turn the ladder!

☞ How many IT assistants does it take to change a light-bulb? Three: one to write the light-bulb removal program, one to write the light-bulb insertion program and one to act as a light-bulb administrator to make sure nobody else tries to change the light-bulb at the same time.

☞ How many librarians does it take to screw in a light-bulb? I don't know, but I can look it up for you.

☞ How many Manchester United fans does it take to change a light-bulb? Three: one to change the light-bulb, one to buy the official Manchester United Light-bulb Changing Memorabilia Pack, and one to drive them all back to Surrey.

☞ How many members of the Royal Family does it take to change a light-bulb? Don't ask stupid questions.

☞ How many Microsoft employees does it take to change a light-bulb? Eight: one to work the bulb and seven to make sure Microsoft gets $2 for every light-bulb ever changed anywhere in the world.

☞ How many midgets does it take to change a light-bulb? That really depends on how high the ceiling is.

☞ How many movie actresses does it take to change a light-bulb? Only one, but you should have seen the line outside the producer's hotel room.

☞ How many pensioners does it take to change a light-bulb? One, but it's going to take all day.

☞ How many politicians does it take to change a light-bulb? Who knows? None of them will ever trust any of the others to hold the ladder steady.

☞ How many search engines does it take to screw in a light-bulb? This page is unavailable.

☞ How many Seventies disco dancers does it take to change a light-bulb? Two: one to boogie up the ladder and one to say "Get down!"

☞ How many sex therapists does it take to change a light-bulb? Two: one to screw it in, and one to tell him he's screwing it in the wrong way.

☞ How many social workers does it take to change a light-bulb? None, but it takes fifteen to write a paper entitled 'Coping with darkness'.

☞ How many sociologists does it take to change a light-bulb? None. Sociologists do not change light-bulbs; they search for the root cause of the last one going out.

☞ How many sound engineers does it take to change a light-bulb? One, two, three. One, two, three...

☞ How many Spaniards does it take to change a light-bulb? Just Juan.

☞ How many surfers does it take to change a light-bulb? Three: one to hold it, one to videotape it and another to say, "Awesome, dude!"

☞ One. How many psychics does it take to change a light-bulb?

LIGHTERS

"I keep a lighter in my back pocket all the time. I'm not a smoker. I just really like certain songs."
Demetri Martin

LIONS

☞ A sex-starved baboon is loitering by a waterhole in Africa when it sees a lion bending over to take a drink. Not being one to miss an opportunity, the randy baboon creeps up behind the lion and buggers it. The lion goes crazy trying to shake the baboon off and when the baboon eventually finishes, the lion chases it across the plain. The baboon nips into some undergrowth where it comes across a game warden sitting on a chair, reading a newspaper. The baboon chases the warden away, sits in the chair and holds up the newspaper in front of its face. The lion comes along panting and wheezing. "Excuse me," he says to the figure behind the newspaper. "You haven't seen a baboon running past here, have you?" "What?" replies the baboon. "You meant the baboon who buggered that lion at the waterhole?" "Oh, my God," says the lion. "It's not in the papers already, is it?"

☞ Out on the grasslands of Africa, a male lion is having sex with a zebra. Suddenly another zebra appears over the hill. "Oh, crap!" says the zebra. "That's my husband. Make like you're killing me."

☞ Two men are on safari. They're out hunting in the bush when one calls to the other, "Here! Look at the size of these lion tracks! The brute that made these must be eight feet long." "Good work," says his friend. "You see where they go, and I'll find out where they came from."

LOGIC

☞ A young man comes back from university after studying logic. "Give me an example of how this logic works," says his father. "Well," says the boy. "I know that you have a dog, so logically I can also say you have a garden to keep it in. If you have a garden then, logically, you have a house. A house would be too large for a single man so, logically, you'd be married and, logically, you would also have children, from which I can logically deduce that you're not gay." "Wow," says father. "I'll try that on Frank at the pub." Later, Father meets up with Frank. "Hey, Frank," he says. "You've got a dog, haven't you?" "No," replies Frank. Father says, "Then piss off, you big fairy."

☞ An old Native American gets a lift in a sports car. As the car zips along, the Indian asks why the engine doesn't overheat. "The engine is air-cooled," says the driver. "The faster you go, the cooler the engine gets." The old man absorbs this information. When he gets back to his house he borrows his son's horse and starts riding it round and round the reservation. It's a hot day, but the old man keeps driving the horse onwards, making it go faster and faster. Eventually the horse has had enough; it collapses into a heap and dies. The son runs up to find out what's going on. "What the hell happened to my horse?" he says. The old man looks at the dead animal and says, "I'm not sure, but I think it must have frozen to death."

☞ Logic is a systematic method of coming to the wrong conclusion with confidence.

LOTTERY

☞ A lottery prayer: Please, Lord, let me prove that winning the lottery won't spoil me.

> **"I figure you have the same chance of winning the lottery whether you play or not."**
> *Fran Lebowitz*

☞ A son from a poor family wins a million pounds in the lottery. He goes home and gives his old dad £100. The old man looks at the cash and says, "Thanks son. This money will mean a lot to me. We've never had much in this family. We've always been poor. Y'know, I couldn't even afford to marry your mother." 'What," exclaims the son. "You mean I'm a bastard?" "Yes," replies dad, "and a bloody tight one, too."

☞ Harry won a three million pound lottery prize. He got a letter officially confirming he will be paid £3 a year for the next million years.

☞ There's a fourteen-million-to-one chance of winning the lottery, and a fifty-thousand-to-one chance of being run over by a car. So why don't more people bet on getting run over?

LOVE

"The only place you're sure to find love is at the end of a letter from your mother."
Bruce Lansky

☞ Love – that magical interval between first meeting a beautiful girl and discovering that, in the mornings, she looks like a haddock.

☞ Have I told you I love you today? No? That's strange – I'm sure I told somebody.

☞ A survey says that two out of every five men would choose love over money and health. This would suggest that the kind of men women find attractive are mostly penniless and sick.

"Money is not the most important thing in the world. Love is. Fortunately, I love money."
Jackie Mason

☞ It's better to have loved a short woman than never to have loved a tall.

☞ Mary, to Charlie: "I can't leave you, my darling." Charlie: "Do you love me so much?" Mary: "No. You're standing on my foot."

LUCK

☞ Harry must be the unluckiest man in the world. He was depressed, so he tried to kill himself. Then he was resuscitated and put on trial for attempted murder. He was found guilty and sentenced to death. Now he's really depressed.

☞ I've always been unlucky. I had a rocking horse once; it died.

☞ Simon meets his old friend Bill in the street. "Hi," says Simon. "How are you doing?" "Terrible," replies Bill. "Last year my house burned down and killed all my family. My dog was run over by a truck. My parents died in a plane crash: and now I've just got back from the doctor. He tells me I have an inoperable brain tumour." "Oh, my God," says Simon. "I'm so sorry." "Well, it's not all bad," says Bill. "Business is still pretty good." "What do you do these days?" asks Simon. Bill replies, "I sell lucky charms."

LUMBERJACKS

☞ A man applies for a job as a lumberjack. "Are you a fast worker?" asks the interviewer. "Sure am," replies the lumberjack. "You won't find faster." "And where was you last job?" asks the interviewer. "I worked in the Sahara Forest," says the lumberjack. "Sarah Forest?" queries the interviewer. "Don't you mean the Sahara Desert?" "Oh, sure," says the lumberjack. "That's what they call it now..."

☞ Did I tell you about the time I was a lumberjack? I was useless; I soon got the axe.

☞ Steve goes for a job as a lumberjack. He has no qualifications for the job but insists he must be paid $400 a day. "That's way too much," says the foreman. "Experienced men don't get half that." "I know," says Steve, "but since I have no idea what I'm doing, I'll have to work twice as hard."

LYING

☞ Governments lie and newspapers lie, but at least in a democracy they are different lies.

☞ A short, fat woman goes to a hospital emergency room to have her cut hand bandaged. The nurse asks for some details, "Your height and weight, please?" she says. The woman replies, "I'm five foot eight and one hundred and twenty-five pounds." The nurse looks at her and says, "I'm sorry, miss, but this is a hospital, not an Internet dating site."

☞ Hazel goes to a casino with her new boyfriend, Peter. They visit the roulette table, but Hazel can't decide what number to choose. "Why not bet on your age?" says Pete. Hazel thinks this is a great idea, so she puts £10 on 26 – then faints when the ball lands on 37.

☞ Mrs Solomon, Mrs Levy and Mrs Lefkowitz are discussing their sons. Mrs Solomon says, "My Sheldon is a world-famous lawyer with big-shot clients, a mansion in Beverly Hills and a summer home in Hawaii. He has a beautiful wife and everything a man could want." Mrs Levy says, "That's nice: but let me tell you about my son Jonathan. He's a doctor: a world-famous researcher. He was nominated for a Nobel Prize in Medicine." Mrs Lefkowitz says, "Well, my Hershel might not be rich or famous, but his pee-pee is so long, ten pigeons can perch on it in a line." The ladies pause for thought. Mrs Solomon says, "Actually, I have a confession to make. Sheldon's an up-and-coming lawyer in Los Angeles, but he doesn't have a mansion or a summer home." Mrs Levy says, "I've got a confession too. Jonathan's is a good doctor but he was never nominated for a Nobel Prize." Mrs Solomon and Mrs Levy look expectantly at Mrs Lefkowitz. "Well, all right," says Mrs Lefkowitz. "The last pigeon has to stand on one leg."

MAGIC, MYTH AND FANTASY

☞ A magician accidentally turns his wife into a sofa and his two children into armchairs. He starts to panic. "What on earth have I done?" he wails. "How am I going to bring them back?" The magician tries every spell in the book, but none of them works, so in desperation he decides to take them to the hospital. Surely the doctors can help them? The magician loads his family into a van and rushes them to casualty. At the hospital, the magician spends a sleepless night while the medical staff run numerous tests on the unfortunate woman and children. Finally, the chief doctor comes out into the corridor to speak to the magician. "How are my family?" sobs the man. "Are they all right?" The doctor replies, "They're comfortable."

☞ A man goes up to a girl in a bar. "Do you want to play 'Magic'?" he says. "How d'you play that?" she asks. "It's easy," says the man. "We go to my house and have sex; then you disappear."

☞ An attractive young woman is sunbathing in her back garden when she sees a little old man crouched in her flower bed, spying on her. She leaps up and grabs him, shouting, "You're a leprechaun! And now I've caught you must give me three wishes! I want a big house, lots and lots of money and a handsome film-star to marry!" "Okay," says the little old man. "I can do all that, but for the magic to work you have to go to bed with me." The woman agrees and they spend the rest of the afternoon in the bedroom. After they've finished, the little old man starts putting on his clothes. "I hope you don't mind me asking," he says, "but how old are you exactly?" "Twenty-two and a half," replies the woman. "Bloody hell," mutters the little old man. "Twenty-two and she still believes in leprechauns?"

☞ George is learning how to be a magician. He's taking a correspondence course and, despite a few setbacks, he seems to be doing okay. One day, he's asked to perform some magic at a garden party. For his first trick, he goes up to the largest man he can find and asks for some help. "I'm going to balance this egg on my head and cover it with a cloth," says George. "Now I want you to take this croquet mallet and hit the egg as hard as you can. Don't worry about hurting me; it's a trick." So the man picks up the mallet and hits the egg with all his might. Three years later, George comes out of his coma, sits up in his hospital bed and shouts, "Ta-daaah!"

☞ The Seven Dwarfs visit Rome and are lucky enough to be granted an audience with the Pope. While they're talking, Dopey asks a question. "Excuse me, sir," he says, "but are there any dwarf nuns in the Vatican?" "No," says the Pope. "There are not." "So are there any dwarf nuns in Rome?" asks Dopey. "No," says the Pope. "There are not." "So are there any dwarf nuns in the whole of Italy?" asks Dopey. The Pope thinks for a second, then says, "No. No there are not." And the other dwarfs start chanting: "Na-na na-na-na! Dopey had sex with a penguin! Dopey had sex with a penguin!"

MANNERS

☞ A woman has her arms full carrying some shopping out of a store. Suddenly the wind blows her skirt up, revealing she's not wearing any underwear. A passing man can't help but look, and gets an eyeful of all she has to offer. "Well!" fumes the woman. "You're certainly no gentleman." "That's funny," replies the man. "I was thinking exactly the same thing."

  ☞ Nothing is quite so annoying as having someone carry on talking while you're trying to interrupt.

☞ A woman wearing a tight miniskirt tries to get on a city bus. However, her skirt is too tight and she can't raise her leg high enough to put her foot on the step. Embarrassed, she reaches behind her and unzips her skirt a little to loosen it up. This doesn't work, so she tries again and unzips a little more. The skirt is still too tight, so she has another go. It still doesn't work. At this point a large man standing behind her lifts her up into the bus. "How dare you touch me?" fumes the lady. "You had no right to go grabbing me like that." "Well, I'm sorry, miss," replies the man, "but after you unzipped my fly three time I figured you wanted to make friends."

> "I'd rather see a pregnant woman standing on
> the bus than a fat girl sitting down crying."
> *Jimmy Carr*

MARINE LIFE

> "Jellyfish: if they're 97 per cent water, why didn't they
> just go all the way with it and become water?"
> *Karl Pilkington*

> "Why does Sea World have a seafood restaurant?
> I'm half-way through my fish burger and I realize,
> 'Oh, my God; I could be eating a slow learner'!"
> *Lynda Montgomery*

MARRIAGE

☞ A husband is someone who, after taking the trash out, gives the impression he's just cleaned the whole house.

> "I love being married. It's so great to find that one special
> person you want to annoy for the rest of your life."
> *Rita Rudner*

☞ A man and two women are sitting in a train compartment. The man decides to strike up a conversation. "Do you know what I am?" he says to his companions. "I'm a SNAG." "So what's a SNAG?" asks one of the women. The man replies, "That means I'm a 'Single, New Age Guy'." "Oh, I get it," says the woman. "I think they call people like me a DINK. That means 'Dual Income, No Kids'." "Are you called anything?" says the man to the other woman. "Yeah," she sighs. "I'm a WIFE." "WIFE?" says the man. "I don't think I've heard of that one. "There's plenty of us around," replies the woman. "It means Wash, Iron, F***, Etc."

☞ A man walks into a police station. He goes up to the desk sergeant and says, "My wife is missing." "How long has she been gone?" asks the sergeant "A month," replies the man. "A month?" exclaims the sergeant. "Why the hell did you wait so long to report it?" "Well," says the man, "until yesterday I thought it was just a dream."

> **"I was cleaning out the attic the other day with the wife. Filthy, dirty and covered with cobwebs – but she's good with the kids..."**
> *Tommy Cooper*

☞ A man comes home and is greeted by his wife dressed in a sexy shortie nightie. "Tie me up," she purrs, "and then you can do anything you want." "Wow," he says: so he ties her up, gets back in the car and drives to the golf course.

☞ A man gets engaged to the woman of his dreams. He goes to tell his father and says, "Daddy! I've found a woman just like mother!" His father gives him a cold stare and says, "So what do you want: sympathy?"

☞ A man goes to a rich banker and asks for the hand of his daughter in marriage. "Tell me," says the banker, "would you want to marry my daughter even if she didn't have a penny to her name?" "Sir," replies the man, "I'd love your daughter if she only owned the clothes she stood up in." "Then you'd better get lost," replies the banker. "You're not marrying my daughter. There are enough idiots in this family as it is."

> **"In my house I'm the boss. My wife is just the decision-maker."**
> *Woody Allen*

☞ A man once told me that his wife was an angel. I said, "Lucky bastard. Mine's still alive."

☞ A man says to his wife, "I had a wet dream about you last night." "Did you really?" says the wife. "Yes," says the husband. "You got run over by a bus and I wet myself laughing."

☞ A man walks into a bar and asks the bartender for a drink. Then he asks for another: and then another: and after that, a few more. The bartender's getting worried. "What's the matter?" he asks. "It's my wife," sobs the man. "We got into a really terrible fight. In the end, she told me she wouldn't talk to me for a whole month." "Don't upset yourself," says the bartender. "I'm sure she didn't mean it." "No; you don't understand," says the man. "Tonight's the last night."

☞ A married man can change his job as often as he likes; he still ends up with the same boss.

"We sleep in separate rooms; we have dinner apart;
we take separate vacations. We're doing everything
we can to keep our marriage together."
Rodney Dangerfield

☞ A woman asks her friend, "Was that your husband who just let me in?" The friend replies, "You don't think I'd hire a butler that ugly, do you?"

☞ A woman comes across her husband poring over a legal document. He keeps reading it over and over again. "What's that you've got?" she asks. He replies, "It's our marriage licence." "Why the interest?" she says. He replies, "I'm looking for a loophole."

☞ Adam and Eve had the ideal marriage. He didn't have to hear about all the other men Eve could have married, and she didn't have to hear about the way Adam's mother cooked.

☞ Before marriage, a man yearns for the woman he loves. After marriage, the 'Y' becomes silent.

**"I've had bad luck with both my wives. The first
one left me and the second one didn't."**
Patrick Murray

☞ David and Jean go to a marriage guidance counsellor. They tell the
counsellor they keep arguing all the time. The counsellor tells them that
they should go away for a few weeks and make a note of all the things they
disagree about and all the things they agree about. In the counsellor's
experience, they will soon find that their agreements outweigh their
disagreements. A few weeks later, David and Jean come back and the
counsellor asks to see the list of things that the couple have agreed on. "We
haven't got one," says David. "In three weeks there's not one thing we've
agreed on." Jean says, "He means four weeks."

☞ Every man should get married. After all, happiness isn't the only thing in
life.

☞ George goes to his doctor and has a check-up. The doctor examines him and
asks a few questions about his home life. The next day the doctor goes round
to George's house to speak to his wife. "Your husband is suffering from
hypertension," says the doctor. "He needs complete rest and relaxation for
the next week." The doctor holds up a bottle of pills. "These are heavy-duty
tranquilisers. I want you to take three a day."

☞ Glenda wakes up with a headache every morning. She has a cure, though;
she sends him to work.

**"The wife's mother has been married three times. Her first
two died through eating poisoned mushrooms. The third
one died with an arrow in his back. I said to her, 'How
terrible! how come he was killed by an arrow?' She said,
"Because he wouldn't eat the bloody mushrooms'."**
Les Dawson

☞ Harry and Thelma get in a small customer lift in a department store. An attractive young woman squeezes in as well and Harry is pleased to find her standing in front of him. The lift goes to the next floor. The young woman is just about to get out when she has her bottom pinched. She turns round, sees Harry ogling her and slaps his face. "How dare you pinch me?" she says indignantly. "You're a dirty old man." The doors close and Harry turns to Thelma. "You've got to believe me," he says. "I never touched her." "I know," says Thelma. "I did."

☞ Harry is reading a newspaper story about a successful, but dim, footballer who is marrying a beautiful model. He calls out to his wife, "I'll never understand how the biggest morons end up with the best-looking wives!" His wife calls back, "Why, thank you, dear!"

"My boyfriend and I broke up. He wanted to get married and I didn't want him to."
Rita Rudner

☞ Harry rings up Dick and asks for his help. Harry is picking up a crate from the docks, and he needs Dick's help to get it into the van. Dick agrees, and he and Harry drive down to the docks. When they get there, they find a large crate waiting for them. "So what's in this thing?" asks Dick. Harry replies, "It's a baboon: all the way from Africa." "What on earth do you want a baboon for?" asks Dick. "To put in my bathroom," replies Harry. "You want to put a baboon in your bathroom?" says the astonished Dick. "Yes," replies Harry. "It's to teach my wife a lesson. She's a great know-all. If the neighbour's cat has just died, I'll tell her and she'll say, 'Yeah, I know'. If the price of bread goes up, I'll tell her and she'll say, 'Yeah, I know'. If my mother has an operation on her knee, I'll tell her and she'll say, 'Yeah, I know'". "I see," says Dick. "But how is putting a wild baboon in your bathroom going to help?" "Tomorrow morning," says Harry, "my wife will get up and go for a pee in the bathroom. Then she'll run out screaming and say, 'Harry! There's a baboon in the bathroom!' And I'll turn over and say, 'Yeah, I know'."

☞ Harry, to George: "I'm getting married next week." George: "Married? She must be desperate. What sort of pathetic idiot would marry you?" Harry: "Your daughter."

☞ Harry's wife lets him subscribe to two magazines: National Geographic and Playboy. Both let him see places he never gets to visit.

☞ I'm two-thirds married. I turned up, and so did the vicar, but the bride didn't.

"Marriage: the only union without a shop steward."
Les Dawson

☞ Jane and Mary are discussing their husbands. Jane says, "My Frank's very fussy. If a steak isn't cooked just the way he likes it, he won't touch it. What about your, Fred? Is he very hard to please?" "I don't know," replies Mary. "I've never tried."

☞ Last night, my wife grovelled before me on her hands and knees. She said, "Get out from under that bed and fight like a man!"

☞ Love is blind, but marriage is a real eye-opener.

☞ Marriage destroys passion; suddenly you're in bed with a relative.

☞ Mike goes to his local priest and says, "Father, you have to help me. My wife's trying to kill me. She's trying to feed me poison in my soup." "My son," says the priest, "I'm sure your fears are exaggerated. There's certain to be a simple explanation. Tell you what; I'll go round to your house and speak to her. I'm sure this can all be sorted out." So the priest goes round to Mike's house and has a word with his wife. A long while later, he comes back to the church. Mike is waiting for him. "Michael," says the priest. "I've spoken to your wife in depth. In fact, I spent four hours in her company: and I'm pretty sure that she is indeed trying to poison your soup." "But what can I do, Father?" pleads Mike. The priest replies, "If I were you, Michael, I'd drink the soup."

☞ My uncle's marriage broke up recently. It was very sad. They'd seemed like the perfect couple; he was a historian and she liked dating.

☞ Tom, to Dick: "I could only marry a girl who had a sense of humour." Dick: "That's the only kind you're going to get."

> **"You always remember the first time you met the woman you'd later marry. I first met the wife in a tunnel of love. She was digging it."**
> *Les Dawson*

☞ My wife and I went to a dinner party last night, but we ended up having a terrible row in front of our friends. She'd had too much to drink and became very abusive; I kept telling her that it was MY turn to get drunk and abusive.

☞ My wife has never been outspoken; no one's ever been able to manage it.

☞ My wife is an angel; she's always up in the air, harping on about something, and never has a thing to wear.

☞ My wife said to me, "You're going to be sorry. I'm leaving you." I said, "Make your mind up."

☞ My wife thinks I'm too nosy; at least, that's what she wrote in her diary.

☞ My wife's the most suspicious person around. If I come home early, she thinks I'm after something. If I come home late, she thinks I've already had it.

> **"Marriages don't last. When I meet a guy, the first question I ask myself is: is this the man I want my children to spend their weekends with?"**
> *Rita Rudner*

☞ Since getting married I've realised that it is better to have loved and lost than to have loved and won.

☞ Girls these days just aren't interested in marriage. I should know; I've asked most of them.

☞ Ted is the mayor of a Midwest town. One day he and his wife Jackie are walking past a construction site when one of the site workers calls over. "Hi, Jackie!" he says. "It's me, Bill!" It turns out that Bill was Jackie's boyfriend in high school, so he and she spend a few minutes reminiscing. After the chat, Ted and Jackie walk on. "Just think," says Ted, "if you'd married that Bill fellow you'd be the wife of a labourer right now." "No," replies Jackie. "I'd still be the wife of the mayor."

☞ The day before Bill's wedding, Harry goes up to him and says, "Treasure this day. In the future, you will look back on this day as the happiest one of your life." Bill replies, "But I'm getting married tomorrow." Harry says, "I know."

"The secret of a happy marriage remains a secret."
Henny Youngman

☞ Tom and Vera are at the local county show looking at the animals. They stop by a bull-pen and see a sign that reads, "This bull mated 50 times last year." Vera nudges Tom. "See that?" she says. "That bull mated 50 times last year. That's almost once a week." They walk to the next pen where there's a sign that reads, "This bull mated 150 times last year." Vera gives Tom a nudge and says, "He could teach you a thing or two. That's more than twice a week!" The couple walk to the third pen where there's a sign that reads, "This bull mated 360 times last year." "Wow!" exclaims Vera. "That's almost every day. He's certainly showing you up." "Really?" sighs Tom. "Well, tell you what; let's go and ask him if it was 360 times with the same cow."

☞ Tom is fishing in the river when he pulls up a huge carp. Another fisherman comes up to congratulate him. "Magnificent fish," says the man. "I doubt even William Smith could have hooked a bigger one in this river." "Was he a champion fisherman?" asks Tom. "Oh, yes," replies the man, "and an all-round sportsman. I get out of breath running for a bus, but old William could have been a professional athlete if he'd wanted to. A very capable man, was William. He was very handy round the house, too. I can barely hammer in a nail straight, but William could fix anything: repair a toaster, a TV, build a wall. He could put his hand to anything. And he was quite a ladies' man by all accounts," continues the man. "He always chose the most appropriate, thoughtful gifts and never forgot an anniversary. And William was a wizard in bed, apparently: always gave the ladies what they wanted: not like me, I'm afraid. I'm a complete duffer in that department." "Really?" says Tom, slightly bemused by this speech. "Was William a friend of yours?" "No," replies the man. "I never met William." "Then how do you know so much about him?" asks Tom. The man replies, "I married his widow."

> **"Whatever you may look like, marry a man your own age; as your beauty fades, so will his eyesight."**
> *Phyllis Diller*

☞ When I first took her out, she looked at me, giggled and smiled. When I asked her to dance, she looked at me, giggled and smiled. When we first made love, she looked at me, giggled and smiled. When I asked her to marry me, she looked at me, giggled and smiled. When I asked her if she'd enjoyed our first wedding anniversary celebrations, she looked at me, giggled and smiled. And that's when it finally dawned on me that she was mentally handicapped.

☞ Tom meets up with George in a bar. "I've found the perfect girl for you," says Tom. "Your days of being single are over." "What's she like?" asks George. "She's young," says Tom, "she's rich and she's beautiful." "I see," says George. "And I'm a dirt-poor, overweight, middle-aged man with a face that could crack a mirror. What's a girl like that going to see in me? She'd have to be a mental case to get married to me." Tom shrugs and says, "Yeah, but you can't have everything."

☞ Two men are sitting on a bench. They get chatting, then start comparing wives. The first says, "My wife's very intelligent. She went to university, has loads of hobbies and reads two or three books a week. She can talk for hours and hours on any subject." The other man sighs and says, "Mine doesn't need a subject."

☞ Two men meet in a bar and start discussing their lives. One says, "I'm getting married. I'm tired of a messy apartment, dirty dishes and no clothes to wear." "That's funny," says the other. "I'm getting divorced for the same reasons."

☞ When a man holds a woman's hand before marriage, it's love; when he holds it after marriage, it's self-defence.

☞ When I argue with my wife I always get the last word. Actually, I get the last two words: "Yes, dear."

MARRIAGE – ADULTERY

"There is one thing I would break up over, and that is if she caught me with another woman. I wouldn't stand for that."
Steve Martin

☞ A boss brings his secretary back from a dirty weekend. "What a great time," he says. "I bet you won't forget that in a hurry." The secretary replies, "I could; what's it worth?"

☞ A man goes to his doctor. "I have a terrible problem," says the man. "My wife's pregnant, but we haven't had sex in over a year. Is there any way that it would be medically possible for her to get pregnant?" "Oh, yes," replies the doctor. "It's a condition we call 'grudge pregnancy'; someone has obviously had it in for you."

☞ A woman finds out her husband is having an affair, so she kills him. To get rid of the body, she decides to bury it in the countryside. She manages to haul his naked body into the boot of her car, but the man's penis is severed when she slams the boot shut. She picks up the severed organ and puts in on the dashboard. The woman is under a great strain and her erratic driving soon attracts the attention of a police car. The woman speeds up to avoid the cops but realises they're gaining on her. Suddenly, she remembers the severed penis sitting on the dashboard in plain view, and flings it out through the sunroof. The penis hits the windscreen of the police car and bounces off into the night. "She's driving like a maniac!" says one of the policemen. "Never mind her," says the other. "Did you see the size of the cock on that fly?"

☞ Tom and his wife June are arguing about adultery. June thinks it's a terrible thing, but Tom isn't so bothered. "Well, really!" says June. "And what would you think if I slept with your best friend?" Tom ponders this for a second, then says: "I'd think you were a lesbian."

☞ A man rushes into the bar and says to the bartender, "The beers are on me! My wife just ran away with my best friend!" The bartender is surprised by this reaction. "Is that good news?" he asks. "Most guys would be devastated if something like that happened." "Not me," replies the guy. "I'm going to save a fortune; both of them are pregnant!"

☞ A man suffering from premature ejaculation goes to his doctor. The doctor suggests that he tries to startle himself when he's about to ejaculate. The man buys a starting pistol, runs home and finds his wife naked in the bedroom. Losing no time, they start having sex. Next day the man goes back to the doctor. "How did it go?" asks the doctor. "Not so good," replies the man. "We were in the 69 position when I felt myself coming, so I fired the gun. My wife crapped on my head, bit three inches off my penis, and my neighbour ran out of the wardrobe with his hands in the air."

☞ A married man is having an affair with his secretary. One afternoon they go to her place and spend the afternoon in bed. Exhausted, they fall asleep and don't wake up until eight in the evening. The man's in a panic. His wife's going to kill him! Suddenly he has an idea. He throws on his clothes, then goes outside and rubs his shoes in the grass and the flowerbed. Once his shoes are thoroughly stained with grass and mud, he drives home. The man's wife greets him at the door. "And where the hell have you been?" she asks. "I can't lie to you," he says, "I'm been having an affair with my secretary. Today we went to her flat and had sex all afternoon." The man's wife looks down at his shoes. "You lying bastard!" she says. "You've been out playing golf again, haven't you?"

☞ At school, little Johnny learns a neat trick from an older boy. "All grown-ups have a secret," says the boy. "All you have to do is pretend you know what it is and you can get anything you want." Little Johnny decides to go home and try it out. When he gets to his house, he's greeted by his mother at the front door. Johnny eyes her sternly and says, "I know the whole truth." His mother blushes and hands him $20. "Just don't tell your father," she whispers. Very pleased at this outcome, little Johnny waits for his father to get home from work. When Dad arrives, Johnny meets him in the hallway and says, "I know the whole truth." Dad hands him $40, saying, "Don't breathe a word to your mother." Johnny is delighted, and can't wait to try the trick on the next adult he comes across. The next morning, he happens to meet the milkman on the front doorstep. Little Johnny goes up to him and says, "I know the whole truth." The milkman smiles broadly, then opens his arms. "Come over here," he says. "Give your daddy a big hug!"

☞ A man goes to a psychiatrist. "Doctor," he says, "my wife's unfaithful. She's a beautiful ex-model and every evening she goes to Larry's Bar to pick up men. She'll sleep with anybody who asks her! She doesn't care what they look like. She just wants sex all the time: nothing but sex, sex, sex! It's driving me crazy. She's a nymphomaniac. What should I do? Can she be treated for it? Help me, doctor! Help me!" "Calm down," says the doctor. "We'll take things one step at a time. Now; where exactly is Larry's Bar?"

☞ Tom discovers that Dick's wife, Sally, is having an affair. He knows he ought to tell him, but can't think how to break the news. One day, Tom arranges to meet Dick in the local pub. On the way there, he walks past Dick's house and sees Sally's boyfriend slipping inside. He hurries to the pub and finds Dick standing at the bar. "Here," says Tom. "Have you ever fancied a threesome?" "You bet I have," replies Dick. "That's always been one of my favourite fantasies." "Well, you'd better hurry home," says Tom. "You might just be in time."

☞ Beryl comes home early, goes into the front room and is horrified to find her husband, naked, mounting the vicar's wife from behind. "My God!" she yells "I knew you'd had affairs, but this time you've gone too far!" "You're right," moans her husband. "I think I'm stuck."

☞ Billy-Bob is drowning his sorrows in a bar. Zeke comes over to see what's troubling him. "I just went to the bathroom," explains Billy-Bob, "and I saw what someone wrote on the wall. It said, 'For a good time with a red-hot chick, call Lulu-Belle LaBlanc'. That's my Lulu-Belle they're talking about. We been engaged for two years." "Don't get all upset," says Zeke. "There's all sorts of morons come in here; someone probably wrote it as a joke." "I'm not upset 'cos they wrote it," says Billy-Bob. "I'm upset 'cos someone came along and crossed her telephone number out."

☞ Dick comes home from a business trip only to be told that his wife, Sarah, has been having an affair. He confronts her and she breaks down, confessing all; she tells him everything – everything except the name of her lover. "Who was it?" cries Dick. "Was it Bill? I bet it was Bill. How could he? He was best man at my wedding!" "It wasn't Bill," sobs Sarah. "I know!" cries Dick. "It must have been Harry. That bastard; we've played golf together every Sunday for the last ten years!" "It wasn't Harry," sobs Sarah. "Hah! Then it was that old goat Tom. He's always had an eye for the ladies, even when we were at school! I'll beat him to a pulp!" "No," sobs Sarah. "It wasn't Tom." Dick pauses for a moment, then says, "So, basically, you're saying that none of my friends is good enough for you."

☞ Donald Duck is talking to his lawyer. The lawyer says, "I understand that you wish to divorce your wife on the grounds of insanity." "I didn't say she was crazy," replies Donald. "I said she was f***ing Goofy."

☞ Glenda goes to the doctor with a strained groin. "How often do you have sex?" asks the doctor. Glenda thinks for a moment, then says, "I have sex on Mondays, Tuesdays, Wednesdays, Fridays and Sundays. So that's five times a week." "It would be better if you cut back a little," says the doctor. "I'd advise you to cut out Tuesdays." "Tuesdays?" exclaims Glenda. "I couldn't possibly do that. My husband's a long-haul pilot; Tuesday's the only night he's at home."

☞ Harry and Pete spend a week with their old friend Simon and his wife. On the day they leave, Harry and Pete pack their car and say their goodbyes. "Thank you for having us," says Harry. "The accommodation was fantastic, the food was great and I really enjoyed screwing your wife." "What did you say?" says the shocked Simon. "I said, I really enjoyed screwing your wife," says Harry. "'Bye now." Harry then starts the car, and he and Pete drive off. After a few moments, the astonished Pete says, "Did you mean that? Did you really screw Simon's wife?" "Yes," says Harry. "Well, why did you have to tell him?" asks Pete. "Why not?" says Harry. "Because you'll have hurt his feelings," says Pete. "Why couldn't you just have lied about it?" "I did lie about it," replies Harry. "I didn't enjoy screwing her all."

☞ George becomes obsessed by golf and takes every opportunity to sneak in a game; in fact, he gets up at six every Sunday morning so he can be the first on the local course. One Sunday, he gets out of bed to find it's pouring with rain. Despite the bad weather, he figures he might get a game in, so he gets dressed, kisses his wife Mildred goodbye and sets off in his car. As he's driving along, he hears a weather forecast saying that severe thunder storms are expected all day. The weather's obviously not going to get any better, and the golf course is the last place you want to be in a thunderstorm, so George reluctantly turns the car around and heads for home. By the time he gets back, it's only seven o'clock. He figures Mildred will still be asleep, so he creeps upstairs, slips into the bedroom, gets undressed and slides into bed next to her. Mildred sleepily says, "Morning, darling." "Morning, dear," whispers George. "Filthy weather outside." "I know," replies Mildred. "And can you believe my idiot husband is out playing golf?"

☞ Harry is having a drink in a bar. He's looking very upset. The barman asks what the problem is. "I'm in terrible trouble," says Harry. "I got caught having sex with my neighbour." "Well, that is pretty bad," agrees the barman. "Did your wife catch you at it?" "No," replies Harry. "*His* wife caught us at it."

☞ Harry is watching Who Wants To Be A Millionaire? with his wife, June. He turns to June and says, "Do you want sex?" June replies, "No." Harry says, "Is that your final answer?" June says, "Yes." Harry says, "Is it all right if I phone a friend?"

☞ Hillary Clinton goes to a fortune-teller. "I see terrible things," says the fortune-teller. "I see that your husband will die a horrible death!" "Oh, my God!" cries Hillary. "Will I be acquitted?"

☞ It's Easter, and little Johnny sneaks into the chicken coop and takes all the eggs. He then sits at the kitchen table, and paints all the eggs in gay Easter colours. When Johnny's mother comes back, she is not best pleased. She tells Johnny to take all the eggs back where he found them. Johnny does as he's told and puts the eggs back in the straw. The rooster his been watching this activity with interest. When Johnny leaves he looks into the chicken coop. After a moment's pause there's an almighty squawk of rage. Then the rooster runs out into the yard and starts kicking the hell out of the peacock.

☞ Jane is married to George, an English professor. One day, she comes home and finds George in bed with the cleaning lady. "George!" she exclaims. "How could you do anything so amazing? I'm surprised at you." "No, no, no," snaps George. "*I* am surprised. *You* are amazed."

☞ Larry comes home early from work, walks into his bedroom and finds his wife in bed with another man. "What's going on?" exclaims Larry. "Who is this man?" Larry's wife thinks for a moment, then says, "That's a good question." She turns to the other man and says, "What exactly *is* your name?"

☞ Little Johnny goes into his parent's bedroom and finds them having sex. "So what's going on?" asks Johnny. Father is taken aback. "I'm… er… I'm just filling your mother's tank," he says. "She must get pretty low mileage," says Johnny. "The milkman filled her up this morning."

☞ Little Johnny is in the school playground when he sees his daddy's car go past and drive into the woods. Little Johnny wants to see what's going on, so he runs into the woods after it. He soon finds the car and sees see his daddy and his mother's sister, Auntie Karen, locked in a passionate embrace. Little Johnny runs straight home to tell his mother. "Mummy, I was in the playground," he says, "and I saw daddy drive into the woods with Auntie Karen. And I went to look. And he was giving Auntie Karen a big kiss and helping her to take her shirt off. Then Auntie Karen helped him take his pants off. And then…" "Stop right there, Johnny," interrupts his mother. "This is such an interesting story, I'd like you to save it until dinner tonight. I'd like to see the look on daddy's face when you tell it to him." That evening, the family sits down for dinner and mummy asks little Johnny to tell his story again. So off he goes once more: "I was in the playground and I saw daddy drive into the woods with Auntie Karen. And I went to look. And he was giving Auntie Karen a big kiss and helping her to take her shirt off. Then Auntie Karen helped him take his pants off. And then Auntie Karen and daddy started doing the same thing that mummy and Uncle Jack used to do when daddy was away in the army…"

☞ Married couples need to have affairs – anything to break the monogamy.

☞ Tom has been having an affair with his Italian secretary. One day, she tells him that she's pregnant and she wants to have the baby. Tom takes this news in his stride and sends the secretary back to Italy. He tells her that, when the baby is born, she's to send him a postcard with the code-word 'spaghetti' on it. He will then fly over to visit her and make arrangements for child support. Nine months later, Tom arrives home and is confronted by his wife. "Tom," she says, "do you know anyone in Italy?" "I don't think so," replies Tom nervously. "Why?" "It's just that we've had a very odd postcard from there," she says. "It seems to have a menu on the back." She hands Tom the postcard. He reads it and faints dead away. The card reads, "Spaghetti, spaghetti, spaghetti: two with meatballs, one without."

☞ Two Aberdeen men, Tam and Jimmie, are talking in a pub. Tam is telling Jimmie a few home truths. "Your lassie's a right old slapper," says Tam. "She's been sleeping with every man in toon!" "Aye, well, it could be worse," says Jimmie. "How could it be worse?" says Tam. Jimmie replies, "Well, we could be living in London."

☞ Two men decide to give up their soft city jobs and try their hand at prospecting in the Canadian wilderness. They go to a supply store in a remote Canadian town, and buy all the things they'll need for the next year. Two huge piles of supplies are assembled for each man, on top of which are two fur-lined boards with holes in them. "What the hell are those?" asks one of the men. "There's no women where you guys are heading," says the storekeeper. "Some guys find those boards mighty handy." "We're not that pathetic," says the other man. "We're not going to need crap like that." His buddy agrees, "You've got to be pretty desperate to use a plank of wood." "Tell you what," says the storekeeper. "You both take a board, and if you haven't used it by the time you come back next year, I'll give you your money back." The two men both agree that this sounds fair, so off they go. A year later, one of the men comes in to buy more supplies. "Howdy," says the storekeeper. "How's it going?" "Not bad," says the man. "Where's your buddy?" asks the storekeeper. "I shot him," replies the man. "I caught the bastard in bed with my board."

☞ What did Harry say when he found his best friend in bed with his wife? "Bad dog!"

MARRIAGE – ANNIVERSARIES

"We've just marked our tenth wedding anniversary on the calendar – and threw darts at it."
Phyllis Diller

☞ An elderly couple revisit their honeymoon hotel every time their wedding anniversary comes round. One year, they're shown to their room, only to find that there's been a mistake; it seems they've been given a whole suite rather than just a double room. "Oh, dear," says the old man to the porter. "I think there's been a mistake in the booking; this is the bridal suite." "Don't worry, sir," says the porter. "There's no pressure to perform. If we put you in the ballroom, we wouldn't be expecting you to dance."

☞ Harry's very cheap. Last week it was his diamond anniversary, so he bought his wife a pack of playing cards.

☞ On our tenth wedding anniversary, my wife and I booked the same hotel suite as we did on our wedding night. Everything was exactly as before, only this time *I* was the one crying in the bathroom.

☞ On their 25th wedding anniversary, a man takes his wife to the hotel where they spent their honeymoon. The couple book the same room as on their wedding night and find it's exactly as they remembered it. "Oh, darling," says the wife, "tonight will be exactly the same as our first night of wedded bliss." "Yeah," said the husband, "except this time it'll be me lying on the bed screaming, 'It's too big! It's too big'!"

MARRIAGE – DIVORCE

☞ A couple are getting divorced, but deciding over the custody of the children is a problem. In the resulting court hearing, the mother protests to the judge that she brought the children into this world, so she should retain custody of them. The judge asks the father what he has to say. The father thinks for a moment, then stands up and says, "Your Honour, when I put a fifty-pence piece in a chocolate machine and a chocolate bar comes out, does that chocolate bar belong to me or the machine?"

☞ A lawyer approaches a witness in court and says, "Are you married?" "No," replies the woman, "I'm divorced." "I see," says the lawyer. "And what did your husband do before you separated?" The woman replies, "A lot of things he thought I didn't know about."

☞ A woman goes to her lawyer to organise a divorce. "And on what grounds do you want to separate?" asks the lawyer. "All my husband wants to do is make love," replies the woman. "Really?" says the lawyer. "Most women would rather enjoy that." "Most women do," replies the woman. "That's why I want a divorce."

☞ How is an ex-husband like an inflamed appendix? It caused you a lot of pain, and after it was removed you found you didn't need it anyway.

☞ Ruby gets pulled over by the police for speeding. She hands over her driving licence. The picture doesn't look much like Ruby, so the policeman decides to test her; he asks her what her age is. "I'm forty-five," says Ruby. "That's incorrect," says the policeman, "According to the date of birth on this licence, you're sixty-five." "Yes; well I'm not counting the twenty years I was married," replies Ruby. "Why not?" asks the policeman. Ruby replies, "You call that *living*?"

☞ The definition of irreconcilable differences: when she melts down her wedding ring to make it into a bullet.

☞ The number one cause of divorce is marriage.

☞ There are two sides to every divorce: yours and shithead's.

☞ Tom is in court trying to divorce his wife. "On what grounds do you want this divorce?" asks the judge. "Adultery," replies Tom. "On one occasion I saw my wife sitting next to the milkman and he put his arms round her three times." "Ridiculous," says the judge. "Who has arms that long?"

MARRIAGE – ECONOMIES

☞ After our last child was born, my wife told me we had to cut back on expenses. She said I had to give up drinking beer: so I gave it up, even though I didn't drink much. Then, the other day, I came across one of her shopping receipts and saw that she'd spent $65 on make-up. "Wait a minute!" I said. "You said we had to cut back. I've given up beer and you haven't given up anything! Why don't you give up make-up? You're spending a fortune on it" "I buy that make-up for you," she says, "so I can look pretty for you!" "Hell," I said, "that's what the beer was for!" I'm not sure when she's coming back.

☞ Tom gets home and finds his wife washing a dress in the sink. "Don't you normally dry-clean your clothes?" asks Tom. "Yes," replies his wife, "but it's getting so expensive I thought I'd do it myself. Cleaning this dress at home has made us £15 richer." "It has?" exclaims Tom. "Quick! Do it again!"

MARRIAGE – NEWLYWEDS

☞ When a man opens the door of his car for his wife, you can be sure of one of two things: either the car is new, or the wife is.

☞ My wife's mother is full of advice. When we got married, she told my wife to preserve her mystique by never appearing before me fully naked – all through our honeymoon she wore a bobble hat and mittens.

☞ Things not to say on your wedding night:
Sure I laughed, but everybody looks funny naked.
You woke me up for that?
Hurry it up. I only rented the room for an hour.
Pass me the remote control, will you?
On second thoughts, this will go better with the lights off.
Hope you're looking as good when I'm sober.
You're pretty good at this; ever thought of doing it for a living?
It's nice being in bed with a chick I don't have to inflate first.
Sorry about the label; I'm terrible with names.
Can you keep it down? Mummy's a light sleeper.

☞ A young bride is having problems with her sex life, so she goes to see her doctor. "Doctor," she says, "I was a virgin on my wedding night and when my husband undressed and revealed his cock – " "Excuse me," interrupts the doctor. "I'd rather call it an 'organ'." "Really?" exclaims the bride. "Well, his looks more like an oboe."

☞ A young couple go on their honeymoon. When they get back, the bride calls her mother. "Mama," she sobs, "it's so horrible. The honeymoon was wonderful and romantic, but as soon as we got home, he started using the most disgusting language – things I'd never heard before: I mean horrible, horrible four-letter words! You've got to come and take me home, Mama!" Mama tries to calm the situation down. "Darling," she says, "don't cry. You need to stay with your husband and work things out. Now, tell me, what was so awful? You're a big girl; you must have heard four-letter words before. What did he say to you?" "Please don't make me repeat them, Mama," sobs the daughter, "They're so disgusting." "You're not a baby," says Mama sternly. "Tell me what these four-letter words were." The daughter gulps back her sobs and replies, "Dust: iron: wash: and cook." There's a second's silence, then Mama says. "Pack your bags. I'll be over in ten minutes."

☞ Dick is staying in a cheap hotel. The walls are very thin and Dick is alarmed to find that the people in the next room are honeymooners. All night long, he's keep awake by the sound of frenzied love-making. Eventually, Dick has had enough. He pounds on the wall and shouts, "Can't you shut up? I'm trying to get to sleep!" There's no reaction: just more sounds of grunting, torrid sex – someone's getting a real pounding! "Damn it!" shouts Dick. "Knock it off! I'm trying to get to sleep!" A man's voice calls back weakly, "For God's sake shout louder. She can't hear you!"

☞ In the first year of marriage, the man speaks and the woman listens. In the second year of marriage, the woman speaks and the man listens. In the third year of marriage, they both speak and the neighbours listen.

☞ June has only been married a week when she tearfully rings her friend Betsy. "Tom and I had such a dreadful fight last night," sobs June. "Don't worry too much," says Betsy. "All newlyweds have silly little arguments." "I know," sniffs June, "but what am I going to do with the body?"

☞ On the first morning of his honeymoon, Harry surprises his new bride with breakfast in bed. He puts down a tray with a plate of bacon, eggs, mushrooms and sausages, fresh orange juice, a rack of toast and a nice pot of tea. "What do you think?" says Harry. "Oh, Harry: it's wonderful," says his wife. Harry continues, "Well, make sure you remember how it's all laid out: because this is how I want it every morning."

☞ A newly-married husband lays down some rules. "I'll be home when I want, if I want, and at what time I want," he insists, "and I don't expect any hassle from you. Also, I expect a decent meal to be on the table every evening, unless I tell you otherwise. I'll go hunting, fishing, boozing and card-playing with my buddies whenever I want. Those are my rules. Any comments?" His new bride replies, "No, that's fine with me: but just understand this; there'll be sex here at seven o'clock every night – whether you're around or not."

☞ On the night before her wedding, an Italian bride-to-be asks her mother how she can make her husband happy. "Well, there's all sorts of things a wife can do with her husband in bed..." replies mother. "Mama," interrupts her daughter, "I know how to make love! What I need is your meatball recipe!"

☞ An Italian couple, Luigi and Julia, are on the first night of their honeymoon. Unfortunately, they are both very naïve and don't have any idea what to do. In desperation, Luigi calls his mother. "Listen," says Mama, "it's easy. Just hold each other in each other's arms. You'll soon get the idea." The couple do as Mama suggests, but nothing happens. Luigi rings home again. "Okay," says mamma, "I want you to both get undressed and get into bed. Then do what comes naturally." The young couple follow this advice, but it still doesn't lead to anything. Luigi phones Mama again. "Mama mia!" she cries. "All right; what you got to do now is get on top of Julia. Then just get on with it! Okay?" Luigi hangs up the phone and gets on top of Julia, but apart from squashing her a little, nothing's going on. Luigi phones home again. "I don't believe it!" cries the exasperated Mama. "What kind of idiot are you? Listen to me. Find her hairy place and put your big sticky-out thing in it. You understand, you moron?" "Yes, Mama," says Luigi. Ten minutes later, Mama's phone rings again. "Hi, Mama," says Luigi. "I've got my nose in her armpit. What do I do now?"

☞ When a newly-married man looks happy, we know why. But when a man who's been married ten years looks happy, we wonder why.

☞ A newly-married couple are in their hotel honeymoon suite when the wife bangs her foot on the bathroom door. "Oh dear, honeybun!" says the husband. "Come here and I'll kiss your tootsie-wootsie better for you." She comes over to him and he kisses her toe better. Things develop, and soon they're making love on the bed. Afterwards, the woman gets up to go to the bathroom and again bangs her foot on the door. Her husband calls out, "Will you watch where you're going, you clumsy cow?"

MARRIAGE – SEX

☞ My wife always closes her eyes when we make love; she hates to see me having a good time.

"My psychiatrist said my wife and I should have sex every night. Now we'll never see each other!"

Rodney Dangerfield

☞ A husband and wife are in bed together. The husband says, "Do you enjoy sex with me – because it doesn't sound like it?" "What do you mean?" asks his wife. The husband replies, "Well, my mates say their wives moan and groan a bit when they're being made love to; you don't." "Okay," replies the wife. "I'll do it, if that's what you want." So the husband gets down to business and his wife says, "Oh, you wouldn't believe the price of bread. The cat's made a mess on the carpet again. Why don't you mow the lawn?"

☞ A husband and wife are in bed together. The wife says, "Do you want to hear something that'll make you happy and sad at exactly the same time?" "All right," says the husband. "Okay," says the wife. "Your dick's much bigger than your brother's."

☞ A man goes to the doctor to ask for help. It seems his wife just isn't interested in sex any more. The doctor gives him a small bottle of pills. "These are experimental," he says. "We don't know all the side-effects, and the tests carried out so far indicate they're very powerful. You mustn't give her more than one!" The man goes home and wonders how he's going to ask his wife to take a pep pill. While he's having dinner, inspiration strikes; he'll just drop a pill in her coffee. He waits until his wife goes into the kitchen, then drops a pill in her coffee cup. Unfortunately, his hand's shaking and he accidentally drops in two pills. The man's very worried; the doctor told him he mustn't give her more than one! Inspiration strikes again. He stirs the pills into the coffee, then drinks exactly half of it. A moment later, his wife comes in and drinks the remaining coffee before taking the empty cup into the kitchen. The man wonders how long the pill will take to work. He doesn't have to wait long. Seconds later, his wife steps into the room dripping with sweat and with a wild look in her eye. Tearing off her blouse, she pants, "I want a man inside me. I want a man inside me right now!" The man gulps and wipes the sweat from his forehead. "You know what?" he squeaks. "So do I."

☞ A man is having a drink in a country pub when he's approached by an old yokel carrying a sack. "You see this sack?" says the yokel. "In here I got a ferret. This ferret'll give you the best blow-jobs you've ever had. If you want, you can buy him for £50." The man's not impressed and tells the yokel to go away. "If you don't believe me," says the yokel, "why not take it round the back and try it out?" The man decides he might as well and goes round the back of the pub with the old rustic. The ferret is brought out of the sack and proceeds to give the man an incredible blow-job. After they've finished, the man gives the yokel £50 and runs home with the ferret. The man finds his wife in the kitchen and hands her the animal. "See that ferret?" he says. "That animal just gave me the best oral sex I ever had." "Oh, yes?" says the wife. "And what do you want me to do with it?" The man replies, "I want you to teach it to cook, then piss off."

☞ A man says to his wife, "You know, from the first time I saw you, I've wanted to make love to you terribly." She replies, "Well, you've certainly done that."

☞ A marriage counsellor is suggesting ways in which a couple can improve their sex life. "Why not vary your position?" he says. "There are all sorts of ways you can do it. For example, you might try the wheelbarrow; that's where your wife gets on her hands and knees, you reach down and lift her legs and off you go!" The husband is eager to try this out as soon as they get home. "Well, okay," says his hesitant wife, "but on two conditions: first, if it hurts, you'll stop straight away: and second, you have to promise we won't go past my mother's house."

☞ A middle-aged couple get married after years of celibate engagement. However, the honeymoon proves to be a disaster. The man confronts his bride at the breakfast table. "I know I promised to fill the void in your life," he says, "but I hadn't realised it was so bloody enormous."

☞ A wife approaches her husband wearing the same sexy negligée she wore on their wedding night. "Honey," she says, "do you remember this? I wore it on our honeymoon." "Yes, I do remember it," replies the husband. "And do you remember what you said to me that night?" asks his wife. The husband replies, "As I recall, I said, 'Baby, I'm going to suck the life out of those big tits and screw your brains out'." "That's right," giggles his wife. "And what are you going to say to me tonight?" The husband looks her up and down and says, "Mission accomplished."

☞ According to a recent survey, what do most men want their wives to do while they're having sex? The cooking and cleaning.

☞ I wouldn't say I was boring in bed, but my wife sets an egg-timer to go off after two minutes in case she dozes off in the middle.

☞ Just before his wedding, a young man goes to his father and asks how he'll know if his bride is a virgin. "It's easy," says dad. "If she appears nervous and confused, then she's a virgin. On the other hand, if she looks like she knows what she's doing, she's probably an old slapper." After the honeymoon, the son comes home with a smile on his face. "She was a virgin," he says. "She was really confused. In fact, she was so mixed up she stuck the pillow under her backside instead of her head."

☞ Murphy and his new bride go to the doctor. "The trouble is," says Murphy, "the wife and I being such good Catholics, we've never had any sex education at all. We're not quite sure how to do it." The doctor obligingly explains the ins and outs of sexual relations, but Murphy and his wife are left scratching their heads. "I'm not sure we got all that, doctor," says Murphy. "Have you not got some pictures?" So the doctor gets out a text-book and shows them a series of diagrams. "No, that's not much clearer," says Murphy. "Have you got anything else?" The doctor happens to have a naughty DVD in his office, so he puts it in his computer and treats the couple to half an hour of hardcore viewing. Murphy and his wife are still not happy. "It was all a bit confusing, doctor," says Murphy, "what with the arms and legs all thrashing about. Could you not make it any clearer?" The exasperated doctor decides there's only one thing left to do. He pulls up Mrs Murphy's dress, pulls down her underwear, leans her over his desk and has it away with her. Finally he finishes and falls back in his chair. "Was that clear enough for you?" he asks. "Very clear: thank you, doctor," says Murphy. "I do have one question, though." "What?" replies the doctor. Murphy says, "How often do I have to bring her in?"

☞ My sex life went downhill after I got married. I use to call our waterbed the Dead Sea.

☞ My wife and I have been into S&M for quite a while now; she snores and I masturbate.

☞ My wife and I were having marital problems, so I bought a waterbed to try and spice up our sex life. It didn't work; we simply drifted further apart.

☞ One morning a woman tells her husband about an odd dream she had. "I was at a penis auction," she tells him, "and big penises were going for £1,000 and little penises were going for £100." "Really?" replies her husband. "And what about a penis like mine?" "No bids," replies the wife. Hurt by this comment, the husband decides to get revenge. Next morning, he says to his wife, "I had a dream about a vagina auction last night. Really big, loose vaginas were going for £1 and small, tight vaginas were going for £10,000." "Oh, yes?" replies his wife. "And what about a vagina like mine? "That wasn't for sale," replies the husband. "They were holding the auction in it."

☞ Sometimes it seems that marriage and paying a call-girl for sex are very similar: except paying a call-girl for sex works out a lot cheaper... and involves sex.

☞ Soon after we were married I discovered that my wife is bisexual; she only does it twice a year.

☞ The three stages of marital sex: honeymoon sex, where you have sex three or four times a night, vacation sex, where you have sex ten or twelve times a year, and oral sex – where you stand on opposite sides of the room and shout, "Screw you!"

☞ Two men are pushing their shopping trolleys round a supermarket. Neither is looking where he's going and their trolleys collide. "I'm sorry," says the first man. "I was looking for my wife." "That's a coincidence," says the second man. "I've lost mine, too. Have you seen her? She has a 40-24-38 figure, blonde hair and blue eyes, and she's wearing a little yellow T-shirt with white hot pants." "Wow," says the first man, his jaw dropping. "So what does your wife look like?" asks the second man. "Screw her!" says the first man. "Let's find yours!"

☞ Why do married men hang strobe lights from their bedroom ceilings? To create the illusion that their wives are moving during sex.

MARRIAGE – WEDDINGS

☞ I'm not saying that Mary gets married too often, but her bridal gown is wash-and-wear.

☞ A woman walks into a church where a wedding's about to take place. An usher says, "Are you a friend of the bride?" The woman replies, "No, I'm the groom's mother."

☞ It's the morning of the wedding, and the young bride is dressing for her big day. Suddenly, the bride realises she can't find her white shoes, so she borrows a pair from one of her bridesmaids. Unfortunately, the new shoes are too small and wearing them is agony, but she hobbles off to the church as best she can. After the wedding her new husband, a retired sea captain, notices that his bride is in distress and offers to carry her to the honeymoon suite. A couple of wedding guests see the captain carry the bride away and, assuming the wedding night is starting early, go and eavesdrop at the couple's door. Standing with their ears pressed against the door, the two guests hear sounds of grunting as the captain struggles to remove his bride's right shoe. It finally comes away, and the young woman gives a cry of relief. "Bloody hell!" exclaims the captain. "That was tight!" "See?" says the first guest to the other. "I told you she was a virgin." Suddenly they hear more grunts and another cry. "And that one was even tighter!" exclaims the captain. The second guest sighs and says, "Once a sailor, always a sailor."

"My fiancée and I are having a little disagreement. What I want is a big church wedding with bridesmaids and flowers and a no-expense-spared reception, and what he wants is to break off our engagement."
Sally Poplin

☞ Tom's very happy. He and his girlfriend have been dating for more than a year, and have decided to get married. Everything's going great, but Tom is a little bothered by his girlfriend's mother, Mrs Jones. Mrs Jones is very sexy and good-looking and she's prone to flirt with Tom, which makes him feel uncomfortable. One day, Mrs Jones calls Tom and asks him over to her house to check the wedding invitations. Tom drives over to her house and finds her all alone, wearing nothing but a pair of high-heeled slippers and a towel. "Tom," she says, "I have desires for you that I can't overcome. I know it's wrong, but just once I'd like you to make love to me: just once before you marry my daughter." Tom gulps. He doesn't have a clue what to say. Mrs Jones slips through her bedroom door and throws out the towel. "I'm waiting for you, Tom," she says, "If you're up for it – if you're man enough – all you have to do is come in here and get me." Tom stands there for a moment, then makes up his mind. He turns around and goes to the front door. Tom opens the door and finds Mr Jones standing there with tears in his eyes. Tom's future father-in-law hugs him. "I'm sorry to put you to that test, my boy," he says, "but I didn't want my little girl marrying an immoral, two-timing skunk. You passed with flying colours. We couldn't ask for a better son-in-law. Welcome to the family!" And the moral of this story? Always keep your condoms in your car.

☞ On the day of her wedding, a bride goes to her mother and confesses that she's not a virgin. "How can I convince my husband he's the first?" she asks. "It's easy," replies mother. "Put an elastic band round your thigh and when he goes into you, snap it against your leg. It'll sound like your hymen breaking." The bride puts this plan into action. That night, when her new husband mounts her, she snaps the band against her thigh. "What the hell was that?" exclaims her husband. "It must have been my hymen snapping," replies the wife. "Then snap it back again!" shouts the husband. "It's caught round my bloody bollocks!"

MENTAL HEALTH

☞ A man phones a mental home and asks the duty nurse if there's anybody in Room 30. The nurse goes and checks, then tells the man that the room's empty. "Thank goodness," says the man. "That means I must really have escaped this time!"

☞ Harry goes up to Dick and says, "Hi there, Dick." "Hi, Harry," replies Dick. "Aren't you going to ask me how I am?" "Sorry," says Harry. "How are you?" Dick says, "Don't ask."

"I have CDO. It's Obsessive Compulsive Disorder – only in alphabetical order, like it should be."
Spike Donner

☞ I was feeling very depressed last week. I went to my psychiatrist and told him I was suicidal. He asked me to pay in advance.

☞ A doctor visits a man in a mental ward. The man has his ear pressed to the wall and is listening intently. The doctor looks at the man's notes and reads that the man has been engaged in this behaviour every day for more than a year. The doctor goes to stand next to the man and presses his own ear to the wall. After a minute, the doctor turns to the man and says, "I can't hear anything." The man replies, "I know. It's been like that for months."

☞ A journalist visits a recently-opened psychiatric hospital to interview the chief psychiatrist for his newspaper. "So how do you decide whether a patient should be institutionalised?" asks the journalist. "Well," replies the psychiatrist, "usually we fill a bath with water; then we offer the patient a teaspoon, a teacup and a bucket, and ask them to empty the bath." "I see," says the journalist. "So a sane person would choose the bucket, because it's bigger than the spoon or the teacup." "Not really," says the psychiatrist. "A sane person would just pull the plug. So, would you like a room with an east view or a west view?"

☞ What happens when a psychiatrist and a prostitute spend the night together? In the morning, both say: "That'll be £120, please."

☞ A man is talking to his psychiatrist, "It was terrible," he says. "I was away on business and I sent my wife a telegram to say I'd be home a day early. When I got back, I found her in bed with my best friend. How could she? How could she do that to me?" "Don't be too hard on her," says the psychiatrist. "Perhaps she didn't get the telegram."

☞ Bernard went to a psychiatrist a couple of weeks ago. He felt people kept taking advantage of him. He finished redecorating the consulting rooms this morning.

☞ A man rushes into his doctor's surgery. "Doctor," he says, "you remember those voices I was hearing in my head?" "Yes," says the doctor. "Well I can't hear them any more," says the man. "I think I'm going deaf!"

☞ Psychiatrists say that one out of every four people is mentally ill. Check three friends. If they're okay, you're it.

☞ A man walks into a psychiatrist's office sobbing his eyes out. He lies down on the couch and says, "Doctor, you've got to help me. I've got the most terrible problem. I just can't seem to make any friends." The doctor nods and starts to make some notes. The man continues, "So come on! What are you going to do to help me, you great, fat, ugly bastard?"

☞ Never get into an argument with a schizophrenic and say, "Just who do you think you are?"

☞ A psychiatrist is feeling depressed and tells his wife that he's making an appointment with a colleague, Dr Bloomfield. "But you're so much better than Bloomfield," protests his wife. "Can't you use your knowledge and experience to cure yourself?" "Of course I could," replies the psychiatrist, "but I charge twice as much as he does."

☞ I suffer from aibohphobia – the fear of palindromes.

☞ A woman goes to see a psychiatrist about her mental problems. After the woman has tearfully described her condition, the psychiatrist nods slowly and says, "I see; I see. Could you please lie on the floor under the window?" The woman complies with this request. The psychiatrist then says, "Now, move over to the space next to the door." Again, the woman does as she is asked. "Thank you," says the psychiatrist. "Now, please go and lie in front of the bookcase." The woman does so, and the psychiatrist mutters to himself as he jots down notes on his writing pad. "Yes, yes," he says. "That's very interesting. Now, please move yourself to the other side of the window..." "Excuse me," says the woman, "but is this part of my therapy?" "Oh no," says the psychiatrist. "I'm having the room redecorated next week and I thought I'd change where I put the couch."

☞ I live in my own little world: but it's okay; they know me here.

☞ A young psychiatrist gets into a lift with an old man. Suddenly, the psychiatrist realises that the old man is Dr Berkowitz, the noted clinical psychologist. "Excuse me, Dr Berkowitz," says the psychiatrist, "but can I ask your advice? How do you remain detached from your patients? I have to listen to lots of terrible stories when patients consult me, and I find it hard to remain objective." "What was that?" replies Berkowitz. The psychiatrist repeats himself, "I was asking how you keep your sense of perspective when you listen to patients." "Listen?" says Berkowitz with a shrug. "Who listens?"

☞ Harry and Tom are walking through the park when a beautiful naked woman runs past them. A few moments later, a man in a white coat hurries past them chasing after the woman. The man is closely followed by a second man in a white coat who is carrying a bucket of sand. "I wonder what that's about?" says Harry. "Oh, I know all about it," says Tom. "That naked woman's a crazy nymphomaniac. She's always escaping from the local asylum." "I see," says Harry. "So the two men in white coats work at the asylum and they're trying to get her back." "That's right," says Tom. "So why was the second man carrying a bucket of sand?" asks Harry. "That's his handicap," explains Tom. "He caught her last time."

> **"People who say they hear voices in their heads are meant to be crazy: as opposed to where, exactly? Hearing voices in your legs – now that's crazy."**
> *Jimmy Carr*

☞ Therapy may help, but screaming obscenities is a lot cheaper.

☞ Man, to psychiatrist: "Doctor, it's terrible. I don't know whether to cut my throat or blow my brains out." Psychiatrist (nodding): "I see, I see. So you have difficulty making decisions?"

> **"Jennifer Aniston goes to Malibu to shout at the sea. I drink Malibu and shout at pigeons."**
> *Bill Bailey*

☞ A general noticed one of his soldiers behaving oddly. The soldier would pick up any piece of paper he found, frown, say, "That's not it," and put it down again. This went on for some time, until the general arranged to have the soldier psychologically tested. The psychologist concluded that the soldier was deranged, wrote out his discharge from the army and handed it to the soldier, who picked it up and said, "Ah! That's it!"

☞ I used to be an arrogant, self-important know-it-all, so I went to a psychiatrist to see if he could help me. Now I'm perfect.

☞ Mrs Cohen is talking to her husband, complaining about their son. "With all the trouble he's been causing recently, and now we send him to a child psychiatrist and find out he's a mental case. He's got the Oedipus Complex! Who heard of such a thing? Where did he catch it? Not from my side of the family: from yours, perhaps? Far more likely, I would have thought, what with your cousin Jacob and his disgusting habits. Oedipus Complex! My life, what am I going to tell the neighbours?" Mr Cohen interrupts. "Ruth – enough already. Oedipus, schmedipus: as long as he loves his mother…"

☞ Once I suffered from a multiple personality disorder, but the doctor gave us some pills and now we're all feeling great.

☞ Three old women are boasting about how much their sons love them. One says, "My son booked me on a £10,000 cruise holiday for my birthday." "That's nothing," says the second woman. "Yesterday, my son bought me a new car that cost £15,000." "I've got you both beat," says the third woman. "My boy goes to Harley Street three times a week where he spends more than £20,000 a year on psychiatrist's fees – and all he talks about is me."

> **"Why is it that when we talk to God, we're said to be praying, but when God talks to us, we're schizophrenic?"**
> *Lily Tomlin*

☞ Three patients are waiting in a psychiatrist's waiting room. The first patient turns to the second and says, "Why are you here, buddy?" The second answers, "I'm Napoleon, but nobody seems to be believe me." "You reckon you're Napoleon?" says the first patient. "Whatever gave you that idea?" The second replies, "I have it on very good authority; God told me." The third patient throws down his newspaper and shouts, "For the last time: no, I did not!"

> **"Being in therapy is great. I spend an hour just talking about myself. It's kind of like being the guy on a date."**
> *Caroline Rhea*

MENTAL HEALTH – MEMORY

☞ A 64-year-old woman has a baby boy with the help of fertility treatment. When she comes out of hospital, her friends come over to say hello to the new arrival. "So when can we see the baby?" asks one of the friends. "We have to wait until it starts crying," says the 64-year-old mother. "Why?" asks the friend. "Can't we look at the baby while he's asleep?" "No," replies the mother, "we have to wait until he cries. I forgot where I put him."

☞ A man takes his sick wife to the hospital. The doctor examines her and says, "We've narrowed it down to two possibilities. Your wife either has Alzheimer's or AIDS." "Oh, my God!" says the man. "What can I do?" "Well, I've discussed it with my colleagues," says the doctor, "and our plan is this; drive her out into the countryside and dump her. Then, if she ever finds her way home, don't sleep with her."

☞ An ageing actor tries to get back into the business after many years of retirement. After a dozen unsuccessful auditions, he finally lands a part in a play. "It's not a large role," the director tells him, "but it's an important one. You play the grandfather, and at the start of the second act you come on stage with a rose held in the fingers of your right hand. You go centre-stage, face the audience, sniff the rose and say, 'Ah: the sweet smell of my mistress'." The actor is happy to take the part, and is quite relieved at the small number of lines he has to learn; his memory is not what it was. Things go well during rehearsals, and on the opening night the old man comes out on cue and says his lines. Unfortunately, the audience reacts to his performance by bursting into laugher. The old man is astonished. He sees the director in the wings and goes over to ask what's happened. "What's the matter?" says the old man. "Did I forget some of the words?" "No, you idiot!" replies the director. "You forgot the rose!"

☞ An Alzheimer's chat-up line: Do I come here often?

☞ An elderly couple are having a drive in the countryside. After stopping for lunch at a restaurant, they head for home. However, after fifteen minutes the woman realises she's left her glasses on the restaurant table. Her husband wearily turns the car round to go back, but doesn't stop moaning at her the whole way. He whines on, telling her she's virtually senile and if her memory gets any worse he'll put her in a home. They get back to the restaurant and the distraught woman steps out to retrieve her spectacles. Her husband shouts after her, "And while you're in there, pick up my hat!"

☞ There are three signs of old age. The first is memory loss...and I can't remember the other two.

MICE

☞ A farmer hears a commotion coming from his barn, so he goes to investigate. Inside, he's astonished to see a sex-crazed mouse having sex with the farm cat. The cat has clearly not consented to this ordeal, and runs off when the mouse is distracted by the appearance of the farmer. The farmer thinks this is the most amazing thing he's ever seen in his life, but is soon even more astonished when the mouse leaps on to his best Jersey cow and starts having his evil way with her. The mouse then repeats the performance with the farmer's mare and his dog. The mouse is momentarily exhausted by all this activity, so the farmer takes the opportunity to catch him and put him in a jar. "My wife's got to see this critter," says the farmer, and he runs into the kitchen. "You'll never believe what I've got here," says the farmer. "It's the most incredible animal I ever saw." "Yeah," replies his wife. "So what is it that's so incredible?" The farmer reveals the jar containing the panting mouse. The farmer's wife screams and jumps on the table. "Get out of here!" she yells, "and take that sex maniac with you!"

☞ A mouse and a lion are drinking in a bar when a beautiful female giraffe walks in. "Wow," says the mouse. "I'd sure fancy some of that!" "Why not try your luck?" says the lion. So the mouse goes over to the giraffe and starts chatting her up. They get along really well, and after a short while they leave together. Next week, the lion's sitting in the bar when the mouse staggers through the door and collapses into a seat next to him. "Holy cow," says the lion. "You look shattered. What happened to you?" "It's that giraffe," replies the mouse. "The giraffe?" says the lion. "But I though you two really hit it off." "We did," says the mouse. "I spent all last week at her house." "But why do you look such a wreck?" asks the lion. The mouse replies, "Because in between all the kissing and the sex, I must've run about a thousand miles."

☞ An elephant and a mouse are talking together. The elephant says to the mouse, "Why do you think it is that I'm so big, strong and heavy, while you're so tiny, weak and puny?" The mouse replies, "I've been ill."

MIDGETS AND DWARVES

☞ A female dwarf goes to her doctor. She tells him that her private parts are sore but she has no idea why. The doctor asks her to remove her underwear and lift her skirts for an examination. The doctor has a look around, then reaches for a pair of scissors. The dwarf hears some snipping sounds; then the doctor asks her to walk around and see if she feels any better. "Oh, yes," she says, "that's much better. What did you do?" The doctor says, "I trimmed two inches off the top of your wellies."

☞ A man is standing at a urinal when he looks to his right and sees a dwarf standing next to him. The dwarf is rhythmically jerking his head to one side. The man asks if he's okay. "It's nothing," replies the dwarf. "I used to work in the circus as a clown. Part of my act was being fired out of a cannon. I did it so many times it damaged my nervous system. It gives me the shakes now and again." The dwarf then zips up his fly and leaves. The man looks round and sees another dwarf peeing in the urinal on his left. This dwarf is also shaking his head violently. "Say," says the man, "were you a circus clown too?" "No," snaps the dwarf. "I'm an accountant, and while you were taking to that other bastard you were pissing in my ear!"

☞ Dave Smith, Britain's smallest man, died in a freak accident last week. He fell into a bowl of muesli and got pulled under by a strong currant.

☞ A midget hires a prostitute and takes her to his motel room. They have twenty minutes of energetic sex, after which the midget slips out from under the sheets and climbs under the bed. The prostitute is puzzled by this odd behaviour, but the midget immediately reappears, climbs into bed and asks for more sex. The prostitute obliges and they have another bout. When the midget has finished, he repeats his curious behaviour; he gets out of bed, crawls underneath it, then crawls out again and asks for more sex. After two hours of this, the prostitute's getting exhausted. She figures that the midget is keeping a bottle of aphrodisiac under the bed, so the next time he finishes she decides to swipe it and have some herself. She waits until the midget has crawled under the bed; then she climbs out, looks underneath – and finds fifteen midgets.

☞ The Seven Dwarfs come back to their cottage after an exhausting day in the diamond mine. They're tired, dirty and hungry, but after a shower and something to eat they all climb into the hot tub and start to feel happy all over. Then Happy reminds them it's Dopey's turn.

☞ Two midgets go to a bar, pick up a couple of prostitutes and take them back to their hotel. Sadly, the first midget finds he is unable to get an erection. His depression is enhanced by the fact that, from the next room, he hears his friend shouting, "One, two, three – uuuh! One, two, three – uuuh!" all night long. In the morning, the second midget asks the first what sort of night he had. "It was so embarrassing," says the first midget. "I tried all night, but I couldn't get an erection." The second midget shakes his head. "You think that's embarrassing? I couldn't even get on the bed!"

MINERS

☞ My granddad was a miner, but as he got older he found he could spend less and less time underground. Towards the end they were lowering him down on a yo-yo.

MISSING

☞ Dick went to the missing persons bureau, but couldn't find anyone there.

MISTAKEN IDENTITY

"I was on the street. This guy waved to me, and he came up to me and said, 'I'm sorry; I thought you were someone else.' And I said, 'I am'."
Demetri Martin

MONARCHY

☞ Tommy Cooper is presented to the Queen after the Royal Variety Performance. "Do you like football, Your Majesty?" he asks. "Not really," says the Queen. "Well, in that case," says Tommy, "can I have your ticket for the Cup Final?"

MONEY

"Money is better than poverty, if only for financial reasons."
Woody Allen

☞ Harry is visiting his grandma. She takes the opportunity to complain about the cost of living. "When I was a girl I could go out with a shilling and come home with a dozen eggs, two pints of milk, a pound of bacon, half a pound of tea and a chicken." "Yes," says Harry. "That's inflation for you." "It's nothing to do with inflation," says grandma. "It's all them bloody security cameras they have nowadays."

"Like a supermodel, I won't get out of bed for less than £20,000. Of course, it does mean I spend an awful lot of time in bed."
Clive Anderson

☞ A fool and his money are a girl's best friend.

☞ What's the name of the richest bear in the country? Winnie the Pools.

☞ A man goes to a car showroom and has a look at the latest models. All the cars have their prices on their windshields except one, a very expensive-looking sports car in the corner. The man knows the car will probably cost more than he can afford, but he really likes the look of its sleek, powerful lines. After a few minutes, the man comes to a decision; if he can possibly afford it, he will buy the car – he must have it! The man beckons a salesman over and, bracing himself, asks the price of the superb sports car. The salesman tells him the bad news. "It's twenty-five pounds, sir: but we'll need three polka-dotted five-pound notes with a fur trim and one ten-pound note made out of balloons." "What?" exclaims the man. "I'm not paying that! That's silly money!"

"Money can't buy you friends, but you get a better class of enemy."
Spike Milligan

☞ A man goes into a dry cleaner to complain about a pair of trousers. "You've ruined them," he says, holding them up. "I only wanted a soup stain removed and you've managed to bleach the crotch and break the zip." "Not much we can do about that, sir," says the man at the counter. The customer replies, "But the sign in the window says 'Money back if not completely satisfied'." "That's right," replies the man. "And when we took your money we were completely satisfied with it."

"Money can't buy you happiness, but it will pay the salaries of a large research staff to study the problem."
Bill Vaughan

☞ A one-dollar bill meets a twenty-dollar bill. "Hey, where have you been?" asks the one-dollar bill. "I haven't seen you around in a while." The twenty-dollar bill replies, "I've been here and there: y'know, hanging out at the casino and places like that. I went on a cruise in January: went round the Caribbean a few times, then back home: went to a couple of football games: did some shopping, the movies, that kind of stuff. So how about you?" The one-dollar bill sighs and says, "Just the same old stuff: church, church, church."

"All I've ever wanted was an honest week's pay for an honest day's work."
Steve Martin

☞ Harry goes to see his solicitor. "My neighbour owes me £5,000," says Harry, "but he refuses to pay up. In fact, he denies borrowing any money from me at all." "Do you have any proof he owes you £5,000?" asks the solicitor. "No," replies Harry. "We did it on a handshake." "Very well," says the solicitor, "I suggest we write him a formal letter asking him to pay the £10,000." "Yes," says Harry, "but I just told you he only owes me £5,000." "True," says the solicitor, "and when he writes back to inform me of that fact, we'll have all the proof we need."

☞ There are bigger things in life than money: but they're mostly bills.

☞ Harry says to Dick, "D'you know, I wish I had enough money to buy a herd of elephants?" Dick says, "What do you want with a herd of elephants?" "I don't," says Harry. "I just wish I had the money."

"All I ask is a chance to prove that money can't make me happy."
Spike Milligan

☞ Dick says to Harry, "If I had the same money as Bill Gates, I'd actually be a bit richer than he is." "How do you work that out?" asks Harry. "Well," says Dick, "I'd do a bit of window-cleaning on the side as well, wouldn't I?"

☞ Money is like fat. There's plenty of it about, but it always seems to be in the wrong places.

☞ If you have to ask the price, you can't afford it: but if you can afford it, make sure you tell everybody what you paid.

☞ Little Johnny asks his dad to buy him a new bicycle. "I'm sorry," says dad, "we can't afford it. Money's tight at the moment. We have a £100,000 mortgage, the roof needs replacing and the foundations are subsiding. It's going to cost us a lot of money to put that right." Johnny nods his head sadly and walks off. Next morning, dad sees Johnny heading for the front door with a couple of packed suitcases. "And where do you think you're going?" asks dad. "I'm getting the hell out of here," replies Johnny. "Why?" asks dad. "I heard you and mum last night in your bedroom," says Johnny. "You said you were pulling out and she said to hang on, as she was coming too. And I'll be damned if I'm going to be left all by myself in a sinking house with a leaky roof and a £100,000 mortgage, with no bike!"

☞ Why did people in Beverly Hills watch Dynasty? To see how the poor folk lived.

> **"Some people get so rich they lose all respect for humanity. That's how rich I want to be."**
> *Rita Rudner*

MONEY – BANKS

> **"24-hour banking? I haven't got time for that."**
> *Steven Wright*

☞ A banker is someone who lends you his umbrella when the sun's shining, then wants it back as soon as it starts to rain.

☞ Harry knows he must have a serious overdraft problem. His letters from the bank used to begin, "Dear Sir." Now they open, "Oi – you!"

☞ George's overdraft is really bad; in fact, the bank wrote to him saying, "Dear Sir, we would be most grateful if we could revert to the old system of *you* banking with *us*."

☞ How come banks charge you for having insufficient funds? Aren't they best placed to realise you don't have the money?

☞ If bankers are so good at figures, how come the average bank has ten windows and only four tellers?

☞ Why do the Irish call their currency the Punt? Because it rhymes with bank manager.

MONEY – INVESTMENTS

☞ A man calls his stockbroker in a panic. "My stocks! Sell all of them! Sell now! Sell everything fast!" The stockbroker tries to explain that the market is cyclical in nature and that the man's stocks are still an excellent long-term investment. "Let me tell you a secret," says the man. "My wife has this thing about the stock market. Her grandparents lost everything in the Great Crash, and when we got married I promised her that I'd never put our money into stocks. Instead, I said I'd always keep it under the mattress." "I see," says the broker. "So you want the money in case she asks for it, because she thinks the market is going down." "No," says the man. "I want the money because she's just about to get a new mattress delivered."

☞ I made a killing in the stock market. My broker lost all my money, so I killed him.

MONEY – MISERS

☞ Misers are no fun to live with, but they make wonderful ancestors.

☞ George's mistress wanted a fur coat and an exotic holiday but George, being a skinflint, bought her a hamster-fur jacket and took her on a weekend to Blackpool. It didn't work out; she spent two days on the big wheel.

☞ An old miser is on his deathbed. He's been hoarding his cash for years and he thinks he's found a way of taking it with him. He instructs his housekeeper to cash a large cheque, then take the money and stuff it into two pillowcases. Once the cases are stuffed with notes, the housekeeper is told to hide them in the attic. The housekeeper does as she's asked, but she can't understand what the old man's up to. The miser explains his idea. "When I die, I'll drift upwards to heaven," he says. "On the way, I'll make sure I waft up through the ceiling. Then I can grab one pillowcase in each hand and take my loot to the afterlife." This sounds a little eccentric to the housekeeper, but she says nothing. A few days later, she takes the miser his breakfast and finds him dead in his bed. After calling the doctor and the undertaker, she goes into the attic to see if the miser's plan was successful. It hasn't; the two pillowcases are where she left them. She says to herself, "That old fool should have told me to put them in the basement."

☞ Dick was a notorious miser who kept all his money under his mattress. Eventually, he'd saved more than a million pounds, but one night he fell out of bed and plunged eighty feet to his death.

☞ Hamish was a notorious miser, but every year he would take his money out of the bank for a holiday. Then, a couple of weeks later, once it had had its holiday, he put it all back again.

MONEY – TAXATION

☞ A fine is a tax for doing wrong. A tax is a fine for doing well.

☞ A penny saved is a government oversight.

☞ An Inland Revenue official pays a visit to a church and speaks to the priest. "Father," he says, "do you know a Mr Albert Smith?" "Why, yes, I do," says the priest. "Is he a member of your congregation?" asks the revenue man. "Yes, he is," says the priest. "Why do you ask?" "I'm from the Inland Revenue and I need to check if Mr Smith actually made the £100,000 donation to your church that he claimed on his tax return." "Well," says the priest, "I can check the parish records but I can tell you one thing now; if he hasn't given it to us already, I can assure you that he will tomorrow!"

☞ It used to be that only death and taxes were inevitable. These days you have to factor in the shipping and handling as well.

☞ The government has just announced it will be introducing a penis tax – the only tax men will willingly overpay.

☞ The Tax Office: we've got what it takes to take what you've got.

☞ The Inland Revenue sends an inspector to audit the books of a synagogue. The inspector looks over the books and asks the Rabbi a question. "I notice you buy a lot of candles," he says. "What do you do with the candle drippings?" The Rabbi says, "We collect the drippings and send them back to the candlemakers. Every now and then they send us a free box of candles." "I see," says the inspector. "And what about all these bread wafers you buy? what do you do with the crumbs?" The Rabbi replies, "We collect the crumbs and send them back to the baker. Every now and then he sends us a free box of wafers." "I see," says the inspector. "You seem to perform a lot of circumcisions here. What do you do with all the left-over foreskins?" "Here, too, we do not waste," replies the Rabbi. "We save all the foreskins and send them to the Inland Revenue, and every year they send us back a complete dick."

MONSTERS

☞ What did Godzilla eat after having his teeth fixed by the dentist? The dentist.

MORRIS DANCING

☞ Why do morris dancers wear bells? So they can annoy blind people as well.

MOTHBALLS

☞ Grandma always said that one of her most enduring memories of childhood was the smell of mothballs. I always wondered how she got their little legs open.

MUSIC AND MUSICIANS

☞ A man goes to the doctor and tells him that he hasn't had a bowel movement in more than two weeks. The doctor prescribes a mild laxative. A few days later, the man comes back. He still hasn't had a bowel movement, so the doctor prescribes something stronger. The man comes back a few days later. Still nothing has happened. The doctor decides to pull out the big guns; he prescribes a huge dose of the strongest laxative he knows of. "If that won't shift him," mutters the doctor, "then nothing will." The next day, the man comes back, but he's as constipated as ever: not a sign of a bowel movement. The doctor's baffled. He decides he'll need to do a detailed check on the man's circumstances to find out what exactly is wrong with him. "What's your age?" asks the doctor. "I'm 39," replies the man. "Are you married?" asks the doctor. "No," replies the man. "And what do you do for a living?" asks the doctor. The man replies, "I'm a professional accordion-player." "Ah," says the doctor. "Problem solved. Here's £5. Go and get something to eat."

☞ A man walks into a jazz club with an octopus on his shoulder. "This octopus in a musical genius," he says. "I'll give £100 to any person who can find a musical instrument my octopus can't play." A number of people give the octopus their instruments – a saxophone, a guitar, a harmonica etcetera – but the octopus can play all of them. Eventually a Scotsman pushes his way through the crowd and hands the octopus a set of bagpipes. The octopus goes frantic and starts pulling the pipes all over the place, but without producing any music. "Ah!" cries the Scotsman. "I knew it. He cannae play the pipes!" "Play it?" says the octopus. "Who wants to play it? As soon as I get its pyjamas off I'm going to screw it."

☞ A musician is walking past a bank when he sees a sign saying 'Musician bank loans. Two per cent.' This is an incredible deal, and the musician rushes inside to borrow some money. He goes to the teller and says, "Can I borrow £2,000 at your two per cent musicians' rate?" The teller replies, "I'm sorry, sir; two per cent isn't the interest rate. That's your chance of getting a loan."

☞ An orchestra is rehearsing a piece when the lead violinist makes a mistake. The conductor signals the orchestra to stop; then they start again from the very beginning. They reach the same part of the music as before, and the lead violinist makes exactly the same mistake again. The conductor sighs and signals the orchestra to start from the top. The musicians play until the same passage of music is reached and, once again, the lead violinist makes exactly the same error. The conductor has had enough; he pulls out a revolver and shoots the violinist through the head. The conductor is tried for murder and found guilty. He is sentenced to death in the electric chair. The day of the execution arrives, and the conductor is strapped to the chair. The prison warden pulls the switch – and nothing happens. All the wiring is checked and the warden tries again: but, again, nothing happens. They try a third time and, as before, nothing happens. They eventually come to the conclusion that the guy's just a really bad conductor.

☞ How do you get a guitar player to play more softly? Give him some sheet music.

☞ How do you improve the aerodynamics of a trombonist's car? Take the pizza delivery sign off the roof.

☞ How do you make a chainsaw sound like a set of bagpipes? Add vibrato.

> **"I was watching MTV and there were girls dancing in suspended cages. That would be an ambivalent situation. 'I'm trapped!... but enjoying the music'."**
> *Demetri Martin*

☞ How do you turn a duck into a soul artist? Put it in the oven until its Bill Withers.

☞ How many guitar players does it take to change a light-bulb? Twelve: one to change the bulb and eleven to say they could do it better.

☞ It's incredible to think the Rolling Stones are on tour again. Apparently their combined age is now 240: and that's just Mick and Keith.

☞ Stevie Wonder is playing his first gig in Tokyo, and the place is packed to the rafters. To break the ice with his new audience, Stevie asks if anyone would like him to play a request. A little old Japanese man jumps out of his seat and shouts at the top of his voice, "Play a jazz chord! Play a jazz chord!" "Well, if that's what you want," says Stevie, who then goes into a long and complex jazz melody on his piano. When he's finished, the little old man jumps up again and shouts, "No, no! Play a jazz chord! Play a jazz chord!" Stevie shrugs his shoulders and dives into a brilliant jazz improvisation with his band. As he finishes, the crowd goes wild at this impromptu display of Stevie's technical expertise, but the little old man jumps up again. "No, no!" he shouts. "Play a jazz chord! Play a jazz chord!" Stevie has been trying as hard as he can to oblige this old geezer and finally loses his temper. "Okay, smartass!" he shouts. "If you think you can play a better jazz chord than me, you'd better come up here and do it!" So the little old man climbs up on to the stage, grabs hold of the mike and starts singing, "A jazz chord to say I ruv you. I jazz chord to shay how much I..."

☞ The doorbell rings. Glenda answers it and finds a blind man holding a tool chest standing outside. "I'm the piano-tuner," says the man. "But I didn't send for a piano-tuner," says Glenda. "I know," says the man, "but your neighbours did."

☞ What did it say on a blues singer's tombstone? "I didn't wake up this morning..."

☞ What do you get when you play New Age music backwards? More New Age music.

☞ What does a trombonist say when he gets to work? "Would you like fries with that?"

☞ What sort of calendar does a trombonist use to keep track of his gigs? Year-at-a-glance

☞ What's brown, smelly and sits on a piano stool? Beethoven's first movement.

☞ What's the best way to tune bagpipes? With a pitchfork.

☞ What's the difference between a cello and a coffin? The coffin has the corpse on the inside.

☞ What's the difference between a chiropodist and a drummer? A chiropodist bucks up your feet.

☞ What's the difference between a conductor and a sack of manure? The sack.

☞ What's the difference between a drum teacher and a drum student? About three days.

☞ What's the difference between a lawnmower and a bagpipe? You can tune a lawnmower.

☞ What's the difference between a musician and a mutual fund? The mutual fund eventually matures and earns money.

☞ What's the difference between a puppy and a singer-songwriter? Eventually the puppy stops whining.

☞ What's the difference between a trombonist lying dead in the road and a country and western singer lying dead in the road? The country and western singer might have been on his way to a recording session.

☞ What's the difference between an accordion and an onion? No one cries when you chop up an accordion.

☞ When I tell people I once produced earth, wind and fire, they think I'm in the music business. I'm not; I just like really hot curries.

☞ Why are drum machines better than drummers? Because they make the right noise at the right time and don't sleep with your girlfriend.

☞ Why did Michael Jackson call his album 'Bad'? Because he couldn't spell 'Awful'.

MYTHOLOGY

☞ A group of mythical creatures decide to form a football league. They form into two teams and meet in the local park the next Sunday. A passer-by happens to notice all the trolls, goblins and fairies etcetera limbering up before the game, but is surprised to see a creature that's half-man and half-horse. The man taps a passing elf on the shoulder and points at the strange creature. "What's that?" he asks. The elf replies, "Oh, that's our centaur forward."

☞ My favorite mythical creature? The honest politician.

NAME DROPPING

☞ A Texan millionaire gets talking to a guy called Bill in a New York bar. During their conversation, Bill tells the Texan that he knows every important person in the world. The Texan doesn't believe him. "So you know everyone important?" he says. "Certainly do," replies Bill. "You know the President of these United States?" asks the Texan. "Yup," replies Bill. "Okay," says the Texan. "I'll make you a bet. I'll fly us to the White House, and if you can get me in to see the President I'll give you $500,000: but if you can't, I get to keep your house and car." "Sounds fair," replies Bill, so they get in the Texan's private jet and fly to Washington. At the airport, they take a car to the White House, and Bill and the Texan are quickly ushered through security. "Good to see you again, Bill," says the Chief of Staff. "The President will see you immediately." Bill and the Texan are then shown into the Oval Office where Bill introduces the Texan to the President. After half an hour in the Oval Office, Bill and the Texan are in a limo being taken to the airport. "I don't believe it," says the Texan. "That really *was* the goddamn President. Who else do you know who's famous?" "Well, I know the Queen of England," replies Bill. "No way!" says the Texan. "I'll bet you don't: double or quits." "I'll take that bet," replies Bill and, as before, they get in the Texan's jet. This time to fly to England. Once in England, the pair take a cab to Buckingham Palace where the guards let Bill and the Texan through the gates. Very soon, Bill and the Texan are having tea with the Queen. After they've eaten, Bill and the Texan are driven back to the airport in the Queen's Rolls-Royce. "Well, that beats all," says the Texan. "You really *do* know the Queen. Who else have you made friends with?" "I know the Pope, too," replies Bill. "That I don't believe," says the Texan. "I'll bet you double or quits you can't get to see him." "I'll take that bet," replies Bill, and within the hour the pair are flying to Italy. When in Rome, Bill and the Texan are driven to Vatican City, but Bill has trouble getting to see the Pope as the guards won't let him through. A Cardinal is called out to see what Bill and the Texan want. Bill tells the Cardinal he wants an audience with his old friend the Pope. "He's very busy," says the Cardinal. "I'll see what I can do, but you can only come alone: not your Texan friend." The Texan is not happy at this. "Listen, Bill," he says. "If I don't see you with the Pope the bet's off. Understand?" Bill agrees to try to sort things out and tells the Texan to wait in the square under the Papal balcony. Half an hour later, the Pope comes out on the balcony to wave at the crowd. Bill comes out to stand beside him and waves down at the Texan. "Dang it!" exclaims the Texan. "He really *does* know everybody!" The Texan turns to a tourist and points at Bill. "See that guy? He seems to know everybody in the goddamn world." "Well, sure he does," replies the tourist. "Everyone knows Bill. But who the hell is that guy in the white dress?"

NAMES

☞ A tourist in New Mexico comes across an old Native American couple sitting on a rug. The tourist says hello and asks what their names are. "My name is White Cloud," says the old man. "This is my wife. Her name is Three Horses. "Three Horses?" says the tourist. "Is that because her father saw three horses soon after she was born?" "No," says the old man. "She's called that because all she does is nag, nag, nag."

☞ George had two sons and named them both Edward. He thought two Eds were better than one.

"My name is Les Dawson. That's a stage name, actually; I was christened 'Friday Dawson' because when my father saw me he said to my mother, 'I think we'd better call it a day'."
Les Dawson

☞ What do you call a goat at sea? Billy Ocean.

☞ What do you call a goat that mimes? Billi Vanilli.

☞ What do you call a man wearing two raincoats in a cemetery? Max Bygraves.

☞ What do you call a man with a large flatfish on his head? Ray.

☞ What do you call a singer with a biscuit on his head? Lionel RichTea.

☞ What do you call a Spanish sheep with no legs? Gracias.

☞ What do you call a vicar on a motorbike? Rev.

☞ What do you call a woman who sets fire to her bills? Bernadette.

☞ What do you call a woman who's good at catching fish? Annette.

☞ What do you call an unemployed goat? Billy Idol.

NEWSPAPERS AND JOURNALISM

☞ A junior reporter for a small-town newspaper is sent out on his first assignment. When he comes back, he submits the following report to his editor. "Mrs Smith was injured in a car accident today. She is recovering in County Hospital with lacerations on her breasts." The editor reads this, then scolds the junior reporter, "This is a family paper, son. We don't use words like 'breasts' around here. Now go back and write something more appropriate!" The reporter thinks long and hard. He tries rewriting the report using words such as 'chest', 'lady bumps' and 'bust', but nothing seems to work. Finally he hands the editor the following: "Mrs Smith was injured in a car accident today. She is recovering in County Hospital with lacerations on her (.)(.)"

☞ A Londoner is staying with his auntie and uncle in Yorkshire. One morning, the man goes out for a stroll and his uncle asks him to buy a newspaper on the way. The man has his walk, then pops into a newsagent's. He goes to the counter to buy the paper but realises he can't remember which one to get. "This is embarrassing," says the man to the newsagent. "I was asked to get a paper but I can't remember which one. I think it began with a 't'." "Well, that's not much use to thee," says the newsagent. "That could be anything: t'Observer, t'Times, t'Guardian..."

☞ A newsboy is standing on a street corner with a stack of papers. He yells, "Read all about it. Fifty people swindled! Fifty people swindled!" Curious, a man walks over, buys a paper and checks the front page. The lead story seems to be about the mayor opening a zoo. "Hey!" says the man. "There's nothing in here about a load of people being swindled." The newsboy ignores him and calls out, "Read all about it. Fifty-one people swindled! Fifty-one people swindled..!"

☞ A newspaper editor is someone who separates the lurid, sensationalist crap from the facts – then prints it.

☞ A reporter gets a job on an Arkansas newspaper and is told to find some human interest stories. The reporter goes into the countryside, finds a remote farmhouse deep in the woods and asks the farmer if he knows of any heart-warming tales. "Well," says the farmer, "one time a neighbour lost himself one of his sheep. We all formed a posse and found it, and after we all screwed that sheep, we took it back to the farmer that lost it." "I can't print a story like that!" says the reporter. "Haven't you got any other heart-warming tales?" "Well, sure," says the farmer. "One time the wife of ma' neighbour got lost, so we all formed a posse and found her, and after all of us had screwed her, we took that gal' back to her husband." "I can't print that!" says the reporter. "Look. Forget heart-warming; have you got any tales that are tragic?" The farmer hangs his head and sighs, "Well," he says, "there was this one time when *I* got lost..."

NON-CONFORMITY

☞ You can always tell a man who's a non-conformist; he looks just like every other non-conformist.

NUCLEAR POWER

"It's been 18 years since the Chernobyl disaster. Is it just me who's surprised – no super-heroes?"
Jimmy Carr

NUDISM, NUDITY AND NUDENESS

☞ A woman is in bed with her boyfriend when she hears her husband's car pull into the driveway. "Hurry!" she yells to the boyfriend. "Grab your clothes and jump out of the window!" The boyfriend looks out of the window and says, "I can't jump out there! It's raining!" "Jump, or he'll kill us both!" shouts the woman, so the boyfriend grabs his clothes and jumps. As he runs down the street, he discovers he's run right into the middle of a town marathon. He starts running alongside the others and – being naked with his clothes tucked under his arm – tries to blend in as best he can. One of the runners says to him, "Do you always run in the nude?" The boyfriend replies, "Oh, yes. It feels so good with the air blowing over your skin." "And do you always run carrying your clothes with you?" asks the runner. "Yes," answers the boyfriend. "That way I can get dressed at the end of the run and not catch a chill." The runner then asks, "And do you always wear a condom?" The boyfriend replies, "Only if it's raining."

☞ Harry gets a job as a door-to-door toy salesman. He knocks on one door and is surprised when a naked woman answers. "I hope you're not embarrassed," says the woman, "but I'm a nudist." "Oh, I see," says Harry. "Well, I'm here to see if you'd like to buy any toys. Do you have any children?" "Oh, yes," says the woman, "I have twelve." "Twelve?" exclaims Harry. "You're not a nudist; you just don't have enough time to get dressed!"

☞ It's a baking-hot Sunday and George has promised to mow the lawn. He calls upstairs to his wife, "It's too hot to mow the lawn. Can't I do it another time?" His wife calls back, "The grass is a foot high. You promised!" George tries to think of a way out of this chore. He calls back, "It's too hot! I'll only mow the lawn if I can do it in the nude!" "Okay!" calls his wife. George is taken aback; he calls out, "What will the neighbours say if they see me starkers on the lawn?" His wife replies, "They'll say I married you for your money!"

☞ Norma was found walking down the high street completely naked apart from contact lenses stuck over each nipple. She was arrested for making a spectacle of herself.

☞ Tom took a trip to a high-class holiday camp for nudists. A nude porter carried Tom's bags to his room, but Tom had no idea how much he should tip him. In the end he reckoned a five-pound note should just about cover it.

THE OCCULT AND SUPERSTITION

> **"One night I stayed up all night playing poker with tarot cards. I got a full house and four people died."**
> *Steven Wright*

☞ I don't think we don't need to worry too much about superstitions – touch wood.

☞ My mother used to be a witch, but she only did it for a spell.

> **"If ghosts can walk through walls, how come they don't fall through the floor?"**
> *Steven Wright*

OCTOPUS

☞ What do you call an octopus with no tentacles? Puss.

☞ What do you get when you cross an octopus with a cow? An animal that can milk itself!

OFFENCE

> **I was surprised how British Muslims reacted to the Danish cartoons of the prophet Mohammed. I thought: "How can you get this worked up about a cartoon?" But then I remembered how angry I was when they gave Scooby-Doo a cousin."**
> *Paul Sinha*

OIL

☞ Harry is in oil in a small way. He's a sardine.

OWLS

☞ What does an educated owl say? Whom!

PAEDOPHILES

☞ What do you give the paedophile who has everything? A new parish.

PANDAS

☞ Chinese scientists have discovered the rare Rock'n'Roll Panda. It will only eat A Wop Bop a Loo Lop a Lop Bamboo.

PARROTS

☞ A couple are in Brazil on their honeymoon. The bride loves parrots, and when she sees a beautiful bird for sale in a local market, she persudes her husband to buy it for her. The couple buy the parrot and take it to their hotel room, where they are delighted to find out it can talk. However, later on, they are less delighted when the bird starts delivering a running commentary on the couple's love-making. Finally, the groom throws a large towel over the cage and threatens to give the parrot to a zoo if it doesn't keep its beak shut. The threat works, and the parrot is silent for the rest of the evening. The next morning, the couple start packing for their return journey. The groom discovers they've bought so many souvenirs he can't close their largest suitcase. "Darling," says the groom, "this just won't fit in. Get on top and I'll try pushing as hard as I can." After some grunting and straining, they give up. "It's no good," says the bride. "It's just too much. Tell you what; you're heavier than me. You get on top and I'll wiggle it around a bit." So the groom gets on top and tries to bounce down on the lid while his wife tries to jiggle the lock shut. After a few minutes of fruitless bouncing and cursing, the couple give up. "Look," says the groom, "we've got to do this. I know; let's both get on top." Suddenly, the parrot yanks away the towel and says, "Zoo or no zoo, this I gotta see!"

☞ A woman goes into a pet shop to buy a parrot. She's shown a beautiful bird for £20. "Why is it so cheap?" she asks. "Well," says the sales assistant, "it used to live in a brothel, and now its language is a bit fruity." "Oh, I don't mind that," says the woman. "I'm very broad-minded." She buys the parrot and takes it home. The parrot looks around and says, "Screw me: a new brothel and a new madam." "I'm not a madam, and this isn't a brothel," replies the woman indignantly. A little later the woman's two teenage daughters arrive home. "Well, screw me," says the parrot, "a new brothel, a new madam and two new whores." "These are my daughters, not prostitutes," says the woman. A short while later the woman's husband comes home. "Well, screw me," says the parrot, "a new brothel, a new madam, new whores, but the same old clients. How ya doing, Dave?"

☞ An old man and a parrot have lived together for more than 40 years. One day, the parrot says: "You know, I've never had sex. I'd really like to try it before I die." The old man agrees to help and takes the parrot to a nearby pet shop. The shop has lots of female parrots, but they're all too expensive. The most the old man can afford is $40, and the cheapest parrot is $250. The shop-owner takes pity on the old man and his horny pet bird. He tells them they can rent a female parrot for the night for $40. The old man and his parrot go home with the female. When they get to the house, the old man puts the pair in a cage in the kitchen, then leaves them to get on with it. After a few seconds, the man hears a terrible squawking. He runs into the kitchen and finds his parrot trying to tear the feathers off the female. "What are you doing?" shouts the old man. "What does it look like?" replies the parrot. "For forty bucks, I should at least get to see the chick naked."

☞ During the days of the Cold War, a Russian man loses his pet parrot. The man looks everywhere. He searches his flat, goes out into the streets and spends hours walking round the park. He goes everywhere, but he can't find the parrot. As a last resort, he goes to his local KGB office and tells an officer his problem. The officer is a little confused. "Look, comrade," he says. "I'm sorry you lost your pet bird, but this is the KGB. We're in charge of security; we don't look for missing animals." "I know," says the man. "I just wanted to say that if you *did* find my parrot, I don't know where he could have picked up all his ridiculous political ideas."

☞ Glenda's dishwasher breaks down, so she calls a repairman. Glenda has to go out, so when the repairman arrives, she gives him some instructions. "After you've fixed the dishwasher, leave the bill on the counter and let yourself out. I'll mail you a cheque tomorrow. Oh! I almost forgot; don't worry about my bulldog. He won't bother you. But, whatever you do, do not under any circumstances talk to my parrot! You've got to take me seriously on this. Do not speak to my parrot! Do not utter a single word to that bird! Do you understand?" The repairman thinks Glenda's a bit crazy, but agrees to do as she asks. Glenda leaves and the man starts fixing the dishwasher. As he's working, he hears heavy breathing behind him and turns round to find the biggest, meanest-looking bulldog he's ever seen in his life. The repairman's terrified, but the dog does nothing; it just stands there watching him. After getting over his shock, the repairman carries on working, but finds himself becoming increasingly annoyed by the parrot. The parrot had been sitting quietly on a perch in the corner of the room, but now the dog has arrived it starts squawking like crazy and throwing its seed around. Even worse, it starts swearing at the repairman calling him a fat-assed bastard and an ugly son of a bitch. The parrot's making so much noise the repairman can't concentrate on his work. Finally he loses his temper. He turns round and shouts, "Shut up, you stupid bird!" There's a pause. Then the parrot says, "Get him, Spike!"

☞ I used to be haunted by the ghost of a parrot. It kept flying around saying, "Oooooo's a pretty boy, then?"

☞ There are three parrots in a cage: one at the top, one in the middle, one at the bottom. Which parrot owns the cage? The one at the bottom; the other two are on higher perches.

> **"Live in such a way that you would not be ashamed to sell your parrot to the town gossip."**
> *Will Rogers*

PENGUINS

☞ A man goes into a brothel and walks up to the madam. "What can I get for $5?" asks the man. "Not much," says the madam, "but I suppose you might get a penguin." The man isn't sure what a 'penguin' is but, being desperate, he hands over his cash. The madam takes him to a back room and tells him to drop his trousers. A prostitute then comes in and starts to do a striptease. Just as the man is getting excited, the prostitute turns her back and leaves. The man waddles after her with his trousers round his ankles. "Hey!" he shouts. "What the hell is a penguin?"

☞ An albatross is sitting on a rock in the South Pacific when it's surprised to see a penguin, high in the sky, flapping its way towards him. The penguin swoops down and takes a seat next to the albatross. "I didn't know penguins could fly," says the albatross. "Neither did we," replies the penguin. "It turned out we just weren't flapping hard enough."

☞ What's grey and lives in the Antarctic? A melted penguin.

PERFORMING ARTS

> **"A fan club is a group of people who tell an actor he's not alone in the way he feels about himself."**
> *Jack Carson*

☞ A seaside holiday camp books a stage hypnotist for the season. His first night goes very well, until he invites thirty people on the stage for a mass hypnosis session. The hypnotist takes a fob-watch out of his pocket and asks his subjects to watch it closely. The hypnotist begins chanting, "Watch the watch. Watch the watch. Watch the watch..." while gently swinging it to and fro. His subjects become mesmerized as the watch swings back and forth, the light gleaming off its polished surface. Thirty pairs of eyes follow the dangling watch until, suddenly, it slips from the hypnotist's fingers and falls to the floor. The watch smashes into a tangle of uncoiled springs, cogs and broken glass. "Crap!" exclaims the hypnotist. It took three days to clean up the mess.

**Great response to a troublesome heckler:
"Excuse me; I'm trying to work here. How would you like it if I stood yelling down the alley while you're giving blow-jobs to transsexuals?"**
Paul Merton

☞ A theatrical agent discovers that one of his clients, an attractive young actress, has taken up prostitution. He asks to sleep with her, and she agrees, but makes the agent pay the full rate for the night. They go to a hotel and the agent hands over the money. Then they go to bed, turn out the lights and make love. Afterwards, the actress falls asleep, but is then woken up for more sex. After half an hour the exhausted girl falls asleep, only to be woken again for yet more sex. After six sessions, the actress can't take it any more. She switches on the light and finds a strange man in bed with here. "You're not my agent!" she cries, "No," replies the man. "He's outside selling tickets."

☞ Epitaph for Liberace: great on the piano, but he sucked on the organ.

☞ Harry and Jill go to Las Vegas on their honeymoon. The hotel they stay in has a number of spectacular shows on, one of which is billed as 'The Incredible Victor'. Harry and Jill decide to see what's so incredible about Victor and take their seats. When the curtain comes up, a middle-aged man strides out on to the stage while a glamorous assistant places a wooden table in front of him. The assistant puts three walnuts on the table and steps back. Victor then takes out his two-foot penis and uses it as a hammer to smash the nuts. Wham! Wham! Wham! Three mighty blows of his dick, and the three walnuts are smashed to pieces. Harry and Jill are very impressed. Thirty years pass, and the couple decide to go back to Las Vegas for their wedding anniversary. Much to their surprise, they see a billboard advertising 'The Incredible Victor' and decide to catch his show again. As before, Victor takes centre-stage in front of a wooden table, but this time, his assistant places three coconuts on it. Victor, now pushing eighty, then drops his pants, extracts his mighty two-foot dick and hits the nuts. Wham! Wham! Wham! Three mighty blows and the three coconuts are smashed to pulp. Harry and Jill can't believe what they've seen. After the show is over, they excitedly chatter about the act at the bar. The barman overhears their conversation. "The Incredible Victor is an institution in this town," he says. "One of Las Vegas' longest-running acts. He really is incredible." "I know," says Harry. "Imagine being able to smash coconuts like that. When we saw him doing that act thirty years ago, he was using his dick to smash walnuts." "Oh, yeah," says the barman, "but let's be fair to the old guy; he's getting on; his eyesight isn't what it used to be."

"I never got the Vagina Monologues. We all know that if vaginas could talk, they'd sound like Enya."
Dylan Moran

☞ Harry really is a terrible actor; he delivers lines the way a one-armed postman delivers aquarium tanks.

☞ My wife always wanted to be a hit on Broadway – which is why I pushed her off the Empire State Building.

"If you shoot a mime, should you use a silencer?"
Steven Wright

☞ Sean goes to the circus. Half-way through the performance, a group of clowns comes out to do their stuff. The chief clown comes over to the stands to pick on a member of the audience. The clown sees Sean and says, "Sir, are you the front end of an ass?" Sean, being shy, gulps at this unwelcome attention, then says, "No, I'm not." The clown then says, "Sir, in that case, are you the back end of an ass?" Shaun nervously says, "No. No, I'm not." The clown then says, "In that case, sir, you are NO END of an ass!" The rest of the audience guffaw with laughter at this jest, but poor Sean is left feeling very downcast and foolish. When the show's over Sean goes home and tells his brother Patrick about his humiliation. Patrick is famous throughout the county for his quick mind, ready wit and razor-sharp retorts, and he decides to get his own back on the cruel clown. The next day, he and Sean go to the circus. Patrick makes sure that he sits where Sean was seated the previous evening. As before, the clowns come out to frolic and the chief clown approaches the audience. The clown sees Patrick sitting there, red-faced and glaring at him, and decides to take him down a peg or two. "Sir," says the clown to Patrick, "are you the front end of an ass?" Patrick says, "No, I'm not." The clown then says, "Sir, in that case, are you the back end of an ass?" Patrick says, "No, I'm not." The clown then says, "In that case, sir, you are NO END of an ass!" Patrick stands up and delivers his devastating retort: "Why don't you feck off, you big red-nosed bastard?"

☞ When a mime is arrested, do cops tell him he has the right to remain silent?

"In the theatrical world, your status and celebrity determines the location of your dressing room; all the biggest and brightest stars have their dressing rooms on the ground floor. It will give you some indication of my popularity when I tell you that my dressing room is partly filled with hawk droppings and the mice keep having black-outs."
Les Dawson

☞ Harry performed his stand-up act at the old people's home. It seemed to go very well; half the audience pissed themselves! But then the nurse told him that happened most days.

PERFUME

☞ A woman gets into an empty lift and lets off a real stinker of a fart. Embarrassed, she takes some perfume out of her bag and sprays it around. A man gets on at the next floor and starts sniffing the air with a sour look on his face. "Can you smell something?" asks the woman innocently. "Yeah," replies the man. "Smells like someone took a dump in a flower shop."

☞ A woman walks up to a perfume counter and picks up a sample bottle. She sprays scent on her wrist and smells it, "That's nice," she says to the sales assistant. "What's it called?" The assistant replies, "It's called 'Viens à Moi'. That's French for 'Come to me'." The woman takes another sniff and says, "Are you sure? It doesn't smell like come to me."

PETS

☞ A man goes into a hardware shop to buy some yellow paint. He gets chatting to the clerk behind the counter and reveals that he wants to use the paint to cheat in a competition. "I've got this small blue parrot," says the man, "but if I paint it yellow, I reckon I can enter it in the local canary competition and win a prize. They're giving $250 to the bird with the best voice, and my parrot sings like an angel." "That'll never work," exclaims the clerk. "If you try to paint a parrot yellow, you'll kill it." "No, I won't," replies the man. "That's one tough bird I've got. It'll be fine. Tell you what; I'll drop by next week and tell you how it went." Next week the man returns, looking downcast. "By the expression on your face, I'd guess the parrot died," says the clerk. "Yes," replies the man, "but it didn't mind the paint at all. It was the sanding between coats that did for him."

☞ Dick is sitting in his living room when he hears the sound of a shot coming from the house of his neighbour, Tom. Dick rushes over to find out what's happened. He finds Tom in his back garden holding a rifle, the body of his pet dog Towser lying at his feet. "What happened?" gasps Dick. "I shot Towser," replies Tom. "Was he mad?" asks Dick. Tom replies, "well, he wasn't exactly pleased about it..."

☞ A woman goes into a pet shop and asks for a canary. "But it must be able to sing," says the woman. "It must sing beautifully." The shopkeeper brings out a succession of canaries, and each of them sings its little heart out, but the woman won't have any of them. Eventually, the shopkeeper brings out an elderly canary sitting on a nest. The old bird might look knackered, but it sings like an angel and the woman is entranced. "I'll take it," she says, "and I'll take the nest too. Is it sitting on some eggs?" "No," replies the shopkeeper. He lifts up the bird and reveals it has no legs. "Good God!" exclaims the woman. "What sort of rip-off merchant are you, trying to sell me a legless bird?" "Listen, lady," snaps back the shopkeeper, "do you want a singer or a dancer..?"

☞ A woman takes her dog to a grooming parlour for a trim. When she gets there, she's astonished to find that a grooming session will cost her £100. "That's ridiculous!" she exclaims. "I only pay £60 when I have my own hair done." "I'm sure you do," says the groomer, "but, then again, I'll bet you've never bitten your hairdresser."

PHARMACISTS

☞ A pharmacist is speaking to an elderly patient, going over the directions on a prescription bottle. "You have to take a pill every four hours," says the pharmacist. "Be careful not to take them more often than that." "No worries there," replies the patient. "It takes me four hours to get the lid off!"

PHILOSOPHY

☞ A philosophy professor gives his class their final exam. He places his chair on his desk and says, "I want you to use everything you've learned in this course to prove to me that this chair does not exist." All the students start thinking out their arguments and writing them down, except Bill. All Bill does is scribble a line on his test paper and walk out. Two weeks later the results are out and Bill gets the highest grade with the shortest answer: "What chair?"

☞ Every time I find the meaning of life, they change it.

☞ I studied philosophy at college. The exam was a piece of cake – which was a surprise, because I'd really been expecting some questions on a sheet of paper.

☞ In Germany, there's an inn with a plaque above the door; it reads 'Heisenberg may have slept here.'

☞ The First Law of Philosophy: for every philosopher, there exists an equal and opposite philosopher. The Second Law of Philosophy: they're both wrong.

PHOBIAS

☞ Tom has claustrophobia and agoraphobia at the same time. He spends most of his time standing in doorways.

PHOTOCOPYING

> **"I once Xeroxed a mirror. Now I have an**
> **extra Xerox machine."**
> *Steven Wright*

☞ Tania spent half an hour photocopying her backside on the office copier. It wasn't for a joke; it was just the only part of her that had come back from holiday without a tan.

PHOTOGRAPHY

"My photographs don't do me justice; they look just like me"
Phyllis Diller

☞ Grandma goes to a photo lab with a photograph of Albert, her late husband. "This picture was the last one taken before he died," says grandma. "But he's wearing that horrid trilby hat of his. Can you use your photography gadgets to get rid of the hat so we can see his head?" "Certainly, madam," says the sales assistant. "We can take the hat off very easily; then we can fill in the missing details. Tell me, what colour hair did your husband have?" Grandma replies, "Why are you asking me? When you take his hat off, you'll be able to see for yourself."

☞ Mr and Mrs Jones are having trouble starting a family. It turns out the fault is with Mr Jones, so they decide to hire a proxy father. They've heard bad things about some sperm donor clinics, so they decide to make sure they're getting the real deal by hiring a man to come round and do the deed himself. The man they choose is a tall, blond college graduate with a high IQ and excellent health. On the day the proxy father is due to arrive, Mr Jones leaves the house early to give his wife some privacy. A few minutes after he leaves, a tall, young blond man knocks on the door – except he's not the proxy father; he's a baby photographer trying to drum up some business by knocking on doors. Mrs Jones lets him in. "Good morning, madam," says the man. "I've come to…" "It's all right," says Mrs Jones. "There's no need to explain. I've been expecting you." "Really?" says the man. "Did you read the flyer I pushed through your door?" "No," says Mrs Jones, "we saw your website." "Great," says the man. "I get a lot of bookings that way. Now, let's see what we can do for you." So Mrs Jones invites him in and they sit on the couch in the living room. "Although I do all sorts of work in this line, I specialise in babies," says the man. "Usually, we do a few round the house: in the bathtub, in the garden, perhaps some on the living room floor – and the bedroom, obviously. But I can't guarantee results every time." "I see," says Mrs Jones nervously. The man continues, "The trick is to try several different positions, shooting from four or five angles." "It sounds like it might take quite a while," says Mrs Jones. "I was hoping we'd be done in ten minutes or so." "Sorry, Madam," says the man. "I could be in and out in five minutes, but you'd be disappointed. We need to take a bit of time at this. The longer I plug away at it, the better the results. I'll show you some of my work." The man pulls out a photo album and opens it. "See here?" he continues, pointing at a smiling baby. "I did this little fellow in the back of a car." He points at another picture. "And this little girl was done in a park." "In a park?" says the astonished Mrs Jones. "Yes," replies the man. "Her mother insisted we did it out in the sunshine with a lot of space around us. It was quite a production. We had quite a crowd watching us at the end of it." "I bet you did," says Mrs Jones. "Though I prefer something more private myself," continues the man. "I didn't feel safe in the park. There were one or two suspicious characters around. One of them kept handling my equipment. He wouldn't stop touching it, even after I asked him not to. I thought he might try to grab it and run off with it." "You don't say?" gulps Mrs Jones. "Anyhow," says the man, "we might as well get started. If you get ready, I'll set up my tripod." "A tripod?" exclaims Mrs Jones. "What do you need that for?" "For support," explains the man. "My equipment's pretty heavy. If I didn't have a tripod to rest my Canon on, I'd probably fall over. And it's too long to handle comfortably when I get started... are you all right, madam? Christ. She seems to have fainted..."

"One time a guy handed me a picture of himself. He said, 'Here's a picture of me when I was younger.' What? Every picture of you is of when you were younger."
Mitch Hedberg

PIERCINGS

☞ Dad arrives home with his ten-year-old daughter after a trip into town to get her ears pierced. When the girl walks through the front door, mum is horrified to see that her daughter has had her ears pierced, a stud put through her nose, a bolt stuck in her eyebrow, a ring in her lip and a chain from her left nostril to her right ear. Dad explains, "The shop had a special offer on."

PIRATES

☞ Why are pirates called pirates? They just Arrrrrrrrrrrrrrrrrrrrr!

PLANES

☞ A passenger jet from Limerick Air is making a landing at a small airport. Murphy, the pilot, turns to his co-pilot and says, "O'Leary, I've landed at this place only once before. It was a few years ago, but I remember that the runway was awful short. Be sure to give me full flaps if I need them." The plane comes in for its landing and sweat begins to bead on Murphy's brow. "To be sure, this is a mighty short runway," he says. "Even shorter than I remember. Give me quarter-flaps." O'Leary turns the landing flaps to one-quarter and the plane drops quickly. "Holy Mother of God!" says Murphy. "This runway's much, much shorter than I remember. Quick! Give me half-flaps!" O'Leary switches the flaps to half and the plane goes into a steep dive. Murphy is now close to panic. "They shouldn't build runways this short!" he fumes. "It's criminal. Hurry now. Give me full flaps!" O'Leary pulls a lever and the flaps go full on. The plane screams down to land on the runway. The wheels touch the tarmac and Murphy throws on the thrust reversers and slams on the brakes. Miraculously, the plane manages to screech to a halt with the front wheel just half an inch from the edge of the runway. Murphy wipes his brow. "Jesus," he says. "I never thought we'd make it. That must be the shortest bloody runway in the world." O'Leary looks out of the side widow. "It's probably the widest, too," he says. "Half a mile, by the looks of it."

PLANTS

> "About a month ago I got a cactus. A week later,
> it died. I was really depressed because I was like,
> 'Damn! I'm less nurturing than a desert'."
> *Demetri Martin*

☞ Scientists say that plants can warn each other of impending danger. What good is a plant warning another plant about danger? What the hell are they going to do about it? Dial 999?

PLUMBERS

☞ A man answers a ring on the doorbell. Outside, he finds a plumber standing on the front step. "Are you Mr Henderson?" asks the plumber. "No," replies the man. "My name's Jones. The Hendersons moved out of here six months ago." "That's typical," fumes the plumber. "These bastards ring for a plumber, tell you it's an emergency, then bugger off to another address!"

☞ Did you hear about the plumber who accidentally swallowed a ballcock and an immersion heater? He's all right now, apart from occasional hot flushes.

POLAR BEARS

☞ A young polar bear comes into his den and says to his mother, "Am I a real polar bear?" "Of course you are," replies his mother. The young polar bear asks his father, "Dad, am I a real polar bear?" "Yes," says Dad. "You are a real polar bear." The young polar bear then says to his parents, "Are grandma and grandpa real polar bears?" "Yes," say his parents. "So are all my relatives real polar bears?" asks the young polar bear. "Yes, they're all real polar bears," says dad. "Why do you ask?" "Because," says the young polar bear, "I'm f***ing freezing!"

☞ Why are polar bears big and furry? Because if they were small and smooth they'd be aspirins.

☞ Why do polar bears like igloos? Because they're crunchy on the outside and chewy on the inside.

POLITICIANS

☞ At a political news conference, a journalist puts his hand up to ask a question. "Sir!" says the journalist. "Your former secretary has stated publicly that you have a small penis. Would you like to comment on that?" The politician replies, "I couldn't really tell you whether it's that large or that small when compared to other men; I just don't know: but what I can say is that my former secretary has a very, very big mouth."

POLITICS

☞ A little old lady phones the police. "Help!" she says. "Send a car to my house right away! There's a damn Democrat masturbating on my front porch!" "How d'you know the masturbator is a Democrat?" asks the operator. The little old lady replies, "It's obvious; if he was a Republican, he'd be screwing somebody!"

☞ A man walks into a bar and orders a drink. It turns out this bar has a robot bartender. The robot serves the man his beer, then says, "So, what's your IQ?" The man replies, "I think it's about 150." The robot then makes conversation about highbrow things such as global warming, quantum physics, spirituality, string theory and nano-technology. The man is very impressed, but decides to test the robot. He'd like to see how flexible its programming is. He comes in the next day and, when the robot asks him his IQ, he says, "Around 100." The robot then starts to make conversation about football, NASCAR, baseball, supermodels and TV shows. Again, the man is impressed, but he decides to give the robot one more test. He comes in the next day, and tells the robot he has an IQ of 50. Speaking slowly, the robot says, "So... are you going to vote Bush again?"

☞ Castro dies and is sent to hell. Unfortunately, his luggage is sent to heaven by mistake, and the devil is forced to send two imps to get it back. When the imps arrive at the Pearly Gates they find that Saint Peter is out to lunch, but they see Castro's bags just inside the gate and decide to climb over and get them. The imps are climbing over the gates when two angels see them. "Typical," says one angel to the other. "Castro's been dead five minutes and already we're getting refugees."

☞ Did you hear about the MP who dreamed he was giving a speech in the House of Commons – then woke up and found he was?

☞ Did you hear about the politician who promised that, if he was elected, he'd make sure everybody got an above-average income?

☞ Did you hear that Monica Lewinsky voted for the Republicans in the last election? She said the Democrats had left a bad taste in her mouth.

☞ How long does a US Congressman serve for? Until he gets caught.

☞ Politics: from 'poli' meaning 'many', and 'tics', meaning 'blood-sucking creatures'.

"The next time we elect a president, for God's sake can we do a background check?"
David Letterman

☞ The Prime Minister made a speech to the TUC today. Ten per cent of the audience booed while the rest applauded. Unfortunately it turned out the ninety per cent who applauded were actually clapping the booing.

☞ Two Florida alligators meet up in a creek. One is very fat, but the other is close to starving. "How did you put on so much weight?" asks the skinny alligator. "I moved in next to a tourist hotel," replies the fat crocodile. "They think I'm harmless, so when no one's looking it's pretty easy to grab one of them. I must've eaten ten tourists this week. What about you? You look like you're half-starved." "I live in a bayou near the Governor's office," says the skinny alligator. "Lots of politicians come my way and I manage to catch plenty, but no matter how many I eat, I get thinner and thinner." "How are you eating them?" asks the fat alligator. "The usual way," replies the skinny alligator. "I grab them by the head, shake the crap out of them and gulp them down." "There's your mistake," replies the fat alligator. "Once you've shaken the crap out of a politician there ain't much left apart from his ears and his underwear."

☞ Why did the Liberal cross the road? To get to the middle.

PORCUPINES

☞ A nun visits a zoo and sees a couple of porcupines in a cage. According to the sign on the cage, one is an African porcupine and one is an American porcupine, but as far as the nun can see they're both the same. The nun goes up to a zookeeper and says, "Excuse me, but what's the difference between a North American porcupine and an African porcupine?" The keeper's in a bad mood and growls, "The African porcupine has a goddamn dick that's three feet long." Shocked, the nun goes to the zoo manager to complain. "I'm sorry you were spoken to so rudely," says the manager. "The keeper should have told you that the easiest way to tell them apart is their quill length. The African porcupine has much longer spines than the North American species. Their dicks are about the same size."

POST AND POST PEOPLE

☞ A 65-year-old mailman in a small town is about to retire, and the community he's served for the past 45 years decides to give him a surprise. On his last day on the job, the mailman goes to the first house on his route and the householder gives him a bottle of Scotch. At the next house they give him a cheque for $100, and in the third house he gets a huge cake. However, when he calls at the fourth house, the door is opened by a beautiful woman in a kimono. The woman takes him upstairs and gives him the best sex he's ever had; then she takes him down to the kitchen and gives him a huge breakfast. Finally, she hands him a five-dollar bill. "Wow," says the mailman. "I've had the best day of my life, but I have to ask; what's the five dollars for?" The woman replies, "Well, when I asked my husband what we should do for you, he said, 'F*** him. Give him five bucks.' The breakfast was my idea."

☞ A post office worker at the sorting office finds an unstamped envelope addressed to God. He opens it and discovers it is from an elderly lady. The old lady has been robbed of her life savings and has no money to pay the bills. She will be cold and hungry for the rest of the month if she doesn't receive some divine intervention. In desperation, she begs God to send her $100. The postal worker is touched by the old lady's plight and organises a collection amongst his colleagues. Everyone digs deep and they come up with $96. Then they send the money to the old lady by special courier to make sure she gets it as soon as possible. A week later, the postal worker finds another unstamped envelope addressed to God. He recognises the handwriting and realises it's from the old lady who was robbed. He opens the envelope and reads the message: 'Dear God; thank you for the $100 dollars. I would have found it very difficult to make it through the next few weeks without your generous gift. PS. The envelope was four dollars short; it was probably those thieving bastards at the post office.'

☞ A woman goes to the post office to buy stamps for her Christmas cards. "What denominations?" asks the assistant. "The woman replies, "I'll need 20 Catholic, 15 Church of England, 10 Baptists and a Presbyterian."

☞ Father O'Leary finds a note pushed through his letterbox. It has only one word written on it: 'Bastard'. Father O'Leary takes the note to mass and holds it up. "Now," he says. "I have had more than one letter where the writer has written a message but forgotten to sign it. However, this is the first time someone has signed the letter and forgotten to write it."

☞ In the last twelve months, the post office has received five million letters complaining about its service. As a result, it's been able to announce record annual profits.

☞ Old Bill's legs are playing up, so he asks his neighbour, old George, if he can walk up the hill to the post office and see if a parcel has arrived for him. Old George was going to the post office anyway to get some tobacco, so he totters slowly to the top of the hill. When he finally gets there, he goes into the post office and, a few minutes later, totters out again. Old Bill watches as George makes his way down the hill, then along the road to Bill's front door. "Was my parcel there?" asks old Bill. Old George nods as he shuffles inside his front door. "Oh, yes," he says, "it's there all right."

POVERTY

"I came from a very poor family; up until the age of fifteen I thought knives and forks were jewellery."
Les Dawson

☞ I came from a very poor family. We couldn't afford a doorbell, so daddy painted a spot on the doorframe; whenever someone pressed it, I had to lean out of the window and shout "Ding-dong!"

"We were so poor, my daddy unplugged the clocks when we went to bed."
Chris Rock

> **"I can't forget the poverty-stricken days of my youth. I never had any shoes; my father used to black my feet and lace my toes up."**
>
> *Les Dawson*

☞ A man visits the home of the local pastor and asks to see the minister's wife, a fine woman well known in the area for her charity and generosity. The man stands before her, holding his hat in his hands. "Ma'am," he says in a voice hoarse with emotion. "I am here to draw your attention to the terrible plight of a poor family in this neighbourhood. There is a destitute woman who is too ill to work, with a dead husband, an elderly father and five young children who are close to starving. They are without a penny and are about to be turned into the cold, empty streets unless someone pays their rent. They need $400 to keep them off the streets." "How terrible!" exclaims the pastor's wife. "Of course they shall have it. I'll take the money round this instant. Are you a friend of theirs?" "No, ma'am," says the man. "I'm their landlord."

PREGNANCY AND CHILDBIRTH

☞ A girl sobs to her mother that she's pregnant. "What? How could you?" screams the mother. "Who's the father?" "How should I know?" sniffs the girl. "You never let me go steady with anyone."

☞ Murphy was devastated when his wife had twins. He's still trying to trace the father of the second child.

☞ A husband and wife are attending a pre-natal class. The instructor is telling the class about the benefits of gentle exercise. "Remember," she says, "a long, slow walk is ideal at this stage in your pregnancy: and, for a bit of company, why not enjoy the experience with your partner?" The husband sticks his hand up and says, "Excuse me: but in her condition, can she actually carry a golf-bag?"

"When I was born, I was so surprised I didn't talk for a year and a half."
Gracie Allen

☞ A pregnant woman goes to the maternity hospital to make arrangements for the birth. "Will the father be present at the delivery?" asks the midwife. "No," replies the woman. "He and my husband don't really get along."

☞ A pregnant woman is at home with her three-year old daughter. Suddenly the woman starts to go into labour, so she calls for an ambulance. A paramedic turns up, but the baby is due any minute, so he decides to deliver it in the house rather than try to get to the hospital. After a lot of pushing, the baby is born; it's a boy. The paramedic lifts him by his little feet and spanks him on the bottom to get him crying. Then he gives the baby to the mother. The paramedic turns to the three-year-old girl and asks her what she thinks of her new baby brother. "I don't think he should have crawled up there in the first place," says the girl. "Smack him again!"

☞ A woman is having a baby. In the delivery room, the father asks the nurse if there's anything he can do to help. The nurse replies, "No; please wait outside." After five minutes, he asks the same question and gets the same reply. This carries on until the baby is born when, once again, the father asks if there's anything he can do to help. This time the nurse says, "Okay; if you want, you can wash the baby." The father is thrilled, and goes off to wash the baby. After a while, the nurse returns to check on the baby and finds the father with his fingers in the baby's nostrils, moving it around in the water as if it were a boat. "What are you doing?" exclaims the nurse. "That's not the way you wash a baby." The father replies, "It is when the water's too hot!"

☞ Dick and Jane buy a house after many years of renting. Their friend George gives them a bottle of champagne as a housewarming present, but during the move it gets lost. Years later, the bottle turns up, just in time to toast the birth of the couple's third child. Jane pours out the champagne to friends and family while Dick reads them the message on the gift label. "Dick, make sure to look after this one. This time it's actually yours."

☞ Following the birth of his daughter, a panicked Japanese father goes to see the obstetrician. "Doctor," he says, "I'm very upset. My daughter has red hair. She can't possibly be my child." "Nonsense," replies the doctor. "Even though you and your wife both have black hair, one of your ancestors may have contributed red hair to the gene pool." "It isn't possible," says the father. "My wife and I have pure Asian ancestry. There's never been a redhead in either of our families." "Well, perhaps there's another explanation," says the doctor. "Let me ask you; how often do you and your wife have sex?" "Not often," says the father. "I've been working very hard for the past year. We've only made love twice in the last 16 months." "Well there you have it!" says the doctor confidently. "It's just rust."

☞ Harry goes up to his boss. "Can I have next week off?" he says. "My wife's expecting a baby." "Sure," replies the boss. "When's it due?" Harry replies, "If everything goes to plan, about nine months from now."

"I want to have children, but my friends scare me. One of my friends told me she was in labour for 36 hours. I don't even want to do anything that feels *good* for 36 hours."
Rita Rudner

☞ Little Jenny catches sight of her mother naked in the shower. Jenny's mother is pregnant and Jenny asks her why her tummy is so large. "Mummy has a baby growing in there," replies mother. Jenny digests this information, then says, "So what's growing in your ass?"

☞ A young girl discovers she's pregnant, and breaks the news to her mother and father. The parents demand to know who's responsible, so the daughter picks up the phone and calls the man in question. Half an hour later, a Ferrari pulls up in front of the house and a distinguished-looking man in an expensive suit steps out of it. He walks into the house and confronts the girl's parents. "Your daughter has informed me of the problem," says the man. "I can only apologise. I'm afraid I can't marry her because of my family situation, but I will take responsibility for the child and make provision for its care. Once it's born I will give you a townhouse and a beach villa, a lump sum of $500,000 and a monthly allowance of $30,000." The parents are astonished at this largesse, and sit there in stunned silence. "However," continues the man, "if there's a miscarriage, I'm not sure what I should do. What do you suggest?" There's a pause; then the father says, "You could try again."

PROCRASTINATION

☞ A procrastinator's work is never done.

☞ If God didn't want me to procrastinate, why did He invent tomorrow?

PROFESSIONS

☞ A doctor, a civil engineer and a consultant are arguing about the identity of the oldest profession in the world. The doctor says, "Well, in the Bible, it says that God created Eve from a rib taken out of Adam. This clearly required surgery. In that case, I can rightly claim that mine is the oldest profession in the world." The civil engineer disagrees. "But even earlier in the book of Genesis, it states that God created the heavens and the earth from out of the chaos," says the engineer. "This was the first and certainly the most spectacular application of civil engineering. Therefore, doctor, I say you are wrong. Engineering is the oldest profession." The consultant leans back in his chair and says, "That's all very well, but where do you think the chaos came from...?"

☞ George trained to be a proctologist, but later he changed his mind and became a dentist. He figured there'd be more business in dentistry; after all, people have 32 teeth but only one arsehole.

☞ Harry bumps into George, an old schoolfriend, in the street. "What are you doing these days?" asks Harry. "I became a fireman," replies George. "Really?" says Harry. "My son'd like to be a fireman. Have you got any career advice for him?" "Sure," replies George. "The most difficult part of our job is sliding down the pole. If you can, install a pole in your garage so your boy can get some practice." A few years later, Harry and George meet up again. "Say," says George. "Did you install that pole like I suggested?" "Yes," says Harry. "And did your son ever become a fireman?" asks George. "No," replies Harry glumly, "but I've got two daughters who became exotic dancers."

☞ My wife spent all the weekend removing panes of glass from our house. I think it's about time we found a window-cleaner who does house-calls.

PROOFREADING

☞ Remember, you should always proofread a document carefully to see if you any words out.

PROTESTS

> **"I'm against hunting; in fact, I'm a hunt saboteur.
> I go out the night before and shoot the fox."**
> *Tim Vine*

PSYCHICS

> **"If it's the Psychic Network, why do
> they need a phone number?"**
> *Robin Williams*

☞ I almost had a psychic girlfriend, but she left me before we met.

☞ Harry goes to see a psychic act at the local theatre. The psychic promises to answer any question truthfully and, true to his word, does manage to give accurate answers to all the questions the audience calls out: for example, "What's my middle name?" "How old is my cat?" "What have I got in my pocket?" Finally, Harry sticks up his hand and shouts, "Where's my father?" The psychic puts his hands to his temples, closes his eyes and says, "Your father is a transvestite barmaid serving drinks in a bar in Bangkok." "Rubbish!" shouts back Harry. "My father is Albert Smith. At this very moment he's at home watching the television with my mother." "Yes," replies the psychic, "Albert Jerome Smith is indeed sitting in number 32 Wigmore Street watching television: but your father is a transvestite barmaid serving drinks in a bar in Bangkok."

PUBLIC SPEAKING

☞ Before I speak, I have something important to say...

☞ A rich businessman is being driven to a conference by his chauffeur. The businessman's moaning about the amount of time he has to spend giving speeches when the chauffeur has an idea. "We look very similar, sir," says the chauffeur, "and I've heard your speeches many times. I bet if we swapped places, I could give some of your talks for you." The businessman thinks this is a great idea. It turns out the people he's speaking to today have never seen him in the flesh before, so they decide to give the plan a go. When they arrive, the chauffeur dresses as the businessman and the businessman puts on the chauffeur's uniform. They enter the lecture hall and the chauffeur prepares his notes. In the meantime, the businessman takes a seat in the audience to see how things work out. The lecture starts and everything goes perfectly; in fact, the chauffeur gives an excellent speech. However, neither he nor the businessman had planned on a question-and-answer session at the end. People raise their hands and the chauffeur manages to answer a few simple questions, but he's soon stumped by a hard one on international economics. The chauffeur keeps his head; he smiles and says, "Well that's a surprisingly simple question from such an expert audience: and, to show you how easy it is, I'm going to ask my chauffeur to come up here and answer it for me."

"When I give a lecture, I accept that people look at their watches, but what I do not tolerate is when they look at it and raise it to their ear to find out if it stopped."
Marcel Achard

☞ In ancient Rome, a pair of Christian slaves is thrown to the lions at the Coliseum. The arena's packed with spectators and they roar in delight at the prospect of bloodshed. The biggest and most ferocious of the lions pads over to the shivering Christians and bares its sharp teeth. Suddenly, one of the slaves leans forward and whispers in the lion's ear. The lion listens, then gives a yelp of alarm and scuttles away with its tail between its legs. The slave's companion turns to him and says, "What on earth did you say to him?" The slave replies, "I told him there was nothing to stop him eating us, but if he did he'd have to give an after-dinner speech to 15,000 people."

PUNS

☞ A grizzly bear walks into a bar and says, "Barman, bring me a beer." The barman replies, "Sorry, sir. We don't serve beer to bears." The bear is furious; it shouts, "Bring me a beer!", belching as it does so. The barman replies, "Sorry, sir; we don't serve beer to bears, and certainly not to bears who belch." "Just get me a goddamn beer!" shouts the bear. The barman replies, "Sorry, sir. We don't serve beer to bears, and certainly not to bears who belch and blaspheme. "I want a beer!" shouts the bear, kicking over some stools. The barman replies, "Sorry, sir. We don't serve beer to bears, and certainly not to bears who belch, blaspheme and behave badly." "Give me a BEER, you moron!" yells the bear. The barman replies, "Sorry, sir. We don't serve beer to bears, and certainly not to bears who belch, blaspheme, behave badly and badmouth the barman. "All I want is one freakin' goddamn beer!" howls the bear, taking a swipe at a passing barmaid. The barman replies, "Sir, we don't serve beer to bears, and certainly not to bears who belch, blaspheme, behave badly, badmouth the barman and beat up the barmaids." "If I don't get a beer in the next five seconds I'll rip off your head!" shouts the bear, biting the bartop in his fury and wolfing down the splintered wood. The barman is outraged; "Listen to me, sir! We do not serve beer to bears, and certainly not to bears who belch, blaspheme, behave badly, badmouth the barman and beat up the barmaids. And never, ever, do we serve beer to bears who take drugs." "What?" says the bear. "Drugs? I haven't had any drugs. "Oh really, sir?" says the barman. "Well what about that bar bit you ate?"

☞ A US company director is in court accused of tax evasion. The prosecuting lawyer asks, "Were you aware that both the FBI and the IRS intended to investigate this CPA, with the assistance of the HMRS?" The director replies, "No, not initially."

☞ Chalky White and Curly Smith both work at the local factory. One day a young, gorgeous woman joins the firm and is given the job of works supervisor. As Chalky is the older of the two men and quite a slow worker, he's afraid that the new woman might cut down his overtime hours. Imagine his delight, then, when he sees her shorten Curly's.

☞ Did you hear about the little Dutch boy who put his finger in the dyke? She kicked the crap out of him.

☞ God decides to cause a great drought as a follow-up to his great flood. He calls Noah to give him some instructions. "Noah," he says, "this drought is going to kill a lot of fish, so I want you to make an ark and fill it with fish tanks. There'll be a lot of fish, so make it at least eight storeys high. Oh: and I really like carp, so forget all the other kinds of fish; just concentrate on saving different kinds of carp. Can you do it?" "Sure," replies Noah. "What you want is a multi-storey carp ark."

☞ Granddad has changed his will fifteen times in the last year. He's a fresh heir fiend.

☞ I was having lunch with a friend when he started coughing and clutching his throat and going red in the face. "What's wrong?" I said. "Are you choking?" "No," he gasped. "I'm serious."

☞ I went into a shop and tried to buy a pack of helicopter-flavoured crisps. I was out of luck; they only had plane.

☞ Japanese authorities have banned the movement of all animals after the discovery of several nibbled sofabeds in Tokyo. It's feared this may indicate an outbreak of Futon Mouse disease.

☞ Mary used to be married to the owner of a fish and chip shop, but she divorced him and married a poet; she went from batter to verse.

☞ Raymond starts work at a zoo. His first job is to clean out a tank of rare fish. However, Raymond slips on a wet patch, smashes the fish tank and watches in horror as the fish flip-flop around on the floor. There are no other tanks nearby, so Raymond flings the dying fish into the lion enclosure, where a hungry lion soon snaps them all up. Raymond does his best to hide the remains of the fish tank, then reports for his second job: delivering a plate of buns to the chimps' tea-party. Raymond arrives with the buns, but slips on a banana skin and falls on two of the chimps, crushing them to death. Horrified, Raymond lobs the dead chimps into the lion enclosure and hopes no one will notice their absence. A hungry lion soon scoffs down the dead chimps. Raymond then reports for his third job; he has to go to the insect house and repair a tank which houses a hive of killer bees. Raymond tries to be careful but, as usual, his clumsiness lets him down. He falls off a ladder and lands on the beehive, squashing it flat. Raymond is terrified that some killer bees will escape, so he stamps up and down on the hive, making sure that every bee is mushed into goo. Once more, Raymond hurries to dispose of the evidence in the lion enclosure. He then leaves the zoo and vows never to return. Next day, a new lion is delivered to the zoo. It walks into the enclosure and starts chatting to the other lions. "So what's the food like in here?" asks the new lion. "It used to be terrible," replies one of the other lions, "but recently it's got a lot better; yesterday we had fish and chimps with mushy bees."

☞ What do you call dinosaurs who suffer from anxiety attacks? Nervous Rex.

☞ Who were the first people to write with fountain pens? The Incas.

☞ Why couldn't the steam train sit down? It had a tender behind.

RACIAL DISHARMONY

☞ A policeman is walking the beat when he comes across a group of schoolchildren fighting at the bus-stop. The children seem to be divided into two groups – black and white – and they're knocking seven bells out of each other. The policeman runs into the fray and breaks up the fight. "Stop it at once!" he shouts. "I can see what this is all about. It's about colour, isn't it? Well, the colour of you skins isn't important. Try to imagine you're not black and white. Try to imagine you're all the same. Why not try to pretend you're all green?" The bus pulls up at the stop. The policeman continues, "Now, imagine you're all green and let's have no more nonsense. Come on; get on the bus: light greens first..."

☞ Down in a Mississippi prison, a new warden is doing the rounds to get to know the inmates. He enters a cell with three convicts in it: two white men and a black man. "So what are you in for?" says the warder to one of the white men. The man replies, "Five years for attempted robbery, sir. The judge said that if I'd actually done it, I would have got ten years!" The warden turns to the other white prisoner. "And what are you in for, son?" The man replies, "I got ten years for attempted murder, sir. The judge said I'd have got twenty if I had actually killed the son of a bitch!" The warder turns to the black prisoner and says, "And how about you, boy? What are you in for?" The man replies, "Twenty years, sir. I didn't have no lights on my bike. The judge said I would've got life if it had been the night-time."

☞ The Pope and his entourage are driving through Alabama as part of a tour of the southern states of the USA. The convoy of vehicles gets lost, and they end up taking a deserted back road. Suddenly, they come across a heart-warming sight of simple humanity; two white men are using a rope to haul a black man out of a river. The Pope gets out of his car to congratulate the two men on rescuing their black brother. "What are your names?" asks the Pope. One of the white guys says, "Ma name's Zeke and this here's Billy-Bob." "And what is the name of your friend?" asks the Pope, pointing to the black guy gasping on the river-bank. "Don't know," replies Zeke. "Marvellous," cries the Pope. "You take the trouble to save this poor man of another race, even though he is a stranger to you. Your actions are most creditable. They remind me of the tribulations of Saint Cecilia when she dived into the churning maelstrom to save the life of a Roman centurion." "Do it?" replies Zeke. "Oh, yes," replies the Pope. "I had heard that Alabama was stricken with the scourge of racism, but you have restored my faith in human nature." With this, the Pope gets back in his car and he and his entourage drive off. Zeke and Billy-Bob look at each other. "That guy sure did know a lot of long words," observes Billy-Bob. "He sure did," replies Zeke, "but he don't know dick about alligator fishing."

RAMBLING

☞ I phoned up to speak to the local branch of the Ramblers' Association; oh, they just went on and on and on...

RECORDS

☞ Every day I beat my own previous record for the number of consecutive days I've stayed alive.

REDNECKS

☞ What has six boobs and three teeth? The night shift at an Arkansas waffle house.

☞ A guy from Alabama passed away and leaves his entire estate to his beloved widow. Unfortunately, she can't touch it until she's 14.

☞ Billy-Bob is being treated by his doctor for VD. "Now listen, Billy-Bob," says the Doc. "This here injection will clear the disease right up, but after I give it you, you can't have sexual relations for a week. You understand?" "Sure, doc," says Billy-Bob. "No sexual relations for a week: but is friends and neighbours okay?"

☞ Billy-Bob is walking down the street with some chicken-wire under his arm. Zeke asks him what he's doing. "It's chicken-wire," says Billy-Bob. "I'm going to use it to catch some chickens." "You dang fool," says Zeke. "You can't catch chickens with chicken-wire." But later that day, Zeke sees Billy-Bob dragging a basketful of chickens down the road. The next day, Billy-Bob is walking down the street with some duck tape under his arm. Zeke asks what he's doing. "I got me some duck tape," says Billy-Bob. "I'm going to use it to catch some ducks." "What kind of idiot are you?" says Zeke. "You can't catch ducks with duck tape." But later that day, Zeke sees Billy-Bob dragging a sackful of ducks down the road. Next day, Billy-Bob is walking down the street with a bundle of sticks under his arm. Zeke says, "What you got there?" Billy-Bob replies, "I got me some pussy willow." Zeke says, "I'll get my hat..."

☞ Experts say there are two reasons why it is nearly impossible to solve a redneck murder: one, all the DNA is the same: two, there are no dental records.

☞ Cletus decides to give his wife Missy-Sue a treat for their wedding anniversary. He buys 24 bottles of champagne and pours them into the tub so she can have a real fancy bubble bath. After she's finished, Cletus decides to be thrifty and carefully pours all the champagne back into the bottles. Cletus gets to the last bottle, fills it, and finds there's still half a bottle of champagne left in the tub. He calls out into the bedroom, "Dang-it, Missy-Sue! Why the hell couldn't you have used the bathroom?!"

☞ Zeke had to go to court before his divorce was finalised. The judge had to decide if his ex wife was still legally his sister.

☞ Did you hear that they've raised the minimum drinking age in Missouri to 32? They want to keep alcohol out of the high schools.

☞ How can you tell if a redneck is married? There's dried tobacco juice on both sides of his pickup truck.

☞ Jed is courting Lulu-Belle out in cattle country. One evening they're sitting on Jed's porch, watching the sun go down, when Jed sees his prize bull mounting one of the cows in the paddock. Jed puts his arm around Lulu-Belle. "Say, sweetcakes," he says. "I'd sure like to be doing what that there bull's doing." "Well, there's nothing stopping you," replies Lulu-Belle. "After all, it *is* your cow."

☞ Three hillbillies are walking down the road when they see the rear end of pig sticking out of a bush. The first hillbilly says, "Gosh, I'm real horny. I sure wish that there was Demi Moore's backside." The second hillbilly says, "Gosh, I'm real horny. I sure wish that was Dolly Parton's backside." The third hillbilly says, "Gosh, I'm real horny too... I wish this was night-time."

☞ Three rednecks are sitting on a porch comparing wives. The first redneck says, "My Cindy's so dumb, she bought a toilet, and we don't even have running water." The second says, "That's nothing! My Maisie bought a ceiling fan, and we don't even have no electricity." The third says, "Aw, that ain't nothing! I was goin' through my Lou-Lou's purse for some whiskey money and I found a box of condoms. And you know what? She ain't even got a pecker!"

☞ What's the similarity between a Texas tornado and an Alabama divorce? Both involve somebody losing a trailer.

☞ Zeke sees Billy-Bob walking around town; he's completely naked except for the boots on his feet. "Billy-Bob," says Zeke, "what the hell you doin' walking around town bare-ass naked like that?" Billy-Bob replies "Well, Zeke, me and Mary-Lou was down on the farm and we started a-kissing. Then Mary-Lou says we should go to the barn, so we did. When we got inside the barn, we starts a-kissing and a-cuddling some more and things got pretty hot and steamy. Then Mary-Lou says we should go up in the hay-loft. So we gets up there, and Mary-Lou takes off all her clothes and says I should do likewise. So I takes off all my clothes except my boots. Then Mary-Lou lies down on the hay and says, 'Okay, Billy-Bob, go to town...'"

☞ Zeke visits Billy-Bob and his wife Lulu-Belle, and stays the night in their shack. The next morning, Billy-Bob goes to get some beer from the store. "Lulu-Belle," he says, "mind you show our guest some real proper hospitality while he's here. If he wants anything, you give it to him, y'hear?" "Sure thing," replies Lulu-Belle. So Billy-Bob goes to the store, but when he returns ten minutes later, he finds Lulu-Belle and Zeke stark naked, having sex. Zeke is lying on the floor, while Lulu-Belle sits on top, pumping away as hard as she can. "Dang it!" cries Billy-Bob. "You call that being hospitable? He's going to freeze his butt off lying on that floor!"

☞ A Texan is driving through the backwoods of Alabama and pulls into a small garage to get some gas. The only person in sight is Zeke, who is sitting in a rocking chair peeling an apple with a Bowie knife. "God damn it!" shouts the Texan. "Do you work here, boy?" "Yup," replies Zeke. "Then get this God-dammed car filled with gas!" "In a minute," replies Zeke. "I just gotta finish peelin' this here apple." "God damn it!" shouts the Texan. "Did you hear me? Get this goddamned car filled with god-damned gas!" Zeke replies, "Round these parts we don't take the Lord's name in vain, mister." "Jesus Christ!" yells the Texan. "If you don't fill this goddamned car, I'll pound you flat and fill it myself!" Zeke looks the Texan straight in the eye and holds up the apple. "You see this here apple?" asks Zeke. "Of course I can see the goddamned apple!" shouts the Texan. "Then look what I can do to it," says Zeke, who then flicks his knife through the air faster than the eye can follow. In a few seconds, the apple is lying in eight equal pieces on the floor. "You got another goddamned apple?" asks the Texan. Zeke nods and holds one up. The Texan whips out a Colt revolver and blasts six bullets through the centre of the apple in less than a second. Zeke jumps to his feet. "Jesus Christ almighty!" he exclaims. "How many goddamned gallons did you want, sir?"

REDNECKS – YOU KNOW YOU'RE A REDNECK IF...

☞ Anyone in your family ever died right after saying, "Hey y'all! Watch this..."

☞ Fewer than half your cars run.

☞ The majority of your teeth are on a chain around your neck.

☞ The diploma hanging up in your living room contains the words 'Trucking Institute'.

☞ The neighbours start a petition to ban your Christmas lights.

☞ The Salvation Army declines your mattress.

☞ You and your friends frequently argue about which county jail has the best food.

☞ You believe the term 'dual air bags' refers to your wife and mother-in-law.

☞ You can entertain yourself for more than an hour with a flyswatter.

☞ You can hunt from your bedroom window.

☞ You have the number of your local taxidermist on speed-dial.

☞ You have to honk your horn when pulling into your driveway to keep from killing a chicken.

☞ You have to walk out of your house to get something out of the fridge.

☞ You judge driving time solely by the number of beers you'll need to put in the pick-up.

☞ You know instinctively that red wine goes with opossum.

☞ You smoked during your wedding service.

☞ You take a beer into a job interview.

☞ You tend to burn your front yard rather than mow it.

☞ You think that women are turned on by animal noises and seductive tongue gestures.

☞ You use a 10-penny nail to pick your teeth after eating roadkill.

☞ You use the phrase 'over yonder' more than once a month.

☞ Your dog doubles as your dishwasher.

☞ Your home has more miles on it than your car.

☞ You're hoping that one day you'll meet 'Cousin Right'.

☞ You've been married three times and still have the same in-laws.

☞ You've ever used weedkiller indoors.

RELIGION

☞ Once there was a time when all people believed in God and the church ruled supreme. We call it the Dark Ages.

☞ I was at a red light behind a car with a bumper sticker that read, 'Honk if you love Jesus'. So I honked. The driver leaned out his window, gave me the finger and yelled, "Can't you see the light's red, you goddamn moron?"

☞ A vicar's car won't start, so he calls the local garage and asks for a tow truck to take it away for repairs. When the truck driver turns up, the vicar says, "I hope this won't be too expensive. I'm only a poor preacher, after all," "I know," says the driver. "I've been to one of your services."

☞ Bill is sitting in the front pew at a rather boring church service. While the choir sings a hymn, the vicar walks over to Bill and says, "Could you wake up the woman sitting behind you?" Bill replies, "You put her to sleep; you wake her up."

☞ What do you get when you mix holy water with castor oil? A religious movement.

☞ A country vicar climbs into his pulpit and is disappointed to see that there is only one person in the congregation: an old farmer. The vicar sighs and asks the farmer if he'd mind if the service was cancelled. "Of course I'd mind," replies the farmer. "If I go out to my hens with a bucket of grain and only one chicken turns up, I don't let that chicken go away hungry, do I?" The vicar is moved by this homespun parable and decides to deliver the best sermon he can for the farmer. The vicar cuts no corners, and after a forty-minute sermon, three readings and five hymns, the vicar goes to greet the farmer as he leaves the church. "And what did you think of the service?" asks the vicar. The farmer gives the vicar a dirty look and says, "Reverend, when only one chicken turns up for its feed, I don't give it the whole bleeding bucket!"

"It's so hard to believe in anything any more. Take religion; it seems so mythological, it seems so arbitrary. But science is based on pure empiricism, and by virtue of its method, excludes metaphysics. I don't think I would believe in anything... if it weren't for my lucky astrology mood watch."
Steve Martin

☞ A priest in a small Irish village has a cock and ten hens, which he keeps in a hen-house behind the church. One Saturday night the cock goes missing, and the priest suspects it's been stolen. During Mass the next day, the priest questions his congregation. "Has anybody got a cock?" he asks. All the men stand up. "No, no," he says. "What I meant to say was: has anybody seen a cock?" All the women stand up. "No," says the priest. "You're getting the wrong idea. What I should have said was: has anybody seen a cock that doesn't belong to them?" Half the women stand up. "I'll try again," says the priest. "What I'm really trying to say is: who here has seen *my* cock?" Six nuns, three altar-boys and a goat stand up.

☞ A vicar has a church in one of the rougher parts of town. Walking into church one day, he greets one of the local prostitutes, who sometimes attends his services. "Good morning, my dear," says the reverend. "I'm sure you'd like to know that I was praying for you last night." "No need for that, vicar," replies the woman. "You could have just rung me up. I wasn't doing anything."

"When I was a kid my dad would say, 'Emo, do you believe in the Lord?' I'd say, 'Yes!' He'd say, 'Then stand up and shout Hallelujah!' So I would – and I'd fall out of the rollercoaster."
Emo Philips

☞ At our house, I always say a little prayer before we sit down to eat. I'm not actually that religious, but my wife's a really lousy cook.

☞ Four women meet at a school reunion and have a chat over a cup of coffee. The first woman says, "My son's now a priest. When he walks into a room, everyone calls him 'Father'." The second woman says, "Well, my son's a bishop. Whenever he walks into a room, people call him 'Your Grace'." The third woman says, "My son's a Cardinal. Whenever he walks into a room, he's called 'Your Eminence'." The fourth woman sighs and says, "Well, my son's six foot six. He's got muscles like Mike Tyson, a face like Tom Cruise and a bulge in his trousers like he's smuggling a salami. Whenever he walks into a room, people say, 'Oh, my God...'"

"I'm completely in favour of the separation of Church and State. My idea is that these two institutions screw us up enough on their own, so both of them together is certain death."
George Carlin

☞ I used to tell a lot of religious jokes, but not any more; they put me on the Sects Offenders Register.

☞ It's Midnight Mass on Christmas Eve, and Father Murphy is shaking hands with his parishioners as they leave the church. O'Leary comes up and proffers his hand. "Mr O'Leary," says Father Murphy. "It's good to see you, but I'd prefer to see you in church more often. When are you going to take up the standard and join the army of God?" "I am in the army of God," says O'Leary. "Really?" says Father Murphy. "Then why is it we only see you at Christmas?" O'Leary looks over both shoulders, then whispers, "I'm in the Secret Service."

"Two guys came knocking at my door once and said: 'We want to talk to you about Jesus.' I said: 'Oh, no; what's he done now'?"
Kevin McAleer

☞ Little Johnny wants a new bike, so that evening he gets on his knees and prays. "Dear Lord Jesus," he says, "I've been really good recently, so as a reward I reckon it would be fair if you arranged for me to get a brand-new bike." Confident of a swift result, little Johnny goes to bed and dreams of his new bicycle. The next day, little Johnny wakes up and is surprised to find that no bike has appeared in his bedroom: and, when he searches the house, he realises that no bike has been left in any of the other rooms, or in the garage, or in the back yard. Little Johnny reckons that Jesus didn't hear him the first time, so that evening he repeats the prayer. "Dear Lord Jesus," he says, "I've been real good recently, so as a reward I reckon it would be fair if you arranged for me to get a brand-new bike." Little Johnny goes to bed, but when he wakes the next morning, there's still no bike to be seen! This goes on for a week, with little Johnny praying as hard as he can in the evening, only to suffer disappointment in the morning. The next Sunday, he decides to try a different approach. He goes to his grandmother's house and swipes her statue of the Virgin Mary. He goes home, blindfolds the statue, ties it with rope and hides it in his wardrobe. That night he prays again. ""Dear Lord Jesus; I got your mom. If you ever want to see her again..."

☞ Our local church accepts all denominations: twenties, tenners, fivers...

☞ The O'Hara twins, Sean and Mike, are well known gangsters in their neighbourhood. They're behind every type of dishonest practice and crime, and their wrongdoings have made them very wealthy. One day Sean dies in a car crash and his brother goes to the local priest to discuss the funeral arrangements. "I know my brother wasn't a good man," says Mike, "but at his service I want you to lie about it. I want you to say he was a saint, and if you do I'll put $10,000 in the poor-box." The priest agrees to this and takes the money. On the day of the funeral, he goes into the pulpit and starts speaking about Sean's life. The priest details all Sean's evildoing, his cheating, his womanizing, his thievery and violence, but ends his tirade by saying, "Mind you, compared to his brother, he was a saint..."

> **"Religious wars – you're basically killing each other
> to see who's got the better imaginary friend."**
> *Richard Jeni*

☞ To see who is the best preacher, a Catholic priest, a Baptist minister and a rabbi decide to set themselves the ultimate challenge. Each of them will try and convert a wild animal: a grizzly bear. After a week of bear-hunting in the woods, they meet up to discuss their experiences. The priest – standing on crutches and with his leg in plaster – goes first. "Well," he says, "when I found my bear I tried saying mass, but the bear didn't like that, so it tried to bite my leg off. Then I sprinkled it with holy water and, praise be to God, it became as gentle as a lamb." The Baptist minister – sitting in a wheelchair with his ribs bandaged – goes next. "When I found my bear," he says, "I grabbed it round the middle, then wrestled it to a lake. That bear fought like fury, but I managed to get it into the water and baptise it before it broke seven of my ribs." The priest and the minister both turn to look at the rabbi. The rabbi is lying in bed with a tube up his nose and his legs in traction. His arms, legs and torso are covered in plaster and his head is wrapped in bandages. The rabbi shrugs his shoulders and says, "Well, if I had to do it again, I probably wouldn't start with the circumcision…"

> **"I would never want to be a member of a group whose
> symbol is a guy nailed to two pieces of wood."**
> *George Carlin*

RELIGION – ATHEISM

> **"I once wanted to become an atheist but I
> gave up. They have no holidays."**
> *Henny Youngman*

☞ An atheist is on a fishing holiday, boating in a Scottish loch. Suddenly, his boat is attacked by the Loch Ness monster. In one easy motion, the beast tosses him and his boat high in the air. Then it opens its frightful maw, preparing to swallow the man whole when he tumbles down. As the man sails through the air, he cries out, "Oh, my God! Help me!" As he says these words, time stops still, and the atheist is suspended in mid-air. A deep voice booms out of the clouds, "Why did you call on me, sinner?" says the voice. "I thought you were an atheist who didn't believe in me!" "Oh, give me a break!" says the man. "Two minutes ago I didn't believe in the Loch Ness monster either!"

"To you, I'm an atheist; to God, I'm the Loyal Opposition."
Woody Allen

RELIGION – BAPTISTS

☞ How do you know that Adam was a Baptist? Only a Baptist could stand next to a naked woman and be tempted by a piece of fruit.

RELIGION – CATHOLICS

☞ The Vatican is to start printing a Catholic edition of *Playboy*. It still has a centrefold, but you have to pull it out just at the right moment.

**"I'm not Catholic, but I gave up picking
my belly-button for lint."**
Emo Philips

☞ Father O'Leary is walking down the road when he passes two nuns coming the other way. He nods in greeting and one of the nuns says, "Ah, Father; I see you got out of the wrong side of bed this morning." Father O'Leary is surprised by this remark, but he walks on. Soon he comes across an altar-boy. "Good morning, Father," says the boy. "I see you got out of the wrong side of bed this morning." Once more, Father O'Leary is puzzled by this comment, but he walks on. The next person the Father sees is Bishop O'Brien. "Hello, O'Leary," says the Bishop. "I see you got out of the wrong side of bed this morning." "Y'know," says Father O'Leary, "you're the third person who's said that to me today. Do I look in a bad mood or something? Because I actually feel very happy." "No," says the Bishop, "you don't look as if you're in a bad mood, but you *are* wearing your housekeeper's shoes."

☞ Our local Catholic church is certainly moving with the times. It has two confessional boxes now: one regular, and one for five sins or less.

☞ Two men are painting the ceiling of a church when they look down and see a little old lady kneeling in prayer. The painters decide to play a prank on her. One of them puts on a deep booming voice and calls out, "Old woman! This is Jesus, thy Lord!" The old lady ignores him. The man thinks she might be deaf, so in a louder voice he calls, "Old woman! This is Jesus, thy Lord!" There is still no reaction, so the man shouts again even louder, "Old woman! This is Jesus, thy Lord!" The old lady shouts back, "Will you be quiet, young man? I'm talking to your mother!"

RELIGION – CATHOLICS AND PROTESTANTS

☞ A Catholic priest and a Protestant minister are having a shower after a game of tennis at a health club. They're both under the hot water, rinsing off the suds, when a fire alarm sounds. The nearest emergency exit is only a few feet away so, stark naked, they hurry through the door, only to find themselves in the club's car park. The door closes behind them, trapping them outside. Highly embarrassed, the pair run round the side of the building to find another entrance. As they run, the minister covers his private parts, while the priest holds both his hands in front of his face. The pair see a side entrance and duck inside. They then hurry to the changing room to retrieve their clothes. The minister turns to the priest says, "I noticed you were running along with you hands over your face." "Well, why wouldn't I?" replies the priest. "That's the part of me most people would recognise."

☞ John takes his pregnant wife Mary on holiday to Ireland. After a week has passed, Mary suddenly goes into labour and she's rushed to a Roman Catholic hospital. While Mary is taken to the labour ward, John waits in the visitors' area. After a little while, a nun comes out to see him. "You'll be glad to know your wife's quite well and you have twin baby girls," says the nun. "Thank goodness," says John. "I'm glad they're girls; we already have seven sons." "Seven sons?" exclaims the nun. "Well, there's nothing like the warmth of a big Catholic family. Congratulations." "Oh, we're not Catholic," says John. "We're Protestant." "Protestant?" exclaims the nun. "You beast! Why, you're nothing but a sex maniac!"

☞ O'Leary the fishmonger decides to get married. The only trouble is that while Mr O'Leary is a Catholic, his intended bride is a Protestant. "She'll be nothing but trouble," says Murphy, O'Leary's business partner. "Marrying a Protestant will cause nothing but problems." "No, it won't," says O'Leary. "She's converting to the Catholic faith. Everything'll be fine." O'Leary gets married, but a few weeks later he goes up to Murphy and says, "My wife doesn't want me to work on Sundays." "What?" exclaims Murphy. "Sunday's one of our busiest days." "I know," says O'Leary, "but the wife wants us to go to Mass in the morning and afternoon and she says I shouldn't be working on the Sabbath at all." "I told you this would happen," says Murphy. "I said marrying a Protestant would cause nothing but trouble."

☞ Patrick and Kevin are digging up the road outside a brothel when they notice a vicar approaching the front entrance. The vicar looks over both shoulders, then ducks inside the brothel. "Did you see that?" says Patrick. "That dirty Protestant sneaking in for his share of sin: the hypocrite!" Ten minutes later, they see a rabbi walking down the road. The rabbi also makes a swift entry into the brothel. "Did you see that?" says Kevin. "Sure, the Jews are no better." A few minutes later, the pair spot Father McGuire walking down the road. The father passes the brothel's entrance, has a quick look round, then doubles back and ducks inside the knocking-shop. "'Tis a terrible thing, Kevin," says Patrick. "Take off your hat. One of them poor girls must be dying in there."

☞ The Reverend Ian Paisley's wife returns from a trip to the shops. She's surprised to find her husband at the bedroom window throwing handfuls of dried petals into the street. "Oh, my God," she thinks. "He's really lost it this time." She dashes upstairs to calm him down. "Ian," she shouts. "For the love of God, what's the matter with you?" The reverend turns to her and says, "I've told you, woman, there'll be no pot-pourri in this house!"

RELIGION – CONFESSION

☞ A little boy goes to confession. He recounts his sins and the priest tells him to say five Hail Marys. The boy goes away. But comes back a few minutes later. "I've got a problem," says the boy. "What's that?" says the priest. The boy replies. "You told me to say five 'Hail Marys', but I only know three."

☞ Father O'Hare and Father O'Leary decide to have a blow-out for their joint 40th birthday party. They agree to let their hair down, then confess to each other the next day and receive their penances. The two go to a casino and spend the night drinking and gambling. Father O'Hare wins a small fortune at roulette and they spend it all on a party in a hotel suite with champagne, caviar and girls by the dozen. The next day, the two hung-over priests go home and return to their duties. First, Father O'Hare hears Father O'Leary's confession. "Bless me, Father for I have sinned," says Father O'Leary. "Yesterday I went to a casino, where I gambled for money, drank to excess and consorted with loose women." "I see," says Father O'Hare. "Well why don't you just say five Hail Marys, and we'll forget all about it, shall we?" Father O'Leary says his Hail Marys, then hears the confession of Father O'Hare. "Bless me, Father for I have sinned," says Father O'Hare. "Yesterday I went to a casino, where I gambled for money, drank to excess and consorted with loose women." "That is outrageous behaviour for a man of the cloth!" bellows Father O'Leary. "You will say 500 Hail Marys, put £1,000 in the poor box and walk barefoot round your parish three times." "What?" exclaims Father O'Hare. "You did exactly the same as I did and I only you gave you five Hail Marys!" "That's totally irrelevant," says Father O'Leary. "What I do in my spare time is my own business, but I take my job very seriously indeed!"

☞ Father O'Leary is hearing the confession of Mr Smith, one of his parishioners. "Last week I committed adultery," says Mr Smith. "I was meant to meet my wife at her parent's house, but my wife wasn't around: just her mother, all by herself – so I slept with her." "Sleeping with your mother-in-law?" exclaims the shocked Father O'Leary. "Say fifty Hail Marys." "That's not all," continues Mr Smith. "The next day, I went to my wife's place of work: but my wife wasn't in, so I slept with her boss, Mrs Grogan." "Disgraceful!" says Father O'Leary. "Say another fifty Hail Marys," "And yesterday," goes on Mr Smith, "I went to meet my wife at her sister's house, but my wife wasn't there – so I slept with her sister." "I think I understand," says Father O'Leary, who then gets up, drops his trousers and bends over. "Let's get on with it." "What are you doing?" says the shocked Mr Smith. Father O'Leary replies, "Well, your wife isn't here, either..."

☞ Four old ladies are playing whist. The first old lady says, "I've known you all for many years and there's something I've got to get off my chest; I'm a kleptomaniac. But don't worry; I've never stolen from any of you and I never will." The second lady also makes an announcement. "Well, since we're confessing, I must tell you I'm a nymphomaniac," she says, "but don't worry; I've never tried to seduce your husbands and I never will." The third old lady decides to make a contribution. "I've something to confess too," she says. "I'm a lesbian: but don't worry; none of you is my type." The fourth old lady stands up. "I, too, have a confession to make," she says. "I'm an incurable gossip. Do you mind if I use the phone?"

☞ A new priest is nervous about hearing confessions, so he asks an older priest to sit in on his sessions. The new priest hears a couple of confessions; then the old priest asks him to step out of the confessional to hear a few suggestions. "When you hear a confession, it's important you appear to be listening very carefully," says the old priest. "I suggest you cross your arms over your chest and rub your chin with your hand to indicate you're deep in thought." The new priest agrees that this is a good idea. The old priest then adds, "And try saying things such as, 'I see; yes, go on,' and 'I understand,' or 'How did you feel about that?'

These phrases will help show that you are paying attention and encourage people to speak from the heart." The new priest jots down these remarks and agrees to give them a try. "Good," says the old priest: "but frankly, I think anything would be an improvement on your current performance. The congregation don't really like it when you slap your knee, laugh, and say 'Cool! What happened next'?"

RELIGION – GOD

☞ A nursery school teacher is observing her class while they draw pictures. She's walking around to see what each child is doing and comes to little Jenny, who is scribbling away diligently. The teacher asks what Jenny's drawing. Jenny replies, "I'm drawing God." The teacher says, "But Jenny, no one really knows what God looks like." Jenny replies, "They will in a minute."

☞ A famous motorcycle designer dies and goes to heaven. The designer's so famous that God himself grants him an interview. The designer comes before the Lord and they start chatting about designs, good and bad. "You're pretty good," says the bike designer. "I've had my successes," says God. "Yeah," continues the bike designer, "but I've got a few beefs about the way you built chicks: you know – women." "What's wrong with them?" asks God, slightly offended. The bike designer runs off a list of complaints, "Well, first, there's a lot of inconsistency in the way they stick out in front. I was always very careful about that on my bikes. Second, they make a heck of a lot of noise. My bikes were always whisper-quiet. Thirdly, a lot of them have rear ends that wobble about like crazy – that's seriously bad. Fourthly, down below, that intake's too damn close to the exhaust." God is annoyed. "Anything else?" he asks testily. "Well, yeah," replies the bike designer. "Their maintenance costs are through the roof!" "I see," says God, keeping his cool. "You may have a few points there: but let's face facts. At the end of the day, most guys would rather be riding one of my inventions than any of yours."

☞ A small boy asks his mother, "Mummy, is God a man or a woman?" "Well," says the mother, "God is both man and woman." The boy says, "And is God black or white?" The mother answers, "God is both black and white." The small boy then asks, "Mummy, is God gay or straight?" The mother says, "Well, some might say that God is both gay and straight." The boy replies "So, basically, you're telling me God is Michael Jackson?"

☞ I found out I was God when I was praying one day; I suddenly realised I was talking to myself.

☞ One day God decides to send an angel to Earth to check on the progress of humanity. The angel comes back and says that, whilst two per cent of the people of Earth are good, kind and decent, the remaining 98 per cent are dishonest, amoral, perverted scumbags who ought to be drowned in a bucket. God is worried by this news; he doesn't want to do anything drastic such as sending down another flood, so instead he decides to give the decent two per cent a bit of encouragement: tell them to keep up the good work. He decides the best way to do this is to send each member of the decent, honest, good 2 per cent of humanity a letter. And do you know what that letter said? No, I didn't get one either...

☞ Sid has driven his car into town to attend a very important business meeting, but he's having trouble finding a parking spot. In desperation he looks up to heaven and says, "Lord, if you help me find a parking space, I promise I'll never lie or cheat again." At that moment a car in front of Sid pulls away from the kerb, leaving an ideal parking place. Sid looks up and says, "It's all right. I just found one."

RELIGION – JEHOVAH'S WITNESSES

☞ How many Jehovah's Witnesses does it take to change a light-bulb? Three: one to screw in the bulb, and two to knock on your door and ask if you've seen the light!

☞ One rainy day, there's a ring on Glenda's doorbell. Glenda opens the door and finds a young girl, a Jehovah's Witness, standing, soaking wet, in her porch. Glenda feels sorry for her, so she asks the young woman into the house for a cup of coffee. While they're having their hot drinks, Glenda makes conversation. "So," she says, "what exactly is this Jehovah's Witness message you're passing along?" The girl shrugs and says, "I'm not sure. I never got this far before."

RELIGION – JESUS

☞ Jesus and Moses get together at a heavenly beach party and have a talk about old times. Moses recalls the occasion he parted the Red Sea and Jesus asks to see him do it again. Moses obligingly taps his staff, holds it over the water and the sea parts in a spectacular fashion. "That's great," says Jesus. "I can do something with water too. I can walk on it." So Jesus takes off his sandals and walks into the surf. However, Jesus takes about ten steps before he starts sinking. He staggers back to the shore, his clothes soaking. "Well, that was embarrassing," says Jesus. "I guess I must have lost the knack." "You might have," says Moses, "but let's not forget, the last time you did that stunt you didn't have holes in your feet."

☞ The Three Wise Men come to visit Joseph and Mary and her new-born son. As the last wise man enters the stable he gives his head an almighty crack on the doorway. He drops his myrrh, puts his hands to his forehead and shouts, "Jesus Christ!" "Hey, Mary," says Joseph, "write that down. It's a damned sight better than Darren."

RELIGION – MORMONS

☞ What do you call a Mormon man with only one wife? A minimalist.

☞ What's the secret for a happy polygamist marriage? Nametags.

☞ Why do Mormon women stop having babies at thirty-five? Because thirty-six is just too many.

☞ Why was the Mormon man upset about his marriage counselling bill? He didn't get a group rate.

> **"A Mormon told me that they don't drink coffee.**
> **I said, 'A cup of coffee every day gives you**
> **wonderful benefits.' He said, 'Like what?' I said,**
> **'Well, it keeps you from being Mormon...'"**
> *Emo Philips*

RELIGION – MUSLIMS

☞ An old Muslim man, living in London, plants some potatoes in his back garden. However, when the time comes to dig them up, he finds the work is too hard for him. He emails his son in Pakistan and asks for his advice. "Don't worry, dad," replies the son. "I'll take care of it." Two hours later there's a squeal of brakes outside the old man's house and a squad of armed police officers run in and start digging up the potato patch. When they've dug it all up, they give the old man a suspicious look and drive off. The old man is intrigued and is about to email his son to ask how he did it, but then notices a new message in his inbox. The message says, "I've buried the stuff in the potato patch. You know what to do."

☞ Did you hear about the Muslim strip club? It features full-facial nudity!

RELIGION – NUNS

☞ A group of novice nuns are in church preparing to take their vows. Just as the service is about to start, four rabbis come in and sit in the right-hand pews. Although there's nothing to stop anyone witnessing the ceremony, having a group of rabbis walk in is very unusual. The priest says, "Can I help you gentlemen?" One of the rabbis replies, "It's all right. We're from the groom's side."

☞ A nun is driving down the road. She's a nursing sister making a delivery of bedpans to a Catholic hospice. Suddenly her car splutters to a halt. It's run out of petrol, so the nun walks up to the nearest garage and asks to borrow a petrol can so she can refill her tank. "Sorry, sister," says the petrol pump attendant. "We don't have any cans to lend out." The sister has a brainwave. She goes back to the car and takes one of the steel bedpans out of the boot. She then goes back to the garage and has the bedpan filled with half a gallon of petrol. The nun walks back to the car with her bedpan full of petrol and carefully starts pouring it into the car's tank. Two rabbis are watching this activity from the other side of the road. One says to the other, "If that car starts, I'm turning Catholic."

☞ A plane crashes into the ocean. The only survivors, a young nun and a pilot, are washed up on a desert island. After many months of isolation, the pair find themselves increasingly drawn to each other. Eventually, it comes to the point where the nun asks the pilot to make love to her. The pilot agrees and they both strip and get down to business. After they've finished, the nun lies back and says, "Thank you; that was wonderful: but I couldn't help noticing something; while we were making love, you kept a tight hold on your trousers. You were gripping them so hard your knuckles were white. Does holding on to your trousers like that give you stamina?" The pilot shakes his head. "No," he says, "it's just that the last time I slept with a nun, she pinched my wallet."

☞ Two Irish nuns go for a walk by the sea. They come across some secluded sand dunes and decide to do a little sunbathing. They both take off their clothes and lie naked on the sand, soaking up the rays. Suddenly, one of the nuns realises that they're being watched by a man with a camera. The man is snapping pictures of the naked nuns, but he's so entranced he's not even looking through the viewfinder. One of the nuns says, "Aren't you going to focus?" The other nun says, "Give him a chance, sister; let him take his pictures first."

☞ A young nun, Sister Agnes, gets a job as assistant to Sister Mary, who works as housekeeper to Father O'Brien. One evening, Sister Agnes comes into Sister Mary's room and tells her that she's found salvation. "Father O'Brien lost the soap in the bath, so I helped him look for it," says Sister Agnes, "but, lo and behold, instead of the soap I found the Key to Salvation between his legs." "Between his legs?" says Sister Mary. "Yes," continues Sister Agnes. "And he fitted it into the lock on the Gates of Heaven which he found between my legs." "Did he now?" sniffs Sister Mary. "That's right," says Sister Agnes. "He spent over half an hour putting the key into the lock, and he says we'll do the same every evening from now on." "I see," says Sister Mary. "Well, I can't pretend to know everything there is to know about theology, but I was given to understand that the thing between Father O'Brien's legs was the Horn of Gabriel." "A horn, you say?" says Sister Agnes. "Yes," says Sister Mary, "and I've been blowing it every night for the last fifteen years."

☞ Father O'Leary is accompanying a group of children and their teacher-nuns on a ferry crossing. One of the children says, "Father, if one of us children fell in the water, what would you do?" "Well," says the Father. "First I'd throw a lifebelt in the river. Then I'd call to one of the crew and tell them there was a person in the water. Then I'd take off my shoes and jacket and jump in the waves to try and save you." The child replies, "And what if one of the Holy Sisters fell in the water?" Father O'Leary eyes the nuns and says, "Which one?"

☞ How do you get a nun pregnant? Dress her as an altar-boy.

☞ Three nuns die and go to heaven. As a reward for their good behaviour, Saint Peter allows them to assume any form they want and return to earth for one week in their new bodies. The first nun says, "I would like to return in the form of Mother Theresa, so that I might know something of her great spirituality." The second nun says, "I would like to return in the form of Saint Catherine, so that I might know what it is to suffer like a martyr." The third nun, a very elderly woman wearing thick pebble glasses, says, "I would like to return in the form of Alice K. Anpipeline." Saint Peter is a bit surprised by this last request. He reaches for a heavenly directory and looks up Ms

Anpipeline. After ten minutes of looking through the 'As' he gives up. "I'm sorry," he says. "I can't find anyone called 'Anpipeline', let alone 'Alice K. Anpipeline'. Where did you hear about her?" The third nun takes an old newspaper cutting out of her pocket. "It mentions her here, Your Holiness." Saint Peter takes the scrap of paper and reads the headline: "Alaskan Pipeline laid by 1,000 men in two months."

☞ Two nuns are riding down a cobbled road on bicycles. One says to the other, "I've never come this way before." The other replies, "Neither have I. It's probably the cobbles."

RELIGION – OBSCURE CULTS

**"Frisbeetarianism is the belief that when you die,
your soul goes up on the roof and gets stuck."**
George Carlin

RELIGION – SERMONS

☞ A crumbling old church desperately needs renovating so, one Sunday, the priest makes an impassioned appeal to his congregation. At the end of the sermon, a rich man stands up and cries, "Father, I will contribute £1,000 to the restoration fund!" There is a smattering of applause and the man sits down. At that moment, some plaster falls from the ceiling and hits the man on the shoulder. The man promptly stands up again and says, "Father, I will increase my donation to £5,000." There's more applause, but before the man can sit down again, an even bigger chunk of plaster falls and hits him on the head. "Okay," says the man. "I'll make it £7,500!" The priest looks up and says, "Hit him again, Lord!"

☞ A little girl and her mother are in church. They are listening to the priest who is droning on and on and on as he preaches his sermon. The little girl leans over to her mother and whispers, "Mummy, if we give him the money now, will he let us go?"

☞ A young priest is having trouble writing his sermons, so he asks his bishop for help. The bishop says, "Well, you might start with something to get and hold their attention, such as, "Last night I was in the warm embrace of a good woman." That will get their attention; then you go on to talk about how warm and accepting she was, and at the end you reveal that she was your mother. That sort of thing's great for sermons about family love." The young priest is impressed and decides to follow this advice. The following Sunday, he gets into the pulpit and starts his sermon. "Last night I was in the arms of an attractive woman," he says. The congregation is totally transfixed – no lack of attention now. Unfortunately, the priest forgets what to say next, so he rambles on and on about how great the woman was and how good she made him feel. The priest is in a real fix now. The original sermon has gone out of his head completely and he's getting desperate to find a way out. Then he's struck by a brainwave; it's pure genius. "Well," says the priest, "that's the end of the story, more or less. I don't recall who exactly the woman was, but I do remember that she was warmly recommended by the bishop!"

☞ After attending church one Sunday, a man says to the priest, "Father, your sermon today reminded me of the peace and mercy of God." The priest is very flattered and asks the man to explain further. The man replies, "Your sermon passed all understanding, and it endured forever."

RELIGION – THE BIBLE

☞ A Sunday school teacher is telling the story of Noah and the flood. Little Jimmy sticks his hand up and says, "Didn't they get bored floating around for 40 days and nights?" "No," replies the teacher. "They had plenty of things to do, like feeding the animals and cleaning out their stalls." "That's not much fun," observes Jimmy. "They probably did fun things as well," says teacher, "like fishing." "That can't have been fun," replies Jimmy, "not if they only had two worms."

☞ Did Noah takes two woodworms on to the Ark? If he did, why didn't it sink?

☞ A Sunday school teacher is discussing the Ten Commandments with her pupils. After explaining the commandment about honouring thy father and mother, the teacher says, "Is there a Commandment that teaches us how to treat our brothers and sisters?" Little Jimmy sticks up his hand and says, "Thou shall not kill!"

☞ Little Johnny and little Suzy are sitting next to each other in Sunday School. Little Suzy isn't paying attention and is staring out of the window. Teacher asks her a question. "Suzy," she says, "who created the Universe?" Little Suzy is stumped, so little Johnny helps her out by jabbing a sharp pencil into her leg. "God almighty!" shouts Suzy. "That's very good," says teacher. Little Suzy goes back to her day-dreaming. Suddenly, teacher asks her another question. "Suzy," she says, "who in the Bible walked on water?" Little Suzy's stumped once more; she has no idea. Little Johnny comes to her rescue and jabs her backside with the pencil. "Jesus Christ!" exclaims little Suzy. "Good," says teacher. "Well done." Little Suzy rubs her sore behind, then starts staring out of the window again. Teacher notices her lack of attention and asks her a third question. "Suzy," she says, "what did Eve say to Adam in the Garden of Eden?" Little Johnny, helpful as ever, sticks the pencil in Suzy's thigh. "You goddamn bastard!" shouts Suzy. "You stick that thing in me one more time and I'll snap it in two and jam it up your ass!"

☞ My wife and I are not religious, but we both obey the Ten Commandments. She obeys one, three, four and nine, and I do the other six.

☞ One day in the Garden of Eden, Eve calls out to God, "Lord, I have a problem!" "What's the matter, Eve?" says God. "Lord," says Eve, "I know you created me and have provided this beautiful garden for me to live in and all these wonderful animals to look at, and that weird talking snake to make things interesting, but I'm lonely." "I have a solution," replies God. "I shall create a man for you." "What's a 'man', Lord?" asks Eve. "Man will be your mate," says God. "He'll be a flawed creature, with aggressive tendencies, an enormous ego and an inability to empathise or listen to you properly. However, he'll be big and fast, really good at hunting fleet-footed animals and making shelters, fires and suchlike, and he'll be not altogether bad in bed." "Well, that sounds interesting," says Eve. "You can have him on one condition," says God. "What's that, Lord?" asks Eve. God replies, "You'll have to let him believe that I made him first."

☞ The children of Israel wandered around the desert for 40 years. Even in Biblical times, men wouldn't ask for directions.

☞ A little girl is talking to her teacher about whales. The girl is worried that a whale might eat her. The teacher tries to comfort her by saying it's impossible for a whale to swallow a human. "Even though a whale is a very large animal," says teacher, "its throat is very small. It couldn't swallow you down." The little girl replies, "But Jonah was swallowed by a whale." "That didn't really happen," says teacher. "Whales can't swallow people." "Yes, they can," says the girl, "and when I die and go to heaven I'm going to ask Jonah how it happened." "Really?" says the teacher. "And what if he went to hell?" The little girl replies, "Then you can ask him."

☞ What did Adam say to Eve when he put his foot down? "I wear the plants in this family!"

☞ Why do we still call it the New Testament when it's over 2,000 years old?

RELIGION – THE CLERGY

☞ A monastery is destroyed in an earthquake and twenty Christian Brothers ascend to heaven at once. At the Pearly Gates, Saint Peter says, "Who amongst you fiddled with children when he was alive?" Nineteen Brothers put their hands up. "Right," says Saint Peter. "You lot get yourselves down to Purgatory – and take that deaf git with you."

RELIGION – THE POPE

☞ If the Pope believes that there is one true God who has inspired him with the Holy Spirit and chosen him as his representative to lead his church on earth, how come there's a lightning conductor installed on the Vatican roof?

"I admire the Pope. I have a lot of respect for anyone who can tour without an album."
Rita Rudner

☞ The Pope and the Queen are standing on a balcony in Vatican City, beaming at thousands of people in the plaza below. The Queen says to the Pope, "I bet you a tenner that I can make every English person in the crowd go wild with just a wave of my hand." "No way," says the Pope. "I'll bet you £20 you can't do it." "Watch this," says the Queen. She waves her hand a little and every English person in the crowd goes crazy, waving little Union Jacks on sticks and cheering and waving. The Pope then turns to the Queen and says. "Double or quits. I bet I can make every Irish person in the crowd go wild with a nod of my head. "Okay," says the Queen. "You're on." So the Pope head-butts her.

☞ The Pope is diagnosed with a rare disease of the testicles. The only cure is sex. The Pope agrees to this treatment to save his life, but insists on four conditions. "Firstly," he says, "the girl I have sex with must be blind so she cannot see me. Secondly, she must be deaf so she cannot hear me. Thirdly, she must be dumb so that she cannot tell anyone what has happened." "And what's the fourth condition?" asks the doctor. The Pope replies, "Massive tits."

☞ They knew the new Pope was going to be a German; apparently he'd had his towel on that balcony for days.

"I have as much authority as the Pope; I just don't have as many people who believe it."
George Carlin

415

RESTAURANTS

☞ A couple are getting ready to go out to dinner. The wife comes out of the bedroom and says, "Darling, shall I wear my Chanel suit or the Gucci outfit?" "They both look nice," replies the husband. The wife goes back into the bedroom and comes out in the Chanel. "Darling," she says. "Shall I wear the Rolex or the Cartier watch?" "I like both of them," replies the husband, "but I suppose the Rolex." The wife goes to find the Rolex and puts it on. "Darling," she says, "what do you think? Should I put on the pearl-rope necklace or the diamonds?" The husband sighs and looks at his watch. "Sweetheart," he says, "it really doesn't matter which one you wear, but if we hang around much longer we're going to miss the Early Bird Half-Price Special."

☞ A depressed-looking man is sitting in a cheap, greasy diner. The waitress comes over to take his order. "I'll have the meatloaf," says the man wearily, "and if you could throw in a few kind words that would be mighty welcome." The waitress leaves and returns a few minutes later with a plate of meatloaf. She plonks the plate on the table in front of the man and starts to walk off. "Hey," says the man. "I got my dinner; how about those kind words?" The waitress turns, takes the cigarette out of her mouth and says, "Don't eat the meatloaf."

☞ A huge leopard and a tiny lamb walk into a restaurant. The waiter comes over and the lamb orders a salad, followed by a nut cutlet with sparkling water. The leopard asks for a cup of coffee. "Nothing to eat, sir?" asks the waiter. The leopard nods at the lamb and says, "If I was hungry, do you think I'd be sitting here with him?"

☞ A man walks into an Indian restaurant and points a gun at the owner's head. "Give me everything you have in the till," says the man. The owner replies, "To take away?"

☞ A new café opens down the street, so Jim decides to give it a go. He goes in, sits down and studies the menu. A gum-chewing waitress comes over to take his order. "Is the coffee fresh?" asks Jim. "I guess so," replies the waitress. "The place has only been open a week."

☞ An elderly couple go to a trendy restaurant, but are turned away because it's full. They return the next night, but again it's full, and they go home disappointed. The next night, the same thing happens again. "Look," says the maitre' d. "To save you time, why don't you make a booking?" The old couple agree this would make sense, but discover that the restaurant is booked solid for the next three weeks. "Tell you what," says the maitre d'. "Try phoning tomorrow. There might be a cancellation." The old man rings the next day and discovers that there haven't been any cancellations; he also discovers that the restaurant is now booked solid for the next five weeks! The old man complains bitterly. "You know," he says, "your restaurant would do a lot more business if you weren't bloody full all the time!"

☞ An old man shuffles into a café and orders a bowl of soup and some bread. The man finishes his meal and goes to pay. The manager takes his money and asks the old man if he enjoyed his meal. "It was very nice," replies the old man, "but I needed some more bread. I only had two slices." Next day, the old man returns and orders the same. The manager remembers that he likes his bread, so he gives him four slices. The old man is finishing his soup when the manager comes over to see how he's enjoying it. "It's very nice," says the old man, "but it really needs more bread." The next day, the old man comes back again. The manager spots him and, determined that the old man should have enough to eat this time, gives him eight slices of buttered bread with his soup. The old man eats it all slowly and goes to pay. "And how was the soup today?" asks the manager, confident that the old man can have nothing to complain about. "It was nice," replies the old man. "It's always nice, but..." "But what?" asks the manager. "You always seem to skimp on the bread," says the old man. "I never have quite enough." "I'll see what I can do about that," replies the exasperated manager. Next day, the manager prepares for the old man's arrival. He goes to the baker and orders the largest French loaf they have – a six-foot whopper that's eight inches across. He carries the loaf back to the cafe, splits it in two, butters both sides, then waits for the old man. Sure enough, the old fellow shuffles in and orders his soup and bread. The soup and the huge sliced loaf are carried to the old man's table and he tucks into his meal. The old man takes ages to eat all the bread, but – incredibly – he manages to stuff it all down. At this point the manager comes over. "So how was that?" he asks. "Was that enough bread for you?" The old man shrugs and says, "Not bad: but I see you're back to two slices…"

☞ George goes on holiday to Italy. On his first night, he goes to the hotel restaurant and orders a meal. The waiter takes George's order, but insists he must try the minestrone soup. "It is most excellent soup," says the waiter, "our speciality." George declines the offer; he's not that keen on soup. A few moments later, the head waiter comes over. "Can we not tempt you with our superb minestrone soup?" says the head waiter. "It is a great favourite with all our guests." Again, George declines the offer. A moment later, the chef comes out of the kitchen and goes to George's table. "Sir," he says. "Can I not implore you to taste our most famous minestrone soup? You will never regret it. It is most wonderful. We at the hotel – we are most proud of this marvellous soup." George shakes his head; he's not keen on soup. After this, George is allowed to finish his meal in peace. He enjoys the rest of the evening, but when he goes to bed he's struck down with terrible stomach pains and starts vomiting uncontrollably. It gets so serious that the hotel manager calls a doctor. George is in a bad way and is on the point of passing out. The doctor needs to get some medicine inside George, but since he can't keep anything down, the doctor decides to give George a dose as an enema. The enema is applied, and the semi-delirious George is taken to the lobby on a stretcher to wait for the ambulance. As they wait, George sees a new guest booking in. "Here, you!" he gasps. The guest comes over. "The minestrone soup!" croaks George. "If they offer it to you, bloody take it! Otherwise they sneak into your room and squirt it up your ass."

☞ Harry goes into his favourite restaurant and orders his favourite dish: a bowl of tomato soup. The soup arrives and Harry looks at it for a moment before signalling the waiter to come back. "Taste the soup," says Harry. "Why?" asks the waiter. "Just taste the soup!" says Harry. "Sir, you've been coming in here almost every day for many years," says the waiter. "You've always enjoyed our soup." Harry says, "I know. Taste the soup!" The waiter protests, "But what's wrong? Is it too hot? Not hot enough?" Harry says, "Taste the soup!" "But I don't understand, sir," splutters the waiter. "Did we leave out the salt? Perhaps you don't have enough bread? Is it the bread? Do you want more bread?" Harry glares at the waiter, "Just –taste – the – god – damned – soup!" he shouts. The waiter gives in, "All right, sir, all right;, I'll taste the soup!" He looks around, "Where's the spoon?" "Aha!" says Harry.

☞ I went to a Chinese restaurant and ordered a meal. Ten minutes later this duck waddles up to me, gives me a single red rose and says, "Your lips are like rubies and your eyes sparkle like diamonds". I called over the waiter and said, "Excuse me. I ordered aro*matic* duck".

☞ It's a busy night at the restaurant. Harry places his order, but waits ages for anything to turn up. Finally, a young man arrives and starts handing out plates. "Are you the waiter who took my order?" asks Harry. "Yes, sir," says the waiter. "Funny," says Harry, "I was expecting someone much older."

☞ Jim and Harry go into a café and order two cups of coffee. Their drinks arrive and the two men proceed to bring out their lunchboxes and eat sandwiches. "Excuse me," says the waitress, "but you can't eat your own food in here." Jim and Harry look at each other, shrug, swap their sandwiches and carry on eating.

☞ My local pizza parlour's getting worse and worse. Last week, I ordered a thin and crispy supreme – and they sent me Diana Ross.

**"The other night I ate at a real nice family restaurant.
Every table had an argument going."**
George Carlin

☞ On Saturday night, Harry and his wife go to a new steak house that's opened in the high street. They each order a steak with all the trimmings and are presented with huge slabs of meat that almost cover their plates. They also have all manner of salads and side dishes: more than they could possibly eat. What's more – it's all delicious! The pair enjoy the best meal they've had in years. For the rest of the week, they rave about the great food they had at the steak house and, when next Saturday comes, they return to repeat the experience. They order the same meal as last time, but are disappointed by the small steaks they're given. The side dishes are also a disappointment; all they're offered is a little green salad and a baked potato. Harry decides to complain to the manager. "We came here last week," he says, "and we had huge steaks and loads of side dishes. It was fantastic. But when we came in today, we were given very little choice and tiny portions." "I know, sir," says the manager, "but last week was different." "But we ordered the same meal!" exclaims Harry. "What was different about last week?" The manager replies, "Last week you were sitting by the window."

☞ Two Chinese men walk out of an Italian restaurant. One says to the other, "I love Italian food, but two days later and you're hungry again."

RESTAURANTS – FAST FOOD

☞ It's not called 'fast food' because it's cooked quickly. It's called fast because you're supposed to eat it fast – otherwise you might taste the damned stuff.

☞ A man walks into a fish and chip shop and asks for the largest cod they have. The guy behind the counter says, "Okay; it won't be long." The customer replies, "Well, it'd better be a bloody fat one, then!"

☞ Bill is standing in line at a fast food restaurant. When he gets to the front, the girl serving him points to a sign. It reads: "We will not accept bills larger than $20." Bill looks at her and says, "Are you kidding? If I had a bill larger than $20 I wouldn't be eating in this dump."

☞ A little old man and woman slowly hobble into a McDonald's one cold winter evening. The old lady takes a seat, while the little old man shuffles up to the counter and orders a burger, fries and a drink. The old man takes the food to his wife's table and sits down. The little old man then unwraps the burger and cuts it in half, placing one half in front of his wife. Then he carefully divides the French fries into two piles and places one pile in front of his wife. The old man then takes a sip of the drink and begins to eat. The old couple and their meagre meal attract pitying looks from the other customers. A young man goes over to ask if he can buy the couple another burger and fries so they don't have to share. "No, thanks, sonny," says the old man. "We're just fine. We're used to sharing. We share everything." The young man then notices that the little old lady still hasn't touched her food. She just sits there watching her husband eat. Again, the young man asks them if he can buy them another meal. "No, thank you, young man," says the old lady. "We're used to sharing. We share everything." "But you're not eating anything," says the young man. "Don't you like it? Shall I get you something else?" "I like burgers and fries just fine," replies the old lady. "They're my favourite. I can't wait to get stuck into them." "But why aren't you eating?" asks the young man. The old woman gives a big toothless grin and says, "I'm waiting for my turn with the dentures!"

RESTAURANTS – WAITER

☞ "Waiter! This coffee tastes like mud." "Yes, sir; it's fresh ground."

☞ "Waiter! I want to complain to the chef about the disgusting meal you've just served me!" "I'm sorry, sir; you'll have to wait. He's just popped out for his lunch."

☞ "Waiter! I ordered a rare steak and this is well done." "Thank you, sir; we aim to please."

RIDDLE ME REE

☞ Every man has one; some are longer than others; the Pope doesn't use his; and a man gives his to his wife when they get married. What is it? A surname.

☞ How do you make a cat go woof? Douse it in petrol and throw a match at it.

☞ How do you spell 'hungry horse' using only four letters? MTGG.

☞ How do you turn a fox into an elephant? Marry it!

☞ How does a wizard tell the time? With a witch watch.

☞ How many legs does a horse have? Six. Forelegs at the front, and two at the back.

☞ If you can make shoes out of crocodiles, what can you make out of bananas? Slippers!

☞ What did the o say to the 8? "Hey, nice belt!"

☞ What do you call a 25-stone woman who is partial to both gentlemen and ladies? A bisexual built for two.

☞ What do you call a dog with two dicks? The judging panel on X-Factor.

☞ What do you call a girl with a frog on her head? Lily.

☞ What do you call a guy with a spade stuck into his head? Doug.

☞ What do you call a guy without a spade stuck into his head? Douglas.

☞ What do you call a man with a number-plate on his head? Reg.

☞ What do you call a man with no shins? Tony.

☞ What do you call an Eskimo lesbian? A Klondyke.

☞ What do you call an Irishman who looks forward to the summer? Paddy O'Furniture.

☞ What do you call the wife of a hippie? Mississippi.

☞ What do you can a woman with a radiator on her head? Anita.

☞ What do you get hanging from cherry trees? Sore arms.

☞ What do you get if you cross a birthday cake with a tin of baked beans? A cake that blows out its own candles.

☞ What do you get if you cross a cat with Godzilla? A town remarkably free of dogs.

☞ What do you get if you cross a chicken with a bell? An alarm cluck.

☞ What do you get if you cross a cocoa bean with an elk? A chocolate moose.

☞ What do you get if you cross a gundog with a phone? A golden receiver.

☞ What do you get if you cross a rabbit with a leek? A bunion.

☞ What do you get if you cross an anthill with a packet of seeds? Ants in your plants.

☞ What do you get if you cross an elephant with an apple? A pie that never forgets.

☞ What do you get when you cross a railway track with a crocodile? Three chunks of crocodile.

☞ What do you get if you cross a kangaroo with a sheep? An ethical debate about the pros and cons of genetic engineering.

☞ What do you sing at a snowman's birthday party? "Freeze a jolly good fellow..."

☞ What has four legs and no ears? Mike Tyson's dog.

☞ What has handles and flies? A dustbin.

☞ What has nine arms and sucks? Def Leppard.

☞ What is a bamboo? The sound of an exploding ghost.

☞ What keeps hot in the fridge? Mustard.

☞ What kind of bee makes milk? A boo-bee.

☞ What was Jack the Ripper's middle name? The.

☞ What you call a man who's scared of Christmas? Noel Coward.

☞ What's blue and has sex with supermodels? Me, in my lucky blue coat.

☞ How do you get two whales in a car? Down the M4 and across the Severn Bridge.

☞ If Martians live on Mars and Venusians live on Venus, who lives on Pluto? Fleas!

☞ What do you call a piece of wood with nothing to do? Board.

☞ What do you get when you cross a monkey with a minefield? A baboom!

☞ What goes "Ooo. Ooo"? A cow with no lips.

☞ What's yellow and smells of bananas? Monkey sick.

☞ What's slow and miserable? Depressed treacle.

☞ What's long and pink and hard in the morning? The Financial Times crossword.

☞ Where do monkey like to do their shopping? At a jungle sale.

☞ What's a hospice? Around three and a half gallons.

☞ What's big and hairy and sticks out of your husband's pyjamas? Your husband's head.

☞ What's big and red and sits in the corner? A naughty bus.

☞ What's black and runny? Linford Christie.

☞ What's black, has long ears and smokes? A rabbit chewing a power cable.

☞ What's blue and smells like red paint? Blue paint.

☞ What's green and misty? Kermit the Fog.

☞ What's green and white and bounces? A spring onion.

☞ What's grey and comes in pints? An elephant.

☞ What's orange and sounds like a parrot? A carrot.

☞ What's red and yellow and looks good on hippies? Fire.

☞ What's short and gets straight to the point? A nymphomaniac midget.

☞ What's small, furry, squeaks and smells like pork? A hamster.

☞ What's ten inches long, two inches thick and starts with a P? A really good crap.

　☞ What's the best way to stop flies from spreading disease? Keep them zipped.

☞ What's the first sign of madness? Suggs walking up your driveway.

　☞ What's the main ingredient of dog biscuits? Collie flour.

☞ What's the opposite of 'omniscient'? I don't know.

　☞ What's the plural of 'baby'? Twins.

☞ What's white, sits by the bed and takes the piss out of you? A dialysis machine.

　☞ What's worse than biting into an apple and finding half a worm? Cancer.

☞ What's yellow and soft and goes around and around and around? A long-playing omelet.

　☞ Where did Napoleon keep his armies? Up his sleevies.

☞ Where do you find giant snails? On the ends of their fingers.

　☞ Where do you go to weigh a pie? Somewhere over the rainbow.

☞ Which Chinese city is famous for it car horn factory? Hong King.

　☞ Who was the first person to wear a shell suit? Humpty Dumpty.

☞ Why did the woman cross the road? Why do women do ANYTHING?

　☞ Why hasn't anyone ever stolen a canal? They have too many locks.

RISING TO THE OCCASION

☞ I won't rise to the occasion, but occasionally I will slide over to it.

SAFETY

☞ Brian was careful to follow all the official safety advice. When he went out in the dark he made sure he was dressed from top to toe in brilliant white clothing. Sadly, he was killed when a snow plough ran over him.

SALES AND RETAILING

☞ Jim's a great salesman. Yesterday, a woman came into his tailor's shop to buy a new suit; it was to bury her dead husband in, and Jim still managed to talk her into buying an extra pair of trousers.

☞ A girl has just started a new job on the hypermarket checkout. As part of her training, the manager comes over to tell her about 'Product Linking'. "I'll demonstrate with the next customer," says the manager. Along comes the next customer, and amongst his shopping he has a bag of grass seed. The manager says, "Sir, I see you have a bag of grass seed in your shopping; have you considered buying a lawnmower? We have some on special offer at £49.99." "What a good idea," says the customer. "I'll take one." "That's Product Linking," says the manager. The checkout girl is impressed. Along comes the next customer, and amongst his shopping he has a box of sanitary towels. The checkout girl says, "Sir, I see you have a box of sanitary towels in your shopping. Are they for your girlfriend?" "Well, yes," says the man. "Have you considered buying a lawnmower?" asks the girl. "We have some on special offer at £49.99." "What's a lawnmower got to do with sanitary towels?" asks the customer. The woman replies, "Well, seeing as your weekend's screwed, I thought you might want to mow the lawn instead."

☞ A man is at the supermarket check-out when he realises he's forgotten to pick up any condoms. He asks the checkout girl if she can have someone bring a packet over. "Sure," says the girl, "but I'll have to check your size." With that, she sticks her hands down the man's trousers and fiddles around. She then shouts out, "One box of large condoms to check-out ten!" The next man in line sees this and decides he'd like to be felt up in the same way. When he gets to the checkout, he also asks for some condoms to be sent over. The girl sticks her hand down his pants, has a quick rummage and shouts out, "One box of medium condoms to check-out ten!" The next customer in line is a teenage boy. He decides to pull the same trick and also asks for condoms. The girl stick her hands down his pants, has a feel around, then shouts, "Clean-up crew to check-out ten!"

☞ A man is walking around a supermarket shouting, "Mazola! Mazola!" The manager comes up to him and says, "Excuse me, sir: but the Mazola's in aisle five." "No, I'm not really looking for Mazola," says the man. "I'm calling my wife." "I see," says the manager. "Your wife's name is 'Mazola'?" "It's sort of a nick-name," says the husband, "but I only call her that in public." "And what do you call her at home?" enquires the manager. The man replies, "Lard-ass."

☞ A sales manager and his boss hire a cabin and go out bear-hunting. The boss stays in the cabin while the sales manager goes out looking for a bear. He soon finds a huge bear and shoots at it, but only manages to wound the animal. The enraged bear charges towards the sales manager and he runs for his life back to the cabin. The manager's running as fast as he can, but the bear's gaining on him with every step. Just as he reaches the cabin door, the sales manager trips and falls flat on his face. Too close behind to stop, the bear falls over the manager and tumbles through the cabin's door. The sales manager jumps up and shouts, "Here you go, boss! You skin this one! I'll go back and get another!"

☞ A store owner hires a young female clerk who likes to wear very short skirts. One day, a young man enters the store and orders some raisin bread. The raisin bread is on the very top shelf, and the girl has to climb a ladder to get it. This gives the young man a great view up her skirt. Others notice, and pretty soon there's a queue of men waiting to order raisin bread. The clerk's getting annoyed at having to go up and down the ladder all the time. She looks down and sees an old man joining the end of the queue. She shouts to him, "Hey! Is yours raisin too?" "No," croaks the old man, "but it sure is startin' to twitch."

☞ An auction's in progress when the auctioneer suddenly stops to make an announcement, "I'm sorry to interrupt," he says, "but I've just been informed that a gentleman in the room has lost a wallet containing £5,000. If you find it, please take it to the main office. There's a £200 reward." There's a second's silence; then a voice calls out from the back of the room, "£250!"

☞ Harry made the mistake of reversing into a car boot sale – but, on the plus side, he managed to sell his engine for a fiver.

☞ George and Harry meet in a pub. "I've got a great deal for you," says Harry. "This circus went bankrupt and I managed to get an elephant. I'll sell it to you for £2,000." "An elephant?" exclaims George. "What am I going to do with an elephant? I live in a ground floor-flat with no garden. I don't have room to swing a cat. Where am I going to put an elephant: in the window-box?" "All right," says Harry. "How about this: I'll let you have two elephants for £3,000." George replies, "Well, now you're talking..."

☞ George decides to open a jeweller's shop in a famous London shopping street. There are three jewellers already in the road, so he goes to check them out. One shop describes itself as 'The best jeweller in London'. The second shop says, 'The best jeweller in the UK'. The third shop has a big sign outside saying, 'The best jeweller in the world'. George thinks about this for a bit, wondering how he can do better. A week later, he opens his shop and hangs up his own sign. It reads, 'The best jeweller in the street'.

☞ George goes to market to sell his prize cow. A local farmer agrees to take it, and they shake hands on the price. The only problem is that the farmer can't pay straight away. He has to raise the money by selling some farm equipment. George is not concerned and agrees to wait a week or two. A couple of weeks pass, and George phones the farmer to ask for his money. The farmer still hasn't made his sale, and asks George to wait a bit longer. Another week passes, and George phones the farmer again. Again, the farmer puts George off, promising to have the money soon. This goes on for weeks and weeks, until George is at the end of his tether. "I'm getting fed-up with this," says George to his wife. "If I'd known that bastard was never going to pay up, I'd have charged him twice as much!"

☞ George takes a job as a second-hand car salesman. His boss tells him to use the standard story about how the car was only ever used by a little old lady to drive to church, but this patter doesn't seem to work. Weeks pass without a sale, and George fears he may lose his job. Then, one day, the flood-gates open and George sells three cars before lunch. "Great work, George," says his boss. "How did you do it? "I changed the patter," says George. "No one was believing that corny 'old lady' story, so I started telling customers about a teenage nymphomaniac who only ever used the back seat."

☞ Harry goes into a greengrocer's. "How much are those melons?" asks Harry. "They're £3 for two," replies the grocer. "So how much for one?" asks Harry. "£2," says the grocer. "OK," says Harry, "I'll take the other one."

☞ Harry goes to his local corner shop to buy a tin of beans. When he gets there, he's surprised to see the shelves are full of boxes of salt. There's salt everywhere: boxes and boxes of it. In vain he searches for beans or, indeed, any other type of grocery item. Baffled, he goes to the till and asks the owner if he has any beans. "We might have a few tins," replies the owner, "but I put them out the back in a shed. I had to make room for all this salt." "I can see that," says Harry, "but if you don't mind me saying, I think you've been a bit short-sighted in your purchasing strategy; you're never, ever going to sell this amount of salt." "I know," replies the owner.

"I know I can never sell this amount of salt; I'm not that good a salesman. But the guy who sold me the salt – you should see HIM sell salt!"

☞ A man goes to see his bank manager. He wants to get a loan to start a business. "I'd like to open a cheese shop in the Netherlands," says the man. "I'm going to call it 'Cheeses of Holland'." "Well, there are quite a lot of cheese shops in the Netherlands already," says the bank manager. "Perhaps you ought to go away and think again." The man comes back the next week. "I changed my mind about the cheese shop in the Netherlands," he says. "I'm going to open it in France instead. I'm going to call it 'Cheeses of Paris'." "That's not a good idea either," says the bank manager. "France is full of cheese shops. Go away and have another think about it." The man comes back the following week. "I've got it this time," he says. "I'm going to open a cheese shop in Israel." "That's much better," says the bank manager: "not much cheese there, I shouldn't think. But what are you going to call it?" The man replies, "Cheeses of Nazareth."

SCAMS

☞ A company takes out a newspaper advertisement claiming to supply hard-core pornography. Its prices seem reasonable, so people place orders and make payments via cheque. Several weeks later, the company writes back to say that it has discovered that, under the present law, it is unable to supply the materials after all and does not wish to be prosecuted. The company then returns all its customers' money in the form of company cheques. However, very few ever bother to pay their cheques in at the bank, the reason being the name of the company printed on the cheques: "Anal Sex and Fetish Perversion Ltd."

☞ Email message: Warning! If someone comes to your front door saying they're conducting a survey on cattle ticks, and they ask you to take all your clothes off and jig around with your arms in the air, don't do it! It's a scam! They only want to see you naked! I only wish I'd got this email yesterday. I feel so stupid.

431

SCIENCE

☞ A physicist, a biologist and a chemist visit the beach for the first time. The physicist sees the ocean and is fascinated by the rippling surge of the surf. He tells the others that he wants to investigate the fluid dynamics of the waves. He walks into the ocean, gets caught by a strong rip-tide and is carried away, never to be seen again. Meanwhile, the biologist tells the chemist that he wants to get a closer look at the fish swimming in the shallows. He walks into the sea, gets caught by the same rip-tide and is also quickly carried away. Unaware of these disasters, the chemist sits on the sand waiting for his friends to come back. At sunset, he gives up and goes home. He explains the mystery by concluding that both physicists and biologists must be soluble in salt water.

> **"Interestingly, according to modern astronomers, space is finite. This is a very comforting thought – particularly for people who can never remember where they've left things."**
> *Woody Allen*

☞ A scientist couple had twin boys. They called one John; they called the other, 'Control'.

☞ How do you generate five random numbers? Ask a sociology graduate to count to ten.

☞ Why did Mr Ohm marry Mrs Ohm? Because he couldn't resistor.

> **"The scientific theory I like best is that the rings of Saturn are composed entirely of lost airline luggage."**
> *Mark Russell*

☞ Why did the chicken cross the Möbius strip? To get to the same side.

☞ A renowned cosmologist is lecturing a group of students on the future of the solar system. He tells his audience that, according to his calculations, the earth will fall into the sun in about a billion years. A nervous voice pipes up from the back of the hall. "Excuse me, P-Professor," the voice stammers, "b-b-ut h-how long d-did you say it w-would be?" "About a billion years," replies the professor. "Thank God for that," says the voice. "For a minute there, I thought you'd said a million!"

☞ An engineer, a mathematician and an arts graduate are given the task of finding the height of a church steeple. A prize of £1,000 is offered for the most accurate answer. The engineer climbs to the top of the steeple and lowers a string on a plumb-bob until it touches the ground. He then climbs down and measures the length of the string. When it's the mathematician's turn, he lays out a reference line, measures the angle to the top of the steeple from both ends and works out the height by trigonometry. However, it's the arts graduate who eventually wins the prize; he buys the vicar a beer in the local pub and asks him how high the steeple is.

> ## "I have just received my degree in Calcium Anthropology – the study of milkmen."
> *Steven Wright*

☞ At a science seminar, fires break out simultaneously in three hotel rooms. In the first room is an engineer. He wakes up, smells the smoke, then dashes to the bathroom and fills the wastepaper bin full of water. He then uses the bin to splash water around until the fire's out, and then goes back to sleep. In the second room is a physicist. He wakes up, smells the smoke, then sits at his desk and calculates how much water will be needed to put out the fire. By the time the calculations are done, the fire has spread considerably; however, the physicist has factored this increase into his calculations. He then walks to the bathroom, fills the wastepaper bin with the required amount of water, puts out the fire and then goes back to sleep. In the third room is a mathematician. He wakes up, smells the smoke, then goes into the bathroom and turns on a tap. "Good," says the mathematician. "A solution does exist." Then he goes back to bed.

☞ How can you tell a mathematician from a physicist? Give each of them a kettle full of cold water, and ask them to make a cup of tea. They will both boil the water, then pour it into their teapots. The next step is to give them each a kettle full of boiling water. As before, the physicist will pour his boiling water into his teapot and make his tea. The mathematician, on the other hand, will empty his boiling water down the sink, and fill the kettle with cold water – thus reducing the problem to one which has already been solved.

☞ How do you know if the car coming towards you is being driven by a physicist? It'll have a red sticker on its bumper, saying: "If this sticker is blue, you're driving too fast."

"It is impossible to travel faster than light, and certainly not desirable, as one's hat keeps blowing off."
Woody Allen

☞ My uncle the scientist has been carrying out some genetics experiments. His latest creation is a cross between a snake and a horse. The bad news is that it can give you a nasty bite; the good news is you can ride it to a hospital.

☞ The two most common elements in the universe are hydrogen and stupidity.

"In awe I watched the waxing moon ride across the zenith of the heavens like an ambered chariot rushing towards the ebon void of infinite space, wherein the tethered belts of Jupiter and Mars hang for ever festooned in their orbital majesty. And as I looked at all this I thought, 'I must put a new roof on this lavatory'."
Les Dawson

SEALS

☞ A seal walks into a club...

SELF-AWARENESS

☞ Becoming aware of your character defects can help lead you to the next step in the healing process – blaming your parents.

SELF-DEPRECATION

> **"I enjoy using the comedy technique of self-deprecation – but I'm not very good at it."**
> *Arnold Brown*

SELF-SUFFICIENCY

☞ I have a computer, a vibrator and a reliable pizza delivery service. Why should I leave the house?

SERVANTS

☞ A butler accidentally spills his master's best snuff into the fire. He has to find a replacement quickly, so he goes out and looks around for something suitable. The butler spots a dried-out dog turd on a path, takes it inside and grinds it into dust. Luckily, it has exactly the same colour and consistency as the snuff it's replacing. That evening, the master of the house is entertaining the bishop. He calls for his snuff. The butler brings it to him and the master takes a noseful. "Good grief," he says. "Y'know, there's a terrible smell of dog mess in this room. Can you smell it, Bishop? "Alas, I can't smell a thing," replies the Bishop. "I have a terrible cold." "Well, the best thing for a cold is snuff," says the master, offering the Bishop his snuffbox. The Bishop stuffs some powder up his nose. "Good heavens," says the Bishop. "You're right. That snuff has cleared my nose completely; in fact, the smell of dog mess is almost overpowering."

SEX

**"I believe that sex is the most beautiful, natural
and wholesome thing that money can buy."**
Steve Martin

☞ A boy needs some help with his English homework. He goes to his father
and asks him to explain the difference between 'potential' and 'reality'.
"Tell you what," says Dad, "to find the difference, go and ask your mother
if she'd sleep with Harrison Ford for a million pounds; then ask your sister
if she'd sleep with Robbie Williams for a million pounds." The boy goes
and asks his questions. The mother replies, "Don't tell your Dad, but I'd
definitely sleep with Harrison for a million pounds." The sister says to him,
"Yeah; I'd love to sleep with Robbie for a million pounds." The boy goes
back to his father and says, "So let's see if I've got this right; 'potentially'
we're sitting on two million quid, but in 'reality' we're living with a couple
of slags."

☞ A bus full of nuns crashes and the sisters find themselves queuing up at
the Pearly Gates. Saint Peter interviews them as they pass through the
portal. To the first nun he says, "Sister, did you ever touch a penis during
your time as a nun?" "Only once, Your Holiness," replies the first nun.
"When I was a nurse I touched one with the tips of my fingers." "I see,"
says Saint Peter. "In that case, dip your fingers in the holy water and you
may pass into Heaven." He then puts the same question to the second
nun. "I did touch a penis, sir," she replies. "When I was a nurse, one
rubbed against my wrist." Saint Peter replies, "In that case, dab the holy
water on your wrist and you may enter the Kingdom of Heaven." At that
moment Saint Peter notices a fight breaking out further down the line.
"What's going down there?" he demands. One of the nuns shouts back, "I
want to get in line before Sister Mary! If I've got to gargle that stuff, I want
to do it before she sticks her ass in it!"

☞ A chubby woman goes to see her gynaecologist. While the woman is in
the stirrups with her legs open, the doctor says, "Are you experiencing any

problems with your love life at the moment?" "Well," says the woman, "my husband doesn't seem to be as interested in it as he used to be. I don't think he finds me attractive any more." "That's a shame," says the doctor. "Have you tried to diet?" "You think I should?" says the woman. "What colour do you think he'd like?"

☞ Harry and Bill walk into a pub and Bill bets everyone there that his mate Harry can make love to 100 women in a row. Lots of people take them up on the bet, and the next day Harry and Bill turn up with 100 women. Harry drops his pants and begins the challenge. True to his word, he moves from one woman to the next, satisfying each one without pausing: 1...2...3... on and on he goes: 49... 50... 51... He slows down somewhat: 83... 84... 85... but he's still moving from one to the next: 97............ 98............. 99........and before he can get to the last woman, Harry has a heart attack and dies. Bill scratches his head. "I don't understand it!" he says. "It went perfectly well in the morning practice!"

☞ A hotel porter is looking through the keyhole of the honeymoon suite. "Holy crap!" he exclaims. "Look at him go!" A passing maid hears him. She pushes the porter out of the way so she can take a peek. "Oh, my God!" she gasps. "Lucky girl. My boyfriend never does that for me." One of the restaurant waiters happens to hear her. He bends down to peer through the keyhole himself. He gives a low whistle and says, "Incredible. He's certainly giving her a good time: and last night he had the nerve to complain about a hair in his soup!"

☞ A little girl comes running into the house crying about a small cut on her finger. She asks her mother for a glass of cider. "Why do you want cider?" asks her mum. "To take the pain away," sobs the little girl. Mum pours her a glass of cider and the little girl puts her finger in it. "It doesn't work!" she yells. "Why did you think it would?" asks mum. "I heard Auntie say so," the girl replies. "She said that whenever she gets a prick in her hand, she can't wait to get it in cider."

☞ A little old lady is being questioned in court. "Describe what happened when the young man sat down next to you on the park bench," says the lawyer. The little old lady replies, "Well, it was then that he started rubbing my thigh." "And were the police called at this point?" asks the attorney. "No," replies the old lady. "So what happened then?" asks the lawyer. "Well, he then started to fondle my bosom," says the old lady. "And is this when the police became involved?" asks the lawyer. "No," replies the little old lady. "What happened after that?" asks the lawyer. "Well," says the little old lady, "that's when he started kissing me and suggested we go into the bushes for intercourse." "I see," says the lawyer. "And is that when the police were alerted?" "No," replies the old lady. "Ma'am," says the lawyer, "when exactly *were* the police called to the scene?" The old lady replies, "After he shouted 'April Fool!', and I shot the son of a bitch."

> ## "I remember the first time I had sex –
> ## I kept the receipt."
> *Groucho Marx*

☞ A man and woman are lying in bed after making love. The man mutters to himself: "Man, oh, man! I finally did it! I'm not a virgin any more!" The woman overhears this. "Wow," she says. "Are you saying that you just lost your virginity to me?" "Yes," says the man. "When I was young, I vowed that I would give my virginity to the woman who was my one true love." Astounded, the woman replies, "What? So you really love me?" "Nah," says the guy. "I just got tired of waiting."

☞ A man goes into an adult store and buys a blow-up sex doll for £25. The doll turns out to be quite badly made, and after half an hour's use it develops a leak and deflates. The man returns the doll to the shop the next day. "I only had it out of the box for an hour," he says to the shopkeeper. "Then it started going down on me." "Wow!" exclaims the shopkeeper. "I'm going to start charging more for these things!"

☞ A man goes out to paint the town red and caps off the festivities by visiting a house of ill repute. A week later, he visits his doctor complaining of a large green lump on the end of his penis. The doctor does a thorough examination, then pulls down a large medical book. He flicks through it until he finds what he's looking for. The doctor looks up and says, "I'm afraid this is serious. We'll have to operate." "Operate?" exclaims the man, "Why? What's the problem?" "Well, you know how boxers can get a cauliflower ear?" says the doctor. "You've developed a similar problem. It seems you have a brothel sprout."

☞ A woman says to a man, "Excuse me; are these your eyeballs? I found them in my cleavage."

☞ A man is drinking champagne in a bar when he sees a woman doing the same. "Are you celebrating?" he asks. "Yes," replies the woman. "After years of infertility my doctor has just told me I'm pregnant." "That's great," says the man. "I'm celebrating too. I'm a chicken farmer, and for months my hens haven't been laying. I solved the problem, and now they're laying eggs like crazy." "So how did you solve the problem?" asks the woman. "I changed cocks," replies the man. "Same here," says the woman.

☞ A man is driving down a country lane when he spots a nude young man hugging a tree. As he gets closer, he realises that the youngster's arms have been handcuffed around the tree, trapping him. He gets out to see what's the matter. "Thank God you pulled over," says the young man. "I'd stopped to give this girl a lift, but when she opened the door, her boyfriend jumped out of the bushes and mugged me. They took my car, my wallet and all my clothes and left me like this." "That's terrible," says the man. "You can say that again," says the youngster. "This must be the worst day of my life." The man starts to undo his trousers. "Yes, sweetie: and it's not getting any better, is it?"

> ## "I don't really enjoy sex. I just pretend I do to get girls to sleep with me."
> *Byron Alley*

☞ An old man joins an exclusive nudist swingers' club. After stripping naked, he wanders around and sees a gorgeous woman. The man gets an erection. The woman notices this, comes over and says, "Did you call for me?" The man replies, "No. Why do you think I called you?" "You must be new here," replies the woman. "Let me explain. It's a rule that, if you get an erection, it implies you called for me." She then leads the man into a chalet where they have incredible sex. Later, the man continues to look around and goes into the sauna. As he sits down, he farts. A huge, fat hairy man lumbers out of the steam toward him. "Did you call for me?" asks the hairy man. "I don't think so," says the newcomer. "You must be new here," says the hairy man. "It's a rule here that if you fart, it implies you called for me." The huge hairy man then bends the newcomer over a bench and has his wicked way with him. Later, the man hobbles back to the club's office and finds the receptionist. "I want to cancel my membership," says the man. "But sir," replies the receptionist. "You've only been here for a few hours; you haven't had the chance to see all our facilities." "I'm not interested," says the man. "I'm 60 years old; I get a hard-on once a month, but I can fart 15 times a day!"

☞ A man starts a new job, but phones in every Monday to say he's sick. Eventually his boss calls him in and says, "Is there anything we can do for you? I'm sure we can find a cure for whatever illness you have." "Well, I'm not exactly ill," replies the man. "Y'see, I like having sex with my mother, but Monday's the only day she has any free time." "What?" cries the boss. "You never come in on Mondays because you're having sex with your mother?" "Hey," replies the man, "I told you I was sick."

☞ A man tells his doctor that his wife hasn't had sex with him for the past seven months. The doctor asks the man to bring his wife in so he can talk to her. The wife comes to the doctor's office, and he asks her why she's lost interest in sex. "I haven't lost interest," she says. "I'm just too tired to have sex. Seven months ago I got a new job and the only way I can get there is by cab. I don't make much money, and the cab driver always says to me, 'So, are you going to pay today or what?' I always give him an 'or what'. Anyway, that makes me late for work. So when my boss sees me, he says, 'You were late again. So are we going to dock your salary, or what?' So I give him the 'or what'. Then, on the way home, it's the same story with the cab driver again. He says, 'So are you going to pay this time or what?' And, again, I do an 'or what' to save some money. So you see, doctor, when I get home I'm just exhausted." The doctor thinks for a second. "I see," he says. "So am I going to tell your husband or what?"

☞ A man walks into a bar and sees his best friend looking miserable. "What's the matter?" he asks. "It's my wife," says his friend. "When we make love she just lies there. I've tried everything, but nothing seems to work. She doesn't moan: doesn't scream: doesn't even move." "Hey; don't worry about it," says the man, patting his friend on the shoulder. "She's exactly the same way with me."

"Love is the answer, but while you're waiting for the answer, sex raises some pretty good questions."
Woody Allen

☞ A man walks into a bar with his girlfriend. A drunk looks at the girl and says, "If you were my woman, I'd lick you from top to bottom like a lollipop." The man is furious and gets ready to punch the drunk, but his girlfriend stops him, telling him she doesn't want a scene. The drunk then walks over and tries to give her a big, sloppy kiss. The man pulls him off and is about to hit him when the girlfriend pulls him away. "If that guy even looks at you again, I'm going to kill him!" shouts the man. After a couple of minutes, the drunk comes over and says, "If you were my woman, I'd turn you upside-down, fill your pussy with beer and drink you dry with one swallow." The man takes the girl's arm and walks her out of the bar. "I thought you were going to beat him up?" says the girl. "I was," replies the man, "but if he can drink that much beer, he's a better man than I am."

☞ A naked woman jumps into the back of a cab and asks to be taken to a nudists' convention. The driver looks at her in the rear-view mirror and says, "Lady, you're naked. How do you expect to pay me?" The woman opens her legs and says, "Does this answer your question?" The driver peers into the mirror again and says, "Got anything smaller?"

☞ A New York man goes on a business trip to Los Angeles. While he's there, he sees a cute puppy and buys it as a present for his daughter. When he's at the airport waiting to go home, he realises it's going to cost a lot of money to take the dog on as excess baggage, so he decides to save himself some cash and slips the puppy down the front of his pants. The man boards the plane and the puppy is undetected. A short while after take-off, a stewardess notices that the man is sweating profusely and is having trouble keeping still. "Are you all right, sir?" she asks. "S-s-sure I am," replies the man. The stewardess is unconvinced, but she leaves him in peace. A while later, she passes the man again and finds him sitting cross-eyed, making small whining sounds in the back of his throat. "Are you sure you're okay, sir?" she asks. "Yes," replies the man in a high squeaky voice. "I'm perfectly fine." The stewardess goes off once more, but returns half an hour later to find the man in an extraordinary state; he's turned bright red, is crossing his ankles tightly, has one fist stuffed in his mouth and is banging the other on the arm rest. "Oh, my God!" says the stewardess. "Are you having a heart attack?" "No," gasps the man. "Stewardess, I... I have a confession to make. I smuggled a puppy down my pants." "What?" exclaims the stewardess. "I'll bet he's not house-trained." "You're right," yelps the man, "and he's not weaned either!"

> **"My friend has the nickname 'Shagger'. Now, you might think that's cool, but she hates it."**
> *Jimmy Carr*

☞ A newspaper conducted a survey of male readers to ask what they enjoyed about having oral sex performed on them. Seven per cent of men said they most enjoyed the sensations; five per cent confessed that their chief enjoyment was the sense of domination it gave them; while 88 per cent said that they were just grateful for a few minutes' peace and quiet.

☞ A priest sees a group of teenage boys sitting on the lawn outside the front of his church. He goes out to ask what they're doing. "Nothing much, Father," says one. "We were just seeing who could tell the biggest lie about their sex life." "Now, lads!" says the priest. "I'm very shocked to hear that. Why, when I was your age, I never even thought about sex at all." "Okay, that's it!" says one of the teenagers. "You win, Father!"

☞ A professor is asked to give a lecture on the subject of 'sex'. When it's his turn to speak he walks to the front of the hall, climbs the stairs to the stage and goes to stand behind the podium. The professor then shuffles his notes into order, adjusts the microphone and says, "Ladies and gentlemen. It gives me great pleasure..." And then he goes back to his seat.

☞ A trainee priest is hearing confessions when one of the parishioners admits to an act of sodomy. The priest can't remember what the penance for this sin should be. He beckons over one of the altar-boys and whispers, "What does Father O'Neill usually give for sodomy?" The boy whispers back, "A choc ice and a Coke."

"Sex alleviates tension. Love causes it."
Woody Allen

☞ A traveller pulls into a hotel around midnight and asks the clerk for a single room. As the clerk fills out the paperwork, the man looks around and sees a gorgeous blonde sitting in the lobby. She's obviously the sort who might show a guy a good time for the right consideration. The man tells the clerk to wait a moment, then nips round the corner to make the girl's acquaintance. After a minute, he comes back with the girl on his arm. "Well, well," says the man. "Fancy meeting my wife here. Guess I'll need a double room for the night." Next morning, the man comes down to settle his bill. He's astonished to find he owes $3,000. "Why the hell are you charging me $3,000?" he yells. "I've only been here one night!" "I know," says the clerk, "but your wife has been here for three weeks."

☞ A vicar visits the house of a young man in his parish and discovers that a sex party is in full swing. All the guests are blindfolded, naked men and they're playing a game where they try to guess identities by fondling each other's genitals. "Oh, dear," says the vicar. "I'd better go. This isn't my cup of tea at all." "Rubbish!" says the young man. "Your name's been called three times already."

☞ A woman goes into a shop and asks if they have any batteries. "Yes, ma'am," says the shop assistant, gesturing with his finger. "Can you come this way?" "If I could come that way," says the woman, "I wouldn't need the batteries."

☞ A woman goes on a quiz show and does very well; in fact, she's invited back the next day to compete for the million-pound prize. That night, the woman's husband sneaks into the studio and steals the answer to the million-pound question. "Listen," he tells her. "When they ask the question, all you have to do is repeat, 'Head, heart and penis'." The woman commits this to memory but, on the day, she's so nervous her memory starts failing her. The time arrives, and the quiz host asks her the million-pound question, "According to tradition, which are the three main organs of the male body?" "Oh, dear," says the woman. "It was the... er... the head... the... um... the heart... and... er..." "Ten seconds to go," says the host. "Oh, dear," says the woman. "What was it? All last night my husband kept drilling it into me, and this morning I had it on the tip of my tongue..." "Close enough!" shouts the host. "You've just won a million pounds!"

☞ A woman is in the bedroom when her husband walks in with a sheep under his arm. He looks at her and says, "This is the pig I have sex with when you've got a headache." His wife replies, "I think you'll find that's a sheep." He replies, "I was *talking* to the sheep."

☞ A woman is talking with her friend. "That bloke I picked up in the bar last night turned out to be a complete bastard. We'd just finished having sex when he called me a slut!" "Never!" says her friend. "What did you do?" The woman replies, "I told him to get out of my bed and take his mates with him."

"Sleeping with prostitutes is like making your cat dance with you on its hind legs. You know it's wrong, but you try to convince yourself that they're enjoying it as well."
Scott Capurro

☞ A woman picks up a Texan in a bar. "Is it true that everything's huge in Texas?" she asks. "Reckon so," replies the Texan. One thing leads to another and they end up in bed, where the woman discovers that everything from Texas really *is* bigger. Next morning, the Texan's getting dressed when he turns to the woman and says, "Hope you don't mind me asking, ma'am, but which part of Texas are you from?"

☞ A woman says to her husband, "I went to the doctor, and he says I must have sex at least five times a week" "Okay," her husband replies. "Put me down for two of them."

☞ A boy rushes home and says to his father, "Dad! Dad! You'll never guess what; I just had sex with the English teacher!" Father is delighted, "You young scamp. You're just like your old Dad – a real ladies' man. Tell you what; now you're so grown up, I think we can let you ride your big brother's motorbike." The boy's face drops, "Aww, I can't," he whines. "My bum still hurts."

☞ After a huge drinking binge, a man wakes one morning to find himself in a strange bed alongside the ugliest woman he's ever seen. Horrified, he slips out of bed and pulls on his clothes as quietly as possible. He's just about to sneak out when he feels a twinge of guilt, so he gets a £20 note out of his pocket and puts it on a table. The man feels a tug on his leg. He looks down to see it's being pulled by another ugly girl who's been asleep under a pile of clothes on the floor. "Oi!" she says. "Nothing for the bridesmaid?"

☞ An explorer is searching the Amazon jungle for a tribe whose women are reputed to have extremely large private parts. The parts are so large – it's rumoured – that they can swallow a whole melon. Eventually, he stumbles across the tribe's village and is granted an audience with the headman. "Tell me," says the explorer, "is it true what they say about women in your tribe?" "Oh, yes," replies the headman. "Each one has a 'mulatata' big enough to swallow a melon or a small pig." "Good heavens!" says the explorer. "But how on earth do you make love to a woman with an organ that size?" "It's not easy," replies the headman with a sigh, "but they do stretch."

☞ An old lady is waiting for a bus that will take her to a pet cemetery. Under her arm she carries a small box containing the body of her deceased cat. As she gets on the bus, the old lady says to the driver, "Is it all right if I bring this box on the bus?" She adds in a whisper, "I have a dead pussy." "Sure," says the driver, jerking his head at a woman sitting behind him, "Why not sit with my wife? You two have a lot in common."

☞ Bob says to Bill, "My doctor says if I don't give up sex, I'll be dead in a week." "Why is that?" asks Bill. Bob replies, "I've been shagging his wife."

☞ Casual sex is great – you don't have to wear a tie!

☞ Chastity is curable, if detected early.

☞ Do you know the scientific name for a female sex change? A Strapadicktome.

☞ Father Christmas asks little Jenny what she wants for a present. "I want a Barbie doll and a GI Joe," she says. "I thought Barbie came with Ken," replies Santa. "No," says Jenny. "Barbie comes with Joe. She fakes it with Ken."

☞ Flower One: "I love you, my darling!" Flower Two: "I love you too, my sweet!" Flower One: "I want you to take me, darling! Take me now!" Flower Two: "I will take you, you delicious temptress! You will scream in ecstasy!" Flower One: "Where the hell are those damned bees...?"

☞ For men, sex is like a bank robbery. You get in, you get out, and you hope you didn't leave something behind that can be traced back to you.

"Sting's always boasting about his eight-hour tantric sex sessions with his wife, Trudie Styler. Imagine how long he could keep it up if she was a looker."
Jimmy Carr

☞ God comes down to the Garden of Eden with a sack. He gathers Adam and Eve together and tells them that he's found a bag of abilities he forgot to share out before. "I can't remember what's in here," says God, "but it's all good stuff." He reaches into the bag, has a rummage and pulls something out. "What's this?" he says. "Oh, right; it's the ability to pee standing up. That's pretty useful." Adam sticks his hand up and stands on tippy-toes, desperate to be given this ability. "Oh, me! Me! Me!" he cries. "Please! Me, me, me! Pretty please?" "Oh, let him have it," says Eve. So God gives Adam the ability to pee standing up. "Now let's see what else is in here," says God. He has a rummage around. "Mmm; not much left: just this." So saying, he pulls something out and says, "Now what the dickens is this one? Oh, yes: multiple orgasms..."

☞ Harry and Dick are walking down the road when they see two dogs mating in a front garden. Harry nudges Dick and says, "That's the way my wife and I like it." "My wife wouldn't go for that," replies Dick. "She's very traditional. We only ever do it the one way." "A drink'll loosen her up," says Harry. "All I have to do is slip my Mary a vodka and she's up for anything." "I think I'll give that a try," says Dick. The next day, the two meet up in a bar. "Did it work?" asks Harry. "Did you pour your wife a drink and try something different for a change?" "Yes," replies Dick. "But it took more drinks than I thought it would. Getting her to try a new position took two whiskies, but she had to down half a bottle before she'd do it in the front garden."

☞ Harry goes to bed, taps his wife on the shoulder and suggests they have a bit of rumpy-pumpy. "Not tonight, dear," says his wife. "I have a headache." Next evening, Harry tries his luck again. "Not now, dear," says his wife. "I'm too tired." The next night, Harry climbs into bed again and, once more, taps his wife on the shoulder. "What?" she exclaims. "That's three nights in a row. Are you some kind of sex maniac?"

☞ Harry is chatting to his ex-girlfriend. "I was having sex with Mary last night," he says, "and all I did was think of you." "Really?" says the ex-girlfriend. "Do you miss me so much?" Harry replies, "No, it stops me from coming too quickly."

☞ Harry is in bed with his new girlfriend. "Your lovemaking's like a newsflash," she says. "Really?" says Harry. "Because it's dramatic, intense and takes you to places you never knew existed?" "No," she says, "because it's quick, unexpected and usually a disaster."

☞ Harry is losing interest in his wife. These days his favourite sexual position is 'next door'.

☞ Harry is walking along one day when he comes across a magic beanstalk. Curious, he begins to climb, and before long he finds the ugliest woman he's ever seen, sitting on a leaf. She beckons to him and says, "Have sex with me, or climb the beanstalk to success." Harry shudders and climbs higher. A bit further on, he comes across a very plain woman sitting on a leaf. "Have sex with me, or climb the beanstalk to success," she says. Again, Harry continues his climb. Before long, he comes upon another woman. This one is very attractive. "Have sex with me, or climb the beanstalk to success," she says. Harry's tempted, but figures that if the women get better-looking the higher he climbs, he might as well keep going. Harry climbs higher and comes across a leaf right at the top of the beanstalk. Standing on the leaf is a dirty, ugly old man wearing nothing but a pair of torn denim dungarees. The old man undoes his buttons and his dungarees fall round his ankles, leaving him naked. "Howdy," says the old man. "Who the hell are you?" asks Harry. The old man replies, "I'm Cess."

"The closest I ever came to a ménage à trois was when I dated a schizophrenic."
Rita Rudner

☞ Harry's wife has just given birth to a son. Harry gets chatting with the doctor who delivered the baby and raises the delicate matter of sex. "Hope you don't minding me asking," he says, "but how soon can my wife and I start having sexual relations again?" "Well, that depends," replies the doctor. "Did they put her on a National Health ward, or has she got a private room?"

☞ I read about a shocking case in the paper the other day. It turns out a woman in our area was sexually assaulted last week. They doubt they'll catch the man; he's got quite a head start. The woman didn't realise she'd been molested until the cheque bounced.

☞ I was walking along a narrow ledge on the side of a mountain when a naked woman came walking towards me from the opposite direction. There was no way for us to squeeze past each other on this ledge. I was in a dilemma; should I block her passage or toss myself off?

☞ I went to the doctor because this mole had appeared on the end of my penis. The bastard reported me to the RSPCA.

☞ It's okay to laugh during sex – just don't point.

☞ Jeff goes to see his doctor. The doctor says, "I have good news and bad news." "What's the bad news?" asks Jeff. "Your wife has syphilis," replies the doctor. "Oh, my God!" exclaims Jeff. "What could the good news possibly be?" The doctor replies, "She didn't get it from you."

☞ Julie and her mother go to the doctor. Julie has been feeling very sick in the mornings and her mother is concerned. The doctor examines the girl and tells her she's pregnant. "What?" exclaims the mother. "That's impossible! Julie's never had a boyfriend. She's never even kissed a man." "That's right!" protests Julie. "What a horrible suggestion. I've never, ever done anything dirty like that." The doctor says nothing; he just picks up a cup of coffee and goes to stare out of the window. After a few moments, the mother says, "Well, what are you doing over there?" "Nothing," says the doctor, "but the last time something like this happened, there was a big star and three wise men turned up. I don't want to miss anything."

☞ Little Johnny goes up to his mother and says, "Is it true that babies come from storks?" "Why, yes," replies mother. "Okay," says Johnny, "So who screws the stork?"

☞ Little Johnny passes his parents' bedroom in the middle of the night. Hearing a lot of moaning and thumping, he peeks in and catches his folks in the act. Before dad can react, little Johnny shouts, "Oh, boy! Horsie ride! Daddy, can I ride on your back?" Daddy, relieved that Johnny's not asking uncomfortable questions, agrees. Johnny hops on and daddy gets back into the rhythm. Pretty soon mummy starts moaning and gasping. Johnny cries out, "Hang on tight, Daddy! This is the part where me and the milkman usually get bucked off!"

☞ Little Johnny, little Mary and little Jane are arguing over what they should play. "I want to play at doctors," says little Mary. "I want to play at nurses," says little Jane. "That's boring," says little Johnny. "I want to play at Presidents and interns – so you two spit out your gum."

☞ One night I managed to make love for an hour and five minutes. It was the day they put the clocks forward.

☞ Practice safe sex; go screw yourself.

☞ The sexual stages of man. In his twenties: thrice weekly. In his thirties: tries weekly. In his forties: tries weakly. In his fifties: tries and tries. In his sixties: tries and cries. In his seventies: tries and dies!

"There's nothing wrong with making love with the light on. Just make sure the car door is closed."
George Burns

☞ Three honeymooning couples settle down for the night in a hotel. One man sees his wife naked for the first time and says, "My god! What a huge fat ass!" His furious bride throws him into the corridor. The second man also sees his wife naked for the first time; he says, "Christ! What floppy, dangling tits!" He too is thrown into the corridor. A few moments later, the third man is also thrown in the corridor. "Did you put your foot in it?" asks the first. "No," replies the third, "but I could have."

☞ Three women are discussing their sex lives. The first says, "I call my husband 'the musician', because he has such an incredible organ." The second woman says, "I call my husband 'the dentist', because he can drill me like no one else." The third woman says, "I call my husband 'the mailman'. The moron always delivers late and most of the time he gets it in the wrong box."

☞ To men, it may be an endless source of fascination but you'll never hear a woman say, "My, what an attractive scrotum!"

☞ What woman think about sex: At age eight – ignore it. At age eighteen – experience it. At age twenty-eight – look for it. At age thirty-eight – ask for it. At age forty-eight – beg for it. At age fifty-eight – pay for it. At age sixty-eight – pray for it. At age seventy-eight – forget it!

☞ What's a man's idea of foreplay? Brushing his teeth.

☞ What's the difference between a bitch and a whore? A whore sleeps with everybody at the party; a bitch sleeps with everybody at the party – except you.

☞ What's the difference between a blimp and 365 blow-jobs? One is a Goodyear, the other is an excellent year.

☞ When God was making the world, he bestowed on man a sex life of 20 years. Man was horrified. "Only 20 years, Lord? Can't I have more?" he begged. God would not be moved – that was all the time he would give man. Then God called upon the monkey and gave him a sex life of 20 years. "I don't need 20 years," said the monkey. "Ten is plenty for me." Man then spoke up and said, "Can I have the monkey's spare 10 years?" God agreed to grant these extra years to man. Then he called upon the lion and gave him a sex life of 20 years. The lion, too, said he only needed 10 years and, again, man asked for the extra time to be added to his account. God agreed to this. Then he called upon the donkey. The donkey was also given a sex life of 20 years, but, like the others, the donkey said that 10 years was enough. Again, man asked for the spare years to be added to his account, and God gave them to him. And that explains why man experiences 20 years of normal sex life, then has 10 years monkeying around, 10 years of lion about it, and spends a final 10 years making an ass of himself.

☞ Why do honeymoons only last seven days? Because seven days makes a hole weak.

☞ Why is a good woman like a good bar? Liquor in the front, poker in the rear.

☞ Zeke is running around in the yard, trying to get his home-made kite to fly. He's not having much luck. His wife, Lulu-Belle, calls out to him from the house. "Zeke!" she shouts. "What you need is a piece of tail!" "That's what I asked you for yesterday!" calls back Zeke. "You told me to go fly a kite!"

> **"I'm still making love at 71, which is handy for me because I live at number 63."**
> *Bernie Clifton*

SEX – APHRODISIACS AND MARITAL AIDS

☞ Jane wants to spice up her love life, so she buys a pair of crotchless knickers. She puts on her new underwear and lies on the bed waiting for her husband to come home. When he opens the bedroom door, she spreads her legs and says, "Hey; fancy a piece of this?" "God, no!" says her horrified husband. "Look what it's done to your pants!"

☞ An old lady totters into a sex shop. "Do you sell things called 'vibrators'?" she asks. "Of course we do," replies the shop-owner. "They're all displayed on the shelving over there." The old woman peers at the weird and wonderful toys on display, then says, "Can I have the big, red one?" "No," replies the owner. "That's the fire extinguisher."

SEX – BETWEEN SWEETS

☞ A jellybaby develops an itchy crotch and goes to the doctor. After the examination, the doctor gives him the bad news; he has VD. "It's my own fault," says the jellybaby. "I've been sleeping with allsorts."

SEX – BISEXUALITY

"Being bisexual doubles your chance
of a date on Saturday night."
Woody Allen

SEX – CONDOMS AND CONTRACEPTION

☞ A man visiting a small country town goes into the pharmacy to buy some condoms. This isn't something he's done in a while, and he's amazed at the variety on offer. He calls over the sales assistant and asks him for some advice. The assistant goes through the various condom brands describing their features, then finally shows the man a packet of condoms made of lambs' intestines. "They're made out of lamb?" asks the incredulous man. "Who the hell wants to use one of those?" "Well, sir," says the sales assistant, "they do say they have a more natural feel." The man eyes the assistant suspiciously, then says, "Not to a city boy they don't."

☞ A woman phones her doctor in the middle of the night. "Doctor! Doctor, come quick!" she says. "My son has just swallowed a condom!" The doctor leaps out of bed and starts pulling on his clothes. The phone rings again; it's the same woman. "It's all right," she says. "The emergency's over. My husband's just found another one."

☞ Condoms should be used on every conceivable occasion.

☞ Two men, one Catholic, the other Protestant are talking. "I don't understand it," says the Protestant. "How is it that my wife and I, who are Protestants and who can use as much birth control as we want, have ended up with nine children while you and your wife, who are Catholics and who can't use any birth control at all, haven't had any?" "Ah, well, you see," says the Catholic, "I'm very careful. I only have sex during the safe period." "Oh, yes?" says the Protestant." And when's that?" "When you're out at work," says the Catholic.

(453)

"Condoms aren't completely safe. A friend of mine was wearing one and got hit by a bus."
Bob Rubin

☞ A young man walks into a chemist's and goes up to the counter. "Could you sell me a pack of condoms?" he says. "My girlfriend's invited me over for dinner and I think she's expecting some action later on! She's pretty hot." The pharmacist gives him the condoms. The young man's on his way out when he thinks of something and comes back. "Tell you what," he says, "you'd better give me another pack. My girlfriend's sister's pretty cute too and I think she likes me. You never know; I might get a chance to roll her in the hay as well." The pharmacist gives the young man another packet of condoms. The young man thinks for a moment, then says, "Y'know what? Give me another pack. My girlfriend's mother's a real fox and she looks pretty horny for an old broad. If I play my cards right, I reckon I could get her in bed as well. Hey, I can dream, can't I?" The pharmacist hands over a third packet of condoms and the young man leaves. The young man turns up for dinner and is seated at the table with his girlfriend, her sister and mother. The father of the house is late getting back from work, so they decide to start without him. The young man offers to say grace and bows his head in prayer. As the young man mumbles his prayers, the father slips into the room and joins them at the table. The prayer continues, the young man bent almost double over the table as he asks for God's blessing on the dinner, the family, the house, the family's pets, the local sports teams etcetera. After ten minutes of this devotion the girlfriend leans over and whispers. "Can you stop now? This is ridiculous. I had no idea you were so religious." The young man replies, "Yeah? Well, I had no idea your father was a pharmacist."

☞ Definition of a birth control pill: the other thing a woman can put in her mouth to keep from getting pregnant!

☞ Every day Julian goes to the chemist and buys a pack of condoms. After a few weeks of this, the chemist comments on the large numbers Julian is purchasing. "You must have quite a lot of success with the ladies," he says. "Women?" replies Julian. "I have nothing to do with women." "I'm sorry," says the chemist. "I didn't know you were gay." "Gay?" replies Julian. "Whatever makes you think I'm gay?" "Well, all the condoms you buy," says the chemist, "and if you don't like women, then I guessed you must like men." "I don't like either," replies Julian, "at least, not in that way." "Then why do you buy condoms?" asks the chemist. "To feed to my pet poodle," replies Julian. "These days, she does all her little jobs in plastic bags."

☞ Girlfriend (to boyfriend): "Mmmmm. These cheese and onion flavour condoms taste really authentic, don't they?" Boyfriend: "But I haven't put it on yet!"

☞ Have you heard about the new super-sensitive condoms? They hang around after the man leaves and talk to the woman.

☞ Have you noticed that all the people in favour of birth control have all been born already?

☞ June is on a train when she sees a man carrying two tiny babies. "Aren't they gorgeous?" she says. "What are their names?" "I don't know," replies the man. "You don't know?" replies June. "What sort of man doesn't know the name of his own children?" "I never said I was their father," replies the man. "Then who are you, and what exactly are you doing with these poor babies?" says the indignant June. "I'm the sales director of the Acme condom company," replies the man, and nods at the babies. "These are complaints."

☞ Mary and four of her friends go out shopping. After a long day at the mall, they pile into Mary's car ready to go home. Suddenly, Mary remembers that she forgot to buy any condoms. Her husband is coming home after a long business trip so she'll be needing them. She leaves the car's engine running and hurries to the nearest pharmacy. Inside, she picks up a packet of condoms, but then finds there's a long queue for the checkout. She runs to the head of the queue, hands over her condoms and says, "Do you mind if I butt in, only I've got four people waiting in my car?"

☞ Mary and Patrick are Catholics who practise the 'stool and saucer' method of contraception. Patrick (five foot three inches) makes loves to Mary (six foot four) upright, while standing on a stool. When Patrick's eyes get as big as saucers, Mary kicks away the stool.

☞ Wear camouflage condoms. Then no one will see you coming.

☞ What do you call a woman who's allergic to latex? Mummy.

SEX – EDUCATION

☞ A nun is teaching a Sunday School class. "Now, children," says the nun, "do you know where little girls and little boys go if they get together to indulge in disgusting, sinful behaviour?" Little Johnny sticks his hand up. "I know, Sister," he says. "We go behind the bike sheds."

☞ Joe's mother asks his dad to tell him about the birds and the bees. Dad sits Joe down in front of the television and puts on a hardcore sex video. After a few minutes, he says, "You see that? Birds and bees do that as well."

SEX – FEMININE HYGIENE

☞ A midget goes up to a woman in a bar and says, "Can I smell your pussy?" "Certainly not!" says the woman. "Oh," says the midget. "Then it must be your feet."

☞ A woman gets on a bus and finds herself sitting opposite an incredibly attractive man. She tries to flirt with him, but he doesn't seem interested. She pouts at him, but gets no response, so she unbuttons her blouse to reveal some cleavage. She still can't get a reaction. Finally she pulls out all the stops; she pulls up her skirt and opens her legs to reveal she's not wearing any underwear. The man sniffs the air, then stands up and pulls out his collapsible white stick. "That was quick," he says. "It's usually half an hour to the fish market."

> ## "Those press-on towels are a real rip-off, aren't they? I used six of them and I couldn't even get my arms dry."
> *Jack Dee*

☞ A crazy bag-lady walks into a fish market and asks a stallholder how much he charges for crabs. The owner replies, "I sell mine for a pound each." "Gracious!" cackles the woman, holding out her paw. "Shake hands with a millionaire!"

☞ One morning in Eden, God is looking for Adam and Eve, but can't find them. Later in the day, God sees Adam and asks where he and Eve have been hiding. Adam says, "This morning, Eve and I were in the bamboo grove making love for the first time." God looks stern and says, "Adam, you have sinned. I knew this would happen. Where's Eve now?" Adam replies, "She's down by the river, having a wash." "Oh, great," mutters God. "Now all the fish'll smell funny."

☞ One day, little Susie gets her period for the first time. Not certain what's happening, she decides to tell little Johnny. Little Susie lifts her skirt and shows little Johnny what's happening. Little Johnny's eyes open wide. "You know," he says, "I'm no doctor, but it looks like someone just ripped your balls off!"

☞ Ted and Joan are on holiday in Australia. Every day they go for a walk on the beach, and every day they see a huge fat woman completely naked, sitting on the sand with her legs wide open, eating a slice of watermelon. This goes on for a week, until one day Joan decides to go over to say hello. "Hi," she says. "It must be very liberating and refreshing to let the fresh air get to your private areas." "Wouldn't know about that," replies the fat woman. "I'm just trying to keep the bloody flies off me watermelon."

SEX – FOR SALE

☞ A boy and his date are parked in a country road, making out in his car. Suddenly, the girl stops the boy. "I really should have mentioned this earlier," she says, "but I'm actually a hooker and I charge £20 for sex." The boy pays her and they do their thing. After they've finished, the girl asks to go home. The boy asks for his fare. "What d'you mean, fare?" asks the girl. "Well, I should have mentioned this earlier," replies the boy, "but I'm actually a taxi driver. The fare back to town is £25."

☞ A Catholic chaplain is walking through a notorious section of town when he sees a soldier leaving a brothel. The soldier pauses on the sidewalk and gestures with his right hand in a manner familiar to the priest. The chaplain approaches the soldier and says, "I'm sorry to see a good Catholic lad like you coming out of a place like that." "I'm not Catholic," answers the soldier. "But I saw you cross yourself," replies the chaplain. "Listen, Padre," says the soldier. "When I come out of a place like that, I always check four things: my spectacles, my nuts, my watch and my wallet."

☞ A class of children is asked what their parents do for a living. Little Johnny sticks up his hand and says, "My mum's a substitute." Teacher knows that little Johnny's mother works in a whorehouse, so she corrects him. "I'm sorry," says teacher, "but your mother isn't a substitute. She's a prostitute." "No," replies Johnny, "my sister's a prostitute, but when she can't make it into work my mum's the substitute."

☞ A cowboy walks into a saloon. He goes up to the barman and says, "I hear Big Bella works here: the roughest, toughest, meanest whore this side of the Colorado." "She sure does," replies the barman. "Upstairs, first door on the right." The cowboy buys two bottles of beer and runs up the stairs to Big Bella's room. He bursts in and says, "Are you Big Bella, the roughest, toughest, meanest whore this side of the Colorado?" "I sure am," says Bella, who then lifts her skirts, lies back on the bed and grabs her ankles. "Don't you want a drink first?" asks the cowboy. "Sure I do;

why d'you think I'm lying like this?" replies Bella. "Hurry up and get the caps off them bottles!"

☞ A farmer has a tame bear which he keeps in his barn. One evening there's a huge storm and the local highway is flooded out, leaving a lot of commuters stranded with no way of getting home. The farmer accommodates a few of these lost sheep, but soon runs out of room. When the next man comes to the farm looking for shelter, the farmer tells him he'll have to use the barn. "Don't mind the bear, though," says the farmer. "He's as tame as they come." The man goes off to the barn. A short while later, another man comes to the farm. The farmer tells him the same story; he can sleep in the barn and mustn't mind the bear. An hour after this, a woman comes to the house. She's a good-looking girl, but is dressed like a hooker. The farmer's not one to make judgements, however, so he tells her she can use the barn as well. After the girl has gone, the farmer realises he didn't say anything about the bear. "Well, so what?" he thinks. "What harm can she come to? Anyway, the guys'll tell her about the bear." A few hours later, the girl reappears with her clothing torn. "Are you sure I can't stay in the house?" she asks. "They're a real rough crowd in that barn." "What happened?" asks the farmer. "Well this tall guy wanted sex and he paid me $40, and that was okay," says the girl. "And the short guy wanted sex and he paid $60, so that was fine. But that bastard in the fur coat – he didn't even say 'Thank you'!"

☞ A hooker mistakes a Salvation Army man for a soldier and propositions him. The Salvation Army gent says, "Ma'am, as a pitiful victim of circumstance, you may be forgiven your mistake: but tell me; are you familiar with the concept of original sin?" "Well, we'll have to see," she replies, "but I ought to warn you; if it's really original, it'll cost you an extra £20."

☞ A man goes to a brothel and knocks on the door. The madam answers. "What can I do for you?" she asks. "What can I get for five quid?" asks the man. "Five quid?" says the madam scornfully. "Why don't you piss off and have a wank?" Two minutes later, there's another knock on the door. The man says, "Who do I pay the five quid to?"

☞ A lumberjack goes to a remote logging station where there are no women for 500 miles. He asks his foreman what the locals do for sex. "Well, if you're feeling lonesome, Old Charlie'll put you right. He's gone sixty, but he can still show you a good time." "Hell, no!" says the lumberjack. "I think I can do without Old Charlie." However, after six long months have passed, the lumberjack changes his mind. "Look," he says to the foreman. "I'm desperate. How much does this Old Charlie guy charge?" "Three hundred and fifty dollars," replies the foreman. "Holy smoke!" says the lumberjack. "How comes he's so expensive?" "Well, Charlie only gets fifty dollars," replies the foreman, "but you have to pay three other guys a hundred bucks each to hold him down."

☞ A man goes to a Bangkok bar but is told that no girls are available. "We do have a pig, though," says the madam. "She very popular. You have her for half price." The man thinks he might as well, so he pays up and is shown to a room with a sow in it. He has sex with the sow and enjoys the experience so much he returns the next day. "Sorry," says the Madam. "No pig today. Why you not try special show? One of our girls is having sex with donkey." The man agrees and is shown to a darkened room which has a wall covered in peep-holes. He looks through one and sees a girl having sex with a donkey. "Wow," he says. "This is great!" One of the other punters turns to him and says, "If you think this is good, you should have been here yesterday. They had this bloke screwing a pig!"

☞ A man goes to a massage parlour for the first time and is invited to lie down on a couch. As the masseuse kneads him, she notices the man has developed an enormous erection. She bends over and whispers, "Would you like a wank?" "Yes, please," replies the young man. The masseuse slip out of the room. Two minutes later, she sticks her head round the door and says, "Have you finished?"

☞ A man goes out shopping with his wife and they decide to split up for a couple of hours. As the man wanders around, he spots a prostitute on a street corner and goes over to see what she charges. "It's £50 for full sex," says the prostitute, "£25 for a blow-job and £5 for one off the wrist." The man checks his pockets and finds he only has £3. "You won't get much for £3." says the prostitute, "and certainly nothing from me." Later, the man and his wife are walking back to their car. The prostitute spots him from over the road and shouts, "Hey! I said you wouldn't get much for £3!"

☞ A man is walking down an alley when he's accosted by a streetwalker. "You want some action?" says the streetwalker. "It's £20 for a hand-job." "I'm not interested," replies the man, "I'm married." "So what if you're married?" says the streetwalker. "Are you afraid your wife will find out?" "Not at all," replies the man. "It's just that my wife only charges £10 for a hand-job."

☞ A man walks into a brothel and says to the madam, "I want to get screwed." The madam tells him to go up to room twelve and knock on the door. The man walks up to the door, knocks on it and says, "I want to get screwed." A sexy voice replies, "Just slide £20 under the door." The man slides £20 under the door and waits... but nothing happens! He knocks on the door again, and says, "Hey! I want to get screwed!" The sexy voice replies, "What? Again?"

☞ A married couple are very short of money, so it's decided that the wife should become a prostitute to make some extra cash. After her first night on the streets, the woman returns home and empties her bag on the kitchen table. Her husband starts to count the takings, putting the cash into neat piles. "There's two hundred pounds and fifty pence in here," says the husband. "That's not bad: but who on earth gave you the fifty pence?" His wife replies, "Well... all of them."

☞ An old man hobbles into a brothel. "How much for a good time?" he asks. "$150," replies the madam. "What!" cries the old-timer. "A hundred and fifty dollars? Are you putting me on?" "I can," replies the madam, "but it's an extra $10."

☞ An old sailor is in a brothel trying to make love with one of the girls. "How am I doing?" he asks. "Three knots," replies the girl. "What d'you mean, three knots?" says the sailor. The girl replies, "You're not hard, you're not in and you're not getting your money back."

☞ I saw a woman standing by the road the other day. She said, "I'll spank you for £20." I didn't know what to do. I went home and phoned my mother. I said, "Mum, you could make a lot of money out here."

☞ Leroy and Jeff decide to have a competition to see who can have the most sex in an evening. They go to a brothel and take the ladies of their choice to their rooms. Jeff energetically makes love to his partner and makes a mark on the wall above the bed to keep score. After a short rest he has sex again, and makes another mark. A little while later, he does it again and makes yet another mark. Then, exhausted, he falls fast asleep. The next morning, Leroy knocks on Jeff's door. "How did you do?" he asks. "Oh, pretty good," replies Jeff. "I'm a regular sex machine." Leroy sees the three marks on the wall. "Holy smoke!" he says. "One hundred and eleven! Damn it! You beat me by three!"

☞ Our MP has promised to get prostitution off our streets and drive it underground – which I suppose is quite good news for miners.

☞ Two city prostitutes, one from New York and one from Chicago, decide to move to California. While driving through New Mexico they stop off at a country store for a break. While they're looking around, they come across two old Native American women selling blankets and beads. One of the prostitutes asks the old ladies where they come from. One of the old ladies says, "I am a Navajo. My friend: Arapaho." "No kidding!" exclaims the prostitute. "Well, ain't that a coincidence. Me a New York ho: my friend, Chicago ho."

☞ Three prostitutes, a mother, daughter and a grandmother, all live together. One night, the daughter comes home looking upset. "How did you get on tonight, dear?" asks mother. "Not good," replies the daughter. "I only got a lousy $20 for a blow-job." "Twenty bucks?" says the mother, "You should be grateful. In my day we gave a blow-job for 50 cents!" "Fifty cents?" exclaims the grandmother. "You should be grateful. Back in the Depression we were happy to get a hot meal!"

☞ Two hookers are talking business. "I feel like a bottle of champagne," says one. "Last night I made $500." "Yeah?" says the other. 'Well, last night I made $5,000 – and I feel like a goddamn pot of glue!"

☞ Two prostitutes are talking about business. One says, "I'm really busy all the time just now. In fact, if I had a second pair of legs, I could open up another branch on the high street."

SEX – GENITAL MISFORTUNE

☞ A man goes to hospital for a circumcision, but ends up having a complete sex change by mistake. When he wakes up, the man goes to pieces and starts crying. "Oh, my God!" he moans. "I'll never be able to experience an erection again!" "Well, of course you will," says the surgeon. "It'll just have to be someone else's."

☞ Do you know what's the worst thing about getting your penis stuck in the fanbelt of a car? It's not the incredible pain, it's not the fear of mutilation, it's not even the agonizing wait for rescue; it's the sickening moment when you realise that, at some point, you will be forced to describe the whole sordid incident on an insurance form.

☞ George wakes up in hospital after a serious operation. "I have good news and bad news," says the doctor. "The good news is that we managed to save your testicles." "Thank God," says George. "And what's the bad news?" The doctor replies, "They're in a bag under your pillow."

SEX – HEALTH

☞ A man goes to the doctor with a yellow penis. "That's extraordinary," says the doctor. "Do you work with dyes or other chemicals?" "No," says the man, "I'm unemployed." "Do you have any unusual hobbies?" asks the doctor. "No," says the man. "So what *do* you do?" asks the doctor. "Well," replies the man, "most days I sit on the sofa, wanking to porn videos and eating Quavers."

☞ The Queen is visiting one of Canada's top hospitals. During her tour, she passes a room where a male patient is masturbating. The doctor accompanying her hurriedly explains. "I'm sorry, Your Majesty," he says, "but this man has a serious condition where the testicles rapidly fill with semen. If he doesn't do that five times a day, they'll explode." On the next floor they pass a room where a young nurse is giving a patient a blow-job. "And what exactly is the problem with this gentleman?" asks the Queen. The doctor replies, "Same problem: better health plan."

SEX – HOMOSEXUALS

☞ Cecil goes to the doctor with a pain up his backside. The doctor looks up his ass and says, "I've discovered the problem. Someone's stuck a bunch of roses up there." "Really?" exclaims Cecil. "Who are they from? Can you see the card?"

> **"For years my mum was convinced I was gay. It was impossible for me to prove I wasn't – until I got the video camera."**
> *Jimmy Carr*

☞ Julian goes up to Harry and says, "If you went to a wild party, got drunk and woke up with a condom sticking out of your arse, would you tell anyone?" "Probably not," says Harry. "I see," says Julian. "Well, in that case, do you want to come to a party?"

SEX – IN OLD AGE

☞ An old man goes for a check-up. The doctor is surprised to find that the old man has friction burns on his penis. "Do you mind explaining these?" asks the doctor. "I just get carried away, doc," replies the old man. "Last night I went out with two twins I met at a social club. At the end of the evening, they invited me back to their place and I ended up banging them all night. I guess I overdid it." "Just take it easier the next time," says the doctor. "And I hope you took precautions." "Oh, yeah," says the old man. "I gave them a false name."

☞ An 85-year-old woman gets married to a 90-year-old man. On their first night of wedded bliss, the old woman goes to bed and lies down. The old man then shuffles into the bedroom and lies down next to her. Then he grasps her hand and the pair drift off to sleep. On the second night, the same thing happens; the old woman goes to bed and lies down. The old man lies next to her, grasps her hand, and they both drift off to sleep. On the third night, the old woman goes to bed and lies down and the old man lies next to her. He reaches out to grasp the old woman's hand, but she pulls it away. "Not tonight, dear," she says. "I'm just too tired."

☞ Eighty-year-old Willy marries 20-year-old Brittany. After a year, Brittany goes into hospital to give birth. The doctor congratulates the old man. "It's amazing," he says. "How do you manage it at your age?" Willy answers, "You've just got to keep that old motor running, doc." The following year, Brittany gives birth again. The doctor comes up to Willy and says, "You're incredible. How do you do it?" Again, Willy says, "You've just got to keep that old motor running, doc." The next year, Brittany goes back yet again. The doctor says, "Three kids at your age; you must be quite a man, Willy." Willy responds with his usual phrase, "You've just got to keep that old motor running, doc." The doctor looks embarrassed. "Well, you might be right about that, Willy," he says, "but I reckon it's time to change the oil; this last one's black."

☞ A little old lady totters into a sex shop. She shakily hobbles the few feet to the counter and grabs it for support. "Ddddoooo yoouuuhhhave aaaaannyyyy vvviiiiibbbbrrattoorrsss?" she says to the sales clerk. The clerk replies, "Yes, we do stock vibrators." The old lady says, "Ddddddooooo yyyouuuu hhhave aaaa pppinkk onnne, tttten inchessss lllong aaaaand aaaaabbboutt ttwwooo inchesss thththththtickkk?" The clerk replies, "Yes, I believe we do." "iiiiinnnn thaaaaat ccaaaassse," says the little old lady, "ccccccoullddd yyyyouuu tellll mmmeeee hhhowwww ttoooo ttturnn tthe ffffriggging thingggg offfffff?"

☞ A ninety-year-old man marries a girl of eighteen. On their wedding night, he slips into bed and holds up four fingers. "Wow," says his bride. "Does that mean we're going to have sex four times?" "No," replies the old man. "It means take your pick."

☞ A young gold-digger marries an elderly millionaire. Her plan is to exhaust him in bed and send him to an early grave. On the wedding night, she decides to go for broke and finish off the old fool there and then, so she puts on her sexiest lingerie and lies on the bed in the most provocative pose she can think of. "Hurry up, honey!" calls the young bride. "I'm waiting!" Her elderly husband shuffles out of the bathroom, and the bride is astonished to see he's wearing a condom over a rock-hard, ten-inch erection. She also notices that the old geezer is wearing a nose-clip and ear-plugs. "What have you got those on for?" she asks. "Two things I can't stand," says the old-timer, "the sound of a women screaming and the smell of burning rubber."

☞ According to the statistics, at the age of seventy there are five women to every man. Which, let's face it, is a little late for a guy to get those kinds of odds.

☞ An old couple get married after many years of courtship. On their honeymoon night, the husband takes off his glasses and goes to clean his teeth, while his bride decides to limber up. She strips naked and does a stretching exercise, lying on her back and lifting her legs up and over her head. Unfortunately, her feet get stuck in the headboard and she cries out for help. Her husband dashes in, peers at her and says, "For God's sake, Muriel; brush you hair and put in your teeth. You look just like your mother."

☞ An old lady is sitting on a bench by a Florida beach. An old man comes to sit next to her and the old lady strikes up a conversation. "I really like the beach," she says. "Do you come here often?" "Now and again," replies the man. "So, do you live around here?" asks the old lady. "Round the corner," replies the man. "I moved in last month." "That's nice," says the old lady.

"Have you got any hobbies?" "Not really," says the old man. The woman struggles to think of something to say. "Do you like pussycats?" she asks. At this, the man growls passionately, grabs the old lady and pulls her behind a bush. He then gives her the ride of her life. When he's finished, the old lady lies back with a smile on her face. "My," she says, "how did you know that was what I wanted?" "Come to think of it," says the old man, "how did you know my name was Katz?"

☞ An old man comes home one night and finds a teenage girl ransacking the place. The old man grapples with the girl, pushes her to the floor, then picks up the phone to call the police. The girl begs him to let her go. "Don't call the police!" she cries. "If you leave them out of it, I'll let you have sex with me. We can do anything you want." The old man agrees, and soon they're both naked in bed. The old man tries very hard to have sex with the girl but, try as he might, he just hasn't got what it takes. Exhausted, he rolls off her and picks up the phone. "What are you doing?" asks the girl." "I'm sorry," says the old man, "but it looks like I'm going to have to call the police after all."

☞ An old man meets up with an old lady at a bingo evening and they end up going back to her place. They have sex, but as a result of this activity the man's penis develops a painful swelling and a persistent, leaky discharge. Disturbed, he goes to see his doctor. "Have you had sex recently?" asks the doctor. "Yes," replies the old man. "D'you know the woman's name?" asks the doctor. "I do," says the old man. "And can you remember where she lives?" asks the doctor. "Certainly," says the old man. "Then you'd better get back there as soon as you can," says the doctor. "You're about to come."

☞ An old man, Bill, and an old woman, Beryl, have got on friendly terms in the retirement home. Things progress to the point where Bill goes to Beryl's room every Friday night and gets jerked off. This goes on for a few months, until Bill meets up with another little old lady and starts hanging around with her instead. "What's she got that I haven't got?" demands Beryl. Bill replies, "Parkinson's."

☞ An old woman calls the emergency services. "Help me!" she shouts. "Two hairy Hell's Angels are trying to climb into my bedroom!" The operator replies. "Hold on, madam. I'll transfer you to the police; you've come through to the fire brigade." "No, you idiot!" shouts the old woman. "They don't need a policeman; they need a longer ladder!"

☞ Despite reaching the grand age of fifty-five, Harry has acquired a new teenage girlfriend. One evening, she whispers in his ear, "Let's go upstairs and make love." Harry eyes the stairs, then says, "Which one would you prefer? I can't do both."

☞ George is chatting to Harry in the pub. "I might be forty-five," says George, "but any time I want, I can get myself an eighteen-year-old." Really?" says Harry. "What's your secret?" George replies, "Chloroform."

☞ George marries a younger lady. They get on very well but, no matter what George does in bed, his wife never has an orgasm. He goes to a doctor for some advice. The doctor thinks for a while, then says, "This might sound a bit unorthodox, but try hiring a young bodybuilder to stand by your bed waving a towel." "A towel?" says George. "Yes," replies the doctor. "Your wife will be able to fantasise about the young man, and waving the towel will cool you down while giving the young man something do to." George shrugs his shoulders and goes out to hire a bodybuilder. A handsome young man is found and George and his wife make love while the bodybuilder enthusiastically waves a towel over them. It doesn't work, however: not on that night, nor on any of the six following nights. George is soon back at the doctor for more advice. "I'd like to suggest a different tack," says the doctor. "I want you and the bodybuilder to swap places. You wave the towel while he makes love to your wife." George, desperate, decides to give it a go. That evening, the bodybuilder climbs on George's wife and they have sex while George waves a towel over them. It soon becomes clear that things are hotting up, and within the hour George's wife has had five earth-shattering orgasms. Eventually the bodybuilder collapses, exhausted, on the bed. George is delighted. He slaps the bodybuilder's bare backside and shouts, "Now *that*, young man, is how you wave a towel!"

☞ Old Fred goes to the doctor for a check-up. After the examination, the doctor proclaims him as fit as a fiddle. "You're in incredible shape for a man of your age," says the doctor. "Tell me; how old was you father when he died?" "Who said he was dead?" replies Fred. "He's ninety-five." "How extraordinary," says the doctor. "Well, how old was your grandfather when he died?" "Who said he was dead?" says Fred. "He's still going strong – one hundred and fifteen on his last birthday. In fact, he got married last week." "Good God!" says the doctor. "I'm astonished that a man of his age would want to get married." Fred replies, "Who said he wanted to?"

☞ Old Hamish and his wife are watching an evangelist preacher on the TV. The evangelist tells them to put one hand on the screen and touch any afflicted part of their body with the other. Hamish's wife totters over to the screen, touches the glass with one hand and places the other on her arthritic hip. Old Hamish decides to get in on the act. He totters over to the TV, places one hand on the screen and sticks the other one up his kilt. "Hamish," says his wife, "were ye no listening? The man's healing the sick, not raising the bloody dead."

☞ Three old geezers are discussing their health. "My eyes are in a terrible state," says the first. "I can barely see the TV these days. The lenses in my glasses must be two inches thick." "You think that's bad?" says the second. "You ought to have my backside. I've got haemorrhoids the size of grapes. I can barely sit down without my eyes watering." "I'm sick of you two moaning," says the third. "You've both got it easy. I've got the worst problem of all; my hands shake like crazy all the time." "Well, that's not so bad," says the first. "Oh, yeah?" replies the third. "Have you any idea how hard it is to pee while you're having an orgasm?"

☞ Two old men are discussing their sex lives. "You know what I do?" says one of the men. "Every morning, I eat half a loaf of rye bread. It gives you really strong erections." The second old man decides to give this a go. He hobbles down to his local bakery and asks for a loaf of rye bread. "Sure," replies the clerk. "Do you want that loaf whole or sliced?" "What's the difference?" asks the old man. "Well," replies the clerk, "if it's sliced, it'll go harder faster." "What?" whines the old man. "How come everyone knew about this except me?"

☞ Two old men visit a whorehouse. The madam takes one look at the pair and figures they're both so senile they won't be able to tell the difference between a real girl and a blow-up doll. She put a doll in each of the old geezer's rooms, turns out the lights and lets them get on with it. After an hour of wheezing sex, the old coots stagger out of the brothel and go to a nearby bar. Over drinks, they compare their experiences. The first man says, "Y'know, I think my gal must have been dead. She never moved, talked or even groaned. How was it for you?" The second man replies, "I think mine was some kind of witch." "What d'you mean, witch?" asks the first. "Well, it's weird," says the second man, "but when I bit her on her tit, she farted and flew out the window!"

☞ Two old men, Joe and Manny, work on an assembly line in a factory. Joe keeps boasting about his sexual prowess and tells Manny that he made love to his wife three times on Sunday. "Three times?" gasps Manny. "How do you do it?" "It's easy," says Joe. "We had sex, then I rolled over and took a ten-minute nap. When I woke up, we made love again and I took another ten-minute nap. Then I put it to her again. The secret is having short rests in between." "I'll have to try that," says Manny. "Ruth won't believe her luck." That night, Manny makes love to his wife. Then he takes a nap, makes love again, takes another nap, wakes up and makes love a third time. Then he falls sound asleep. When he wakes up, he realises he's overslept, so he pulls on his clothes and runs to the factory. Outside the factory, he finds his boss waiting for him, fuming. "What's up, boss?" says Manny. "Why are you so cross? I've worked here for twenty years and I've never been late before. You aren't going to hold twenty minutes against me, are you?" "What d'you mean, twenty minutes?" shouts the boss. "Where the hell were you on Tuesday and Wednesday?"

SEX – MASTURBATION

☞ A father takes his spoilt son to the funfair. It's the boy's birthday so, as a treat, Dad says he can do whatever he likes. The boy wants to go on all the rides, so they go on all the rides. The boy wants to play all the games, so they play all the games. The boy wants a giant teddy bear, so Dad spends a fortune on the shooting range until he wins one. The boy wants to call the giant bear 'Wanker', so all day he does so, much to his father's embarrassment. Finally, it's time to go home. Dad straps Wanker to the roof-rack of the car and they drive away. Wanker is not fixed securely, however, and the boy spots the bear as it tumbles over the side of the car. "Dad," he whines, "Wanker's off." "Not now, son," sighs Dad. "Perhaps on your next birthday."

☞ A few months after his parents' divorce, little Johnny passes his mother's bedroom and sees her rubbing her body and moaning. "Ohh," she says, "I need a man; I need a man!" Over the next couple of months, he sees her doing this several times. One day, he comes home from school early and hears her moaning again. He peeks into her bedroom and sees his mother with a man lying on top of her. Little Johnny runs into his room, tears off his clothes and starts stroking himself. "Ohh," he moans, "I need a bike! I need a bike!"

☞ A shy young couple invent a name for making love: 'doing the laundry'. One night, the husband wakes up and asks his wife if she wants to 'do the laundry'. His wife complains she's got a headache, so the husband goes back to sleep. In the morning, he again asks if she'd like to 'do the laundry', but his wife complains she's too tired after having a restless night. That afternoon, he asks if she's ready to 'do the laundry', but she's too busy with her chores. That evening, his wife snuggles up to him on the sofa and asks if he still wants to 'do the laundry'. "No, it's okay," he replies. "It was a small load, so I did it by hand."

☞ Add some variety to your sex life; use the other hand!

☞ Antonio comes home from school and walks into the kitchen. His grandma says, "Antonio, what did you learn in school today?" Antonio replies, "We learned about penises, and vaginas, and sexual intercourse, and masturbation." Grandma slaps Antonio hard, and he runs crying to his room. Antonio's mother walks in and says, "Mama! Why did you go and hit Antonio!" Grandma replies, "I asked him what he learned in school today and he started talking about sex and penises and masturbation!" Mother replies, "That's what they learn these days. It's called sex education!" Grandma feels guilty about hitting Antonio, so she goes to apologise. She opens his bedroom door and finds him masturbating. "Antonio," she says, "when you've finished your homework, come downstairs and talk to me."

☞ Father O'Reilly is having a quiet wank in the cathedral vestry when a tourist spots him and takes a picture. "Oh, my God!" says Father O'Reilly. "That picture must never be seen. How much d'you want for that camera?" "Five hundred pounds," says the tourist. This is extortionate, but he has no choice, so Father O'Reilly pays up. Later, Sister Mary sees him with his new camera. "That's very nice, Father," says the Sister. "How much did you buy it for?" "Five hundred pounds," replies Father O'Reilly. "Christ!" exclaims the Sister. "Someone must've seen you coming."

☞ If a woman is uncomfortable watching me play with myself, should she: a) Accept it as a form of self-expression? b) Try to become more broad-minded? c) Find another seat on the bus?

☞ In order to stop me masturbating, my father used to put something in my tea: my penis.

☞ Little Johnny becomes a real nuisance and keeps interrupting his Dad's Saturday afternoon poker game. Dad tries every way possible to keep Johnny occupied – television, ice cream, homework, video games – but nothing will keep him quiet. Eventually Johnny's Uncle Harry takes him by the hand and leads him out of the room. A few minutes later, Uncle Harry returns and the poker game recommences. Hours later, Dad asks Harry what he said to Johnny to have kept him quiet for so long. "I didn't say anything," replies Harry. "I just showed him how to masturbate."

☞ Little Johnny's mother walks by his room and sees him masturbating. Later, she has a talk with him and tells him that good little boys save it until they're married. A few weeks later, she says, "How are you doing with that problem we talked about, Johnny?" Little Johnny replies, "Great! So far I've saved nearly a quart!"

☞ Name the most abused and neglected part of the male body... No! Hold it right there! It might be abused, but it's certainly not neglected.

☞ Two men are crossing Mexico in a car when they're ambushed by bandits. The bandit chief pulls them out of the car and orders them to masturbate. They do so, and they are then told to masturbate once more. Again they masturbate to completion: and, once again, they are told to repeat the performance. This goes on and on until the two men are exhausted and totally unable to get erections. "Bueno," says the chief. "Now you can give my sister a lift into town."

☞ When I was 12, my father told me that if I masturbated I'd go blind. I said, "I'm over here, dad."

☞ Why did early men learn to walk upright? To leave their hands free for masturbation.

SEX – ORAL

☞ A little boy tells his friend that his father has two penises. "That's impossible!" says the friend, but the boy insists he's seen them. "What do they look like, then?" asks his friend. "Well," says the boy, "one's small and floppy and he uses it for peeing, and the other's long and stiff and he uses it for brushing mummy's teeth."

(473)

☞ A man loses all his cash at a Las Vegas casino and tries to beg a ride to the airport from a cab driver. The man promises to send back the cab fare when he gets home, but the cab driver very rudely tells him to go to hell. A year later, the man returns and sees the cab driver waiting last in line at a taxi rank. The man decides to get revenge on the rude driver. The man approaches the first driver at the taxi rank and says, "How much to the airport?" "Fifteen dollars," is the reply. "And how much for a blow-job on the way?" asks the man. The cab driver is disgusted. "Get away from my car, you pervert!" he shouts. The man continues down the line of cars, asking each driver the price to the airport and how much for a blow-job. Each driver is disgusted and tells him to get lost. Finally, the man approaches the last cab in line and speaks to the driver who'd been nasty to him. "How much to the airport?" he asks. "Fifteen dollars," replies the driver. The man gets in the car and off they go. As they pass the line of waiting drivers, the man leans out of the window with a grin on his face and gives them the thumbs-up.

☞ A man walks into a rough New Orleans bar with an alligator. "Who wants to see a cool trick?" he shouts, then proceeds to stuff his genitals in the alligator's mouth. "Now how about this?" he shouts, and starts hitting the alligator over the head with a stick. The alligator is extremely annoyed by this and everyone is astonished when the man finally pulls out his genitals without a scratch on them. "Anyone else got the guts to try it?" shouts the man. "Sure!" shouts a little old lady, "but don't hit me with the stick."

☞ A nun gets into a minicab. After a few minutes, the cab driver says, "I hope you won't be offended, sister, but it's always been a fantasy of mine to have a nun perform oral sex on me." The nun replies, "That could be arranged, but only on two conditions; you must be a Catholic, and you must be single. "The cab driver says, "Well, I'm both! I'm single, and I'm Catholic too!" "Okay," says the nun. "Pull over." The cab driver pulls over, and the nun fulfils his fantasy. When they get back on the road, the driver says, "Thanks for that, but I ought to confess; I'm not single and I'm not

Catholic. I'm a married Protestant." The nun replies, "That's all right. I also have a confession to make; my name's Nigel. I'm on my way to a fancy-dress party."

☞ An unhappy-looking man walks into a bar and orders nine double martinis. The barman lays out the drinks in a line and watches as the man knocks them back one after the other. "Why all the drinks?" asks the barman. "I'm celebrating my first blow-job," says the man. "Congratulations," says the barman. "Let me give you one on the house to make it an even ten." "No, thanks," replies the man. "If nine can't get the taste out of my mouth, one more won't help."

☞ A woman goes to the doctor with green stains on the inside of her thighs. The doctor looks at them and says, "Is your boyfriend a gypsy?" "Why, yes," replies the girl. "How did you know that?" "I've seen this problem before," replies the doctor. "You're going to have to tell him his earrings aren't real gold."

☞ A young man, Bill, drops off his girlfriend at her home. They reach the front door and Bill leans casually on the doorframe. "So," he says, "how about you give me a blow-job?" "What?" says the girl. "Are you crazy?" "Don't worry; it'll be quick," says Bill. "No," says the girl. "Someone might see us." "It's just a blow-job," insists Bill. "You might like it." "No," says the girl. "Don't be disgusting." "Aww, come on," whines Bill. "Just take it in your hand..." At that moment the front door opens. It's the girl's mother. "Honey," she says. "Either blow him, or tell him to get lost: but either way, daddy wants him to take his hand off the intercom."

☞ An Eskimo is driving through the frozen wastes when his car breaks down and he has to push it to the nearest garage. While he's waiting for his car to be fixed, the Eskimo buys a vanilla cornet from the garage shop. The mechanic calls him over, so the Eskimo gulps down his snack as quickly as he can and walks to the car. The mechanic gestures at the car's engine and says, "Looks like you blew a seal." The Eskimo wipes his mouth and says, "Nah, it's just ice-cream."

☞ How do you get a woman to stop giving you oral sex? Marry her.

　☞ It's a warm summer night and a young couple are having sex in a meadow. The man is giving his girlfriend oral sex. "Wow," he says. "This is great. I wish I had a torch." His girlfriend replies, "So do I; for the last five minutes you've been eating grass."

☞ Little Johnny is out walking with his mother when they see two birds mating. Little Johnny asks what they're doing and mummy, embarrassed, tells him they're making sandwiches. A little while later, they see two dogs mating. Again, little Johnny asks what they're up to and, again, mummy tells him they're making sandwiches. That night, little Johnny hears strange noises from his parents' room. He bursts in and switches on the light. "Mummy!" he cries. "You were making sandwiches!" "No, I wasn't!" protests mother. "Yes, you were," says Johnny. "You've got mayonnaise all down your chin."

　☞ Little Johnny passes his parents' bedroom and sees them having sex. Next day, he asks his mother why she was doing what he'd seen her do. "I was doing that because I want a baby," replies mother. Next night, little Johnny sees his mother giving his dad a blow-job. The next day he asks her about it. "Were you doing that because you want another baby?" he says. "No," replies mother, "I was doing that because I want a BMW."

☞ Sherlock Holmes is walking through a park with Watson. They spy three women eating bananas and Holmes says, "See there, Watson: a spinster, a prostitute and a new bride." "Heavens!" says Watson. "How the devil did you deduce that?" "Observe their banana-eating habits," says Holmes. "You'll see that the spinster breaks her banana into pieces before placing them in her mouth. The prostitute holds her banana with both hands and eats it whole, while the bride swallows hers while slapping the back of her head with her free hand."

☞ Tom, to Harry: "Did I tell you about the worst blow-job I ever had?" Harry, "No, I don't think you did." Tom, "It was great."

☞ What's 69 plus 69? Dinner for four.

☞ What's the square root of 69? Eight something.

☞ What do oral sex and lobster Thermidor have in common? You don't get either of them at home.

☞ What's the difference between love, true love and showing off? Spitting, swallowing and gargling.

☞ Why are pubic hairs curly? So they don't poke you in the eye.

☞ Why is getting a blow-job from an eighty-year-old like walking a tightrope? In both cases, you really don't want to look down.

SEX – ORGASMS

☞ How can you tell when an Essex girl's having an orgasm? She drops her bag of chips.

"The only time my wife and I had a simultaneous orgasm was when the judge signed the divorce papers."
Woody Allen

☞ The organisers of National Orgasm Week suffered a disappointment. They discovered that the majority of women who'd participated had only pretended to celebrate.

SEX – ORGIES

☞ Larry and Dick are having a drink. "I've got an idea," says Larry. "Why don't we get some people together and have an orgy?" "Who did you have in mind?" asks Dick. Larry replies, "I was thinking of me and my wife, you and your wife, and my neighbour and his girlfriend." "Naa," says Dick. "I'm not sure I'd like that sort of thing." "Okay," says Larry. "I'll take you off the list."

SEX – PENISES

☞ A husband and wife are cooing over their newborn baby son. "Look at the size of his todger," says the man. "It's massive!" "Yes, dear," says his wife, "but at least he's got your ears."

☞ A little boy and girl are talking. "What's a penis?" asks the little girl. "I'm not sure," says the boy. "I'll ask my dad." The boy goes off and finds his father lying on the couch. "What's a penis?" asks the boy. Dad unzips his fly and shows him. "That's a penis," he says. "As a matter of fact, this is the perfect penis." The boy takes a look, then runs off to find his friend. The boy unzips his fly and shows the little girl what's inside. "This is a penis," says the boy. "And if it was two inches shorter, it would be the perfect penis."

☞ I told my new girlfriend that I had a four-incher. When she saw it, she almost fainted. I guess some girls don't like them that wide.

☞ What's the difference between medium and rare? Six inches is medium; eight inches is rare.

☞ What's the difference between purple and pink? The grip.

SEX – PENISES (LARGE)

☞ A big Texan ambles into the men's room of a Dallas hotel. As he stands at the urinal, he notices that a small, skinny guy standing next to him has an enormous penis. "Hoowee!" exclaims the Texan. "Just how long is that critter?" "Fourteen inches," replies the little guy. "Goddamn!" says the Texan. "Fourteen inches soft?" "That's right," says the little man. "So how long is it when y'all get heated up?" asks the Texan. The little guy shrugs, "I don't know. Every time I have an erection, I pass out."

☞ A good-looking young man walks into a pharmacy owned by a couple of spinsters. "This is very embarrassing," says the man, "but I have a problem with my penis; it never gets soft, even after making love for hours at a time. It never seems to go down. It's insatiable. Can you give me anything for it?" The spinsters go to the back of the shop and have a muttered conversation. Eventually they come back to the counter. One says, "The best we can offer you is £500 a week, and a third interest in the store."

☞ A husband and wife are having a bitter argument. The husband yells, "When you die, I'm getting you a headstone that reads, 'Here Lies My Wife – Cold As Ever'." "Yeah?" she replies. "Well, when you die, yours will read, 'Here Lies My Husband – Stiff At Last'."

☞ A man goes into a shop selling artificial penises. "I had mine cut off in an accident and I'm looking for a replacement," says the man. "I see, sir," says the shop assistant. "Well our six-inch models are very popular." "Have you got anything larger?" asks the man. "We do have this seven-incher," replies the assistant, putting a large penis on the counter. The man sighs and says, "My wife was hoping for a bit more than that. Anything bigger?" The assistant reaches under the counter and comes out with a monster penis. "This is the Dreadnought" he says. "It's the largest penis we stock." "Fantastic!" says the man. "Do you have one in white?"

☞ A man has his impotence cured with an elephant muscle transplant that increases the strength of his erections. On his first day out of hospital, he takes his girlfriend to dinner. The meal is going well until the man starts to feel aroused. At this point, his fly bursts open and his huge new penis snakes out of his trousers, grabs a bread roll and disappears under the table. "Wow!" says his girlfriend. "Can I see that again later, in the bedroom?" "I don't know," replies the man. "There must be a limit to the number of bread rolls it can stuff up my ass."

☞ A man sits in his garden reading a paper and drinking a beer, while his wife struggles to push the mower across the lawn. A neighbour looks over the fence and says, "It's a disgrace, the way you make your wife work while you just laze about. You ought to be bloody well hung!" "I am," replies the man. "That's why she does all the work."

☞ A man sunbathes in the nude and ends up burning his penis. His doctor tells him to ease the pain by bathing it in a saucer of cold milk. Later, his wife comes home and finds him crouched on the floor with his todger in a saucer of milk. "Good heavens," she says. "I always wondered how you reloaded those things."

☞ A married couple fall on hard times. They decide that the only way they can keep the wolf from the door is if the wife becomes a prostitute. The wife decides to work from home and, after putting an ad in the paper, she gets her first client. She takes the man upstairs and he asks her how much she charges for full sex. The wife doesn't have a clue, so she nips downstairs where her husband is waiting in the kitchen. "Charge him £70 for full sex," he tells her. Back upstairs, the wife tells the man the cost, but he says he only has £20. The wife nips downstairs and asks her husband what she should give him for £20. "Tell him he can have a blow-job for that," says the husband. The wife nips upstairs again. She tells her customer what he can expect for £20, and he starts to strip off. He removes his trousers and underwear and the wife is astonished at the size of his erect member. She nips downstairs and says to her husband, "Here, you couldn't lend us £50, could you?"

☞ A milkman knocks on Mrs Smith's door. He's come to settle her £5 bill. Mrs Smith answers the door wearing a sexy nightie and suggests she pays the £5 she owes with sex. The milkman agrees and they go to the bedroom. There, the milkman strips off and reveals he's got the biggest penis Mrs Smith has ever seen. The milkman then takes some large rubber washers out of his pocket and starts slipping them over the end of his monster. "There's no need for that," says Mrs Smith. "It might be big, but I'll take all of it." "Oh, yeah?" replies the milkman. "Not for a bloody fiver you won't."

☞ A sergeant calls a surprise medical inspection on a group of Marines. He lines them up outside their hut in three rows, then looks over each man before the doctor arrives. The sergeant sees a man in the back row scratching his arm, so he whacks the man's elbow with a stick. "Did that hurt, soldier?!" bellows the sergeant. "No, sir!" is the reply. "Why not?" shouts the sergeant. "Because I'm a Marine, sir!" yells back the soldier. The sergeant then sees a man in the middle row rubbing his nose. The sergeant whacks the man over the head. "Did that hurt, soldier?" bellows the sergeant. "No, sir!" is the reply. "Why not?" shouts the sergeant. "Because I'm a Marine, sir!" yells back the soldier. The sergeant then sees a man in the front row with a huge erection. The sergeant whacks the erection with his stick and bellows, "Did that hurt, soldier?!" "No, sir!" replies the soldier. "Why not?" shouts the sergeant. The soldier says, "Because it belongs to the man behind me, sir!"

☞ A spinster hears a knock on her front door and opens it to find a tramp begging for food. She's about to turn him away when she notices the tramp has huge shoes on. Remembering the theory that men with big feet have equally large penises, she invites the tramp in. Next morning, the tramp wakes up after a night of passion and finds a £50 note and a letter pinned to his pillow. The letter reads, 'Buy some shoes that fit.'

☞ A Texan walks into a bar and says, "Last week my wife gave birth to a 20-pound baby boy. I'd like to buy everyone a drink!" The Texan buys drinks for everyone and the barman says, "Twenty pounds is a pretty big baby. What does he weigh now?" "15 pounds," replies the Texan. "How could he lose so much weight in a week?" asks the barman. The Texan replies, "Easy. We had him circumcised."

☞ A woman takes her two dachshunds, a male and a female, to the vet for a check-up. "Has the male been neutered?" asks the vet. "There's no need," replies the woman. "At home, I keep the female upstairs and the male downstairs. There's no chance they'll have puppies." "Can't the male climb stairs?" asks the vet. "No," replies the woman, "not when he's got a hard-on."

☞ A young couple have just got married and are about to spend their first night together. The man says, "There's something you ought to know – I'm hung like a baby." His bride is disappointed but tells him that sex isn't the important thing; love is what makes a marriage special. Hearing this, the husband takes off his trousers, and the woman faints. When she's recovered, the woman says, "What the hell was that? You said you were hung like a baby!" "I am," replies her husband. "It weighs seven pounds."

☞ A young man is so well endowed that it's interfering with his walking. Three doctors are consulted to solve the problem and they all recommend reductive surgery. The first doctor says, "I think the best course of action is to take a piece off the end." However, it's decided that this will affect the sensitivity of the penis, so the idea is dropped. The second doctor says, "We'll just have to take a section out of the middle." This idea is discussed, but it's decided this surgery will reduce the strength of the organ, so they try to think of something else. The third doctor says, "Why not take a section out of the base?" This solution is also discussed, but the doctors decide it will cause erection problems. Finally, a group of nurses presents a petition saying, "Can't we just make his legs longer?"

☞ After many years of married life, a man becomes impotent. After seeking help everywhere, he eventually turns to a witchdoctor. The witchdoctor casts a powerful spell and tells the man that all he has to do to get an erection is say, "One, two, three." He'll then be stiff for as long as he wants. To make the erection disappear, someone has to say, "One, two, three, four". There's a catch, however; once the spell has been used, it cannot be used again for another year. The man rushes home, gets into bed with his wife, and says "One, two, three". His puzzled wife says, "What did you say 'One, two, three' for?"

☞ Harry and Tom are changing in a locker room when Tom remarks on the huge size of Harry's penis. "It's a beauty, isn't it?" says Harry. "It's a transplant job: cost me £10,000." A few months later, they're back in the locker room. Tom drops his trousers and says, "You were ripped off with that transplant. I had a new one fitted last month and it only cost me £500." Harry peers at Tom's new penis and says, "No wonder it was so cheap. That's my old one!"

☞ Harry has a crush on a girl at work. He's dying to ask her out on a date, but every time he sees her he gets a huge, uncontrollable erection. One day, he summons up the nerve to phone her and they arrange to go on a date. To prepare for their evening, Harry straps his penis to his leg so he won't embarrass himself. He arrives at the girl's house and rings on her doorbell. Unfortunately, she answers the door in her underwear and Harry kicks her in the face.

> **"In my opinion, women who only like well-hung men are shallow – though admittedly that might not be the right term."**
> *Jimmy Carr*

☞ Lorenzo, a well-known ladies' man, dies suddenly of a suspected heart attack. As it happens, his old friend Harry is the coroner given the task of examining Lorenzo's body. As the examination proceeds, Harry is astonished to discover that Lorenzo had an absolutely enormous todger. It really is a prize specimen and Harry is reluctant to see it meet a fiery end in the crematorium. Harry makes a decision; looking around to make sure no one's watching, he whips off the organ with a scalpel and drops it in his medical bag. Harry intends to take the huge organ home and pickle it. When he gets back to his house, he can't resist showing off his trophy to his wife. He calls her over, opens his medical bag and tells her to peek inside. She does so, then reels back in horror. "Oh, my God!" she wails. "Lorenzo's dead!"

☞ Three men are exploring a remote island when they're captured by cannibals. The cannibals take the men back to their village where they're told that the cannibal chief has the longest penis on the island. If the combined lengths of the men's penises beat the chief, the men can go free; otherwise they'll be eaten. The chief lifts his grass skirt and the men are horrified to see that his penis is 20 inches long. The first man drops his trousers, and his penis is measured at ten inches. The second man drops his trousers, and is measured at nine inches. The third man drops his trousers, and he's measured at one inch. Since the final tally equals the chief's, they're allowed to go. The first man breathes a sigh of relief, "Good job for us I had a ten-inch penis," he says. The second man says, "Well, it was a good job I had a nine-inch penis." The third man says, "It was a good job I had an erection."

☞ Three men, an American, an Australian, and a German, are bragging about how long their penises are. To put it to the test, they go to the top of a fifty-storey building and flop their tackle over the side. The German goes first and his penis dangles down 15 stories. The Australian goes next and his flops 30 stories. The American goes last, flops his over the side, then starts frantically twitching his hips about. "What are you doing, mate?" asks the Australian. The American replies, "Dodging traffic."

☞ To save money, Jane and Tom have their honeymoon at the home of Jane's mother. Jane has never seen Tom naked before and is very nervous. When Tom takes off his shirt, she runs downstairs to her mother. "Mum," she says. "Tom has a hairy chest. Is that normal?" "Yes," replies mother. "All good men have a hairy chest." Back upstairs, Tom takes off his trousers. Jane runs downstairs again. "Mum," she says. "Tom has hairy legs. Is that normal?" "Yes," replies mother. "All good men have hairy legs." Back upstairs, Tom takes off his underpants. Jane runs downstairs and says, "Mum, Tom's thingy is over a foot long. Is that normal?" "You stay down here, dear," replies mother. "This sounds like a job for me."

☞ Two brothers, Jake and Bill, decide to enlist in the army. During their physical examination, the doctor is surprised to discover that both of the brothers possess incredibly long, oversized penises. "How do you account for this?" says the doctor. "It's hereditary, sir," replies Jake. "I see," says the doctor, writing in his file. "So you think you inherited your elongated penises from your father?" "No, sir," says Bill. "It was our mother." "Your mother?" exclaims the doctor. "Don't be an idiot, son. Women don't have penises!" "I know, sir," replies Bill, "But mum only had the one arm, and when it came to getting us out of the bathtub, she had to manage as best she could."

☞ What does a man with a ten-inch penis have for breakfast? I had toast; why do you ask?

☞ What's the difference between 'light' and 'hard'? You can sleep with the light on.

☞ What's the difference between CS gas, an onion and a two-foot dick? Nothing; they all make your eyes water.

☞ What's white and fourteen inches long? Absolutely nothing!

SEX – PENISES (LARGE) – MY DICK IS SO BIG...

☞ A homeless family lives underneath it.

☞ Clowns climb out of it when I come.

☞ I have to call it Mister Dick in front of company.

☞ I have to cook it breakfast.

☞ It can chew gum.

☞ It has a basement.

☞ It has a personal trainer.

☞ It has an opening act.

☞ It has its own dick.

☞ It won't return Spielberg's calls.

☞ King Kong is going to climb it in the next remake.

☞ Michael Jackson wants to build an amusement park on it.

☞ My mother was in labour for three extra days.

☞ Right now it's in the other room fixing us drinks.

☞ Stephen Hawking has a theory about it.

☞ There's still snow on it in the summertime.

SEX – PENISES (SMALL)

☞ What do you call a man with a one-inch penis? Justin.

☞ Have you heard the one about the guy with no dick? He went home and gave his wife a good bollocking.

☞ A man goes to a doctor and asks him to take a look at his penis. "But you must promise not to laugh," says the man. The doctor agrees to this, but when the man drops his pants the doctor can't help but giggle. "I'm sorry," he says, "but that's the tiniest penis I ever saw. It's minute. It's so incredibly small I can barely see it." The doctor recovers his composure, then says, "So, anyway, it looks okay to me. What seems to be the matter with it?" The man replies, "It's swollen."

☞ A man is at a pub playing on the slot machines when his wife rings him on his mobile and tells him to come home. "I can't leave now," he says. "I'm on a winning streak. I've got a pile of 50p pieces as long as my dick." "What?" exclaims his wife. "You mean you're down to three quid?"

☞ A man makes an obscene phone call to a woman. "Hello, darling," he gasps. "If you can guess what's in my hand, I'll give you a piece of the action." "Forget it," says the woman. "If you can hold it in one hand, I'm not interested."

☞ A man with a tiny penis finds a shop that sells extra-small condoms. He goes to the shop every month or so, but is always very embarrassed to be seen buying small-sized condoms. One day, the man is browsing online when he sees that he can buy the same brand of condom direct from the supplier. The man is delighted that his days of humiliation are finally over and uses his computer to put in an order. A week later, there's a ring on the doorbell and the man takes delivery of a discreet, small brown parcel from a courier. As the man signs for his condoms, the courier asks for direction to the next town. The man tells the courier where to go and then watches him drive off – in a large white van with the words, 'MICRO CONDOMS. PROTECTION FOR THE UNDERSIZED GENTLEMAN' written on the side in big red letters.

☞ A wealthy woman is discussing Christmas presents with her maid. "Now, what gift should I get the butler?" asks the woman. "A set of wine glasses?" suggests the maid. The woman frowns. "He doesn't need that. A butler never entertains. He'll get a tie. Now what about Jenny, the scullerymaid?" The maid replies, "What about a dress?" The woman tuts, "She doesn't need a new dress. We'll get her another apron. Now, what about my husband?" "I assume you want to get him something he really needs, madam?" says the maid. "Of course," says the woman. The maid replies, "Then how about five more inches?"

> **"I hate those emails where they try to sell you penis enhancers. I got ten just the other day: eight of them from my girlfriend. It's the two from my mum that really hurt."**
> *Jimmy Carr*

☞ Tom has such a small penis he often has trouble finding it when he wants to pee. It's not such a problem in bed, though; then the search party consists of two people.

SEX – PERVERSIONS

☞ Mary's a masochist. When she gets home from work, she changes into something less comfortable.

☞ Mum is cleaning little Johnny's room when she finds a bondage magazine hidden under his bed. She's very upset and shows the magazine to her husband. "What should we do about this?" she asks. Her husband flicks through the magazine, looks at all the pictures of chains, whips and manacles, and says, "Well, I certainly don't think we should spank him."

☞ Two men are shipwrecked on a desert island. They get talking and discover that one is a sadist and the other is a masochist. The masochist is delighted. "This is great," he says. "You can punch me and pinch me. You can kick me. You can walk all over me. You can be as mean as you like." The sadist looks at him coolly and says, "Nah."

☞ What's the difference between erotic and kinky? Erotic is using a feather; kinky is using the whole chicken.

SEX – POOR PERFORMANCE

☞ My new girlfriend and I had sex for the first time last week. After it was over, she had the nerve to say I was lousy in bed! It's outrageous! How can she have any sort of qualified opinion after only fifteen seconds?

☞ One Sunday morning, George puts on his dressing gown and walks into the kitchen. Here, he finds his wife Beryl preparing breakfast. She turns round when he comes in and says, "Don't say a word. Ravish me right now!" So saying, she whips off her own dressing gown and lies back naked on the kitchen table. Always one to rise to a challenge, George throws off his own clothing and gets to it. After they've finished their torrid activity, George gasps and says, "That was fantastic: but what's the occasion? We don't often make love in the kitchen." "There's no occasion," replies Beryl, walking over to the stove. "I'm boiling an egg and the timer's broken."

☞ Why do so many men suffer from premature ejaculation? Because they have to rush back to the pub to tell their mates what happened.

SEX – PORNOGRAPHY

☞ I took my wife to see a raunchy movie the other night. She didn't mind the graphic depictions of sex, but found the masturbation very off-putting; she kept slapping my hand to make me stop.

☞ I would never buy pornography; I haven't got a pornograph to play it on.

☞ Tom gets to play his guitar on a movie soundtrack. He's very proud of his work, but finds out that the movie's a porno film. Normally, Tom wouldn't be seen dead watching hardcore movies, but he wants to hear his music so he sneaks into the local porno cinema. Tom takes a seat near a little old lady and watches as the film starts. Tom is horrified by the non-stop orgy on the screen and, when he can't imagine things getting any more depraved, a large Alsatian joins the action and proceeds to have sex with all the women and most of the men. When the film finally ends, the lights go up and Tom puts on his coat. He catches the eye of the old lady and says, "I don't normally watch these sorts of films. I only wanted to hear my music on the soundtrack." "I understand," replies the little old lady. "I don't care for this type of film myself; I only came here to see my dog."

SEX – POSITIONS

☞ A woman goes to see her doctor with inflamed knees. "Can you think of any reason why they might hurt?" asks the doctor. The woman replies, "My husband and I make love nine times a week and we always do it doggy-style." "There are other positions, you know," replies the doctor. "Yes," says the woman, "but not if you want to watch TV."

☞ Two cowboys are talking in a bar and the conversation turns to sex. The first cowboy says, "Say, have you ever heard of the Rodeo Position?" "No," replies the second cowboy. "How does that work?" "It's a lot of fun," replies the first cowboy. "You mount your wife from behind, grab her tits, and say, 'Hey, these are almost as good as your sister's'. Then you see if you can stay on for more than eight seconds."

SEX – PROBLEMS

☞ A man goes to his doctor and says, "I've got this sex problem. It all starts in the middle of the night. My wife always wakes me up at about three in the morning for nookie, and then again at about five so we can make love before I go to work." "I see," says the doctor. "There's more," says the man. "When I get on the train to work I meet this girl every day. We get a compartment to ourselves and have sex all the way into town. Then I get to the office, where I have to give my secretary one in the storeroom." "I see," says the doctor. "No, there's more," says the man. "When I go to lunch, I meet this lady in the cafeteria and we nip out the back for a quickie." "Now I understand," says the doctor. "There's more," says the man. "When I get back to the office in the afternoon my female boss has to have me or she says she'll give me the sack." "Ahh," says the doctor. "Now I see." "No, there's more," says the man. "When I get home, my wife's so pleased to see me, she gives me a blow-job before dinner and then we have sex until it's time to go to bed." "Okay," says the doctor. "Have you finished now?" "Yes," says the man. "So what *is* your problem?" asks the doctor. "Well, y'see, doc," says the man, "it hurts when I masturbate."

☞ A woman goes to her doctor. "Can you help me?" she says. "My husband's 300 per cent impotent." "I'm sorry," says the doctor, "but I'm not sure I understand what you mean." The woman replies, "Well, he can't get an erection. Last week he burned his tongue, and now he's gone and broken his fingers!"

☞ Harry and Jane are trying for a baby, but Harry has no lead in his pencil. He goes to the doctor, who gives him a course of monkey gland injections. These do the trick, and within a month Jane is pregnant. Nine months later, Harry rings the doctor to tell him the good news. "My wife had a baby last night, doctor. It was seven pounds eight ounces." "Congratulations," says the doctor. "Is it a boy or a girl?" "We're not sure," replies Harry. "Once we get a ladder we'll be able to pry it off the ceiling fan and find out."

☞ Tom goes to his doctor complaining of impotence. After an examination, the doctor says, "I can restore your sex drive, but it'll require surgery. I can do it in a series of operations over a month that will cost twelve thousand dollars, or I can do it in one operation right away that will cost thirty thousand dollars. I suggest you go home and discuss the options with your wife." The next day, Tom rings up the doctor and says, "We're going to have a new kitchen."

SEX – SPERM DONATION

☞ I've tried to help childless couples by making anonymous donations of my sperm. However, I've now been told I should really be doing this through a clinic – not just straight through their letterboxes.

☞ London's first sperm bank was a total disaster. There were only two potential donors; one missed the tube, and the other came on the bus.

SEX – VIAGRA

☞ My doctor's refused to give me Viagra. He said it would be like putting a new flagpole on a condemned building.

☞ A little old man goes into a chemist's shop to buy some Viagra. "Can I have 12 tablets, please?" he says, "and could you cut them into quarters for me?" The assistant says, "A quarter of a tablet won't be enough to give you a full erection, you know." "That's all right," says the old man. "I'm 96 years old; I don't have much use for an erection. I just want to make it stick out far enough that I don't pee over my shoes."

☞ Did you hear about the man who took a course of iron tablets along with his Viagra? Now, no matter where he is, his penis always points due north.

☞ A man gets a prescription for Viagra. He goes home, but finds his wife's out shopping, so he calls her on the phone. "I've just taken some Viagra," he says. "Get home as soon as you can." His wife gets in her car and starts making her way home, but gets stuck in traffic. An hour passes, then another, and the man starts to get frustrated. He calls his doctor for advice. The doctor replies, "Well, it's a shame to waste an erection. Do you have a housekeeper? Maybe you can use it on her instead?" The man replies, "But I don't need Viagra with the housekeeper."

☞ A man gets some sex pills from his doctor with instructions to take only one a week. The man ignores this advice and swallows the whole bottle as soon as he gets home. Next day, the man's son rings the doctor. "What's up, Jimmy?" says the doctor. The boy wails, "Doc, you've got to come over. Grandma's died of exhaustion. Mom's passed out. Sis has locked herself in the garage. My butt's sore as hell: and now Dad's stark naked up a tree shouting 'Here, kitty, kitty'!"

☞ What do the Dirt Devil and Viagra have in common? They both put the power of an upright in the palm of your hand.

☞ A man goes to his doctor asking for a Viagra prescription. "But I'll need an extra big dose," explains the man. "I've got two young nymphomaniacs spending a whole week at my place." Later that week, the man comes back asking for some pain-killers. "What's the matter?" asks the doctor. "Have you strained your penis with all that fooling around?" "No", replies the man, glumly. "It's for my wrist; they never showed up!"

☞ Did you hear that the first Viagra baby has been born? It could stand up right away.

☞ A man goes to his dentist with a bad tooth. After the examination, the dentist tells the man he needs some serious root canal work. The dentist prepares some anaesthetic, but the man tells him that he's allergic to it. "Okay," says the dentist. "I'll give you some laughing gas instead." "Sorry, doc," says the man, "but I'm allergic to laughing gas too." The dentist thinks for a bit, then gives the man two pills and a glass of water. "What kind of anaesthetic is this?" asks the man. "It's not an anaesthetic," replies the dentist. "It's Viagra." "Viagra?" exclaims the man. "Why the hell are you giving me that for? Does it work as some sort of painkiller?" "No," says the doctor. "It'll still hurt, but now you'll have something to hang on to."

☞ What do you get when you smoke pot and take Viagra? Stiff joints!

☞ A man is picking up his Viagra prescription at the chemist. "£10 for a prescription?" he whines. "That's a disgraceful price!" "Cheer up," says his wife. "£20 a year isn't too bad."

☞ Viagra claimed its first victim last week. A man overdosed on pills and his wife died of exhaustion.

☞ An old couple are sitting at the breakfast table. The old man is peering at bottle of pills. "Aren't you ever going to try those Viagra pills I got for you?" asks his elderly wife. The old man grimaces at his wrinkled partner and drops the bottle in a bin. "Nope," he grunts. "No sense putting lead in your pencil if there's no one worth writing to."

☞ A wife is distraught because her husband's 'little soldier' can't salute any more. She goes to her doctor and explains the situation. The doctor thinks for a while, then hands her a slip of paper. "Listen," he says, "I don't do this for everyone, but get this prescription and put three drops in his milk before he goes to bed." Two weeks later, the woman returns and the doctor asks how it went. "He's dead," sniffs the women. "I put thirty drops in his milk by accident. Now we're looking for an antidote so we can close the coffin."

☞ There's a new type of coffee on the market: Viagraccino. One cup and you're up all night.

☞ Generic Viagra is sold under the name Fix-a-Flat.

☞ An old man is putting on his coat. "Where are you going?" asks his wife. "To the doctor," replies the old man. "I'm going to get some of those new Viagra pills." Hearing this, his wife starts pulling on her coat. "I'm coming with you," she says. "Why?" asks the old man. His wife replies, "If you're thinking of putting that rusty old thing inside me, I'm going to get a tetanus shot."

"Old men don't need Viagra because they're impotent. Old men need Viagra because old women are very, very ugly."
Jimmy Carr

☞ An old man walks into a pharmacy and asks for a bottle of Viagra. The pharmacist says, "Do you have a prescription?" "No," says the old man, "but here's a picture of my wife."

☞ If you think you might need Viagra, see a professional. If that doesn't work, see a doctor!

☞ For years, the medical profession has been looking after the ill to make them feel better. Now, with Viagra, they're raising the dead!

☞ Have you seen the new Viagra smiley face? :-----)

☞ I know a man who spent all his savings on Viagra – now he's really hard up.

☞ I started my new diet this morning. It consists of Viagra and prune juice – now I can't tell if I'm coming or going!

☞ A woman asks her husband if he'd like some breakfast. "Bacon and eggs? Perhaps a slice of toast?" she says. "Or maybe some grapefruit, and a cup of coffee?" Her husband declines. "It's this Viagra," he says, "it's really taken the edge off my appetite." At noon, she asks if he would like some lunch. "A bowl of soup, perhaps? A cheese sandwich?" she says. "Or how about a bowl of chilli and a beer?" Again the husband declines. "No, thanks," he says. "It's this Viagra. I really don't feel hungry at all." At dinner-time, she again asks if he wants anything to eat, "Would you like a pizza? How about a stir-fry? That'll only take a couple of minutes." Once more, her husband declines. "No, thanks. It's this Viagra. I really don't feel like eating anything." "Okay," says his wife, "I understand. But would you mind getting the hell off me for a minute? I'm STARVING!"

SEX – VIAGRA – YOU KNOW YOU'RE TAKING TOO MUCH VIAGRA WHEN...

☞ At work, they call you the 'Spiritualist', because when you sit down at a meeting, the table starts floating.

☞ When you sunbathe in the nude, people can use you to tell the time.

☞ You always come last in limbo contests.

☞ You can make drawings in the sand without having to find a stick.

☞ You don't have to use your hands to open doors when you're at the sauna.

495

☞ You have to remove the ceiling fan before you can sleep on your back.

☞ They only ever let you go at the front of the rumba line.

☞ You find it dangerous to stand in a lift facing the doors.

SEX – VOYEURISM

☞ An elderly couple, Terry and June, rent out a room to a young woman. Their house is quite old, however, and the bathing arrangements consist of a tin bath in the parlour. One evening, while Terry's out playing darts at the pub, the lodger has a bath and June accidentally catches sight of her naked. Later, in bed, June tells Terry that their lodger has shaved privates. "Blimey," says Terry. "I wonder what that looks like." "Tell you what," says June. "When you go to play darts tomorrow I'll leave the curtains open a crack and you can look into the parlour when she's having her wash." Next evening, June leaves the curtains slightly open and stands near the window while the lodger has her bath. Sure enough, the lodger's privates are in full view and, by way of comparison, June lifts her skirts to reveal her own hairiness to Terry watching outside. Later, in bed, June asks Terry what he thought of the experience. "It was interesting," says Terry, "but why did you have to lift your skirts like that?" "Well, why not?" says June. "It's nothing you haven't seen before." "Well, I know *I've* seen it before," replies Terry, "but the rest of the darts team hadn't."

SEX – WITH ANIMALS

☞ A man joins the Foreign Legion and is posted to a remote desert fort. The sergeant explains to the man that the legionnaires rely on camels for sex and, that evening, a whole herd of them are to be released in the grounds of the fort. Night comes, and the camels arrive. The men go wild, chasing camels all over the place, desperate to have their wicked way. The new recruit loiters by the gate watching the goings-on with disgust. The sergeant sees him and shouts, "Hey! What are you waiting for? Get stuck in!" "What's the hurry?" replies the recruit. "There must be over a hundred camels here." "Suit yourself," says the sergeant, "but don't blame me if you get stuck with an ugly one."

☞ A man shuffles into a doctor's office and asks to be examined. It turns out the man has severe bruising of the buttocks and a ruptured anus. "How did this happen?" asks the doctor. "It's very embarrassing," says the man, "but when I was on safari I was raped by a bull elephant." "How extraordinary," says the doctor. "However, from the little I know about the subject, I understood that male elephants have long, but very thin, penises." "They do," replies the man, "but this one fingered me first."

☞ A preacher is making a sermon about the supernatural. "Has any one of you ever seen a ghost?" he asks his congregation. "No!" they reply. "Has any one of you ever spoken to a ghost?" asks the preacher. "No!" replies the congregation. "Has any one of you ever made love to a ghost?" asks the preacher. "Yes!" cries a voice from the back of the chapel. "What?" says the preacher. "You've made love to a ghost?" "Sorry," says the man. "I thought you said a goat."

☞ A prospector goes to a remote mining community and is horrified to find there aren't any women in the area. He's even more horrified when he finds out that the locals use sheep for sex. For months the man resists temptation, but the day arrives when he can't stand it any more; he goes out, finds a pretty young sheep and takes it to bed. Next day, he decides to show off his new girlfriend and takes it to the town saloon. As soon as he enters the saloon with the sheep the place goes silent, and everyone stares at him in horror. "What's the matter with you all?" cries the man. "You all do it, so don't pretend you don't!" "Sure we do it," says the barman, "but never with the preacher's wife!"

☞ A zoo acquires a female gorilla, but a few weeks after she arrives the gorilla becomes very difficult to handle. A vet examines her and discovers the gorilla is in heat. However, since there's no male gorilla around, satisfying her will be a problem. After some discussion it's decided to approach Big Zeke, one of the keepers, to see if he'll sleep with the gorilla for £500. Zeke goes off to think about it. The next day he walks into the zoo office and says, "I'll do it: but I've got three requests. Firstly, I don't want to have to kiss her on the lips, and secondly, I won't be responsible for any children she has." The zoo officials agree to this, then ask what his third request is. "I'll need to put it off for another two weeks," says Zeke. "It'll take me that long to raise the £500."

☞ How does a New Zealander make a U-turn? He winks at it.

☞ Little Johnny visits his Uncle's farm and sees a bull mounting a cow. "Wow!" says Johnny. "Look at that bull screwing that cow!" "Don't use that word," scolds his Uncle. "If you have to refer to that sort of behaviour say that the bull is 'surprising' the cow." That evening, little Johnny and his Uncle's family are sitting down to dinner. Johnny glances out of the window and says, "Holy smoke! That bull is really surprising those cows!" Uncle says, "You mean 'cow'. A bull can't surprise more than one cow at once." "Oh, yes, he can," replies Johnny. "They're watching him screw that horse."

☞ Mary goes to the doctor with back pain. After examining her, the doctor says, "Hope you don't mind me asking, but what position do you have sex in?" Mary replies, "Doggie-style." The doctor says, "Have you ever considered the Missionary Position?" "You've got to be joking," says Mary. "Have you ever smelled a labrador's breath?"

☞ There's a new commander at the Foreign Legion fort. The captain is showing the commander around when he spots a small blue hut. "What's in there?" asks the commander. The captain replies, "That's where we keep the camel. There are no women here, so whenever the men feel the need for female company, they use the camel." The commander is disgusted by this idea, but after six months of celibacy he decides to give it a try. He goes to the captain, gets the key and sneaks over to the blue hut. On opening the hut door, the commander finds the camel with its back to him, so he climbs on a stool, drops his pants and starts to have sex with it. After a few minutes, the commander realises that the captain is standing behind him holding a saddle. "Begging your pardon, sir," says the captain, "but I thought you might like to borrow my saddle. You see, if the men want a woman, they usually ride the camel into town."

☞ Tom, to Harry: "I saw a man having sex with a dog the other day." Harry: "Really?" Tom, "Yeah: but you know how the tail always gets in the way...?" Harry: "Yes." Tom: "I thought so."

☞ What do you get when you cross an elephant with a poodle? A cross-eyed poodle that has to sit on a cushion.

☞ What is Osama bin Laden's idea of safe sex? Marking the camels that kick.

☞ What's the best way to give your dog a bone? Tickle his balls!

☞ What's the difference between a poodle humping your leg and a pitbull humping your leg? You let the pitbull finish.

☞ Why is a sheep better than a woman? A sheep doesn't care if you date her sister.

SHARKS

☞ Shark experts say you should avoid swimming alone. Always try to swim with a group of people – or as sharks call it, a buffet.

SHEEP

☞ My pet sheep has a gambling problem. It got so bad I decided it needed professional help; I sent it to Gambollers Anonymous.

SHOES

> ## "If high heels were so wonderful, men would still be wearing them."
> *Sue Grafton*

☞ A newly-married couple go to Tunisia for their honeymoon. One day, they're wandering through a market when they're invited into a shop selling slippers. They have a look at the wares, but can't see anything they like. They're just about to leave when Abdul the shopkeeper takes a pair of slippers from a high shelf. "Please, sir," he says, "before you go, try on these special slippers. They have the magical ability to increase your sex drive. If you put these on, you will be insatiable. You will never tire of the sexual act." The couple are dubious, but to humour Abdul the man takes off his shoes and puts on the slippers. Immediately, the man's eyes bulge out of their sockets. He gives a great roar, rips off his shorts, bends Abdul over a chair and starts tearing off his robes. "No, no!" shouts Abdul. "Wrong feet! Wrong feet!"

> ## "Act your age, not your shoe size; that means something different on the Continent."
> *Richard Herring*

☞ What do people with two left feet wear on the beach? Flip-flips!

SHOPPING

☞ Veni, Vidi, Visa: I came. I saw. I did a bit of shopping.

☞ All my wife does is shop; once she was sick for a week, and three stores went under.

"I went into a clothes store, and a lady came up to me and said, 'If you need anything, I'm Jill'. I've never met anyone with a conditional identity before."
Demetri Martin

☞ A man goes into a supermarket to buy some toilet rolls. He's astonished by the variety on display and calls over a shop assistant for some advice. "This brand is called Gossamer," says the assistant. "It's quite expensive, but it's very strong and soft. This next brand is called Luxo. It's not as soft as the other stuff, but it's quite strong and it's a bit cheaper." The assistant holds up another roll. "This is Ripley's toilet paper. It's not very soft, but it is very strong and much cheaper than the other ones." "What's that?" asks the man, pointing to a cheap-looking roll. The assistant lowers his voice and says, "I wouldn't recommend that brand, sir. It doesn't have a proper name, but we all call it 'John Wayne'." "Why 'John Wayne'?" asks the man. The assistant replies, "Because it's rough, tough and doesn't take shit from anyone."

☞ By using the 'money off' labels found on their groceries, Dick and Tina have managed to save enough money to decorate and furnish one of the rooms in their house. They'd like to do the same with the other rooms in the house, but they're all full of tins, jars and boxes.

☞ A policeman is walking a new beat when he comes across a front garden piled high with shopping trolleys. Curious, he rings the doorbell. A man answers and the policeman asks where the trolleys came from. "I got them at the supermarket," says the man. "It's silly to have so many, but I can't resist a bargain; they're only a pound each!"

☞ A woman goes into a hardware shop to buy a hinge. She takes it to the counter. The assistant says, "Want a screw for that hinge?" "No," replies the woman, "but I'll give you a blow-job for a toaster."

☞ My wife'll buy anything marked down. Last year she bought an escalator.

☞ Glenda goes to a high-class clothes shop and sees a lambswool sweater for sale at £500. She calls over a sales assistant. "This price is outrageous," she complains. "I could go into any shop in the high street and get the same jumper for £50." "No, madam," says the assistant. "Most ordinary knitwear is made from recycled wool, whereas this sweater is one hundred per cent virgin lambswool." "Big deal," says Glenda. "For an extra £450, who cares what the lambs get up to at night?"

"I love to shop after a bad relationship. I don't know; I buy a new outfit and it makes me feel better. It just does. Sometimes, if I see a really great outfit, I'll break up with someone on purpose."
Rita Rudner

☞ Harry is out shopping with his wife at a big supermarket. They split up and Harry arranges to meet his wife at the check-out. When he turns up, she notices he's carrying a music CD. "What do you want that for?" asks his wife. "Why on earth do you want to buy a CD when we don't have a CD player?" Harry shrugs and says, "Did you hear me complain when you bought that bra?"

"I like to go into the Body Shop and shout out really loud, 'I've already got one'!"
Norman Lovett

☞ My wife left me for religious reasons. She worships money and I don't have any.

"I was in a convenience store reading a magazine when the clerk comes up to me and says, 'This isn't a library'. So I say, 'All right; I'll talk louder, then'!"
Mitch Hedberg

☞ The other day at the supermarket, I saw a man and a woman wrapped in a barcode. I said, "So, are you two an item?"

SIGNS

☞ Advertisement: Cleaner required, two hours a day, to clean small officers.

☞ Advertisement: Rings by post. State size or enclose tape tied round finger.

☞ Advertisement: Since taking your medication I have felt like a new woman (original may be seen on request).

☞ Advertisement: To let – small mouse.

☞ Advertisement: Wanted – person to wash dishes and two waitresses.

☞ Advertisement: Widows made to your specification.

☞ At a doctor's surgery in Italy: Specialist in women and other diseases.

☞ At a drive-through fast-food restaurant: Parking for drive through only.

☞ At a dry cleaner's: We do not tear your clothing with machinery. We do it carefully by hand.

☞ At a gas station: We will sell gasoline to anyone in a glass container.

☞ At a hospital: Family planning advice – use rear entrance.

☞ At a hotel in Acapulco: The manager has personally passed all the water served here.

☞ At a railroad station: Beware! To touch these wires is instant death. Anyone found doing so will be prosecuted.

☞ At the bottom of the menu in a German restaurant: After the main course we suggest that you sample the tart of the house.

☞ For sale: Boys' bicycle, also two girls. Perfect order.

☞ For sale: Sofa. Converts to double bed. Covered in mustard.

☞ In a Bangkok dry cleaner's: Drop your trousers here for best results.

☞ In a café: Special today – no ice-cream.

☞ In a cemetery: Persons are prohibited from picking flowers from any graves except their own.

☞ In a church hall: The ladies' group have cast off clothing of every kind and may be seen in the basement.

☞ In a church hall: Weight Watchers will meet at 7pm. Please use the large double door at the side entrance.

☞ In a clothing store: Wonderful bargains for men with 16 and 17 necks.

☞ In a health-food shop window: Closed due to illness.

☞ In a hotel: In case of fire, warm the chambermaid.

☞ In a Japanese hotel: You are invited to take advantage of the chambermaid.

☞ In a launderette: Automatic washing machines. Please remove all your clothes when the light goes out.

☞ In a loan company window: Now you can borrow enough money to get completely out of debt.

☞ In a London department store: Bargain basement upstairs.

☞ In a Maine restaurant: Open seven days a week and weekends.

☞ In a Norwegian hotel: Ladies are requested not to have children in the bar.

☞ In a Parisian hotel: Guests are asked to leave their values at the desk.

☞ In a safari park: Elephants please stay in your car.

☞ In a sperm bank: Men, please take your hat and jacket off.

☞ In the toilet of a London office: Toilet out of order. Please use floor below.

☞ In a Tokyo bar: Special cocktails for the ladies with nuts.

☞ In a Zurich hotel: Because of the impropriety of entertaining guests of the opposite sex in the bedroom, it is suggested that the lobby be used for this purpose.

☞ In an electrical shop: Ladies, we can quickly and economically repair anything your husband has already tried to repair with no questions asked.

☞ In an office: After tea-break, staff should empty the teapot and stand upside-down on the draining board.

☞ In the window of an Oregon store: Why go elsewhere and be cheated when you can come here?

☞ Notice in a farmer's field: The farmer allows walkers to cross the field for free, but the bull charges.

☞ On a box of light-sensitive photographic paper: Open only in total darkness. See further instructions inside.

☞ On a church notice board: Will those who have relatives buried in graves in the churchyard please keep them in order?

☞ On a repair shop door: We can repair anything. Please knock hard – bell doesn't work.

☞ On a road sign: When this sign is under water, this road is impassable.

☞ On an Atlantic City hotel restaurant: Have your next affair here.

☞ On the door to an optical research lab: Do not look into laser with remaining good eye.

☞ Outside a country shop: We buy junk and sell antiques.

☞ Outside a dry cleaner's: Customers leaving garments longer than four weeks will be disposed of.

☞ Outside a Hong Kong tailor's shop: Ladies may have a fit upstairs.

☞ Outside a restaurant: Where good food is an unexpected pleasure.

☞ Seen in a conference facility: For anyone who has children and doesn't know it, there is a day-care centre on the first floor.

☞ In a bar: Guys: No shirt – no service. Gals: No shirt – no charge.

☞ In a newsagent's window: To let. One-bedroom furnished flat. £300 per month. Electricity and rats included.

SKELETONS

☞ Why didn't the skeleton go bungee-jumping? He didn't have the guts.

☞ How did the skeleton know it was raining? He could feel it in his bones.

SKIING

☞ Glenda is on a skiing holiday. She's just been lifted to the top of a slope when she realises she desperately wants a pee. There's no rest-room in sight, so Glenda scoots off to a small clump of trees and drops her ski pants. She breathes a huge sigh of relief as her bladder starts to empty, but doesn't realise that she's started slowly sliding backwards. Suddenly, Glenda does notice that she's moving, but by this time she's left her ski sticks behind. She picks up speed and, still peeing, slips down the slope, going faster and faster. Glenda's backside turns blue as it's pelted by flying snow, and her ordeal only ends when she crashes backwards into a post. An hour later, Glenda is being admitted to hospital with a broken arm. In the waiting room, her wheelchair is parked next to a man in skiing clothing who has his leg in plaster. "Hi," says Glenda. "Looks like we've both had some bad luck today. How did you break your leg?" The man shakes his head, "You'll never believe it," he says. "I was in the ski lift when I looked down and saw this crazy woman skiing backwards down the mountain with her trousers round her ankles, having a whizz. I leaned over to take a better look, and fell out of my chair. So, how did you break your arm?"

"Cross-country skiing is great if you live in a small country."
Steven Wright

☞ How many ski instructors does it take to screw in a light-bulb? None; they screw in the hot-tub.

☞ How many skiers does it take to change a light-bulb? Ten; one to screw it in and another nine to stand around saying, "Nice turn, nice turn..."

SKYDIVING

☞ A skydiving instructor is answering questions from a group of first-time jumpers. A nervous beginner asks, "So, if my chute doesn't open, and the reserve chute doesn't open either, how long do I have until I hit the ground?" The instructor replies, "You have the rest of your life."

☞ Murphy is taking skydiving lessons. On his first day he's told to jump, count to three, then pull the cord. Murphy jumps. He mutters to himself as he plummets to the ground, "One. Two... Ah, Jaysus. One. Two... Sure enough, it's on the tip of my tongue. One, two. Holy Mother! I remembered it yesterday. I was word-perfect. One..."

SLAVE LABOUR

☞ The slaves are pulling the oars on a Roman galley when one of the older slaves suddenly has a heart attack and dies. The overseer comes over, unchains the dead slave and, without ceremony, pushes him through an oar-hole into the sea. He then goes around the galley with his whip lashing everyone he comes across. One of the newer slaves turns to the man next to him and says, "That's a bit much. Why is he whipping everyone? We didn't do anything." "It's always the same," replies his companion. "Whenever somebody leaves, there's always a whip-round."

SLEEP

> **"Man is the only animal that goes to sleep when he's not sleepy and gets up when he is."**
> *Dave Gneiser*

☞ I'm exhausted. I couldn't get to sleep last night. I tried counting sheep, but by the time I'd got to 180,876 it was time to get up again.

> **"I slept like a log last night. I woke up in a fireplace."**
> *Tommy Cooper*

☞ I phoned up Harry late last night. "Hello," I said. "I didn't wake you, did I?" "No," said Harry. "Do you want to call back later?"

> **"The good people sleep much better at night than the bad people. But, of course, the bad people enjoy the waking hours much more."**
> *Woody Allen*

SMELL

☞ I was hosting a cocktail party the other day, but I noticed that people were avoiding me. Then my wife came over and told me my feet really stank, so I nipped upstairs and changed my socks. I didn't solve the problem, though; people still kept clear of me. On reflection, perhaps I shouldn't have stuffed the old socks in my jacket pocket.

SMOKING

☞ A captain is inspecting the guard at an army camp. He walks to the sentry box and sees a new recruit slouched inside. At the man's feet is a cigarette butt. It looks fresh and, since smoking on duty is an offence, the captain decides to investigate. "You, there," he says. "Is that your cigarette?" The soldier looks down at the butt and says. "Nah. Go on, mate, you have it; you saw it first."

  ☞ Good news for smokers! Clinical tests have shown that if you smoke cigarettes, it dramatically reduces your risk of developing Alzheimer's Disease – you drop dead before you get a chance to get it.

☞ Harry finally managed to stop smoking. He discovered that the only way to control his cravings was by continuously chewing on toothpicks. Sadly, he later died of Dutch Elm Disease.

  ☞ Harry wants to give up smoking, but is very weak-willed. Finally, his wife gives him an ultimatum. He'll get no sex until he gives up. Harry discusses this development with his friend Bill. "So how long can you hold out?" asks Bill. "Not sure," replies Harry. "I suppose until she dies and I remarry, or I get repetitive strain injury."

☞ Mary wants to help her husband give up cigarettes. She asks her friend June for advice. June suggests that Mary limits her husband's smoking to a post-sex cigarette. Mary decides to give it a go and tells her husband that, in future, he can only smoke a cigarette after making love. A week later, June meets Mary in the street. Mary is slowly hobbling down the road on bow-legs, using two canes to support herself. "You look terrible," says June. "What happened to you?" "I took your advice about the smoking," replies Mary, "but so far, I've only been able to get him down to 20 a day."

☞ To help me with my smoking problem, I've been using passive smoking patches. You stick them on other people.

SMUGGLING

☞ A man rides up to the border on his bicycle. He has two large bags over his shoulders. The border guard stops him. "What's in the bags?" he asks. "Sand," says the man. The guard asks the man to hand the bags over for inspection. The guard empties the bags out, but finds nothing but sand. He sends the man on his way. A week later, the same man cycles up to the border again. Like last time, he has two bags slung over his shoulder. "What have you got in the bags?" asks the guard. "Sand," says the man. The guard examines the bags again and finds they contain nothing but sand. He gives the bags back to the man and sends him on his way. This goes on every week for three years. Finally, the man stops appearing at the border crossing. Years go by and the border guard eventually retires. One day, he's walking through a nearby town when he sees the man sitting in a cafe. "Hey," says the guard. "I remember you. I'm sure you were smuggling something through my crossing station. I'm positive you were, but I never figured out what your angle was. It used to drive me crazy. Just between you me, were you smuggling stuff?" "Yes," says the man. "Hah!" says the guard. "I knew it. But I always searched you so thoroughly. What on earth were you smuggling?" The man replies, "Bicycles."

SNAILS

☞ What did the snail say when it sat on top of the tortoise? Wheeeeeeeeee!

> ☞ Yesterday, I came across two snails having a fight. I thought about stopping it, but then left them to slug it out.

SNAKES

☞ An old snake goes to have his eyes checked. It turns out he needs glasses quite badly, and slithers away wearing a pair of thick spectacles. A week later, the snake returns to enquire about contact lenses. The snake looks very depressed, so the optician asks him what's wrong. "Everything all right?" asks the optician. "Are the glasses okay?" "They're fine," replies the snake, glumly. "They're a real help when it comes to catching food and looking out for eagles wanting to eat me, and suchlike." "So why the long face?" asks the optician. The snake sighs and says, "Well, when I got home, I slithered over to show my wife my new glasses, and I discovered I'd spent the last two years living with a hose-pipe."

SNOBBERY

☞ Bill Smith is a rag-and-bone man. He's a poor, illiterate fellow with very little education. For years he scrapes a living collecting scrap, but one day his luck changes; he makes a deal to salvage metal from an old shipyard and when the price of steel rockets, he finds he's made it rich! Soon after his good fortune, Bill's bank manager rings him. "Mr Smith," says the bank manager. "I have a query about your account. For years you've signed your cheques with two crosses, but now we're receiving cheques marked with three crosses. Is this your signature?" "Yes," says Bill. "It's the wife's idea. She reckons that now we've gone up in the world, I ought to have a middle name."

☞ My aunt's a terrible snob. She went on a cruise and refused an invitation to dine at the Captain's table; she didn't want to be seen eating with the crew.

SNOWMEN

☞ There are two snowmen in a field. One says to the other, "Can you smell carrots?"

SOCIAL BLUNDERS

☞ I went to a tea party at the vicarage yesterday. While I was standing there, the vicar's cat came along and started licking its back. I said, "Wow, reverend. I wish I was agile enough to do that. Don't you?" Which would have been all right, except that by the time the vicar turned round to look, the damned cat was licking its ass

SOCIAL WORK

☞ One social worker goes up to another social worker and says, "Hey! Do you know what the time is?" "Sorry," says the second social worker. "I don't have a watch." "Never mind," says the first social worker. "The main thing is that we talked about it."

☞ What's the difference between a social worker and a pitbull terrier? You can usually manage to get your baby back from the pitbull.

SOCIOLOGY

☞ A sociologist is someone who, when a beautiful women enters the room and everybody looks at her, looks at everybody.

SORT OF

"'Sort of' is such a harmless thing to say. 'Sort of.' It's just a filler. 'Sort of.' It doesn't really mean anything. But after certain things, 'sort of' means everything: like after 'I love you' or 'You're going to live', or 'It's a boy'."
Demetri Martin

SPEECH IMPEDIMENTS

☞ A huge hairy biker goes into a gas station and asks where the bathroom is. "W...W...W...Wh...Where's t...t...t...the j...j...j...john?" stutters the biker. The man at the check-out says nothing. The biker repeats the question. "W...W...W...Wh...Where's t...t...t...the j...j...j...john?" The check-out man remains silent. The biker tries again. "W...W...W...Wh...Where's t...t...t...the g...g...god...d...d...damn j...j...j...john?" he yells, banging his fist on the counter. The check-out man says nothing at all. The biker is furious. "T...t...then I...I...I'll p...p...piss on y...y...y..your g...g...god...d...d...amn p...p...pump!" he shouts, and storms out. Another customer goes up to the check-out guy and says, "Why didn't you tell him where the bathroom is? It's only round the back." "I...I...I w...w...w...would h...h...h...have," replies the check-out guy. "B...b...b...but I d...d...d...didn't w...w...w...want t...t...t...t g...g...get b...b...beaten u...u...up."

☞ A man goes to a speech therapist. "I hea-hea-heard th-th-that you can he-he-help t-t-to cu-cu-cu-cure st...st-st...stammering," says the man. The therapist replies, "The cure is very simple. Just sit down in this chair, look into my eyes, and count slowly to ten." The man does so and counts, "O-o-o-o-one, t-t-t-t-two, th-th-th-th-three, f-f-f-four, f-f-five, s-six, s-seven-eight, nine, ten. Hey! That's incredible!" says the man. "I don't stammer any more!" "I said it was simple," says the therapist. "So how much do I owe you, doc?" asks the man. "The bill comes to four thousand dollars," says the therapist. The man replies, "Wh-wh-what th-th-the fu-fu-fu-"

☞ A man walks into a pub and goes up to the barman, who's a hunchback. "H-h-h-how mu-mu-mu-much is a b-b-b-beer?" he asks. "Six dollars a bottle," replies the hunchback barman. "S-s-s-s-six d-d-d-d-dollars?" says the man. "Th-th-th-that's a-a-a b-b-b-it st-st-st-steep. H-h-ho-how mu-mu-much for a-a-a co-co-coke?" "Four bucks," replies the barman. "J-j-j-jeez," says the man. "Th-th-th-that's p-p-p-pre-pretty p-p-p-ricey t-t-t-t-to-too." "How about a lemonade for two-fifty?" says the hunchback barman. "That's the cheapest drink we've got." "O-o-o-ok-ok-okay," replies the man. "B-b-b-b-but t-t-th-th-that's r-r-r-real e-e-exp-p-pens-s-s-sive a-a-as w-w-well." So saying, the man hands over two-fifty and the barman pours him a glass of lemonade. "B-b-bye t-t-the w-w-way," says the man, "t-t-t-th-th-tha-thanks f-f-f-for n-n-n-no-not la-la-la-aughi-i-i-ing a-a-at m-my st-st-st-stutter." "Don't mention it," says the barman. "Thank you for not laughing at my hump-back." "A-a-a- hu-hu-hu-hump-b-b-ba-back?" says the man. "C-c-c-Christ. W-w-w-wi-wi-with ev-ev-everyth-th-rh-thing e-e-else b-b-being s-s-s-s-so hi-hi-high a-a-around h-h-h-he-here, I r-r-reckoned th-th-th-that w-w-w-was y-y-y-your a-a-ass!"

☞ A midget with a speech impediment goes to buy a horse from a farmer. The farmer shows the midget the horse in question. The midget says, "Can I see her mouf?" The farmer lifts up the midget so he can examine the horse's mouth. The midget then says, "Can I see her eerth?" The farmer lifts up the midget so he can look in the horse's ears. The midget then says, "Can I see her ostwils?" So the farmer lifts up the midget so he can see the horse's nostrils. Then the midget says, "Can I see her twat?" The farmer, who is now pretty sick and tired of the midget, lifts up the little man and sticks his head up the horse's rear end. After a few seconds, he pulls the midget free and puts him down. The midget wipes goo off his face and says, "Pewhaps I can wephrase the wequest. Can I fee her walk about a bit?"

☞ Three Irishmen are being treated by a speech therapist for stuttering. The therapist is a lady, and she's a real looker, with lots of curves in all the right places. Unfortunately, she's not making much progress with her patients, so she decides to encourage them with a reward system. She tells them that she will have sex with the first man who can name the place of his birth without stuttering. The first Irishman stands up, and says, 'B-B-Belf-f-f-f-ast." The second Irishman says, "D-D-D-Dublin." The third Irishman says, "London." True to her word, the therapist takes the man into the next room and makes passionate love with him for the next hour. Eventually, the Irishman stumbles out of the room and collapses into a chair. The therapist also reappears, fussing with her hair and buttoning up her white coat. "Well, that was productive," she says. "Now, before we close today's session, is there anything any of you would like to say?" The third Irishman raises his hand and says, "D-d-d-d-derry."

☞ Yesterday a severe stutterer was sent to prison for drunk driving. He was given six months, but police say it's unlikely he'll finish his sentence.

SPEED

"To give you an idea of how fast we travelled, we left with two rabbits and when we arrived, we still had only two."
Bob Hope

SPIDERS

☞ I got home yesterday and found a spider in the bath. It was absolutely enormous. I wouldn't have minded, but it was using all the hot water.

SPORT

"I used to play sports. Then I realised you can buy trophies. Now I'm good at everything."
Demetri Martin

☞ A new report has forecast there will be long-term changes in the sports that are played in Britain. For example, it suggests that by 2015 England will not have a cricket team: so no change there, then.

"If a woman has to choose between catching a flyball and saving an infant's life, she will choose to save the infant's life without even considering if there is a man on base."
Dave Barry

☞ A tug-of-war contest between British and French teams had to be cancelled recently; no one could find a rope twenty-six miles long.

"When my husband watches sports on television, he thinks that if he concentrates he can help his team. If the team is in trouble, he coaches the players from our living room. And if they're really in trouble, I have to get off the phone in case they call him."
Rita Rudner

☞ I was terrible at gymnastics. I couldn't even stand on my head; I could never get my feet high enough.

"The depressing thing about tennis is that no matter how good I get, I'll never be as good as a wall."
Mitch Hedberg

☞ Jim won a gold medal at the last Olympics. He's so proud of it, he's had it bronzed.

"I said to my girlfriend, 'You shouldn't eat before you swim.' She said, 'Why not?' I said, 'You look fat'."
Jimmy Carr

☞ The luge is the only sport where you can die during the event and still win.

"Swimming is a confusing sport because sometimes you do it for fun and other times you do it to not die."
Demetri Martin

☞ A Jew, a Catholic and a Muslim are boasting about their families. The Jewish man says, "I have four sons. One more, and I'll have a basketball team." The Catholic says, "So what? I have ten sons; one more, and I'll have a football team." The Muslim says, "That's nothing. I have 17 wives. One more and I'll have a golf course."

> **"Cricket is a game which the British, not being a spiritual people, had to invent in order to have some concept of eternity."**
> *Lord Mancroft*

☞ Did you hear who won the Bangkok marathon? It was a Thai.

☞ Why do American football stadiums have Astroturf? It stops the cheerleaders grazing.

STATISTICS

☞ A statistician is someone who is good with numbers, but lacks the personality to be an accountant.

☞ I once asked a statistician for her phone number. She gave me an estimate.

☞ Statistics are like bikinis. What they conceal is more important than what they reveal.

STRANDED

☞ A married couple, Terry and June, have been stranded on a deserted island for many years. One day another man, Joe, washes up on shore. Joe and June become attracted to each other, but realise they must be creative if they're to engage in any hanky-panky. Terry is also pleased that Joe has arrived on the island. "Great," he says. "Now we'll be able to have three people doing eight-hour shifts in the watchtower." Joe volunteers to do the first shift, and climbs up the tower. Terry and June start making a fire to cook supper. Joe yells down, "Hey, stop having sex!" Terry yells back, "We're not having sex!" A few minutes later, the couple start repairing a fishing net. Joe yells down, "Hey, stop having sex!" Again, Terry yells back, "We're not having sex!" Later, Terry and June are putting palm leaves on the roof of their hut. Again, Joe yells down, "Hey, stop having sex!" Terry yells back, "We're not having sex!" Eventually, Joe's shift in the watchtower is over. Joe climbs down the tower and Terry takes over. Terry climbs to the top of the tower, looks down and says, "Well I'll be... he was right! From up here it *does* look like they're having sex."

STRESS

☞ Stress is when you wake up screaming, and suddenly realise that you hadn't actually fallen asleep.

STUPIDITY

☞ A blonde phones her redhead friend. "Could you come over and help me?" she says. "I have this big jigsaw puzzle of a tiger, but I can't figure out how to start it." The friend goes over and finds the blonde with the jigsaw pieces scattered across the kitchen table. The blonde shows her redhead friend the picture of the tiger on the box, then points to the pieces. "I can't make head or tail of it," says the blonde. "All the jigsaw pieces look the same colour to me." The friend starts sweeping the pieces into a pile. "Tell you what," says the redhead. "You go and have a lie down while I put these Frosties back in the box."

☞ A coastguard receives a mayday over the radio. "Help!" says a voice. "We're in the water!" "Capsize?" says the coast guard. There's a pause, then the voice says, "Five and five-eighths."

☞ After his wife died, Bill found that he had a lot to learn about household appliances. For example, he put a load of laundry in the washing machine, but it all disappeared when he pulled the chain.

☞ An Alabama football player gets pulled over by the police. The cop goes up to his car and says "Got any ID?" The football player replies "Bout whut?"

☞ Bill and Simon are two rather unsuccessful fishermen. One day, they're walking down by the harbour when they see a boat full to the brim with fish. They go aboard and beg the captain to tell them the secret of his success. Finally the captain relents. "'Tis easy, lads," he explains. "Just sail out of the harbour and keep going until you hit a stream of fresh water; then throw out your nets. You'll catch all the fish you want." So Bill and Simon jump in their boat and set sail. After a few minutes, Simon tells Bill to pull up a bucket of seawater and taste it. "It's still salty," says Bill, so they sail on some more. After another few minutes, Simon tells Bill to taste the seawater. "It's still salty," says Bill, so they sail on some more. Another five minutes pass, and Simon tells Bill to taste the sea water again. "It's still salty," says Bill, so they sail on some more. This goes on for half an hour and the boat is almost out of sight of land. Again, Simon says: "Bill, taste the seawater again." Bill calls back, "I can't; the bucket's empty."

☞ Dick and Jane are having a row. "And you know what?" says Dick. "You're stupid too." "How dare you?" says Jane. "You take that back. Say you're sorry." "All right," shouts Dick, "I'm sorry you're so stupid!"

"Don't argue with a fool. The spectators can't tell the difference."
Charles J. Nalin

☞ I find it difficult to concentrate these days; my mind keeps wandering. Luckily it's too weak to get very far.

☞ Murphy made a fortune with his last invention; it was a 'Stop' sign for the tops of ladders.

☞ George and Mike have got jobs on a building site. One day, they're having a breather after shifting a tonne of bricks. George taps Mike on the shoulder and points to Mr Smith, their boss, who's sitting down having a cup of tea. "Look at him there," says George. "How come we do all the hard work while he sits there relaxing and getting all the money?" "I don't know," says Mike. "Why don't you ask him?" So George goes over and says, "Can I ask you a question, boss? How come it's us poor idiots who do all the sweaty hard work, while you sit there like Lord Muck and take all the money?" Mr Smith thinks for a moment, then says, "Intelligence." George is offended. "What do you mean 'intelligence'?" says George. "I'm just as smart as you are." "Okay, George," says Mr Smith, "let's test that, shall we? I want you to punch my hand as hard as you can." Mr Smith puts his hand in front of a steel girder and George takes a swing at it. Mr Smith pulls his hand away at the last second and George lands a blow on the girder. "Aaaargh!" he cries. "There you go," says Mr Smith. "Intelligence." George stomps back to Mike nursing his bruised hand. Mike says, "So, did you discover the secret of Mr Smith's success?" "Yes," replies George. "It's intelligence." "What do you mean by that?" asks Mike. "Was he saying we're thick or something?" "I'll show you," says George. He looks around for a steel girder, but can't find one, so he puts his hand in front of his face. "Go on," says George, "hit my hand as hard as you can."

☞ George never had a head for business. Last year he set up as a loan shark; he gave out £3,000 to four people, then skipped town.

☞ Gerry isn't that bright. We bought him a disposable camera for his birthday; when we got the prints back, we found 24 snapshots of his right eye.

☞ My mother-in-law may be a little stupid, but she does have a kind heart. Last week, she was in a restaurant which had a tank of live lobsters. She couldn't bear to see them all killed, so she sneaked a couple into her handbag, then released them – into a wood.

☞ My uncle Silas is illiterate. He once tried to sue the local baker for forging his signature on a hot-cross bun.

☞ No one gets too old to learn a new way of being stupid.

☞ Patrick and Sean have been out on the town and now they're walking home. Both are the worse for wear for drink and there isn't a taxi in sight. "I know what," says Patrick. "Down the next street is the bus station. I'll keep watch outside while you nip in and pinch a bus. We can ride it home." "That sounds like a good plan," says Sean: so, while Patrick loiters outside, Sean nips inside the station to find a bus. Ten minutes later Sean still hasn't reappeared, and Patrick's starting to get nervous. A few more minutes pass, and Patrick's thinking of making a run for it. Suddenly, Sean sticks his head round the door. "It's no good," he says. "I can't find one." "You can't find a bus?" says Patrick. "There must be dozens in there." "There are," replies Sean. "But I can't find a number 19." "We don't need a 19," replies Patrick. "Just grab a 14A and we'll get off at the bakery. It's only a five-minute walk from there."

☞ Patrick goes up to Sean and presents him with a problem. "I have a pig I want to sell at the market," says Patrick, "but the big scale on the farm's broken. How can I find out how much the pig weighs?" "We'll use the old country method," says Sean. "First, you have to get a long pole and tie two identical baskets to either end. Then you take the pole and put it across a stone wall. Next, you put the pig into one of the baskets and start to fill the other basket with rocks. The basket of rocks will become heavier and heavier as you fill it; then there'll come a point when the rocks and the pig weigh the same, and the two baskets balance each other out. You follow?" "Yes," says Patrick. "What do I do then?" "Then," says Patrick, "you have to guess the weight of the rocks."

☞ Pete goes to the local DIY store, but comes homes with a black eye. "What happened to you?" asks his wife. "When I got to the store, the man at the counter asked me if I needed decking," replies Peter, "so I thought I'd get my punch in first."

☞ The easiest way to appear wise is to say the opposite of whatever first pops into your head.

  ☞ The figures for average American life expectancy and IQ passed each other recently – going in opposite directions.

☞ The other day I got to thinking about chickens. Why do we call them chickens? Then I thought, "Well, they look like chickens, they sound like chickens and they taste like chickens, so calling them chickens does actually make a lot of sense."

  ☞ The University of Alabama has reduced the length of its degree courses from four to three years, the reason being that tractors now come with automatic transmission.

> **"Think of how stupid the average person is, and realise half of them are stupider than that."**
> *George Carlin*

☞ What did the Florida quarterback get on his IQ test? Beer. What did the Kentucky quarterback get on his IQ test? Bourbon. What did the Alabama quarterback get on his IQ test? Drool.

  ☞ Zeke applies for a job as Deputy Sheriff. Zeke isn't known for his intellect and the Sheriff doesn't really want him on the force, so he tries him out with a simple IQ test. "I'll ask you three questions," says the Sheriff, "but get one wrong and I'll send you straight home." "Fire away," replies Zeke. "What's one and one?" asks the sheriff. Zeke replies, "Eleven." The Sheriff admits that this could be considered a legitimate answer, so he asks another question. "Zeke," he says. "Which two days of the week start with the letter 'T'?" Zeke thinks for a second, then says, "Today and tomorrow." Again, the Sheriff reckons that Zeke might have a point here, so he asks another. "Zeke," he says.

"Who shot Abraham Lincoln?" Zeke scratches his head and thinks really hard. After ten minutes, he eventually gives up. "Gee," he says, "I don't rightly know." "Well, tell you what," says the Sheriff. "Why don't you go home and have a think about it?" Zeke goes home, and his mom asks him how his interview went. "It was swell," says Zeke. "I ain't had the job for five minutes and already they got me working on a murder case!"

SUICIDE

☞ A man is driving across a bridge when he sees his girlfriend getting ready to jump over the side. "What are you doing?" he shouts. "I'm going to end it all!" she shouts back. "You got me pregnant and now I'm going to commit suicide!" A tear comes to the man's eye. "You're one in a million," he says. "Not only are you a fantastic shag, but you're a great sport too."

> **"I come from a very traditional family. When I was seven, my Uncle Terry hanged himself on Christmas Eve. We didn't take his body down until the sixth of January."**
> *Nick Doody*

SUMO

☞ Why do Sumo wrestlers shave their legs? So they won't look like feminists.

SURVIVAL

☞ We heard some very sad news about Harry this week. He went on a survival course and didn't pass.

SWEARING

☞ A mother is working in the kitchen, listening to her son Jimmy play with his new train set in the dining room. She hears the train stop, then Jimmy say, "Okay. All you sons of bitches who want to get off, get off now. This is the last stop! So piss off! All you sons of bitches going back, get your butts on the train right now!" Mother is furious; she goes into the dining room to give Jimmy a good telling-off. "We don't use that kind of language in this house," she says. "Go to your room right now and stay there till seven o'clock. When you come out, you can play with your train again, but only if you behave yourself." At seven, Jimmy is back in the dining room playing with his train. This time, when the train stops, mother hears him say, "All passengers disembarking, please remember to take all your belongings with you. Thank you for travelling with us today and we hope you will travel with us again soon." Mother is very pleased to hear that Jimmy has cleaned up his act. Then she hears Jimmy say, "And for those of you pissed off about the delay, see the bitch in the kitchen."

> ## "People who say they don't swear haven't had the right sex or food."
> ### *Russell Howard*

☞ A priest buys a lawnmower from his neighbour. Unfortunately, he can't get it to work. He complains to his neighbour, who says, "It's temperamental. To get it to work, you have to swear at it." The priest replies, "But I haven't sworn in over thirty years!" "Don't worry," says the neighbour. "Just keep trying to start the damn thing and it'll soon come back to you."

☞ Harry says to Tom, "Testicles. Balls. Nuts. Plums. Gonads." Tom replies, "Harry, now you're just talking bollocks."

☞ Mary and her mother are sitting in the parlour. Mary has just delivered some shocking news to her father. "So," says mother, "what did your father say when you told him you were pregnant?" Mary says, "Do you want me to leave out the profanity?" "Yes please," replies mother. "Oh," says Mary. "In that case, he didn't say anything."

☞ Two brothers are sent home from school for swearing. Their father gives them a hiding and sends them straight to bed. In the morning, father asks them what they'd like for breakfast. The first boy says, "I'll have f***ing cornflakes." Father gives the boy a thrashing and sends him back to his room. He then turns to the second boy and asks what he'd like for his breakfast. "I'm not sure," says the boy. "But I tell you one thing – it's not going to be f***ing cornflakes."

TABLOID TARGETS

> **"People are always saying that we should move travellers on – but isn't that playing into their hands?"**
> *Jimmy Carr*

☞ How do you confuse a Daily Mail reader? Tell them that asylum-seekers are the natural predator of paedophiles.

TALKING

☞ A husband and wife have an argument about who talks the most: men or women. The husband maintains that it's women who talk the most, and he's pleased to come across a newspaper article that seems to prove his point. The article reports a scientific study that shows that men speak an average of 15,000 words a day, while women speak an average of 30,000 words a day. "That proves it," crows the husband. "Women speak twice as much as men." "Rubbish," replies his wife. "All that proves is that men are so bad at listening, women have to say everything twice."

TECHNOLOGY

☞ A female secretary is helping her new boss set up his computer. She asks him what word he'd like to use as a password. Being a bit of a Jack the Lad, the boss tells her to use the word 'penis.' The secretary does as she's asked and enters the password. The computer's response is 'Password rejected. Not long enough.'

☞ A geek meets a girl in an Internet chatroom. They start dating, and he's soon invited to meet the girl's parents. The girl's father is a jovial sort. He gives the geek a beer and slaps him on the back. "Say, son," says Dad, "what sort of fancy line did you use to pick up my beautiful daughter?" The geek pushes the glasses up his nose and replies, "Nothing special: just a regular 56k modem."

☞ Acme Computers has announced a breakthrough in personal music. It has developed a sound chip that can store music in a woman's breast implant. This invention solves an old problem; women have long complained that men stare at their breasts and don't listen to them.

☞ Bill walks into a bar and sits down. He starts punching numbers into the palm of his hand as if it was a telephone keypad; then he starts talking into his hand. The bartender sees this and thinks Bill's drunk or on drugs. He goes over and asks Bill what he's doing. "I've had a phone installed in my hand," says Bill. "I was tired of carrying a mobile around." "That's crazy," says the barman. "No, I'll prove it," says Bill. "What's your mother's telephone number?" The barman tells him, and Bill dials the number on his hand, then holds up his palm to the barman's ear. The barman is amazed to hear the voice of his mother and they have a short conversation before Bill hangs up. "That was incredible," says the barman. "Yeah, it's great," says Bill. "I can keep in touch with my office, my broker, my accountant – anybody. By the way, where's the bathroom?" The barman directs him to the gents'. Ten minutes go by, and Bill doesn't reappear. The barman starts to get concerned; he fears that someone has seen Bill's unusual gadget and mugged him for it. When twenty minutes have gone past, he goes into the bathroom to see what's happened. There, the barman is horrified to find Bill spread-eagled on the floor with his pants round his ankles and a roll of toilet paper up his butt. "Oh, my God!" says the bartender. "Did they rob you? Are you hurt?" Bill turns to him and says, "No, I'm fine. I'm just waiting for a fax."

☞ Computers help us to do stupid things faster.

☞ Give a person a fish and you feed them for a day; teach that person to use the Internet and they won't bother you for weeks.

☞ Janice calls the IT helpdesk to complain that there's something wrong with the password on her computer. "The problem is that whenever I type in the password, it just shows stars," says Janice. "Those asterisks are to protect you," says the helpdesk technician. "It means that if someone was standing near you, they wouldn't be able to read your password." "Yeah," says Janice. "I understand that; I'm not stupid. The thing is, they come up even when there isn't anyone standing behind me!"

> **"I want to know what good is a web search engine that returns 324,909,188 'matches' to my key word. That's like saying, 'Good news; we've located the product you're looking for. It's on Earth'."**
> *Bruce Cameron*

☞ Peter decides to introduce his elderly mother to the advantages of the Internet. He sits the old lady in front of his computer and gives her a quick lesson in logging on and searching for information. However, his mother is reluctant to have a go; she feels nervous about communicating with a machine. "It's easy," assures Peter. "Pretend the search engine is a person and ask it a question. It'll answer anything you want." Peter's mother decides that this sounds fairly easy, so she sits down and begins typing a question: "How are Aunt Mary's varicose veins?"

TEENAGERS

☞ What's the definition of a teenager? God's punishment for enjoying sex.

☞ Adolescence is a period of rapid changes. Between the ages of 12 and 17, for example, a parent ages 20 years.

☞ A girl starts dating and her mother sits her down to see if she needs any advice. "Is there anything you need to know about boys?" asks mother. "I know you're not very experienced, so feel free to ask me anything you want. I went out with lots of boys before I met your father, so I won't be embarrassed." "I'm too shy to ask," simpers the daughter. "Don't be silly," says mother. "We're both grown-ups, so ask me anything you want." "Okay," says the daughter. "So, you know when a boy is... y'know... getting fresh with you?" "Yes?" says mother. The daughter blushes, "How do you get the cum out of your hair?"

☞ Spiderman is the ultimate teenage boy. One day, he wakes up with muscles, finds hair in new places and discovers he can spray sticky goo around the house.

☞ Paddy and his wife are searching the room of their teenage daughter, Mary. They find a pack of cigarettes hidden in a drawer. "Oh, Lord!" cries Paddy. "Our Mary's a smoker!" A few moments later, they find a bottle of vodka. "Saints preserve us!" exclaim Paddy's wife. "Our little girl's an alcoholic!" Next, they find a packet of condoms. "God help us!" cries Paddy. "And she has a penis!"

T-SHIRT SLOGANS AND BUMPER STICKERS

☞ All men are idiots – and I married their king.

☞ Ask me about microwaving cats for fun and profit.

☞ Ask me about my vow of silence.

☞ Assassins do it from behind.

☞ Be kind to donkeys – kiss my ass!

☞ Beer; it's not just for breakfast any more.

☞ Body by Nautilus: brain by Mattel.

☞ Boldly going nowhere.

☞ Calm down; who lit the fuse on your tampon?

☞ Cat: the other white meat.

☞ Caution – driver legally blonde!

☞ Caution! I speed up to run over small animals.

☞ Conserve toilet paper; use both sides.

☞ Constipated people don't give a crap.

☞ Cover me; I'm changing lanes.

☞ Discourage inbreeding; ban country music.

☞ Do not wash this vehicle – undergoing scientific dirt test.

☞ Don't be sexist; broads hate that.

☞ Don't drink and drive; you might hit a bump and spill your drink.

☞ Earth first! We'll strip-mine the other planets later.

☞ Eat right: exercise: die anyway.

☞ Eschew obfuscation.

☞ Fight crime! Shoot back!

☞ Forget the flag; burn a politician.

☞ Friends don't let friends drive naked.

☞ Go to church this Sunday; avoid the Christmas rush.

☞ God put me on Earth to accomplish a certain number of tasks. Right now I'm so far behind, I'll live for ever.

☞ Good girls get fat; bad girls get eaten.

☞ Gravity; it's not just a good idea, it's the LAW!

☞ Gravity always gets me down.

☞ Gravity is a myth; the Earth sucks.

☞ Have a nice day... somewhere else.

☞ He who hesitates is not only lost, but miles from the next exit.

☞ Heart attacks: God's revenge on you for eating his animal friends.

☞ Honk if anything falls off.

☞ Honk if you like obscene gestures!

☞ Honk if you've never seen an Uzi fired from a car window.

☞ Honk if you want to see my finger.

☞ Horn broken; watch for finger.

☞ How many roads must a man travel down before he admits he's lost?

☞ I brake for hallucinations.

☞ I brake for... no apparent reason.

☞ I can handle pain until it start hurting.

☞ I do whatever my Rice Krispies tell me to.

☞ I fart to make you smell better.

☞ I have the body of a god: Buddha.

☞ I just let my mind wander, and it didn't come back.

☞ I lost my virginity, but I still have the box it came in.

☞ I love everybody – and you're next!

☞ I need someone real bad; are you real bad?

☞ I said 'No' to drugs, but they didn't listen.

☞ If at first you DO succeed, try not to look surprised.

☞ If sex is a pain in the ass, you're doing it wrong.

☞ If that phone was jammed up your butt, maybe you could drive a little better.

☞ If you can read this, I can hit my brakes and sue you.

☞ If you can read this, please flip me back over. (Seen upside-down on a jeep.)

☞ If you can read this, thank a teacher: and, since it's in English, thank a soldier!

☞ If you can read this, the bitch fell off. (Seen on the back of a biker's vest.)

☞ If you can't dazzle them with brilliance, riddle them with bullets.

☞ If you don't believe in oral sex, keep your mouth shut.

☞ If you drink, don't park; accidents cause people.

☞ If you're not a haemorrhoid, get off my ass.

☞ I'm as confused as a baby in a titty bar.

☞ I'm not as think as you drunk I am.

☞ I'm objective; I object to everything.

☞ Impotence: nature's way of saying 'No hard feelings'.

☞ It's not how you pick your nose, but where you put the bogey.

☞ Jesus is coming! Everyone look busy!

☞ Jesus paid for our sins – so let's get our money's worth.

☞ Keep honking; I'm reloading.

☞ Laugh alone and the world thinks you're a moron.

☞ Men are proof that women can take a joke.

☞ Montana: at least the cows are sane.

☞ My folks went to Turin and all I got was this lousy shroud.

☞ My karma ran over your dogma.

☞ Necrophilia: the urge to crack open a cold one.

☞ Next time you wave, use all your fingers.

☞ No hand signals: driver on Viagra

☞ No radio: already stolen.

☞ Nobody's perfect. I'm a nobody.

☞ If you see me running, try to keep up. (Seen on the back of a T-shirt worn by a bomb disposal expert.)

☞ On the other hand, you have different fingers.

☞ Please tell your pants it's not polite to point.

☞ Porn; it's cheaper than dating

☞ Reality is a crutch for people who can't handle drugs.

☞ Remember when air was clean and sex was dirty?

☞ Save a tree; eat a beaver!

☞ Save gas; fart in a jar.

☞ Save your breath; you'll need it to blow up your date!

☞ Saw it – wanted it – had a screaming fit – got it!

☞ Snatch a kiss, or vice versa.

☞ So many pedestrians: so little time.

☞ So you're a feminist; ain't that cute?

☞ Some day you'll look back on all this and crash into a parked car.

☞ Sticks and stones may break my bones, but whips and chains excite me!

☞ Support your local undertaker; drop down dead.

☞ Taxation WITH representation isn't so hot either!

☞ Thank you for pot smoking.

☞ The Earth is full – go home.

☞ The face is familiar, but I can't quite remember my name.

☞ The more you complain, the longer God makes you live.

☞ They told me I was gullible... and I believed them.

☞ This would be really funny if it wasn't happening to me.

☞ Those who live by the sword get shot by those who don't.

☞ To all you virgins – thanks for nothing.

☞ Wanted: meaningful overnight relationship.

☞ Warning! Driver only carries $20 in ammunition.

  ☞ Warning: I drive like you.

☞ Where are we going, and why am I in this hand-basket?

  ☞ Why be difficult? With a bit of effort you could be impossible.

☞ You! Out of the gene pool!

TELEPHONES

☞ Bill and his wife June are having dinner when the phone rings. June picks it up and chats away for twenty-five minutes. "Just under half an hour!" says Bill when she finally hangs up. "That's pretty good for you. What happened?" June says, "It was a wrong number."

  ☞ There's a new premium-rate telephone service that tests your IQ. It costs £2.50 a minute. Apparently, if you call it at all, you're an idiot. If you stay on for three minutes or more, you're a moron.

> ### "So I got home, and the phone was ringing. I picked it up, and said, 'Who's speaking, please?' And a voice said 'You are'."
> *Tommy Cooper*

☞ "Good afternoon: incontinence hotline. Can you hold, please?"

TELEPHONES – SUPPOSEDLY GENUINE CALLS TO DIRECTORY ENQUIRIES

☞ A caller asks for a knitwear company in a place called Woven. Operator: "Woven? Are you sure?" Caller: "Yes. That's what it says on the label; Woven in Scotland."

☞ Caller: "I'd like the number for a reverend in Cardiff, please." Operator: "Do you have his name?" Caller: "No, but he has a dog named Ben."

☞ Caller: "I'd like the number of the Argoed Fish Bar in Cardiff, please." Operator: "I'm sorry; there's no listing. Is the spelling correct?" Caller: "Well, it used to be called the Bargoed Fish Bar but the B fell off."

☞ Caller: "I'd like the RSPCA, please." Operator: "Where are you calling from?" Caller: "The living room."

☞ Caller: "The Water Board, please." Operator: "Which department?" Caller: "Tap water."

☞ Operator: "How are you spelling that?" Caller: "With letters."

☞ A man makes a call to directory enquiries and asks for a number. The operator starts to give it to him, when she hears the man making heavy breathing sounds. "Sorry," says the man. "I'm in a phone box and I haven't got a pen. I'm steaming up a window to write the number on."

TELEVISION

☞ Harry didn't bother buying a new TV licence this year. He thought he could get away with a photocopy of the old one; after all, he only watches repeats.

☞ Why do news bulletins begin with the words 'Good evening' or 'Good morning', when the news is so depressing? Shouldn't it be 'Crappy morning' or 'Godawful evening'?

TEMPTATION

"I generally avoid temptation unless I can't resist it."
Mae West

THE WAR ON TERROR

> ## "I don't worry about terrorism. I was married for two years."
> *Sam Kinison*

☞ Good news; Saddam Hussein is facing the death penalty. Bad news; Beckham's taking it.

☞ A man comes across a little boy buying a Valentine's Day card. "You're a bit young to have a girlfriend," says the man. "It's not for a girl," replies the boy. "It's for Osama Bin Laden." "Bin Laden?" says the stunned man. "Why do you want to give him a Valentine's Day card?" The boy replies, "Because if he gets a card for Valentine's Day from a little boy from the West, he might think we're not so bad after all, and he might come out and try and make friends with us." The man is very touched by this sentiment. He wipes a tear from his eye. The little boy continues, "Then, when he's out in the open, the marines can blow the crap out of the lousy bastard."

> ## "Men who blow themselves up are promised 72 virgins in paradise. That's a high price to pay for a shag. In real life you'd be hard-pushed to find one virgin. It begs the question; what on earth do they all look like? That's a lot of hairy women."
> *Shazia Mirza*

☞ Osama Bin Laden is pottering around in his cave while his Al Qaeda deputy, Ayman al-Zawahiri, is outside feeding the goats. Suddenly, Ayman hears an explosion in the cave and rushes in to see what's happened. He finds Osama lying on the ground with his face covered in blood and half his beard burnt off. "What happened?" exclaims Ayman. "It was a letter bomb," says Osama. "A letter bomb?" says Ayman. "But surely a letter bomb would have wounded your hands, not your mouth?" Osama replies, "You idiot; I was licking the envelope!"

☞ Recent terrorist attacks have resulted in France increasing its terror alert status from 'Run' to 'Hide'. The two higher levels are 'Surrender' and 'Collaborate'. In Italy, similar concerns have raised the terror status from 'Shout Loudly and Excitedly' to 'Elaborate Military Posturing'. Further attacks might prompt changes to the higher levels of 'Ineffective Combat Operations' and 'Change Sides.' In Germany, the alert level has gone from 'Disdainful Arrogance' to 'Dress in Uniform and Sing Marching Songs'. Germany's next level is 'Invade a Neighbour'; its highest is 'Lose'.

☞ What did Saddam Hussein say when he climbed out of his hidey-hole? "Did I beat David Blaine?"

TIME

☞ For sincere personal advice and the correct time: call a random telephone number at 3am.

"Half our life is spent trying to find something to do with the time we rushed through life trying to save."
Will Rogers

☞ What happens when a clock is hungry? It goes back four seconds.

"My watch is three hours fast and I can't fix it. So I'm going to move to New York."
Steven Wright

TIME OF THE MONTH

☞ How do you know if you have PMS? Your husband suddenly starts agreeing with everything you say.

> **"Women complain about premenstrual syndrome,
> but I think of it as the only time of the
> month that I can be myself."**
> *Roseanne Barr*

TOILETS AND SEWAGE

> **"I was in a restaurant. I asked the waiter where the
> gents' were; he said, 'Just go down the stairs...'"**
> *Jimmy Carr*

☞ A couple are trying to save money on their water bills by not flushing their toilet so often. After a few days, the woman says, "We're going to have to go back to flushing the toilet, you know. The smell's getting really bad." "You're right," says the man, "And pressing the toilet seat all the way down is getting harder and harder."

☞ A woman is walking through the woods when she comes across a duck with a brown mark running down its back. The duck is in some distress, and when the lady investigates further she discovers the brown stain is actually faeces. She takes pity on the poor creature and uses a tissue to wipe away the effluent. Walking farther on, she comes across another duck. This one is also covered in poop and, again, the lady cleans off as much as she can with a tissue. The woman walks on and comes across a third duck, also covered in evil-smelling manure. She uses the last of her tissues to clean off the mess and wonders what can be going on. She walks on and soon notices a horrible smell coming from a large bush. Someone groans pitifully and the sound of a long, bubbly fart can be heard. From the bush, a voice calls out weakly, "Hey, lady." "Yes?" replies the woman. "You got any more tissues?" asks the voice. "No; sorry," replies the lady. The voice says, "You seen any more ducks?"

☞ Bob goes into a public toilet and sees a man with no arms standing next to the urinal. Bob has a pee and is about to leave when the man says, "Can you help me out and unzip my fly?" "Er, sure," says Bob, undoing the zip. Then the man says, "Could you take it out for me, please?" Bob says, "Um... okay." He pulls out the man's penis and sees that it's covered in all kinds of mouldy red bumps, oozing yellow sores and brown scabs. "Could you point it for me?" asks the man. "Sure thing," says Bob, holding it steady. "Could you put it back in?" asks the man when he's finished. "Will do," says Bob, shaking it dry and putting the horrible thing back inside the man's pants. "Thanks. I really appreciated that," says the man. "No problem," says Bob. "But I've got to ask you; what the hell is wrong with your penis?" The man pulls his arms out from inside his jacket and says, "Damned if I know – but I sure ain't touching it."

☞ Britain's longest-serving sewage engineer, who has spent eight hours a day for the past sixty years up to his neck in effluent, was today knighted by the Queen – using a ten-foot bargepole.

☞ My uncle's very mean. To save money, he wipes his backside with old newspaper. He does like to keep up appearances, though; if he has guests round, he rents a toilet roll from the corner shop.

☞ Prince Charles goes down the sewers to meet some drainage workers. The Prince is introduced to old Alf, who's been down the sewers for forty years. "This work is more interesting than you might think," says Alf to the Prince. "For instance, you see that turd over there? You can tell that's from the hairdressers in the High Street because of all the bits of cut hair stuck to it." "How fascinating," says the Prince. "And you see that one over there?" says Alf. "That's from a garage toilet. You can tell by the oily sheen on it." "Extraordinary," says the Prince. "And how about that large one over there in the corner?" "Why," says Alf, "that's from my very own house. That's one of my wife's turds." "How on earth can you tell?" asks the Prince. "Easy," replies Alf. "It's got my sandwiches tied to it."

☞ Tom is always getting hold of the wrong end of the stick – which wouldn't be so bad, except he works in a sewage farm.

☞ Tom is standing at the urinals in a public toilet. Suddenly, the man in the next stall starts talking. "Hi. How are you?" he says. "Um… I'm fine," answers Tom. "So, what are you up to?" asks the man. "I'm on holiday," replies Tom, hesitantly. "Mind if I stop over for the night?" asks the man. "What?" exclaims Tom. "But I hardly know you!" "Hey, I'll call you back," says the man. "The idiot in the next stall keeps talking to himself."

☞ "What's the difference between a shower curtain and toilet paper?" "I don't know." "Oh: so it was you!"

☞ Why is it called 'raw sewage'? Does that mean that someone, somewhere, is cooking the stuff?

☞ You know how some people have a little bit of rug sitting on the lid of their toilet seat? Why do they do that? Do they think if they have a party there's not going to be enough standing room?

"If you stay in a house, go to the bathroom and find there's no toilet paper, you can always slide down the banisters."
Paul Merton

TRANSPORT, TRAVEL AND TOURISM

"I want to hang a map of the world in my house. Then I'm gonna put pins into all the locations that I've travelled to. But first, I'm going to have to travel to the top two corners of the map so it won't fall off the wall."
Mitch Hedberg

"The other day I went to a tourist information booth and said, 'So, tell me about some of the people who were here last year'."
Steven Wright

TRANSPORT, TRAVEL AND TOURISM – AIR TRAVEL

☞ The first piece of luggage out of the chute at the airport; why does it never seem to belong to anyone?

☞ The three basic rules of flying:
   1) Try to stay in the middle of the air.
   2) Try to avoid the edges of the air.
   3) The edges of the air are marked by things like house, trees, cows and outer space; it is much, much harder to try to fly through these things.

☞ What's the ideal staffing complement on the flight deck of a modern airliner? A captain, a co-pilot and a dog. The dog bites the captain if he ever tries to touch the controls, and the co-pilot feeds the dog.

☞ Did you hear about the jumbo jet that had an all-woman crew? They had to change the name of the cockpit to 'the box office'.

☞ Dick won second place in an airline's 'Most Travelled Passenger' contest after travelling four hundred thousand miles in a year. First prize was won by his luggage, which had done seven hundred thousand miles.

☞ A girl and her parents are flying to San Francisco. The family have a seat overlooking the wing. As they near the airport, the plane banks to one side, giving the passengers a view over the bay. The mother points out of the window and says to her daughter, "Honey, can you see the water?" The girl tries to peer over the wing. "No," she says, "but I can see the diving board."

☞ A passenger jet en route to New York begins to shudder violently half-way across the Atlantic. There's the sound of an explosion, and the horrified passengers look out of the cabin windows to see that one of the engines has just blown up. The aircraft is then rocked again as a second engine explodes on the other wing. The passengers are starting to panic now. To calm their fears, the pilot strides out from the cockpit and stands at the head of the aisle where everyone can see him. He assures the passengers that there is nothing to worry about, and that all the relevant safety procedures are in place. His soothing words and confident manner make the passengers feel a lot better. The passengers then watch as the pilot puts on a parachute and walks calmly to the forward exit door. The rest of the flight crew – also wearing parachutes – join him and form an orderly queue. "Hey," says one of the passengers. "You just stood up there and told us there was nothing to worry about." "There isn't," replies the pilot, opening the door. "We're just popping out to get some help."

☞ A plane is flying from LA to New York. About an hour into the flight, the pilot makes an announcement. "Ladies and gentlemen," he says. "I'm afraid we have lost the use of one of our engines. Please don't be concerned, as we still have three left. However, instead of three hours, it will now take us four hours to get to New York." A little later, the pilot makes another announcement. "Ladies and gentlemen," he says, "I'm afraid a second engine has just failed, but don't worry; we still have two left. However, it will now take us five hours to get to New York." A little later, the pilot comes on the intercom yet again. "Ladies and gentlemen," he says, "our third engine has now died. Please do not be alarmed, as the plane can fly perfectly well on a single engine. However, it will now take us at least six hours to get to New York." A passenger leans over to his wife and says, "Jeez, I hope we don't lose that last engine; we'll be up here for ever!"

☞ George is sitting at an airport bar waiting to board his flight. A beautiful young woman sits next to him and George tries to think of a way to strike up a conversation. He reckons she might work as a stewardess, so he tries a few airline slogans to see if she responds to one of them. First he tries Delta Airlines: "We love to fly, and it shows." There's no response from the girl. Next, George tries American Airlines: "Doing what we do best." The girl gives George a funny look, but says nothing. George then tries United Airlines: "Fly the friendly skies." The girl is starting to look a bit irritated now. George tries British Airways: "The world's favourite airline." Suddenly the girl turns on him and snaps, "What the hell do you want?" "Ahh," says George. "Aeroflot."

☞ There's been some severe cost-cutting at our local airline; the last time I took a flight they asked us to fasten our Velcro before take-off.

☞ Mike and Mary are at the airport, waiting for a flight. Suddenly Mary slaps her forehead and lets out a deep sigh. "What's the matter?" asks Mike. "I wish we'd brought your briefcase," replies Mary. "Why?" asks Mike. "We've got three huge suitcases, two shoulder-bags and your handbag. They're all stuffed full. What on earth would you want to put in my briefcase?" "Nothing," replies Mary. "It's just that the tickets are in it."

☞ A pilot is a confused soul who talks about women when he's flying and about flying when he's with a woman.

☞ Avoid jetlag; take an earlier flight.

☞ Harry and Larry are on a flight to New York. The plane has just taken off and the pilot is talking to the passengers over the intercom. "Good morning, ladies and gentlemen," he says. "This is Flight 324 for New York. The estimated time of arrival is 2.40pm local time. We'll be cruising at 35,000 feet and – OH, MY GOD! OH, MY GOD!..." The intercom is suddenly switched off, leaving the passengers sitting in stunned silence. Harry and Larry look at each other and gulp. The intercom is switched back on and the pilot's voice returns. "I'm sorry about that, ladies and gentlemen," he says. "I was drinking some coffee and I tipped the whole lot in my lap." He chuckles, "As you may have guessed, it was very hot. You should see the stain down the front of my trousers..." Harry turns to Larry and says, "Yeah? Well he should see the stain down the *back* of mine!"

☞ I took a flight last week. I happened to look under my seat and I saw this life-jacket. So what's going on; do the ferries have all the parachutes?

☞ The airline I used last week was terrible; when they came round to take my order for dinner, they said I had two choices: yes or no.

☞ The control tower calls the pilot of Flight 2345, "Attention 2345. Turn right 45 degrees for noise abatement." "Roger," replies the pilot, "but, tower, we are currently at 35,000 feet. How much noise can we make up here?" The tower replies, "Have you ever heard the noise a 727 makes when it hits a 747?"

> ### "I booked a flight the other day and the clerk asked, 'How many people will be travelling with you.' I said, 'I don't know; it's your plane'."
> *Steven Wright*

☞ I wouldn't say it was a cheap airline, but you couldn't get on a plane without the exact change.

☞ Tom is taking a flight to America. He's just settled into his seat when another man sits next to him. The man has a Labrador dog on a leash. "I didn't know dogs could travel with the passengers," says Tom. "Normally they don't," replies the man. "But I'm a DEA agent and this is a sniffer dog. His name is Bingo. Rather than check out everyone when they arrive at the airport, me and Bingo are seeing if we can save time by checking them during the flight." So saying, the agent releases Bingo, who goes down the aisle sniffing people as he goes. Bingo comes to one man, sniffs him and barks twice. "That means Bingo can smell cocaine," explains the agent to Tom. "I'll write down his seat number." Bingo then sniffs a woman and barks once. The agent says, "One bark is for marijuana. I'll make a note of her seat number too." Suddenly Bingo runs back up the plane and jumps into the agent's lap. The dog then lets off an evil-smelling fart, does a huge crap and starts peeing all over the place. "Oh my God!" exclaims Tom. "That's disgusting!" "True," says the agent, "but that's the least of our problems. Looks like Bingo just found a bomb."

TRANSPORT, TRAVEL AND TOURISM – ROAD AND RAIL

☞ Harry was never much good at hitch-hiking. For a start, he always used to get up early to avoid the traffic.

☞ A posh man gets into a taxi. "Where to, guv?" asks the driver. "Honestly!" says the posh man. "Do you really think I'd give my address to the likes of you?"

> **"So I said to this train driver, 'I want to go to Paris'. He said, 'Eurostar?' I said, 'I've been on telly, but I'm no Dean Martin'."**
> *Tim Vine*

☞ A man gets into a cab and asks to be driven to the airport. Ten minutes into the journey, the man discovers he needs to stop at an ATM and get some cash. He reaches over and taps the driver on the shoulder to get his attention. The driver's reaction is startling; he lets out a high-pitched scream, jumps a foot in the air, loses control of the cab and crashes it into a tree. The shaken passenger manages to crawl out of the wreckage and pulls the driver free of the now burning cab. The man props the driver up against a tree. "What the hell was that about?" asks the man. "All I did was tap you on the shoulder." "I'm sorry," replies the driver, "but this is my first day as a cab driver. For the last 25 years I made a living driving a hearse."

☞ A passenger train is crossing the American plains. Suddenly the front engine breaks down. The engineer makes an announcement to the passengers. "Ladies and gentlemen, I have some bad news and some good news. The bad news is that we lost an engine. The good news is that we have two engines, so we can continue our journey at half-power. This means we will be arriving at our next stop 40 minutes late." The train continues on its way and, for an hour, all is well. Then the overloaded second engine packs up as well. The engineer makes another announcement to the passengers. "Ladies and gentlemen," he says. "I have some bad news and some good news. The bad news is that our second engine has broken down and it will take an hour for another locomotive to come and get us moving. The good news is that we've lost both engines and you're *not* sitting in an airplane."

☞ An Indian train is slowly chugging its way to Bombay. The journey is taking hours longer than it ought to and, eventually, one of the first-class passengers goes to the front of the train to complain to the driver. "I say, driver," he says, "can't you go any faster than this?" "Most certainly, sir," says the driver, "but unfortunately I am not allowed to leave the train."

☞ Bert, the most idle and bad-tempered railway porter in the country, retired the other day. For his retirement present, his boss gave him a beautiful set of expensive matching luggage; Bert asked him what he thought the bloody trolleys were for.

☞ Harry is driving down the road behind a truck. At every red light, the truck driver gets out of his cab, runs back and bangs on the truck door. This happens several times and Harry, curious about this behaviour, follows the truck into the parking area of a roadside cafe. The truck driver parks his rig and, as before, gets out and starts banging on the back door of the truck. Harry comes over. "Excuse me," he says. "I don't mean to be nosy, but why do you keep banging on the door of your truck?" The driver replies, "I'm carrying 20 tonnes of canaries and this truck has a 10-tonne limit; I have to keep half of them flying."

☞ Jack retires from the railway after 50 years' service. The train company asks him what he'd like as a gift, and Jack replies that it's always been his dream to have his own railway carriage installed on a bit of track in the back garden. The carriage would be his den where he could sit and reminisce about the many happy years he'd spent working on the railway. Since Jack has been such a faithful employee, the company finds a luxury carriage that has just been taken out of service and presents it to the old man as a retirement gift. A few months after the retirement party, an old mate from the railway stops by Jack's house to see how he's getting on. Jack's wife answers the door and tells him that Jack's in the back garden. The mate goes round the side of the house and finds Jack sitting in a deckchair in the pouring rain, smoking his pipe. "What are you doing getting wet?" asks Jack's mate. "Why aren't you sitting inside your lovely carriage?" "I can't," replies Jack. "It's only got non-smoking compartments."

☞ Jim is waiting at the bus-stop at the end of a long queue. A bus arrives and everyone troops inside except Jim; the conductor puts his arm out to stop Jim getting on. "Sorry," says the conductor. "We're full. You'll have to wait for the next one." "And how long will that be?" asks Jim. The conductor replies, "The same as this one: about thirty feet."

☞ Mike missed the number 10 bus, so he took a number 20 and got off half-way.

☞ Solly, an old Jewish man, gets on a train. The second-class compartments are full, so he takes a peek into first-class and sees an empty seat temptingly close to the door. The train is about to leave, so Solly reckons it's a safe bet the seat won't be taken. He slips inside the carriage, sits down and gets out a copy of the Jewish Chronicle. He happily spends the next half-hour reading his paper while munching on a salt beef sandwich and dipping into a jar of pickled herrings. Suddenly, he's tapped on the shoulder by a steward. "Excuse me, sir," says the steward, "but this seat is reserved for the Archbishop of Canterbury." "So?" says Solly. "Who says I'm *not* the Archbishop of Canterbury?"

☞ Tommy Cooper is getting out of a taxi. As he does so, he slips something into the driver's breast pocket and says, "There you go, mate. Have a drink on me!" When the driver reaches in his pocket, he finds a teabag.

☞ What did the bus driver say to the man with no arms or legs waiting at the bus stop? "How are you getting on, mate?"

TREASURE

☞ A man is walking along a beach. He's completely broke and feeling very depressed: almost suicidal. Suddenly, he hears a booming voice call from the heavens. "Dig!" booms the voice. The man looks around, a little confused. "Dig!" booms the voice once again. The man's not sure what's going on, but starts digging in the sand by his feet. After a couple of seconds, he unearths a wooden box. He opens it and finds it contains hundreds of gold coins. The heavenly voice booms out again. "Casino!" it says. The man decides to do what he's told, and runs up the beach to the nearby casino. As soon as he walks through the door, the man hears the voice boom the words, "Roulette table!" So the man walks over to the roulette table. When he gets there, the voice booms out, "Sixteen, black!" The man puts all the gold coins on sixteen black. The wheel is spun, and the ball jerks around, flipping from number to number. Eventually the wheel slows and the ball comes to rest on five, red. "Bugger!" booms the voice.

TWINS

☞ A musician starts talking to a couple of girls in a bar. Much to his surprise, they turn out to be Siamese twins, joined at the hip. One thing leads to another and the girls wind up back at the man's apartment. They have more drinks and the man eventually talks the twins into bed. He makes love to one girl, then starts to make love to the other. The first girl sees a trombone lying on the floor and asks if she can have a go. The man doesn't mind, so he hands it to her. The girl turns out to be a great trombone player and she serenades the man as he makes love to her sister. A few weeks later, the twins are walking past the man's apartment building. One of the girls says, "Hey, let's stop by and see that guy." The other girl says, "Gee, do you think he'd remember us?"

☞ Harry was dating a Siamese twin, but after a while he started seeing her sister behind her back.

☞ I used to know identical twins. They looked so alike, it was incredible; sometimes they'd even manage to borrow money from each other without the other knowing about it.

☞ John and Joe are identical twins. John has a wife, and Joe has a boat, and they're both lost on the same day; John's wife has a heart attack, and Joe's ancient boat sinks. A week later, an old lady sees Joe in the street and mistakes him for John. She walks over to commiserate with him on the loss of his wife. "I'm so sorry for your loss," says the old lady. Joe smiles and says, "Well, I'm not that sorry myself; it was bound to happen sooner or later. She was pretty ancient, her bottom was all chewed up and she really stank of fish. From the first time I got into her, she made water faster than anything I ever saw. She had a pretty big crack in her front, too, and it got bigger every time I used her. It got so I could barely handle her, and if anyone else used her, she'd leak like anything. The thing that finished her off was these four Japanese guys over here on holiday. They came here looking for a good time and asked if I could lend her to them. I warned them she wasn't so great, but they could have a go on her if they liked. And d'you know what? Those crazy idiots all tried to get inside her at once. It was too much for the old girl. She cracked right up the middle." And the old lady faints.

UGLINESS

> **"We used to play Spin the Bottle when I was a kid. A girl would spin the bottle and if it pointed to you when it stopped, the girl could either kiss you or give you a dime. By the time I was 14, I owned my own home."**
> *Gene Perret*

☞ A man gets chatting to a woman at a party. "Don't look," he says, "but standing by the punchbowl is the ugliest man I ever saw in my life." "That's my husband," says the woman. "I'm so sorry," says the man. The woman replies, *"You're* sorry?"

☞ A rather homely-looking aunt goes to visit her sister and young niece. The little girl sits quietly in the corner for much of the visit. Eventually, the aunt goes over to say hello. "You've been very quiet," says the aunt. "Has a cat got your tongue?" "No," replies the girl. "Mummy gave me a pound not to mention your yellow teeth and cross-eyes."

☞ An ugly woman walks into the supermarket with her two kids. The store greeter says, "Are they twins?" "No," replies the woman, "he's nine and she's seven. Why? Do you think they look alike?" "No," replies the greeter. "I just can't believe you managed to get laid twice."

☞ Fred gets on a bus. After a few stops, a man gets on – the ugliest man Fred has ever seen in his life. The man is so spectacularly ugly that Fred feels he has to say something. He reaches over and taps the ugly man on the knee. "I can truly say," says Fred, "that your face is the most horrible dog's dinner I have ever seen in my life." "Well, that's not very nice," replies the man. "I can't help the way I look, can I?" "No," says Fred, "but you could have stayed at home."

☞ Harry was a very poor physical specimen; he even failed the medical for the Mickey Mouse Club.

☞ I was never what you'd call attractive; one of my first jobs was posing nude for 'get well soon' cards.

UNDERWEAR

"I got some new underwear the other day: well, new to me."
Emo Philips

☞ A young woman buys some lingerie and asks if the panties can be embroidered with a special message. The message she wants written is, 'If you can read this, you're too close.' "We can do that if you like, madam," says the sales assistant. "Do you want that in block capitals?" "No," replies the woman. "Braille."

US PRESIDENTS

☞ During his presidency, Bush has created 10 million new jobs, nine million of which are comedians.

☞ Five ex-presidents are taking an Antarctic cruise when they hit an iceberg. Gerald Ford cries out, "Oh, my goodness! What do we do?" Reagan shouts, "Man the lifeboats!" Jimmy Carter says, "Women and children first!" Nixon shouts, "Screw the women!" Clinton says, "Do we have time?"

☞ For some reason, George W. Bush is convinced he's really a pubic wig. He keeps telling people, "I'm proud to be A-mer'kin."

☞ George Bush dies and goes to hell. The Devil says to him, "I'm short on space and I've got three people here who weren't quite as bad as you. I'll let one of them go, and you can take their place. As a favour, I'll even let you decide who leaves." First, the Devil takes George to a room where Richard Nixon is bobbing in a pool of water. "No," says George. "I wouldn't like that. I'm not a good swimmer." Next, the Devil leads George to a room where Tony Blair is hammering a never-ending pile of rocks. "No," says George. "I wouldn't like that much. I've got a bad back." The Devil opens the final door. Inside, Bill Clinton is tied to a bench while Monica Lewinsky bends over him giving him a blow-job. George says, "That looks good. I'll take it." "Finally!" exclaims the Devil. "Okay, Monica. You're free to go!"

☞ George Bush is visiting the Queen. While they're having tea, he says, "Your Majesty, how do you run such an efficient government?" "Well," says the Queen, "the most important thing is to surround yourself with intelligent people: and to make sure they really are clever, you ask them a riddle. I'll show you." The Queen pushes a button on her intercom. She speaks into it and says, "Please send for the Prime Minister." A few minutes later, Tony Blair walks into the room. "Answer me this, please," says the Queen. "Your mother and father have a child. It's not your brother and it's not your sister. Who is it?" Without pause, Blair answers, "That would be me, your Majesty!" "That's right," says the Queen. George is impressed by this display and, back at the White House, he calls Dick Cheney to the Oval Office. "Dick," he says. "Answer this question for me. Your mother and your father have a little baby. Now, this baby is not your brother and it's not your sister. So who is it?" "I'm not sure," says Dick. "Let me think... um... well, I guess that the baby would have to be me. Is that right?" "No, it isn't, you idiot!" exclaims George. "It's Tony Blair!"

☞ Hillary Clinton and Janet Reno are having a girl-to-girl talk. "You're lucky you don't have to have sex," says Hillary. "I have to have sex with Bill all the time and I never feel good about it; there's no telling who he last had his pecker in. God knows what he's picked up." Janet replies, "Just because I'm not that good-looking doesn't mean I don't have sex. In fact, I often have to fight off unwelcome sexual advances." "So how do you do that?" asks Hillary. "It's easy," replies Janet. "Whenever a guy's getting too fresh with me, I squeeze out the loudest, nastiest fart I can. That soon puts them off." That night, Hillary's lying in bed with Bill when he starts to get frisky. Hillary's not in the mood, so she decides to put Janet's advice into action. She tenses up and lets out the most disgusting fart imaginable. Straight away, Bill is wafting up the sheets to get rid of the stench. "Jesus Christ!" he says. "Janet? Is that you?"

☞ President Bush is being given his daily briefing on world affairs. An aide says to him, "Sir, yesterday, three Brazilian soldiers were killed in an accident." "Oh, dear God, no!" wails Bush. "That's terrible! That is absolutely awful! Oh, God, please, no!" Devastated, he falls back in his chair and says, "So exactly how many is a brazillion?"

☞ President Bush is visiting a primary school. He drops in on one of the classes and finds they're learning about words and their meanings. The teacher asks the president if he'd like to hear some thoughts on the word 'tragedy', so the president stands up and asks the class for an example of a 'tragedy'. Little Billy says, "If my best friend, who lives on a farm, was playing in a field and a tractor ran over him and killed him, then that would be a tragedy." "No," replies Bush, "that would be an accident. Can anyone else give me an example?" Little Mary raises her hand and says, "If a school bus carrying 50 children drove over a cliff, killing everyone inside, would that be a tragedy?" "I'm afraid not, little girl," explains the president. "That's what we would call a great loss." Little Johnny sticks his hand up and says, "If Air Force One was carrying you and Mrs Bush, and it was hit by a 'friendly fire' missile and blown to bits, I guess that would be a tragedy." "Very good!" exclaims the president. "That's right, little boy. But can you explain why that event would be considered a tragedy?" "Well," says little Johnny. "I suppose it has to be a tragedy – because it certainly wouldn't be a great loss and it probably wouldn't be a f***ing accident either."

☞ Why does President Bush walk around with his fly open? Occasionally he has to count up to eleven.

USA

> **"I think that's how Chicago got started; a bunch of people in New York said, 'Gee, I'm enjoying the crime and the poverty, but it just isn't cold enough. Let's go west'."**
> *Richard Jeni*

☞ How do you know when you've entered into a serious relationship with a Californian? They take you to meet their Tarot reader.

☞ Why don't San Francisco blondes wear miniskirts? Because then you could see their balls.

VAMPIRES

☞ Dracula is walking down the street one evening, when he's suddenly pelted by smoked salmon sandwiches, ham rolls, pitted olives, chicken wings, chippolatas, pizzas slices and any number of similar easy-to-handle, bite-sized nibbles. Dracula then collapses to the ground with a miniature Thai chicken satay kebab stuck in his chest. "Curses!" he cries with his dying breath. "It's Buffet the Vampire Slayer!"

☞ I once knew a midget who thought he was a vampire – he was a real pain in the arse.

VASECTOMIES

☞ A man goes to his doctor. "I'm thinking about getting a vasectomy," says the man. "That's a pretty big decision," says the doctor. "Have you talked it over with your family?" "Yes," says the man. "They're in favour of it, 15 to two."

☞ Mary says to Gladys, "I have to be really careful not to get pregnant." Gladys says, "But I thought your husband just had a vasectomy?" "That's right," says Mary, "and that's why I need to be really careful."

VENDING MACHINES

☞ A man puts some money into an automatic vending machine. He watches as a cup fails to drop into place properly and the nozzle squirts all his coffee down a grille. "Great," says the man. "It's so automated it even drinks the damn stuff for you!"

VENTRILOQUISM

☞ Harry is a very good ventriloquist, but arthritis means he can't work his puppet any more. Looking around for something to do, he decides to become a medium. He sets up shop in a basement and soon greets his first customer, a widow. "Can you help me get in contact with my husband Stanley?" sniffs the widow. "He passed away last month." "Sure I can," says Harry. "I can guarantee it." "And how much do you charge?" asks the widow. "I'm very reasonable," replies Harry. "You can either have a £40 session, or a £60 session." "What's the difference?" asks the widow. Harry replies, "For £40 you get to hear his voice. For £60 you get to hear his voice while I drink a glass of water."

☞ Harry was a lousy ventriloquist; his lips moved when his dummy was speaking, and his ears moved when it was listening.

VIOLENCE

"I got in a fight one time with a really big guy, and he said, 'I'm going to mop the floor with your face.' I said, 'You'll be sorry.' He said, 'Oh, yeah? Why?' I said, 'Well, you won't be able to get into the corners very well'."
Emo Philips

"The world is a dangerous place; only yesterday I went into Boots and punched someone in the face."
Jeremy Limb

WAR AND THE MILITARY

☞ I knew a war was going to break out soon; I was going past Vera Lynn's house and I heard her gargling.

☞ A General, an Admiral and an Air Marshal are asked to speak at a dinner. The General and Admiral decide to have a dig at the Air Marshal, and both of them patronizingly describe the air force as the 'Cinderella' of the armed forces during their speeches. When it's the Air Marshal's turn, he stands up and starts his speech by saying, "I don't know much about Cinderella, except for the fact she had two ugly sisters..."

☞ The army has been trying to cross a messenger pigeon with a woodpecker. They want a bird that will deliver messages, but knocks on the door first.

☞ A soldier is driving a jeep near the front line when he comes across a shaded pool. It's a hot, sweaty day, so he strips off and dives in. While he's standing in the water, a shot rings out and the soldier faints. Hours later, he comes round in a military hospital. "What happened?" he croaks. "I'm sorry, son," says the doctor, "but a sniper shot your balls off." "It could have been worse," says the soldier. "It was lucky I was thinking of my wife's sister at the time."

> **"I can't forgive the Germans for what they did to my granddad in the last war – passed over for promotion time and time again..."**
> *Jimmy Carr*

☞ When I was in the army, we were taught to shoot first and ask questions later. Mind you, we never got many answers.

☞ A US Colonel happens to bump into his old army valet, Private Jackson, a man who'd been with him throughout his tour of Vietnam. Seeing that Jackson is down on his luck, the Colonel offers him his old job back. "It'll be just like it was back in the army," says the Colonel. "Just do everything that you used to do for me back then." So the next morning, Jackson puts on the Colonel's coffee, goes into the Colonel's bedroom and tells him that it's an hour before dawn. Then he slaps the Colonel's wife on the backside and shouts, "Rise and shine, Tiger Lily! Time to get back to the bar!"

☞ Did you hear about the Rear-Admiral who fell into a vat of whipped cream? Later that day he was piped aboard ship.

☞ Why are armies predominantly made up of men, when men can't even aim accurately at a toilet rim?

☞ My uncle had his tongue shot off during the war. He never used to talk about it, though.

> **"I think Iran and Iraq simply had a war because their names are so similar they kept getting each other's post."**
> *Paul Merton*

☞ On the battlefield, an officer orders a soldier to try to save a military warehouse that's been set on fire by the enemy. To get to a hose, the soldier dodges bullets, wipes out a machine-gun nest and blows up an enemy tank. On the way back he kills three men bare-handed, shoots down an enemy helicopter and wipes out a bunker. He then climbs all over the burning building with his hose, extinguishing every flame he can find. The officer salutes him. "That was the most heroic thing I ever saw," says the officer. "You'll get a medal for saving that warehouse." "Warehouse?" exclaims the soldier. "Dang! I thought you said 'whorehouse'!"

WASTE DISPOSAL

☞ Tom doesn't pay the council to collect his rubbish. He just gift-wraps it all and leaves it in an unlocked car.

"Is it fair to say that there'd be less litter in Britain if blind people were given pointed sticks?"
Adam Bloom

☞ Bill needs to get rid of his old fridge. He puts it in his front garden and sticks a sign on it saying, 'Free to good home. If you want it, take it!' For three weeks, the fridge sits there without anyone looking twice at it. Eventually, Bill decides that no one is ever going to take it, so he sticks up a different sign. This one reads, 'Fridge for sale, £50.' And sure enough, the next time he looks in the garden, it's been stolen.

"My wife is always trying to get me out of the house. The other day, she told me to put the garbage out. I said to her I already did. She told me to go and keep an eye on it."
Rodney Dangerfield

WEATHER

☞ As Noah once famously said, "Scattered showers, my ass!"

☞ Bill and Harry are walking down the road when it starts to pelt with rain. Luckily, Harry has brought his umbrella. He opens it, but Bill is horrified to see that it is full of holes and half the struts are broken. It can hardly keep itself upright and most of the water is pouring straight through the fabric. "Why on earth did you bring along that piece of junk?" says Bill. Harry replies, "I didn't think it would rain."

"I said to the First Officer, 'Gad, that sun's hot!' to which he replied, 'Well, you shouldn't touch it'."
Spike Milligan

☞ A tornado rips across the Kansas plain. In its path is a small homestead. The farmer and his wife see the mighty wind bearing down on them and take shelter in the cellar. The tornado strikes and the wooden house is unable to withstand its terrible force. First the roof, then the first-floor timbers and then the ground floor are whipped up into the sky. The foundations start to go and the tornado penetrates as deep as the cellar, lifting the farmer and his wife high into the sky. Their terrible ordeal lasts for many long minutes until, suddenly, the wind drops and the unfortunate couple hurtle downwards. However, their luck changes, and instead of landing on the hard ground they plummet into a swamp where the water and mud break their fall. The farmer and his wife drag themselves to firm ground. The farmer's wife is sobbing uncontrollably. "It's okay, Mary," says the farmer. "We made it." The farmer's wife ignores these words of comfort, and tears continue to pour down her face. "Ah, dang it, Mary!" says the farmer. "Will you quit crying? We're both fine, ain't we?" "It's not that," sobs his wife. "Then what?" asks the farmer. His wife says, "This is the first time we've been out of the house together for five years, and I'm wearing an old dress."

> ## "You know it's summer in Ireland when the rain starts to get warmer."
> *Hal Roach*

☞ We had two windmills on our farm, but we had to take one of them down. We found we didn't have enough wind for two.

☞ Mary tells Brian to go and water the lawn. "Are you mad?" he says. "It's raining!" Mary replies, "So take an umbrella!"

WORDS OF WISDOM

☞ A day without sunshine is like... well, night.

> ## A wise old man once said to me, "People don't listen; they just wait for their turn to speak'. At least, I think that's what he said."
> *Jimmy Carr*

☞ After all is said and done, a hell of a lot more is said than done.

☞ Always remember to pillage *before* you burn.

> ## "Common sense is the collection of prejudices acquired by age 18."
> *Albert Einstein*

☞ Confession is good for the soul, but bad for your career.

☞ Education teaches us how things work; experience teaches us how they fail.

☞ Friction is a drag.

☞ Give a man a fish, and he eats for a day. Teach a man to fish, and he eats for a lifetime. Give a man a fire, and he's warm for a day. Set a man on fire, and he's warm for the rest of his life.

☞ Have you ever noticed how nothing is impossible for those who don't have to do it?

> **"Expecting the world to treat you fairly because you're a good person is a little like expecting a bull not to attack you because you're a vegetarian."**
> *Dennis Wholey*

☞ Help a man when he's in trouble and he'll remember you when he's in trouble again.

☞ If in doubt, make it sound convincing.

☞ If it jams, force it. If it breaks, it needed replacing anyway.

☞ If the grass is always greener on the other side, it's because they use more manure.

☞ If the world didn't suck, we'd all fall off.

☞ If there is a problem, most people would prefer to have a good scapegoat than a solution.

☞ If you can't be kind, at least have the decency to be vague.

> **"If you're not part of the solution, you're part of the precipitate."**
> *Steven Wright*

☞ It is better to be pissed off than pissed on.

☞ It's always funny until someone gets hurt, and then it's just hilarious.

☞ Just when I was getting used to yesterday, along came today.

☞ Life is like a roll of toilet paper; the closer it gets to the end, the faster it goes.

> **"Life is all about ass; you're either covering it, kicking it, kissing it, busting it, trying to get a piece of it or behaving like one."**
> *Stephen Jolly*

☞ Life is like being in a dog-sled team. If you're not the lead dog, the scenery never changes.

☞ Look out for number one: and don't tread in number two, either.

☞ My mind not only wanders, sometimes it leaves completely.

☞ Never let any mechanical object realise you are in a hurry.

☞ Never marry a beautiful person; they might leave you and break your heart. Of course, an ugly person might leave you too. But who gives a damn?

☞ Never say anything to a woman that suggests you think she's pregnant unless you can actually see the baby coming out.

> **"My father always used to say, 'What doesn't kill you, makes you stronger'... before the accident."**
> *Jimmy Carr*

☞ No matter what happens, somebody will find a way to take it too seriously.

☞ One word identifies the reason why the human race has not achieved its full potential, that word is 'meetings'.

"It's never just a game when you're winning."
George Carlin

☞ People who get too big for their britches will be exposed in the end.

☞ People who say they don't let little things bother them have never slept in a room with a mosquito.

☞ People who want to share their religious views with you almost never want you to share yours with them.

☞ Some minds are like concrete – thoroughly mixed up and permanently set.

☞ Sometimes I think I understand everything; then I regain consciousness.

☞ Streakers beware; your end is in sight.

"It's a small world...but I wouldn't like to paint it."
Steven Wright

☞ Take my advice; I don't use it anyway.

☞ Take out the fortune before you eat the cookie.

☞ The best way to forget all your troubles is to wear tight shoes.

☞ The easiest way to find something you lost is to buy a replacement.

☞ The main accomplishment of organised protests is to annoy people who are not in them.

☞ The most powerful force in the universe is gossip.

☞ The nice part about living in a village is that when you don't know what you're doing, someone else will.

"Things should be made as simple as possible, but not any simpler."
Albert Einstein

☞ The older you get, the better you get (unless you're a banana).

☞ The only time the world beats a path to your door is when you're in the bathroom.

☞ The problem with reality is the lack of background music.

☞ There is a fine line between 'hobby' and 'mental illness'.

☞ They say the darkest time is just before dawn. So that's definitely the best time to steal your neighbour's newspaper.

☞ Time is the best teacher. Unfortunately, it kills all its students.

"Throwing acid is wrong... in some people's eyes."
Jimmy Carr

☞ Under no circumstances take a sleeping pill and a laxative on the same night.

☞ When trouble arrives and things look bad, there is usually one person who is willing to take charge of the situation. Very often, that person is completely crazy.

☞ Wisdom comes with age, but sometimes age comes alone.

☞ You can pick your friends and you can pick your nose, but you can't pick your friend's nose.

"You do not really understand something unless you can explain it to your grandmother."
Albert Einstein

WORDS OF WISDOM – CONFUCIUS SAY...

☞ Girl who sits on judge's lap gets honourable discharge.

☞ He who places head in sand will get kicked in the end!

☞ He who walk through airport door sideways going to Bangkok.

☞ Man who leap off cliff jump to conclusion.

WORK AND BUSINESS

☞ A businessman gets a bill from a supplier, but can't make head or tail of it. As far as he can tell, it's been calculated incorrectly, but before he contacts the company he wants to double-check his mental arithmetic. He knows his secretary has a good head for figures, so he asks her into his office. "Jane," he says, "if I were to give you $10,000, minus 15 per cent, how much would you take off?" The secretary replies, "Everything but my earrings."

☞ A company is hosting a family barbecue for its workforce. One of the employee's wives goes up to the chief executive and says, "You're the boss aren't you?" "That's right," he says. "How did you guess?" "It was easy," she says, "My husband is always doing imitations of you to amuse the children."

"A good rule of thumb is that if you've made it to thirty-five and your job still requires you to wear a name tag, you've made a serious vocational error."
Dennis Miller

☞ A female employee tells her boss there's something she'd like to get off her chest. "What's that?" he asks. She says, "Your eyes!"

☞ A new man joins the office. He's given a desk next to Jim. The new boy decides to break the ice. He leans over to Jim and says, "Hi. So, how long have you been working here?" Jim replies, "Ever since my manager threatened to fire me."

> **"Employee of the Month is a good example**
> **of how somebody can be both a winner**
> **and a loser at the same time."**
> *Demetri Martin*

☞ A railway worker is lying on the floor in a train station, clutching his stomach and rolling around in pain. "Are you all right?" asks a passenger. "Yeah," says the worker, "but I'm busting to go to the toilet and I don't start work for another seven minutes."

☞ An uncle of mine used to work in a shoe factory; try as he might, he never really fitted in.

☞ Harold goes for a job as a toilet cleaner, but when it's discovered he can't read or write he's sent packing. On his way home, Harold sees a box of bananas on sale for £10. He buys the bananas, takes them to the local market and sells them for £15. From this small beginning, Harold establishes an international business as a grocer. One day, he's being interviewed for the TV and the reporter is astonished to discover that Harold can't read or write. "That's amazing," says the reporter. "You've done so much as an illiterate; just imagine what you might be doing now if you could read and write!" "I know exactly what I'd be doing," replies Harold. "I'd be mopping floors in a shithouse."

☞ Harry has a booming business; he exports American flags to Arab countries. They come in a special gift pack with a box of matches.

☞ "How long has your father been in his present position?" "Three months." "And what is he doing?" "Six months."

☞ Bill is sitting in a hotel bar when an attractive young lady comes over and sits on the stool next to him. "Hi," she says, "Would you like a little company?" "I might be interested," says Bill. "What's its turnover?"

☞ Harry told me he'd never had a day's illness in his entire working life; he's always managed to stretch it out to last a week.

☞ George was a workaholic. Every time someone mentioned work, he got drunk.

☞ Nigel worked in a completely paperless office. He thought it sounded like a really good idea – until he had to go the toilet.

☞ I went into partnership with a friend of mine. It should have been the perfect arrangement; I had the money and he had the business experience. Unfortunately, it didn't turn out so well; now I have the experience and he has the money.

☞ I'm very religious. I won't work in any week that has a Sunday in it.

> **"I lost my job. No, I didn't really lose my job.**
> **I know where my job is. It's just when I go**
> **there, there's this new guy doing it."**
> *Bobcat Goldthwait*

☞ It's evening in the meeting room of a large multinational company. A group of cleaning ladies are relaxing round the director's table. One cleaning lady turns to her neighbour and says, "Here, do you think the directors ever pretend to be us?"

☞ My ex-wife was a career woman. She brought her work home with her night after night. In the end, I asked for a divorce. I wouldn't have minded so much, but she was a prostitute.

☞ A magazine does a survey of a thousand women. It asks them what they'd do if they had a penis for a day. The majority reply, "Get a pay rise."

☞ Negotiations between union members and their employer are at an impasse. The employers are accusing the workers of flagrantly abusing the sick-leave provisions of their contract. At the bargaining table, the company's chief negotiator holds up the current edition of the local newspaper, "This man," he announces, "is an employee who called in sick yesterday! Yet here on the sports page is a photo of this same, supposedly ill, employee winning a semi-professional golf tournament with a score of seven under par." The union negotiator thinks quickly and breaks the stunned silence: "And just think of the score he *could* have had if he hadn't been on his deathbed!"

☞ You do the work of three men: Larry, Moe and Curly.

WORK AND BUSINESS – EFFICIENCY SAVINGS

☞ An efficiency expert is lecturing a group of business people about workplace productivity. The expert concludes his lecture with a note of caution. "These techniques are very valuable in the office," he says. "However, you must be careful about trying them at home. For example, last year I began to study my wife's breakfast routine. I noticed that she made many trips to the refrigerator, oven, table and pantry cupboard, often carrying only a single item at a time. I pointed this out to her and said that, with a little thought and planning, she could significantly reduce the amount of walking and carrying she did. And I was right; it did save an awful lot of time." "How much?" asks a member of the audience. "Thirteen minutes," replies the expert. "She used to make breakfast in twenty minutes. Now I do it in seven."

☞ Tom takes on a new job as a factory manager. Productivity is low, so Tom decides to make an example of someone. He's walking round the factory floor when he sees a young man lounging on a bench picking his nose. "Here! You!" says Tom. "I don't pay you to sit around all day. How much do you earn in a week?" The young man replies, "£200."

Tom takes a wad of money out of his pocket, peels off ten £20 notes and gives them to him. "Here's a week's wages. Now piss off; you're fired." The young man walks off, and Tom turns to the foreman. "We'd better find someone to replace that slacker," he says. "What exactly was he doing here?" The foreman replies, "He was delivering our lunch."

WORK AND BUSINESS – INTERVIEWS AND APPLICATIONS

☞ According to a survey, 40 per cent of people applying for jobs said they had some lies on their resumé. The rest said it was all lies.

☞ A boy applies for a job delivering newspapers. However, the newsagent decides the lad is too young and tells him he's looking for someone a little older. A week later, the boy comes back and applies for the job again. "You again?" says the newsagent. "I though I told you I wanted someone older." "You did," replies the boy. "And here I am – a week older."

☞ Tom is being interviewed for a job. The personnel manager says, "Our firm is looking for a person who is going to work hard for less than average pay, come to work early and stay all night if necessary. Do you think you're that kind of person?" "Well, no," says Tom, "but if you hire me, I'll help you look for one."

☞ A woman goes for a job interview. The interviewer asks her to give an example that illustrates how she uses her mental dexterity. "Well," says the woman, "I like crossword puzzles; in fact, I've completed a number of very complex prize-winning puzzles." "I see," says the interviewer, "but what I really want are examples of mental dexterity within the workplace." The woman replies, "Well, they are. I spend most of my office time doing crossword puzzles."

☞ Harry applies to become the handyman at the local old people's home. At his interview, the home's manager runs through Harry's skills and qualifications. "Can you do plumbing?" asks the manager. "No," replies Harry. "Are you any good at carpentry?" asks the manager. "No," replies Harry. "Are you qualified to carry out electrical repairs?" asks the manager. "No," replies Harry. "Do you do any decorating?" asks the manager. "No," replies Harry. "How about gardening?" asks the manager. "No," replies Harry. The manager recaps: "So you don't do any plumbing, carpentry, electrical work, decorating or gardening. Why on earth do you call yourself a handyman?" Harry replies, "Because I only live round the corner."

☞ Bill goes into a Job Centre and tells the employment advisor he wants to get a job in a bowling alley. "Ten-pin?" asked the advisor. "No," says Bill, "permanent."

☞ Harry is interviewed for a job in a hardware store. "Where were you working before this?" asks the interviewer. "I was at Mason's Hardware on the high street. I worked there for forty years." "Forty?" exclaims the interviewer. "It says on your CV that you're 50 years old. Did you start work at 10?" "No," replies Harry, "but I did put in a lot of overtime."

☞ Simon sees a job advert for a 'fanny shaver'. He rings up the employment agency which placed the ad, and discovers that he'll be required to shave the bikini lines of supermodels at photoshoots in the world's most glamorous locations. Moreover, the job pays £40,000 a year! "Do you think you'd be up to it?" asks the man at the agency. "Sure," says Simon. "Where do I go for the interview?" The man says, "Can you be at Croydon bus station by eleven o'clock on Monday?" "Yes," replies Simon, "but the advert said the job was based in Oxford Street." "It is," replies the man, "but Croydon is where the queue for the interview starts."

WORK AND BUSINESS – OFF WORK

☞ One of Bill's employees doesn't turn up for work, so Bill gives him a call. He dials the employee's number and the phone is picked up by a small girl. "Hello," whispers the girl. "Hi," says Bill. "Is your daddy home?" "Yes," says the girl. "Can I speak to him?" asks Bill. "No," says the girl. Bill says, "So is your mummy there?" "Yes," says the girl. "May I talk with her, then?" asks Bill. Again, the girl whispers, "No." "Well, is anybody else there?" asks Bill. "Yes," says the girl. "A policeman is here." "So can I speak with the policeman?" asks Bill. "No," whispers the girl. "He's busy." "Busy doing what?" asks Bill. "He's talking to daddy and mummy and the fireman," replies the girl. Bill hears what sounds like a helicopter coming over the phone. "Is that a helicopter?" he exclaims. "Yes," replies the girl. "What on earth is going on there?" demands Bill. The girl replies, "The search team just landed." Bill, alarmed, says, "Oh, my God! What are they searching for?" The girl whispers back, "Me."

WORK AND BUSINESS – OFFICE LORE

☞ Executive ability is about making quick decisions – and getting somebody else to do the work.

☞ What's the difference between this company and a cactus? The cactus has its pricks on the outside.

☞ Getting anything done around here is like watching elephants mate. It's all done on a very high level, there's a lot of stomping and screaming involved and it takes two years to get a result.

☞ If you ain't makin' waves, you ain't kickin' hard enough!

☞ The 11th commandment: Thou shalt not whine!

☞ The management hierarchy is like a pair of legs. Anyone who gets to the top becomes a complete asshole.

☞ The opulence of the front office decor varies inversely with the fundamental solvency of the firm.

WORLD AFFAIRS

☞ The United Nations conducts a worldwide survey. The only question asked was: "Please give your honest opinion about solutions to the food shortage in the rest of the world." The survey was a colossal failure. In Africa they didn't know what 'food' meant. In Eastern Europe they didn't know what 'honest' meant. In Western Europe they didn't know what 'shortage' meant. In China they didn't know what 'opinion' meant. In the Middle East they didn't know what 'solution' meant. In South America they didn't know what 'please' meant, and in the USA they didn't know what 'the rest of the world' meant.

ZOOS

☞ Nigel was the only short-sighted skunk in the zoo. Once, he managed to fall in love with a gas leak.

☞ Tom and his wife were visiting the zoo when they accidentally got locked in one of the cages. They were stuck there all night – but, on the plus side, it was the first time they'd successfully mated in captivity.

ZZZZEEEE FINAL FEW THOUGHTS

☞ A final thought; there are three types of people in the world: those who make things happen, those who watch things happen and those who wonder what the hell just happened.

☞ A final final thought; have you ever wondered whether the world is being run by smart people who are putting us all on, or by imbeciles who really mean it?